Special Protection of Trade Marks with a Reputation under European Union Law

Special Protection of Trade Marks with a Reputation under European Union Law

Edited by

Michal Bohaczewski

Wolters Kluwer

Published by:
Kluwer Law International B.V.
PO Box 316
2400 AH Alphen aan den Rijn
The Netherlands
E-mail: international-sales@wolterskluwer.com
Website: lrus.wolterskluwer.com

Sold and distributed in North, Central and South America by:
Wolters Kluwer Legal & Regulatory U.S.
7201 McKinney Circle
Frederick, MD 21704
United States of America
Email: customer.service@wolterskluwer.com

Sold and distributed in all other countries by:
Air Business Subscriptions
Rockwood House
Haywards Heath
West Sussex
RH16 3DH
United Kingdom
Email: international-customerservice@wolterskluwer.com

ISBN 978-94-035-2021-6

e-Book: ISBN 978-94-035-1991-3
web-PDF: ISBN 978-94-035-2004-9

Table of Contents

Foreword

As Advocate General of the Court of Justice of the European Union where I issue Opinions for the benefit of the judges on how cases should be resolved, I sometimes get the impression that in relation to some domains of European Union (EU) law everything is in the legal writings. Trade mark law is surely one of those areas, at least as far as substantive (as opposed to procedural) law is concerned. This cannot be said about the book of Professor Bohaczewski who explores a highly controversial subject and sheds new light on several aspects of trade mark protection under EU law.

It is common knowledge that the essential function of a trade mark is to safeguard the communication of accurate information about marked goods or services to the consumer or end user. A trade mark serves a specific purpose which is to transmit objective information on the origin of goods or services within the relevant market where it exists, often alongside a plethora of other trade marks. This explains why it is granted protection under both national and international laws.

Due to the very reason that the trade marks are present in the market, the public may also familiarise with certain trade marks, which would then become well-known or reputed trade marks. It is precisely this phenomenon, with its profound legal implications on the protection granted to a trade mark, which Professor Bohaczewski analyses in his book.

The author addresses the dual system encompassing trade marks registered at national and EU levels in this book. Indeed, the book deals with both the Trade Marks Directive and the EU Trade Mark Regulation. In his book, the author delves into the case law of the EU courts as well as the European Union Intellectual Property Offices decision-making practice. It is, in particular, this latter aspect which I consider as a crucial feature of this publication.

It is against this legal background that Professor Bohaczewski examines the controversies surrounding the scope and very existence of the special regime of protection of trade marks with a reputation. He deals with the ambiguity of the notion of 'trade marks with a reputation' and its interplay with the concept of a well-known trade mark. The author also presents the criteria and forms of the trade marks possessing that quality. In this regard, he contends that the recognised forms of infringement, commonly referred to as 'blurring', 'tarnishment' and 'free-riding', serve different purposes and, as such, are independent from each other. His views are very well argued.

The in-depth analysis by the author results in numerous opportunities to highlight the issues that in future may be brought before the EU courts and which should nourish the doctrinal debate and catch the attention of legal practitioners. It is also important to notice that the author is clearly addressing the readers as both scholars and practicing lawyers. This strengthens my belief that the present volume will become an essential reference and daily tool for both academia and legal practice.

Maciej Szpunar
First Advocate General at the Court of Justice of the European Union
Professor at the University of Silesia in Katowice (Poland)

List of Abbreviations

AIPPI	Association internationale pour la protection de la propriété industrielle (International Association for the Protection of Intellectual Property)
Ann. dr. comm.	Annales de droit commercial
Ann. propr. ind.	Annales de la propriété industrielle et artistique
ATRIP	Association for the Advancement of Teaching and Research in Intellectual Property
BoA	Board of Appeal
Bull.	Bulletin des arrêts de la Cour de cassation
CA	Cour d'appel (French Court of Appeal)
Cah. dr. entr.	Cahiers de droit de l'entreprise
Cass. civ.	Cour de cassation Chambre civile (French Court of Cassation, Civil Chamber)
Cass. com.	Cour de cassation Chambre commerciale (French Court of Cassation, Commercial Chamber)
CFI	Court of First Instance of the European Communities (nowadays, General Court of the European Union)
CJ	Court of Justice of the European Union (previously of the European Communities)
Columb. L. Rev.	Columbia Law Review
Comm. com. électr.	Communication – Commerce électronique
Contrats conc. cons.	Contrats concurrence consommation
D.	Recueil Dalloz
D. IP/IT	Recueil Dalloz IP/IT
ECHR	European Court of Human Rights
EConvHR	European Convention on Human Rights
EEA	European Economic Area

EIPR	European Intellectual Property Review
EPS	Europejski Przegląd Sądowy
EU	European Union
EUIPO	European Union Intellectual Property Office
Gaz. Pal.	Gazette du Palais
GC	General Court of the European Union
GRUR	Gewerblicher Rechtsschutz und Urheberrecht
Harv. L. Rev.	Harvard Law Review
ICC	International Chamber of Commerce
IIC	International Review of Intellectual Property and Competition Law
INTA	International Trademark Association
IPQ	Intellectual Property Quarterly
IRPI	Institut de recherche en propriété intellectuelle
JCP	Semaine juridique, édition générale
JCP E	Semaine juridique, édition Entreprise
JDI	Journal du droit international privé
JIPLP	Journal of Intellectual Property Law & Practice
NSA	Naczelny Sąd Administracyjny (Polish Supreme Administrative Court)
OHIM	Office for Harmonisation in the Internal Market
OSN	Orzecznictwo Sądu Najwyższego
OSP	Orzecznictwo Sądów Powszechnych
PI	Revue Propriété industrielle (WIPO review)
PIBD	Propriété industrielle – Bulletin documentaire
PiP	Państwo i Prawo
PPH	Przegląd Prawa Handlowego
Propr. ind.	Revue Propriété industrielle (LexisNexis review)
Propr. intell.	Revue Propriétés intellectuelles
PS	Przegląd Sądowy
RDI	Revue de droit international
RDPI	Revue du droit de la propriété intellectuelle
Rev. Inter. Dr. Comparé	Revue internationale de droit comparé
Rev. soc.	Revue Droit des sociétés
RFPI	Revue Francophone de la Propriété Intellectuelle
RIPIA	Revue internationale de la propriété industrielle et artistique
Riv. Dir. Comm.	Rivista di diritto commerciale
Riv. Dir. Ind.	Rivista di diritto industriale
RJDA	Revue de jurisprudence de droit des affaires
RLDI	Revue Lamy droit de l'immatériel

RTD civ.	Revue trimestrielle de droit civil
RTD com.	Revue trimestrielle de droit commercial
RTD eur.	Revue trimestrielle de droit européen
S.	Recueil Sirey
SA	Sąd apelacyjny (Polish Court of Appeal)
SN	Sąd Najwyższy (Polish Supreme Court)
SO	Sąd okręgowy (Polish District Court)
TGI	Tribunal de grande instance (French Grand Instance Court)
TMR	Trademark Reporter
Trib. com.	Tribunal de commerce (French Commercial Court)
TRIPS	Agreement on Trade-Related Aspects of Intellectual Property Rights
Univ. Pen. Law Rev.	University of Pennsylvania Law Review
WIPO	World Intellectual Property Organization
WSA	Wojewódzki sąd administracyjny (Polish Regional Administrative Court)
ZNUJ	Zeszyty Naukowe Uniwersytetu Jagiellońskiego (Universitas Iagellonica Acta Scientiarum Litterarumque)

Introduction

1. Distinctive function of the trade mark and principle of speciality. According to the traditional definition, the trade mark is a distinctive sign whose primary aim is to indicate the commercial origin of a product.[1] There is no doubt that the distinctive function is therefore the essential function of the trade mark.[2]

In European law, the trade mark rights, as all the intellectual property rights, based on the concept of property right to tangible objects, serve to protect above all the individual interests of their owners. By their very nature, the monopolies conferred by registration limit the freedom of trade and industry and the related freedom of competition of others. Nevertheless, trade mark rights are at the same time necessary for all undertakings to carry on their economic activity. Indeed, trade marks ensure the proper functioning of the market and make progress possible, by encouraging the owners to invest in the quality of goods or services in order to satisfy the consumer.[3]

Under European trade mark law, the distinctive function of the trade mark traditionally delimits the scope of its protection. Trade mark rights do not confer exclusivity over the sign per se. In other words, they do not refer to the sign envisaged in itself, but in so far as it designates the goods or services concerned.[4] Hence, trade mark rights protect the sign to the extent that its reservation constitutes a necessary and justified limitation of the freedom of trade and industry. In trade mark law, this freedom is reflected in the so-called principle of 'speciality' which traditionally governs this area of law. The right to the trade mark was indeed always considered essentially relative and narrowly limited to the industry in which it served as a distinctive sign.[5] Few opinions questioned the relativity of the trade mark right and favoured an absolute

1. Eugène Pouillet, *Traité des marques de fabrique et de la concurrence déloyale en tous genres*, 6th ed., Imprimerie et Librairie Générale de Jurisprudence Marchal et Billard, Paris 1912, pp. 13-14.
2. According to the well-established case law of the Court of Justice, the 'essential function' of the trade mark is 'to guarantee the identity of the origin of the trade-marked product to the consumer of final user by enabling him to distinguish without any possibility of confusion between that product and products which have another origin'. CJ, 3 December 1981, case 1/81, *Pfizer v. Eurim-Pharm*, para. 8.
3. Cf. Jérôme Passa, *Traité de droit de la propriété industrielle*, t. I, 2nd ed., LGDJ, Paris 2009, p. 9.
4. Cf. Fernand Jacq, *Subtilités dans le domaine des marques*, PI 1955, p. 232.
5. Pouillet, *Traité des marques de fabrique ...*, pp. 249-250.

protection of the mark, allowing the owner to prohibit its use in any sector of industry or trade.[6]

Consequently, trade mark law, as conceived in the 19th century, granted protection only against the use of the trade mark by third parties that infringed the distinctive function, likely to appear in the event of a risk of confusion among the public.[7] This was because the protection conferred on the mark was considered to be an effective means of protection against unfair competition.[8] The purpose of the special trade mark legislation was to ensure that manufacturers were able to protect their interests against unfair competitors, which would be more effective than the protection sought on the basis of general civil tort liability.[9]

2. Quality function of the trade mark. Over time, it was observed that trade marks known to the public are likely to transmit to the consumer information going beyond the mere indication of the commercial origin of the good or service, in other words, may fulfil functions other than the distinctive function. First, it was accepted that a known mark provides customers with information on the quality they can expect from the product bearing the mark. As early as 1868, the Paris Court noted that the trade mark is the distinctive sign of the good serving to guarantee its 'quality, reputation and origin'.[10] The doctrine thus recognised what is referred to as the 'quality function', which is therefore fulfilled when a trade mark, as a result of its exploitation on the market, generates positive associations among customers with regard to the characteristics and quality of the good or service.[11] It is particularly when a mark acquires a reputation that it becomes a true indication of quality. As one author pointed out a

6. Cf. Georges Marry, *De la contrefaçon en matière de propriété industrielle, littéraire et artistique*, thesis Paris 1899, pp. 32-33. According to the author, it is in the interest of the trade mark owner that the sign adopted by him remains absolutely his own and cannot be employed in a totally different area of industry or trade. The author based his opinion on a judgment of the French Court of Cassation of 1 December 1890, according to which the ownership of a trade mark is absolute and entirely independent of the use to which it may be applied. Cass. com., 1 December 1890, PI 1891, p. 22. Also in Italian doctrine, this judgment was presented as favouring the idea of an absolute protection of the trade mark against its use for any product. *See* Moise Amar, *Dei nomi, dei marchi e degli altri segni e della concorrenza nell'industria e nel commercio*, Unione Tipografico-Editrice, Turin 1893, pp. 157-158. Nevertheless, the authors misinterpreted the decision. The Court of Cassation only stated that the trade mark owner could bring action for infringement of his right even if he did not use the trade mark for the goods for which it was registered. Pouillet, *Traité des marques de fabrique ...*, pp. 249-250. The idea of an absolute protection of the trade mark was also defended by some Italian authors at the beginning of the 20th century. Cf. Cesare Galli, *Funzione del marchio e ampiezza della tutela*, Guiffrè, Milan 1996, p. 2.
7. *See* Robert Perent, *Marques notoirement connues et marques dites 'de haute renommée'*, thesis Paris 1960, p. 279.
8. Jassuda Bédarride, *Commentaire des lois sur les brevets d'invention, sur les noms des fabricants et des lieux de fabrication, sur les marques de fabrique et de commerce*, t. III, Imprimerie et Librairie Générale de Jurisprudence Cosse et Marchal, Paris-Aix 1869, pp. 12-13 and 56.
9. Ambroise Rendu, *Traité pratique des marques de fabrique et de commerce et de la concurrence déloyale*, Imprimerie et Librairie Générale de Jurisprudence Cosse et Marchal, Paris 1858, pp. I-II and 2.
10. CA Paris, 16 January 1868, Ann. propr. ind. 1869, p. 336.
11. Ryszard Skubisz, *Funkcje znaku towarowego*, in: *Księga pamiątkowa z okazji 80-lecia rzecznictwa patentowego w Polsce*, Polska Izba Rzeczników Patentowych, Warsaw 2001, p. 170.

century and a half ago, everyone is able to appreciate a mark that has become famous, while the number of those who know and can judge at first glance the real quality of the merchandise is very small. It is therefore above all the mark that is the focus of fame. Hence, he said, what indeed gives value to a good is not so much its intrinsic perfection as the mark it bears.[12] However, it must be noted that the quality function depends on the origin function, being only an aspect of the latter.[13] The quality function is indeed protected indirectly, through the distinctive function,[14] since the trade mark gives no guarantee as to the quality of the product bearing it.[15] Consequently, although the reputed trade mark is likely to perform the quality function, like any trade mark used on the market and known to customers, this function of the trade mark does not justify the extension of its protection because of its notoriety.

3. Advertising function of the trade mark. From the second half of the 19th century, as a result of the economic progress linked to the development of the means of production, and in particular thanks to the development of advertising, trade marks could become widely known by consumers, in other words they could acquire a reputation, also outside the clientele targeted by the owner. From then on, the trade mark could become a means by itself to encourage the public to buy any good or service designated by it. Indeed, the fame allows the mark not only to inform about the quality of the good or service that customers can expect but also to attract and direct public attention to the good or service,[16] to 'seduce' the consumer.

This effect is traditionally referred to as the 'advertising' function. In general, this function may be performed by the trade marks that are known to the public.[17] The advertising function is often presented as specific to the trade marks having a reputation. According to several authors, the trade mark fulfils the function of indication of source and the quality function, but when it reaches a certain degree of

12. Bédarride, *Commentaire des lois sur les brevets ...*, p. 153.
13. Dominique Brandt, *La protection élargie de la marque de haute renommée au-delà des produits identiques et similaires. Étude de droit comparé*, Librairie Droz, Geneva 1985, pp. 117-118; Sara Caselli, *Il marchio che gode di rinomanza*, thesis Parma 2014, pp. 14-18. Indeed, the quality function makes it possible to justify protection of the trade mark against the likelihood of confusion, since the quality of the third party's goods, over which the proprietor has no control, is likely to be associated with him. Skubisz, *Funkcje znaku towarowego ...*, p. 171.
14. Adriano Vanzetti, *Funzione e natura giuridica del marchio*, Riv. Dir. Comm. 1961, I, pp. 32-33. *See also* Annette Kur, Martin Senftleben, *European Trade Mark Law: A Commentary*, Oxford University Press, Oxford 2017, p. 14. Cf. Brandt, *La protection élargie de la marque ...*, p. 120.
15. Giuseppe Sena, *Brevi note sulla funzione del marchio*, Riv. Dir. Ind. 1989, I, p. 8. Indeed, the trade mark owner is not required to maintain a particular quality, which results from the fact that trade mark law only serves to protect the owner's interests and, if the law protects the consumer, it is only indirectly and because it protects the owner first. Pouillet, *Traité des marques de fabrique ...*, pp. 15-16.
16. *See* Yann Basire, *Les fonctions de la marque: essai sur la cohérence du régime juridique d'un signe distinctif*, LexisNexis, Paris 2014, p. 140.
17. Nevertheless, it was observed that the advertising function can sometimes be fulfilled by a trade mark, thanks to its inherent originality. Perent, *Marques notoirement connues ...*, p. 279. The *ab initio* distinctiveness may give the mark an important advertising value. Georges Dassas, *L'élargissement de la protection des marques en droit français, allemand et international*, Librairies techniques, Paris 1976, p. 88.

fame, it can then perform the advertising function.[18] This function can therefore, in principle, be achieved, thanks to the reputation embodied in the mark, which makes it possible not only to retain customers but also to expand the clientele.

There is little doubt that a reputed trade mark, through the associations it brings to mind, often determines the consumer's decision. Some trade marks turn into real symbols that convey specific ideas or values,[19] are communication tools which can be used to raise particular associations and expectations in the minds of consumers.[20] As a result, from a simple sign indicating the commercial origin, the trade mark became a 'power in itself',[21] 'an independent support for the constitution of a clientele',[22] 'inspiring the buyer's confidence',[23] having a 'magnetism'.[24] Nowadays, it is perhaps even more true to say that the trade mark is often more important to customers than the quality of the designated good. As Vivant said, today's consumer can pay a lot of money for a branded product, whether it is good or not, because he pays for the mark.[25]

The economic importance of the trade mark is undeniable and this phenomenon is not recent.[26] Nowadays, the trade mark is essential in the marketing of any kind of good or service, giving its owner a major advantage on the market. The owner may charge higher prices than his competitors. In addition, he can easily extend its field of activity to new sectors. The mark is likely to have a high value which can be the main element of the proprietor's assets. The company's market position will depend in large part on the commercial value of the mark linked to its ability to attract the public. This is why significant investments are directed at promoting the mark to the public.

Consequently, the trade mark with a reputation exerts a power of attraction and suggestion that leads the consumer to choose a good or a service not because of its qualities but because of its mark.[27] For this effect to occur, the consumer does not need to be misled as to the commercial origin of the good or service. The trade mark fulfils the function of advertising independently of the distinctive function. In other words, the consumer may be seduced and encouraged to buy even if he does not attach the origin of the good or service to the trade mark owner. Thus, it was recognised that the reputed trade mark acquires an advertising value that is likely to be threatened by acts

18. *See* e.g. Georges Dassas, *Conditions et effets de la notoriété*, in: *Le nouveau droit des marques en France*, Colloque IRPI, Paris 1991, No. 10, p. 27.
19. On the role of trade marks today cf. Jean-Pierre Clavier, *Marques et droits des tiers – (vers un droit des 'marques-médias')*, Propr. ind. 2004, No. 7, étude 13, paras 2 et seq.
20. Martin Senftleben, in: Annette Kur, Martin Senftleben, *European Trade Mark Law: A Commentary*, Oxford University Press, Oxford 2017, p. 339.
21. Hélène Portet, *Les marques notoirement connues ou de haute renommée selon la Convention de Paris et la loi française du 31 décembre 1964*, thesis Paris 1975, p. 16.
22. Herman Cohen Jehoram, *La protection des marques contre l'usage pour des produits différents: la loi Benelux, un exemple pour l'Europe?*, PI 1978, p. 225.
23. Michel Jaton, *La protection des marques de haute renommée au regard du droit suisse*, thesis Lausanne 1961, p. 30.
24. Senftleben, *European Trade Mark ...*, p. 337.
25. Michel Vivant, *Marque et fonction sociale de la marque. Ou quand la réalité passe par le rêve?*, in: *Les défis du droit des marques au XXIe siècle. Actes du colloque en l'honneur du professeur Yves Reboul*, LexisNexis, Paris 2011, p. 153.
26. *See* e.g. Yves Saint-Gal, *Importance économique des droits de propriété industrielle*, RIDIA 1968, No. 76, p. 50.
27. Brandt, *La protection élargie de la marque ...*, p. 122.

other than traditional acts of trade mark infringement.[28] Indeed, with the emergence of reputed trade marks, third parties began to abuse the freedom to use others' marks outside the speciality. The third party could benefit from the attractive power resulting from the public's knowledge and recognition of the mark, and from the public's trust in the mark acquired through the owner's efforts. At the same time, the owner risked suffering damage because the use of the mark by the third party was likely to reduce the attractiveness of the sign.

National European trade mark legislations were however traditionally aimed at preserving only the function of indication of origin. It was accepted that, even if the trade mark fulfilled several functions, only the distinctive function was subject to protection.[29] Hence, trade mark law, governed by the principle of speciality, tending to condemn the risk of confusion, quickly proved insufficient to ensure effective protection of trade marks and no longer always corresponded to the particularities of the economic context,[30] appearing as a simplistic conception of the subject. As a result, in many countries, the courts began to condemn the use of famous trade marks outside the speciality and in the absence of a likelihood of confusion, on the grounds of general civil liability. The jurisprudential practice, supported by the doctrine that developed several concepts to enhance the trade mark protection, led the legislator to establish a special regime for the protection of trade marks having a reputation.

4. Consecration of special protection of trade marks with a reputation by the European legislator. At the European Union (EU) level, a regime of enhanced protection of the trade mark with a reputation was introduced by the trade mark Directive 89/104 of 21 December 1988[31] and by the Regulation on the Community trade mark 40/94 of 20 December 1993.[32] Today, the special regime is provided for by the trade mark Directive 2015/2436 of 16 December 2015[33] and by the Regulation on the EU trade mark 2017/1001 of 14 June 2017.[34] All the current Member States of the EU provide for the extended protection of the trade mark with a reputation which, under Directive 2015/2436, is mandatory.[35] Under the special regime, the trade mark with a reputation benefits from enhanced protection since the law condemns acts of use made

28. Cohen Jehoram, *La protection des marques ...*, p. 225.
29. *See* Caselli, *Il marchio che gode di rinomanza ...*, p. 13.
30. Brandt, *La protection élargie de la marque ...*, p. 198.
31. First Council Directive 89/104/EEC of the Council of 21 December 1988 to approximate the laws of the Member States relating to trade marks, Official Journal L 040 of 11 February 1989; replaced by Directive 2008/95/EC of the European Parliament and of the Council of 22 October 2008 to approximate the laws of the Member States relating to trade marks, Official Journal L 299 of 8 November 2008.
32. Regulation (EC) No. 40/94 of the Council of 20 December 1993 on the Community trade mark, Official Journal L 11 of 14 January 1994; replaced by Regulation (EC) 207/2009 of the Council of 26 February 2009 on the Community trade mark, Official Journal L 78 of 24 March 2009.
33. Directive (EU) 2015/2436 of the European Parliament and of the Council of 16 December 2015 to approximate the laws of the Member States relating to trade marks, Official Journal L 336 of 23 December 2015.
34. Regulation (EU) 2017/1001 of the European Parliament and of the Council of 14 June 2017 on the European Union trade mark, Official Journal L 154 of 16 June 2017.
35. *See* Georges Bonet, *La très prochaine réforme du droit des marques dans l'Union européenne*, Propr. intell. 2015, No. 54, p. 6.

by third parties outside the speciality and independently of the existence of a likelihood of confusion. These are acts of reproduction or imitation of reputed marks that are detrimental to the distinctive character of the trade mark or its repute, or that allow third parties to take unfair advantage of the distinctive character or repute of the mark. All these cases constitute forms of infringement of the trade mark under the special regime. Once a form of infringement has been demonstrated, the third party may avoid liability only if he establishes that he had due cause to lawfully use another person's trade mark. Moreover, a risk of violation of a trade mark with a reputation constitutes a ground for refusal or invalidity of a younger trade mark. In those cases, the conditions for infringement apply *mutatis mutandis*, with the main difference that the assessment is made based on the application for registration of the younger mark and not based on the use of a sign by the third party on the market.

Since the subject of this book is par excellence harmonised at the level of the EU, the examination of the special protection of trade marks with a reputation requires that account be taken in particular of the case law of the Court of Justice and General Court of the European Union. To some extent, refererence will also be made to the practice of the European Union Intellectual Property Office (EUIPO) and to the jurisprudence of some of the Member States which apply the special regime resulting from the EU law in civil infringement proceedings. It should be noted that the European trade mark law functions in many national legal systems and the interpretation and application of rules derived from the European legislation are sometimes affected by legal practices and traditions adopted in the Member States. It should be, however, noted that, given the objective of harmonisation, there is very little room for divergence in this area of law.

5. Plan of the study. The right holder who invokes trade mark infringement beyond the limits of the speciality must demonstrate that the mark deserves the benefits of extended protection and is therefore covered by the special regime provided for trade marks with a reputation. Thus, in the first chapter, I will set out the framework of that regime, which will allow me to determine the assumptions on which that special protection is based. The allegedly unlawful use of a trade mark with a reputation must constitute a use which is subject to sanctions on the basis of extended protection irrespective of the form of infringement established by the proprietor of the mark. Therefore, in the second chapter, I will present the prerequisites for infringement of the right to a reputed mark common to all forms of infringement recognised by the legislature. The different types of infringement of the right to the trade mark with a reputation will be the subject of the third chapter, in which I will characterise the forms of infringement, trying in particular to explain the role of each of them and to analyse how they can be demonstrated in civil infringement and administrative proceedings.

CHAPTER 1

Special Regime of Protection of Trade Marks with a Reputation

6. Evolution and current regime. A proper understanding of the current regime of special protection of trade marks with a reputation (§1.02) requires a thorough study of its evolution (§1.01). Indeed, the European regime of enhanced protection is the result of several doctrinal theories and conceptions implemented by courts in many countries over the course of a few decades. The different national praetorian practices and theoretical visions of the extension of the protection of the reputed trade mark developed in the past have not been without an impact on the model of special protection adopted by the European legislator which, in a way, brought them together and combined in a single system. The study of the evolution of the special protection will enable us to better frame and understand the current regime and to identify some of the distortions present in the current case law of the concepts which are at the origin of the enhanced protection of the reputed trade mark.

§1.01 EVOLUTION OF THE SPECIAL REGIME OF PROTECTION OF TRADE MARKS WITH A REPUTATION

7. Sources of the principle of speciality. The trade mark laws adopted in the 19th century, such as the French Trade Mark Law of 23 June 1857, the first modern trade mark legislation, condemned only two cases of infringement of trade mark rights, namely infringement *stricto sensu* in the case of servile reproduction of the mark and the 'fraudulent imitation likely to mislead the buyer'.[36] Apart from the situation of reproduction of the mark for the goods designated in the registration, an act of infringement of trade mark right could therefore only be established in the event of use of a similar sign causing a likelihood of confusion. The legislator thus provided for a

36. Respectively, in Articles 7 and 8 of the French law of 23 June 1857. *See* Pouillet, *Traité des marques de fabrique ...*, p. 242.

relative protection of the trade mark, within the limits of the distinctive function, as a means of protection against unfair competition and the resulting damage. It was admitted that for both to occur, the later sign had to be more or less easily confused with the prior mark. Otherwise, prohibition of use of the second sign would have no rational basis in terms of equity or justice.[37] Hence, in order for the mark to perform its function of indication of origin, and thus guarantee that all the goods under the mark come from its owner, the legislator conferred on the mark a scope of protection going beyond the use of an identical sign for goods designated in the registration.[38] However, since the law only preserved the distinctive function, trade mark protection only extended to goods that could be associated with the same commercial origin.[39]

Taking into account the economic reality of the time, it was accepted that a likelihood of confusion was only possible when the trade mark was used by the third party for goods that were similar in their nature. It was considered that the reproduction of a trade mark in another industry excluded any risk of confusion, and therefore in no way infringed the trade mark right.[40] In this respect, Bédarride held that from the purpose of the law followed that the trade mark belonging to one manufacturer was protected in his favour only against use in similar industries, since there was no competition and hence no risk of harm when, for instance, a manufacturer of silk used a mark of sheets or lace.[41] Since the purpose of the law was to prevent unfair competition and therefore the likelihood of confusion, and not the trade mark itself, the principle of speciality was born, limiting the scope of protection of the trade mark to its use for identical or similar goods. This is how the similarity between the goods in dispute became a necessary condition for infringement of the trade mark right.

At the time, in order to assess the similarity between the goods, the case law attached crucial importance to their nature and sought confusion between the goods themselves. In a decision of 6 April 1866, a French court ruled that there was no similarity between the pins and needles, and in a judgment of 9 April 1888, another French court decided that the sewing linen thread and the sewing cotton thread were not similar. According to the latter judgment, their strength and appearance were not the same; for there to be confusion between these two goods of a different nature, it would be necessary to have a very inexperienced buyer and at the same time a very unscrupulous seller.[42] Thus, at first, the judges tended to qualify as similar goods which were mutually substitutable. This approach was generally approved by the scholars. In French doctrine, Rendu considered that since the purpose of the trade mark was to prevent confusion between similar goods, it was not possible to prohibit the use

37. Bédarride, *Commentaire des lois sur les brevets ...*, p. 56.
38. Cf. Paul Mathély, *Le droit français des signes distinctifs*, Librairie du Journal des notaires et des avocats, Paris 1984, p. 600.
39. *See* Galli, *Funzione del marchio e ampiezza ...*, p. 6.
40. *See* Amar, *Dei nomi, dei marchi e degli altri segni ...*, pp. 100-102; Henri Allart, André Allart, *Traité théorique et pratique des marques de fabrique et de commerce*, Arthur Rousseau, Paris 1914, p. 82.
41. Bédarride, *Commentaire des lois sur les brevets ...*, p. 57.
42. Cited by Paul Fauchille, *De ce qu'il faut entendre par des industries ou des commerces similaires en matière de marques de fabrique*, Ann. dr. comm. 1890, pp. 268-269. The judgment of 9 April 1888 was cancelled by the Court of Cassation. Cass. com., 1 December 1890, PI 1891, p. 22.

of a mark of threads by a manufacturer of candles. How could confusion be possible? - he was asking. Will we ever take a candle for thread, and vice versa?.[43] Also in Italian doctrine, some authors considered that trade mark infringement required the likelihood of confusion not only as to the origin but also between the goods themselves.[44] This interpretation of the legal provisions was sometimes criticised.[45] Rendu himself admitted that it was possible that the industry in which the mark was first applied was close enough to the industry in which the later sign was used, and that could lead to confusion.[46]

Over time, the assessment of the criterion of similarity between the goods evolved, moving away from the search for confusion between the goods themselves. Nevertheless, the nature of the goods remained the main factor when examining the similarity and hence the infringement of the trade mark right. However, over the decades, the economic context changed. On the one hand, companies began to extend the scope of their activities, focusing on neighbouring or even very distant industries, which was likely to justify a likelihood of confusion understood more broadly. On the other hand, production possibilities evolved, allowing for 'mass production'. In addition, advertising, which needed a distinctive sign as a support, experienced a great expansion, so that marks could more easily expand their notoriety and market value.[47]

First, it was doctrine and case law that filled the gap in trade mark law perceiving the trade mark exclusively as a sign indicating the commercial origin of the good bearing it. In several cases, the decisions concerned trade names, company names, etc. They were however perfectly transposable to trade marks.[48] The origins of the special protection of the reputed trade mark date back to the last decade of the 19th century. At that time, courts in various countries began to condemn the use of marks with a particular reputation despite the absence of similarity of the goods, assessed in the strict sense of the term, which therefore escaped the qualification of infringement of trade mark rights (§1.01[A]). This practice required to find a legal basis on which the decisions could be founded (§1.01[B]).

[A] Types of Use Falling under the Special Protection

8. Two main types of infringing use. The study of the case law and doctrine of the time allows to distinguish two main situations in which a wider protection was granted to famous trade marks outside the speciality. The first consisted in a likelihood of confusion in the broad sense of the term, i.e. in a danger of misleading the consumer as to the commercial origin of the good of the third party, notwithstanding the differences in nature between it and the good designated by the trade mark (§1.01[A][1]). In the second case, protection was granted against use of a sign by a

43. Rendu, *Traité pratique des marques de fabrique* ..., p. 24.
44. Cf. Galli, *Funzione del marchio e ampiezza* ..., p. 17.
45. *See* in particular Fauchille, *De ce qu'il faut entendre par des industries* ..., pp. 270-271.
46. Rendu, *Traité pratique des marques de fabrique* ..., p. 25.
47. Portet, *Les marques notoirement connues* ..., pp. 8-10. Cf. Mathély, *Le droit français des signes* ..., p. 18.
48. Perent, *Marques notoirement connues* ..., p. 166.

third party which, in the absence of any likelihood of confusion, was likely to undermine the attractive power of a trade mark having a reputation (§1.01[A][2]).

In both cases, the use of a reputed trade mark was generally condemned when it caused damage to the trade mark owner, in accordance with the general rules of civil liability. However, it should be noted that, apart from these two main situations, courts sometimes also condemned taking an unfair advantage of the reputation of a famous trade mark, in the absence of any risk of confusion or damage to the attractive power of the mark, as the current law expressly provides. However, this idea can be found in more recent case law, in particular German decisions from the 1980s, condemning the mere transfer of the image of reputation to the goods of the third party.[49] This type of infringement of a reputed trade mark was also considered in the draft amendments to the Paris Convention drawn up in the 1950s, which will be discussed further.[50] Nevertheless, at the origin of the special protection of a reputed trade mark, there is first and foremost the idea of condemning unfair conduct by third parties likely to cause damage to the owner of the trade mark.

[1] *Likelihood of Confusion* Lato Sensu

9. Broadening of the principle of speciality. At the end of the 19th century, courts in Europe began to condemn the likelihood of confusion *lato sensu*, which was widely appreciated in the sense that it was sufficient for the public to believe that the trade mark owner had extended his field of economic activity or that the two companies were linked. It was also referred to as the 'likelihood of confusion between the companies', to distinguish it from the classic situation of likelihood of confusion between the goods. Thus, the reputation of the sign made it possible to escape the rule of speciality in the strict sense of the term. This approach was favoured by some authors at the time, who pointed out that a danger of confusion outside the strict similarity of the goods justified an extended trade mark protection.[51]

Such likelihood of confusion allowed the third party to take an unfair advantage of the mark's reputation, which characterised the latter's fault, a necessary condition for general civil liability (§1.01[A][1][a]). In some decisions of the time, the prejudice was clearly determined, resulting in the degradation of the image of the trade mark (§1.01[A][1][b]).

[a] Likelihood of Confusion as an Unlawful Act

10. Early case law. To our knowledge, the oldest decision in which an extended protection of a reputed designation was admitted is the judgment of the Paris Commercial Court of 1 October 1891.[52] In this case, a company operating under the

49. *See* Ilanah Simon Fhima, *Exploring the Roots of European Dilution*, IPQ 2012, No. 1, pp. 31-32.
50. *See* para. 31 *infra*.
51. *See* Perent, *Marques notoirement connues ...*, pp. 178 et seq.
52. Trib. comm. Paris, 1 September 1891, confirmed by CA Paris, 24 February 1892, Ann. propr. ind. 1893, p. 319, *Bureau Veritas*.

name *Bureau Veritas*, whose purpose was to inform the public about the value and seaworthiness of seagoing vessels, objected to the use of the name *Agence Veritas* by a commercial information agency. According to the Paris Commercial Court, the defendant, by usurping part of the company name of the plaintiff, pursued only one purpose, that of taking advantage, thanks to confusion caused, of the indisputable notoriety on the market enjoyed by *Bureau Veritas*. The Court expressly admitted that the two companies operated in different industries, but the similarity between the two names was sufficient to cause confusion. As Brandt observed, this judgment remained in France for a long time an isolated decision.[53] A likelihood of confusion in the broad sense was accepted almost forty years later, in a judgment of the Paris Court of Appeal of 21 January 1930, concerning a well-known name *Urbaine*.[54] Nevertheless, it should be noted that in the two cases mentioned above, to quote the terms of the *Veritas* judgment, there existed 'a certain analogy between the types of industries operated by the parties in dispute'.

Thus, as the first case in which the idea of enhanced trade mark protection clearly going beyond the speciality appeared is often cited a dispute that took place in the United Kingdom in 1898, in which the manufacturer of cameras known under the name *Kodak* brought an action against a third party using that name for bicycles. The Court condemned the manufacturer of the bicycles on the basis of the passing off action, stating that there was a likelihood of confusion outside the speciality, which was possible, according to the decision, since the two goods were often sold in the same stores.[55] In another case, in 1902, an English judge ruled that the use of the sign *Times* by a manufacturer of bicycles was likely to lead the public to believe that there was a link with the owner of the trade mark of the famous newspaper.[56] In both cases, the courts identified a likelihood of confusion in order to base their decisions on the provisions on unfair competition, but, as it has been observed, the reasoning appears somewhat artificial.[57]

At that time, famous marks began to enjoy extended protection in the Scandinavian countries. In 1909, a Swedish court condemned the use of the sign *Aladdin*, renowned in relation to alcohol stoves, for oil. The owner of the trade mark *Ford*, reputed with respect to automobiles, was granted enhanced protection against the use of his mark in 1924, in Denmark, for cigarettes and in 1925, in Norway, for tobacco.[58]

The Dutch courts also condemned the likelihood of confusion *lato sensu* in several cases since the 1930s, for example, in 1931, the use of the mark of pharmaceutical articles *Rheumasan* by a manufacturer of bed sheets advertised as a remedy for rheumatism, and, in 1932, the use of the mark of cigarettes *Turmacq* for razor blades.[59]

53. Brandt, *La protection élargie de la marque …*, p. 196.
54. CA Paris, 21 January 1930, Ann. propr. ind. 1930, p. 101, *Urbaine*.
55. Cited by John Wolff, *Non-competing Goods in Trademark Law*, Columb. L. Rev. 1937, vol. 37, No. 4, p. 588; David S. Welkowitz, *Trademark Dilution*, Bloomberg, Washington 2002, p. 9.
56. Cited by Simon Fhima, *Exploring the Roots …*, p. 26.
57. Simon Fhima, *Exploring the Roots …*, p. 26.
58. Brandt, *La protection élargie de la marque …*, p. 196.
59. Cited by Leo Wichers Hoeth, *Étude comparative de quelques aspects de l'usage de la marque*, thesis Leyden 1963, pp. 143-144; Brandt, *La protection élargie de la marque …*, p. 196.

By a judgment of 11 March 1949, the Turin Court condemned the use of the mark of cigarettes *Lucky Strike* by a manufacturer of perfumes, recognising for the first time in Italy an extended protection of reputed marks.[60] According to the judgment, the use of a famous trade mark for different goods was likely to create confusion among the public as to the origin of these goods.[61] In a judgment of 29 January 1954, the Court of Arezzo decided that the use of a reputed trade mark entailed a likelihood of confusion since the consumer could believe that the companies in dispute were linked.[62]

This jurisprudential trend was not specific only to Europe. In the United States (US), in three cases decided in the 1920s, the owners of the trade marks *Rolls-Royce*, *Vogue* and *Dunhill* raised the reputation of their marks to successfully oppose their use for, respectively, radio sets, headgear and shirts.[63]

Since in the above-mentioned *Veritas* and *Urbaine* cases, between the activities of the litigants, although not competing, there existed a certain analogy, it was in a judgment delivered by the Paris Court on 23 November 1937, concerning the designation *Paris Soir*,[64] that a French court granted for the first time a special protection to a distinctive sign against its use for a totally different good.[65] In this case, the title of the famous newspaper was used by a manufacturer of aperitifs.[66] The Court noted that the priority of use of this title conferred on its holder the right to prohibit any abusive and harmful use, even for different goods, and that such abuse could constitute a civil fault. This judgment deserves particular attention. As Dassas noted, although the likelihood of confusion was mentioned by the Court, it was unlikely that the public could believe that the publishing house of *Paris Soir* had embarked on the production of aperitifs. According to the author, it was therefore not a question of the likelihood of confusion, either between the goods or between the companies, in other words, the likelihood of confusion in the narrow or broad sense, but of a simple association of ideas, possible thanks to the attractive power and notoriety of the name *Pars Soir*.[67] Moreover, it should be noted that, on the one hand, the Court expressly condemned only the third party's intention to create confusion and not the likelihood of confusion as such and, on the other hand, the reasoning of the decision does not allow to identify the damage suffered by the holder. That is why, Fernand-Jacq criticised the decision, insisting on

60. Cited by Remo Franceschelli, *Dei marchi notori, del modo come si construiscono i principi giuridici consolidati, e della fortuna delle sentenze*, Riv. Dir. Ind. 1961, II, p. 396.
61. The Court also specified that even if confusion did not appear, the use of the mark *Lucky Strike* was, nevertheless, a means for the third party to unduly benefit from the notoriety of the mark. Thus, the idea of punishing the sole fault of the usurper consisting in taking unfair advantage of the trade mark's reputation is also present in the judgment.
62. Cited by Galli, *Funzione del marchio e ampiezza …*, p. 37.
63. Cited by Wolff, *Non-competing Goods …*, pp. 601-603; Rudolf Callmann, *Unfair Competition Without Competition?*, Univ. Pen. Law Rev. 1947, vol. 95, No. 4, p. 446. The courts condemned their use by retaining a risk of confusion in the broader sense, without referring to dilution of trade marks, a concept which, as we shall see, was already discussed in doctrine. *See* paras 15-16 *infra*.
64. CA Paris, 23 November 1937, Ann. propr. ind. 1939, p. 269, comment of Fernand Jacq, *Paris Soir*.
65. Dassas, *L'élargissement de la protection …*, pp. 136-137.
66. It should be noted that the title of a work was, according to Pouillet, in fact the designation of the good. Pouillet, *Traité des marques de fabrique …*, pp. 998-999.
67. Dassas, *L'élargissement de la protection …*, p. 137.

the importance of the principle of speciality and on the absence of any indication in the decision as to the possibility of confusion likely to cause prejudice to the plaintiff.[68] Therefore, the decision appears particularly modern, as it corresponds to the current model of protection of reputed trade marks, which condemns the mere fault resulting from an association of signs, irrespective of the likelihood of confusion.

[b] Likelihood of Confusion Detrimental to the Repute of the Trade Mark

11. Early case law. In part of the case law of the time, the harm resulting from the creation of a likelihood of confusion was clearly identified. It consisted in the degradation of the mark, in other words in tarnishment of its image.

The idea of protecting the image of the sign (precisely of a trade name) appeared in French jurisprudence in a famous judgment rendered by the Commercial Court of Seine of 5 January 1940, concerning the designation of pens *Waterman* used by a manufacturer of razor blades.[69] According to the Court, the fact that a manufacturer of razor blades presented its goods under the name of another undertaking, namely *Waterman*, a company with a high reputation in the pens industry, was likely, notwithstanding the differences between the goods, to create confusion that benefited it and to cause the holder of the name a sensitive commercial disorder, as well as significant damage if the goods were of poor quality, or sales processes contrary to local practices. In the judgment, therefore, the idea of prejudice in the form of damage to the image of the name resulting from the likelihood of confusion assessed extensively appears clearly.[70] The Bourges Court of Appeal referred to the *Waterman* decision in a judgment of 28 January 1958, concerning the use of the trade name of the manufacturer of famous sewing machine *Singer* by a manufacturer of bicycles.[71] The Court held that there existed a likelihood of confusion likely to cause harm to the Singer companies, in particular if the bicycles were of inferior quality, or if the selling conditions were contrary to fair trade practices.[72] The idea of degradation reappeared in French case law in a decision rendered on 26 June 1974 by the Nancy Court of Appeal concerning the trade mark *Anne de Solène*.[73] According to the judgment, the owner of a reputed trade mark has the greatest interest in defending it not only against direct competitors but also against abusive use, exposing that famous mark to deterioration and to losing, by becoming banal, its attractive power with the clientele that considered it as a prestigious mark.[74] The damage to the mark image is indeed the central point of the decision.

The damage consisting in the degradation of the trade mark image resulting from the likelihood of confusion *lato sensu* was condemned in other countries. As Wolff

68. Fernand Jacq, *Note sous CA Paris 23 nov. 1937*, Ann. propr. ind. 1939, p. 271.
69. Trib. com. Seine, 5 January 1940, Ann. propr. ind. 1940-1948, p. 289, *Waterman*.
70. On this judgment *see* Perent, *Marques notoirement connues …*, pp. 160-161.
71. CA Bourges, 28 January 1958, PI 1959, p. 32, *Singer*.
72. Regarding a trade mark *see* CA Paris, 3 November 1958, Ann. propr. ind. 1959, p. 24, *Lu*.
73. CA Nancy, 26 June 1974, Ann. propr. ind. 1975, p. 161, JCP 1975, p. 18178, comment of Georges Bonet, *Anne de Solène*.
74. On this judgment *see* Portet, *Les marques notoirement connues …*, p. 192.

observed, despite the application in Germany of the theory of dilution, which will be presented below, courts even more frequently condemned the use of reputed trade marks, based on the concept of likelihood of confusion in the broad sense, namely that the public could believe that the companies were related. The damage to the owner of the famous trade mark consisted in harm to its reputation if the goods of the third party were of inferior quality.[75]

The idea of degradation linked to the likelihood of confusion in the broad sense was present also in Dutch case law. In a decision of 8 December 1948, a court condemned the use of the mark of cigarettes *Players* by a manufacturer of sugar cigarettes, in the absence of danger of confusion within the speciality. The judge found that the defendant caused damage, by the fact that its packaging was of poor quality, to the image of the *Players* mark. In a judgment of 5 May 1953, the Court of Appeal of Bois-le-Duc condemned the use of the sign *Lucky Smile* for chewing gum, as infringing the rights of the owner of the trade mark *Lucky Strike*. According to the decision, if the third party's goods were of inferior quality, the goods of the trade mark owner would be discredited in the eyes of the public. In consequence, the trade mark owner would sell less than previously. Thus, the latter would run the risk that his mark would lose its value since it would no longer have the same advertising effectiveness.[76]

[2] Harm to the Attractiveness of the Trade Mark in the Absence of a Likelihood of Confusion

12. Two types of harm. Another group of cases of use of reputed trade marks condemned outside the speciality are the situations in which, in the absence of any likelihood of confusion in the minds of customers, the attachment of a famous mark to a third party's good undermined the attractiveness of the mark. These cases include two forms of harm caused to the trade mark, referred to in European doctrine as, on the one hand, 'dilution',[77] 'whittling away' or 'blurring' of the distinctive character (§1.01[A][2][a]) and, on the other hand, 'tarnishment' or 'degradation' of the mark's image (§1.01[A][2][b]). These concepts gave rise to two forms of infringement of reputed trade marks, which are now enshrined by the European legislator, namely detriment to the distinctive character and detriment to the repute of the trade mark. Although tarnishment seems currently more important in practice, we will see that it is above all dilution that is at the origins of the extended protection of the trade marks.

75. Wolff, *Non-competing Goods* ..., p. 588.
76. Cited by Wichers Hoeth, *Étude comparative* ..., pp. 144-145.
77. This term, in particular under American law, may cover all forms of infringement of reputed trade marks. In this book I will use it in a narrow sense, as synonym for the detriment to the distinctive character, as the Court of Justice understands it. *See* CJ, 27 November 2008, case C-252/07, *Intel*, para. 29.

[a] *Dilution of the Distinctive Character of the Trade Mark*

13. History of dilution. The concept of dilution consists in granting a special protection to a reputed trade mark against the blurring of its distinctive power. At first, it appeared in German case law (§1.01[A][2][a][i]). It was developed by Anglo-Saxon doctrine (§1.01[A][2][a][ii]) and then enjoyed some success in other European countries (§1.01[A][2][a][iii]). It should be stressed that the concept of dilution is based on the idea that there is no likelihood of confusion.[78] However, as we will see, this concept was distorted in some countries by courts which linked it to the likelihood of confusion *lato sensu*.

[i] Origins of the Concept of Dilution in German Jurisprudence

14. First court decisions. The origins of the theory of dilution can be traced back to German case law of the 1920s. A judgment of 11 April 1923 concerning the use of a famous mark of perfume *4711* by a manufacturer of stockings and starch products and a judgment of 11 September 1924 concerning the reproduction of the mark *Odol*, reputed in relation to toothpaste water, by a producer of cutlery, should be mentioned.[79] In both cases, there was no danger of confusion.[80] The judge in the *Odol* case held that 'Odol' was a 'word-force' (*Schlagwort*) that has conquered an advertising force going beyond the usual meaning of trade mark so that anyone reading or hearing the word 'Odol' thinks of the plaintiff's toothpaste water. The latter therefore has the greatest interest in ensuring that his trade mark is not diluted. It would lose its advertising power if anyone used it to designate products that were totally different. According to the decision, appropriation of the fruits of the labour of others in this way is contrary to commercial honest practices. The defendant must also consider that if everyone could call his products 'Odol', the plaintiff's word 'Odol' would lose its value.[81] In the above judgments, the use of the disputed signs by third parties was condemned on the grounds of the existence of a risk of dilution of the distinctive character of the famous trade marks (*Verwässerung*). This case law enabled German doctrine to develop the theory of *Verwässerungsgefahrt*, literally danger of diluting of highly reputed trade marks.[82]

The notion of dilution reappeared in German case law after the Second World War in a judgment of 14 May 1952 concerning the use of a trade mark *Kaffee Hag*.[83] This trend is also reflected in a judgment of 11 November 1955 by the German Federal

78. Wichers Hoeth, *Étude comparative ...*, p. 150; Brandt, *La protection élargie de la marque ...*, p. 155. Cf. Eric D. Offner, *International Trademark Protection*, Fieldston Press, New York 1965, p. 75.
79. Cited by Ludwig Baeumer, *La protection de la marque de haute renommée en droit français et en droit allemand*, Rev. Inter. Dr. Comparé 1962, p. 550.
80. Perent, *Marques notoirement connues ...*, p. 167.
81. *See* Dassas, *L'élargissement de la protection ...*, p. 155. On this judgment *see also* Wolff, *Non-competing Goods ...*, p. 588.
82. *See* Baeumer, *La protection de la marque ...*, pp. 550-551.
83. Cited by Marie-Angèle Pérot-Morel, *L'extension de la protection des marques notoires*, RTD com. 1966, p. 33.

Court of Justice in the *Magirus* case, according to which the danger of blurring was not linked to the likelihood of confusion that the existence of similar marks could cause. In the light of the judgment, trade marks known in a very general way, beyond the circle of potential buyers, should be protected, even when any danger of confusion on the part of the public is excluded because of a totally different nature of the goods, against the use of identical or similar signs, likely to harm the unique situation that those marks occupy on the market, and at the same time, the attractive power they exercise over the public, thanks to their uniqueness.[84]

[ii] Development of the Concept of Dilution by Anglo-Saxon Scholars

15. Schechter's theory. The concept of dilution was then developed in Anglo-Saxon doctrine by an American lawyer Schechter who, in his famous article of 1927, called for special protection for trade marks, aimed at preserving their distinctiveness, regardless of the likelihood of confusion in the public mind. Schechter pointed out that, apart from the essential function of the mark to indicate the commercial origin of goods, its role was to stimulate purchases by influencing consumer choices. He considered that the traditional trade mark protection was inadequate because it ignored this fundamental aspect of the nature of the mark.[85] According to the author, the idea that trade mark law should be based on the preservation of the function of indication of origin, and that, consequently, the only prejudice for the owner consisted in the likelihood of confusion, was archaic. He noted that, in the modern world, it was no longer the designation of commercial origin but the 'creation and retention of custom' that constituted the mark's objective.[86]

Hence, Schechter pointed out that the use of a mark by non-competitors may also be harmful to the proprietor. This harm consisted in the 'whittling away' of the trade mark. According to the author, the more distinctive or unique the trade mark, the more important the effect it has on the public, and therefore the greater the need for its protection against dissociation from the good for which it was originally used.[87] It should be noted that Schechter proposed enhanced protection precisely not for reputed (famous) trade marks, but for 'coined, invented, arbitrary or fanciful' marks.[88]

16. Influence of Schechter's theory. Schechter's theory was criticised by many Anglo-Saxon authors who considered that it granted on coined, invented, arbitrary and fanciful trade marks a property right, thus an absolute right similar to copyright or

84. Cited by Perent, *Marques notoirement connues ...*, p. 171.
85. Frank I. Schechter, *The Rational Basis of Trademark Protection*, Harv. L. Rev. 1926-1927, vol. XL, p. 818.
86. Schechter, *The Rational Basis ...*, p. 822.
87. Schechter, *The Rational Basis ...*, p. 825.
88. This idea was recently approved by an author who questions the principle of speciality and considers that the owner of each unique trade mark should be able to extend its protection to any product. Danny Friedmann, *The Uniqueness of the Trade Mark: A Critical Analysis of the Specificity and Territoriality Principles*, EIPR 2016, vol. 38, No. 11, pp. 677 et seq.

patent.[89] In Wolff's view, Schechter's idea was too revolutionary because it proposed to abandon the criterion of likelihood of confusion on which American trade mark and unfair competition laws were based. Wolff considered that the same objective could be achieved relying on the theory of likelihood of confusion in the broad sense, applied by an American court in the *Vogue* case, or earlier by an English court in the *Kodak* case.[90] Notwithstanding the criticism of his theories in later doctrine, the ideas raised by Schechter contributed considerably to the development of the concept of dilution,[91] which was eventually enshrined in law, *inter alia*, by the European legislator. The quotation of Schechter's work by Advocate General Jacobs in the *Adidas Salomon* case, as the first to articulate the notion of dilution, clearly shows his impact on trade mark law.[92]

In the US, one of the first cases in which the concept of dilution was implemented was the *Tiffany* case between the famous jeweller and a film production company. Reiterating Schechter's words, the judge pointed out that in such cases, concerning non-competitive goods, the real damage was to be found in the 'gradual whittling away or dispersion of the identity' of the mark.[93]

Schechter's theory was then approved by Callmann who pointed out the difference between the situations of likelihood of confusion and dilution and proposed to apply the latter in the absence of any confusion. According to this German-American author, 'The dilution presages a process of attrition that slowly but surely destroys the uniqueness or singularity of a trademark.'[94] Like Schechter, Callmann limited the protection of the distinctive power of famous trade marks to unique or highly distinctive signs.[95]

[iii] Reception of the Concept of Dilution in Europe

17. Jurisprudence. Outside Germany, the concept of dilution was to some extent successful in Europe. An excellent example of a decision in which the theory of dilution was applied can be found in Polish case law. In a judgment of 4 October 1938, a court

89. *See* Ilanah Simon, *Dilution by Blurring: A Conceptual Roadmap*, IPQ 2010, No. 1, pp. 48 et seq. The author presents several theories relating to the protection of famous trade marks developed in Anglo-Saxon doctrine.
90. Wolff, *Non-competing Goods* ..., pp. 602-603. Regarding the *Vogue* and *Kodak* cases *see* para. 10 *supra*.
91. On the influence of Schechter's work *see* Graeme B. Dinwoodie, *Dilution as Unfair Competition: European Echoes*, Oxford Legal Studies Research Paper 2013, No. 37, pp. 1 et seq.
92. Opinion of Advocate General Francis Geoffrey Jacobs in case C-408/01, *Adidas Salomon*, para. 37. In addition, Advocate General cites the American model of dilution protection as an example. In American doctrine, this passage in the conclusions was considered surprising since Schechter developed his theory on the basis of German case law. *See* J. Thomas McCarthy, *Dilution of a Trademark: European and United States Law Compared*, TMR 2004, vol. 94, No. 6, pp. 1165-1166.
93. Cited by Welkowitz, *Trademark Dilution* ..., p. 10. It should be, however, noted that the question of confusion is also raised in the *Tiffany* decision. *See* Wolff, *Non-competing Goods* ..., pp. 601-602.
94. Callmann, *Unfair Competition* ..., p. 448.
95. Callmann, *Unfair Competition* ..., p. 461.

condemned the application for registration of an image of a coffee grinder, registered as a trade mark in relation to coffee, by a manufacturer of sewing thread.[96] Given the long-lasting use, the judge qualified the mark as well known and noted that the harm suffered by the owner consisted in dilution of the mark's power of attraction. According to the judgment, the image of the coffee grinder would lose its distinctive force if it was used by several companies to distinguish several goods of a different nature. As a result, the trade mark was likely to become more common; hence the distinctive character could be diluted.[97] The decision perfectly applies the concept of dilution. The attractive power of the trade mark is linked to its fame and not to a particular image it would convey, and the harm of the interests of the trade mark owner is characterised by the blurring of the distinctive character of the sign.

French case law applied the theory of dilution restrictively since it was considered to be a mere corollary of the likelihood of confusion.[98] However, French doctrine integrated this theory correctly. Pérot-Morel explained that, in the event of simultaneous use of marks, even in the absence of any likelihood of confusion, the interplay of the association of ideas on which the trade mark's commercial value is based is distorted. The author pointed out that if the sign represents several goods of a different nature, the spontaneous association with the sign, therefore, the suggestive effect of the trade mark deteriorates considerably. Moreover, the fascination that the mark exerted because of its uniqueness fades as soon as it becomes a common sign. Pérot-Morel concluded that what is commonplace no longer has any appeal. As a result, the economic value of the mark is degraded.[99] The Paris Court of Appeal referred for the first time to the idea of dilution in a judgment of 3 November 1958, in a case between the owner of the mark of biscuits *Lu* and a manufacturer of rusks and gingerbread using a similar sign *Luc*.[100] According to the decision, it is not acceptable for third parties to take advantage of the reputation of a well-known mark in order to sell under its name more or less similar goods to buyers misled as to the origin of the goods, thus reducing the value of the mark through too frequent and diverse use. In a judgment of 8 December 1962,[101] the Paris Court of Appeal explicitly condemned the damage caused to the distinctiveness of a trade mark.[102] By that decision, the Court punished the use of the famous mark of automobile *Pontiac* by a manufacturer of refrigerators.[103] The Court observed that by choosing, to sell refrigerators, a name known to a wide public as the mark of the American manufacturer of cars, without

96. SO Nowy Sącz, 4 October 1938, case I C 180/28, PI 1939, p. 99.
97. On this judgment *see* Brandt, *La protection élargie de la marque* ..., pp. 185-186; Joanna Piotrowska, *Renomowane znaki towarowe i ich ochrona*, C.H. Beck, Warsaw 2001, p. 178.
98. Brandt, *La protection élargie de la marque* ..., pp. 137 et seq.
99. Pérot-Morel, *L'extension de la protection* ..., p. 30.
100. CA Paris, 3 November 1958, Ann. propr. ind. 1959, p. 24, *Lu*. *See* Dassas, *L'élargissement de la protection* ..., p. 176.
101. CA Paris, 8 December 1962, D. 1963, p. 406, comment of Henri Desbois, Ann. propr. ind. 1963, p. 156, comment of Raymond Dusolier, *Pontiac*.
102. Cf. Marie-Angèle Pérot-Morel, *Notoriété et renommée: unité ou dualité de concept en droit des marques?*, in: *Mélanges offerts à Jean-Jacques Burst*, LexisNexis, Paris 1997, p. 469.
103. On the judgment *see also* Albert Chavanne, *Les marques notoirement connues ou de haute renommée*, in: *Études de droit contemporain*, Éditions Cujas, Paris 1966, p. 306; Pérot-Morel, *L'extension de la protection* ..., p. 37.

doing anything to ensure that customers were well informed that it was a French production with no connection to the American firm, the French company caused a prejudice to the foreign firm by weakening the distinctive character and appeal of the mark. In addition, the Court pointed out that in particular, potential buyers of high-quality, expensive cars may be reluctant to contact a firm which, in their opinion, also launches on the market different articles, undoubtedly of good quality, but which are very widely available to the general public.[104] The French judges applied the concept of dilution in several subsequent decisions.[105] An express reference to dilution of the distinctive power of the trade mark appears in particular in decisions rendered on 12 October 1967 and 19 October 1970,[106] in a case widely commented in doctrine between the owner of the mark *Mazda*, renowned in France in relation to lamps, and the Japanese manufacturer of cars. The courts raised that the use of the famous *Mazda* mark by another undertaking weakened the distinctive character and attractiveness of the mark. The decisions mentioned above prove the presence of the concept of dilution in French case law. Nevertheless, as we have pointed out, the condemnation of dilution was closely linked to the fact that the use of the disputed sign was likely to lead the public to believe that there was a kind of conjunction of interests, of dependence between the owner of the earlier trade mark and the user of the disputed sign. Indeed, Desbois pointed out that the judgment of the Paris Court in the *Mazda* case was based on the idea that customers could attribute a common origin to the signs, which was a type of the likelihood of confusion.[107]

Relating dilution to the likelihood of confusion was not specific to French case law. In the above-mentioned judgment of the Court of Appeal of Bois-le-Duc in the Netherlands of 1953, rendered in the *Lucky Strike* case, the Court retained, regardless of the danger of confusion, another consequence, namely that the trade mark owner risked seeing his mark diluted and thus losing its attractive power.[108] Similarly, in the above-mentioned judgment of 11 March 1949 concerning the use of the mark *Lucky Strike* in Italy, the Turin Court expressly referred to dilution.[109]

[b] Tarnishment of the Image of the Trade Mark

18. Role of the concept of tarnishment. The second form of infringement of a reputed trade mark condemned by courts in the absence of a likelihood of confusion constitutes the detriment to the reputation, in other words, tarnishment (degradation) of the trade

---

104. It is also interesting to read that Desbois criticised the Court for attaching too much importance to an opinion in which 'snobbism' plays a part. Henri Desbois, *Note sous CA Paris 8 déc. 1962*, D. 1963, p. 411.
105. *See* CA Lyon, 18 May 1967, Ann. propr. ind. 1968, p. 177, *Nobel-Bozel*.
106. TGI Paris, 12 October 1967 and CA Paris, 19 October 1970, Ann. propr. ind. 1971, p. 1, comment of Dusolier, *Mazda*.
107. Henri Desbois, *La protection des marques notoires ou de haute renommée en l'absence de confusion entre les produits, à propos de l'affaire Mazda*, in: *Mélanges en l'honneur de Daniel Bastian*, t. II, Librairies techniques, Paris 1974, p. 16. Cf. also CA Paris, 5 June 1986, Ann. propr. ind. 1987, p. 189, *Liberty*.
108. Wichers Hoeth, *Étude comparative* ..., pp. 144-145.
109. Galli, *Funzione del marchio e ampiezza* ..., p. 38.

mark's image. For a long time, the doctrine attached much less importance to this type of damage and the old case law recognising extended protection is definitely more modest in this respect. As we have seen, trade mark degradation was often related to the likelihood of confusion and was effectively condemned on the basis of trade mark infringement within the speciality. It should therefore be noted that the protection of the famous trade mark outside the risk of confusion has its origins more in the theory of dilution than in the idea of condemning the harm caused to the trade mark's repute.

To a certain extent, taking into account degradation, in the absence of a likelihood of confusion, appears to be a consequence of the recognition of the detriment of dilution. Indeed, since it is considered that the use of a reputed trade mark should be condemned in the event of blurring of its distinctive power, it seems logical to admit that it should also, or even *a fortiori*, be repressed when the association of the mark with the goods of the third party is detrimental to its repute, in particular to its image of excellence or prestige.

Nevertheless, tarnishment, as an autonomous form of infringement of a reputed trade mark, should not be considered only as a mere development of the concept of dilution. Indeed, the idea of condemning the detriment to the reputation of the trade mark in the event of use for dissimilar goods, in the absence of any confusion, was not completely ignored by the old doctrine and jurisprudence. In his study of 1899, Marry argued that when a mark is used for even completely different goods of inferior quality, discredit will be associated with the sign and consequently the owner will suffer a damage.[110]

19. Jurisprudence. Polish jurisprudence provides an example of a case in which degradation was claimed and condemned, in the absence of a likelihood of confusion. By a judgment of 30 November 1934, the Polish Supreme Court condemned the use of the famous mark of chocolate *Suchard* by a manufacturer of soap of poor quality.[111] Having ruled out the qualification of trade mark infringement because of the differences between the goods, the Supreme Court condemned the prejudice consisting in the fact that the plaintiff's customers, exposed to soaps of poor quality under the same trade mark, risked losing confidence in the quality of the plaintiff's chocolates. The fact that chocolate was associated with a lower quality soap was thus detrimental to the former, reducing customer's interest due to the degradation of the mark's image.[112]

European case law, however, contains few examples of cases in which detriment to the image of the trade mark was condemned. German jurisprudence, as Brandt observed, focused on the theory of dilution, very rarely mentioned the damage to the reputation of the mark.[113] Moreover, as a general rule, in several countries, detriment

110. Marry, *De la contrefaçon en matière de propriété* ..., p. 32. The author considered that this situation should constitute an infringement of the right to trade mark since he was in favour of the idea of absolute and non-relative protection of the trade mark.
111. SN, 30 November 1934, case C II 1744/34, OSN 1935, No. 5, p. 461, *Suchard*.
112. *See* Piotrowska, *Renomowane znaki* ..., p. 177.
113. Brandt, *La protection élargie de la marque* ..., p. 177. As an exception, the author cites a decision of 10 May 1951, by which the Stuttgart Court acknowledged tarnishment of the reputation of the mark because of the nature of the defendant's product, namely condoms.

to the image was strongly linked to the likelihood of confusion.[114] This was, for example, the position of French case law. Tarnishment was only retained regardless of the risk of confusion in more recent decisions.[115]

[B] Legal Grounds for the Special Protection

20. General and special grounds. It is now necessary to examine the grounds on which use of reputed trade marks outside the speciality *stricto sensu* was condemned prior to the harmonisation of trade mark law by Directive 89/104. At first, in the absence of special provisions, judges in various European countries only disposed of general legal grounds (§1.01[B][1]). Since the latter were not sufficiently adapted to ensure effective protection of reputed trade marks, several initiatives were taken to adopt special provisions expressly providing for extended protection (§1.01[B][2]).

[1] General Provisions

21. Trade mark law and tort liability. In the absence of a special ground of protection for reputed trade marks, one of the possibilities for granting enhanced protection was to interpret the provisions of trade mark law in a more flexible way (§1.01[B][1][a]). A second method was based on the use of the general tort civil liability or provisions on unfair competition based on tort liability principles (§1.01[B][1][b]).

[a] General Provisions of Trade Mark Law

22. Infringement of trade mark right: France. The method of granting enhanced protection against acts of use of reputed trade marks on the basis of trade mark law was to make the principle of speciality more flexible through an extensive interpretation of the concept of similarity of the goods. As we have seen, in assessing the similarity of the goods, the old case law was often very restrictive.[116] It focused above all on the intrinsic character of the products, seeking confusion between the goods themselves.[117]

---

114. Brandt, *La protection élargie de la marque ...*, p. 179.
115. *See* e.g. CA Paris, 21 February 1989, PIBD 1989, No. 461, III, p. 450, *American Express*. According to the judgment, the use of the mark *American Express* for clothing and shoes was likely to diminish the prestige of the mark with which the public associated ideas of seriousness and quality. Cf. regarding appellations of origin, CA Paris, 5 March 1984, Ann. propr. ind. 1985, p. 121, comment of Georges Bonet, *Champagne*. The Court condemned the use of the notion *Champagne* to designate tobacco, pointing out that this may have made the appellation, applied to inimitable and prestigious products, less radiant and more widespread, thus have the effect of weakening the reputation and attractive power of the appellation. On this judgment *see* Georges Bonet, *La protection des marques notoires dans le Code de la propriété intellectuelle*, in: *Jean Foyer, auteur et législateur: leges tulit, jura docuit: écrits en hommage à Jean Foyer*, PUF, Paris 1997, p. 199.
116. *See* para. 7 *supra*.
117. Apart from the above-mentioned examples found in 19th century case law, in French jurisprudence were considered different: tea and coffee, Trib. civ. Seine, 30 April 1936, Ann. propr. ind. 1939, p. 61, *Magellan*; champagne and sparkling wines, CA Paris, 30 December

Already in 1890, Fauchille criticised this jurisprudence, arguing for a more subjective examination of the similarity of the goods. It is worth recalling his words, which reflect a very modern approach to trade mark law. The author considered the definition of the similar industry based solely on the intrinsic nature of the products to be excessively narrow and not taking into account the spirit and purpose of the law. In Fauchille's view, as soon as there is a possibility of damage, the usurpation of the mark must be repressed, and the situation in which the goods bearing the mark are mistaken for each other is not the only case in which damage may occur. The use of the same trade mark for two different goods may still, in some cases, mislead the public as to their origin and therefore harm the owner of the mark. According to the author, are similar also goods which, although different in their production, are sufficiently closely related to each other that the public can reasonably believe that they come from the same person, from the owner of the mark. It is only if this belief is impossible that two goods can be considered not similar.[118]

There are examples of old French case law in which the similarity between the goods was appreciated more liberally. The Lyon Court adopted this approach in a judgment of 25 November 1936, according to which it is sufficient for the public to be naturally inclined to attribute the same origin to the two goods.[119] Earlier, in a judgment of 8 January 1930, the Rouen Court of Appeal qualified chocolates and liqueurs as similar and consequently upheld the infringement of a trade mark, emphasising its notoriety within the public.[120] Some subsequent decisions used this method, which had the advantage of respecting the principle of speciality and condemning abusive use based on trade mark law infringement.[121] This trend in case law was, however, criticised by some authors who considered that it was leading to a distortion of the concept of similarity.[122]

1929, Ann. propr. ind. 1932, p. 231; CA Paris, 19 mai 1930, Ann. propr. ind. 1933, p. 3. *See also* the cases cited by Dassas et Brandt. In 1883, a French court ruled that toilet soaps and Marseille soaps were not similar. Cited by Dassas, *L'élargissement de la protection ...*, p. 106. French courts denied similarity between stamping fats and car oils or between vanilla pods and vanilla sugar, and Belgian courts considered hard soaps and packaged soaps or cheeses and milk products different. Cited by Brandt, *La protection élargie de la marque ...*, p. 215.

118. Fauchille, *De ce qu'il faut entendre par des industries ...*, pp. 270-271. In addition, the author noted that in practice companies cumulated several industries and this circumstance could be taken into account when assessing the likelihood of confusion.
119. CA Lyon, 26 November 1936, Ann. propr. ind. 1938, p. 300, *Ozo*.
120. CA Rouen, 8 January 1930, Ann. propr. ind. 1930, p. 139, *de l'Abbaye de Fécamp*.
121. The judgment of CA Paris, 3 November 1958, Ann. propr. ind. 1959, p. 24, *Lu*, by which the Paris Court considered biscuits and rusks and gingerbread to be similar, is sometimes cited as an example. *See* Pérot-Morel, *L'extension de la protection ...*, p. 21. However, it must be admitted that the similarity of the goods in question did not pose a real problem. In this direction Raymond Dusolier, *Note sous CA Paris 8 déc. 1962*, Ann. propr. ind. 1963, p. 152.
122. *See* Pérot-Morel, *Notoriété et renommée ...*, pp. 466-468; Julien Canlorbe, *L'usage de la marque d'autrui*, Litec, Paris 2008, p. 111. Indeed, some authors preferred to reserve trade mark protection in the context of the speciality for its use for identical or similar goods in the restrictive sense of the term, i.e. goods of the same nature or destination. In this direction Sylviane Durrande, *Note sous CA Paris 27 mai 1987*, D. 1986, p. 528.

Nevertheless, as Dusolier observed in his commentary on a judgment of 12 July 1955,[123] the French courts were generally very restrictive in assessing the similarity of the goods, focusing rather on their intrinsic nature.[124] In the said case, in which the proprietor of the mark *Conté*, registered for pencils and, in general, office items, opposed to the marketing of calculating machines under the sign *Contex*, the Court held that if the calculating machines are part of the office machines, and are sold at paper mills, it is also true that they are devices which, by their clever construction and high precision, are manufactured differently. In consequence, the goods in question were not considered similar.[125]

Dassas noted that even in cases where the use of reputed trade marks could have been condemned under trade mark law, by using a flexible interpretation of the concept of similarity of the goods to determine the likelihood of confusion, the courts preferred to grant extensive protection in the field of tort liability.[126] Commenting on the above-mentioned judgment in the *Pontiac* case,[127] Chavanne noted a 'particular vigour' of the judges in affirming the principle of speciality. According to the author, it could be assumed that in the public mind, a certain link could exist since many companies manufactured both goods at the same time.[128] Hence, the author seemed to favour a less rigorous assessment of the notion of similarity of the goods. According to Pérot-Morel, the subjective assessment involved taking into account the consumer's point of view to determine whether he was exposed to a likelihood of confusion as to the origin of the goods. The author pointed out that this likelihood, depending on the intensity of the advertising and the reputation of the mark, could exist even for goods of a very different nature.[129]

The jurisprudence subsequently evolved, focusing less on the objective similarity, derived from the intrinsic nature of the goods, to take greater account of the public's state of mind. Thus, goods, even of a different nature, were considered similar if the consumer could believe that they came from the same manufacturer.[130] A judgment of the Court of Cassation of 16 January 1990 illustrates this approach.[131] In this case, the mark *Bulgari*, renowned in the field of jewellery, was used by a

123. CA Paris, 12 July 1955, Ann. propr. ind. 1956, p. 128, *Conté*. On this judgment *see* Pérot-Morel, *L'extension de la protection* ..., p. 35.
124. Raymond Dusolier, *Note sous CA Paris 12 juill. 1955*, Ann. propr. ind. 1956, p. 134.
125. However, it should be noted that in this decision the Paris Court adopted a flexible interpretation of the relative character of the famous trade mark. The Court granted the latter a more extensive protection ruling that the more the mark was known to the public, the more possible was the likelihood of confusion. On this judgment *see* Baeumer, *La protection de la marque* ..., p. 553.
126. Dassas, *L'élargissement de la protection* ..., p. 112. Cf. para. 15 *infra*.
127. CA Paris, 8 December 1962, D. 1963, p. 406, comment of Henri Desbois, Ann. propr. ind. 1963, p. 156, comment of Raymond Dusolier, *Pontiac*.
128. Chavanne, *Les marques notoirement connues* ..., p. 306. In this case, the conflicting goods were refrigerators and automobiles. Also according to Dusolier, the two goods were such that the public could attribute them to the same producer, since both were high-tech goods in which mechanics and electricity play an important role. Dusolier, *Note sous CA Paris 8 déc. 1962* ..., p. 152.
129. Pérot-Morel, *L'extension de la protection* ..., p. 22.
130. Durrande, *Note sous CA Paris 27 mai 1987* ..., p. 528.
131. Cass com., 16 January 1990, No. 88-10.856, Ann. propr. ind. 1990, p. 5, *Bulgari*.

manufacturer of perfumery, glasses, clothing, etc. According to the decision, a general trend towards diversification led to the creation of jewellery and perfumes by leading fashion designers, while famous jewellers market women's perfumes and accessories, so that the public has become accustomed to attributing the same origin to items which, although very different, have in common their luxury character and their destination, which is to give women a finery and an added attraction. Consequently, there was, in the present case, a similarity between the goods making it possible to establish infringement of the trade mark right.

23. Infringement of trade mark right: Italy. The subjective assessment of the likelihood of confusion, through a more liberal examination of the condition of similarity of the goods, was favoured by the Italian courts which considered that many large companies manufactured goods of various kinds and extended their activities to goods that objectively had no points in common with those for which they were originally known. As a result, the public, used to seeing the same mark on several different goods, risked linking the origin of the third party's good to the owner of the mark. Indeed, by a decision of 15 March 1952, the Italian Court of Cassation established a formula, many times repeated in subsequent case law, according to which the trade mark is protected against use for similar goods either by their intrinsic nature or by their destination for the same clientele or the satisfaction of the same needs (*affini per la loro intrinseca natura o per la loro destinazione alla medesima clientela o alla soddisfazione dei medesimi bisogni*).[132] In particular, the expression 'intended for the same clientele' made it possible to broaden very clearly the legal notion of similarity between the goods.[133] Thus, in the light of the jurisprudence of the Italian Court of Cassation, in the case of a reputed trade mark, the likelihood of confusion had to be assessed more broadly, covering the cases in which the public could associate the origin of third party's goods with the owner of the reputed trade mark.[134]

Italian case law subsequently developed a concept of 'marks that create tastes and fashions' (*marchi creatori del gusto e della moda*). According to this concept, all goods were similar if, although different in nature, they had relationships which could, in the public opinion, testify to their common origin. The theory was likely to apply in particular to luxury goods, perfumes, clothing, accessories, etc. It allowed the courts to consider similar goods, such as perfumes and clothing, totally different given their intrinsic nature.[135]

---

132. Cited by Galli, *Funzione del marchio e ampiezza …*, p. 40.
133. Galli, *Funzione del marchio e ampiezza …*, pp. 48, 71.
134. Remo Franceschelli, *È proprio vero che il nome Champagne è in Italia di libera appropriazione come marchio a designare qualunque prodotto che non sia vino spumante?*, Riv. Dir. Ind. 1989, II, pp. 36-37. On the evolution of the Italian jurisprudence *see* Caselli, *Il marchio che gode di rinomanza …*, pp. 37-41.
135. Gioacchino Sotriffer, *Protezione allargata del marchio di rinomanza e prodotti affini*, Riv. Dir. Ind. 2010, II, p. 116. This was, e.g., the solution adopted by the Milan Court in a decision of 6 November 1978 concerning the mark *Cartier*. Cited by Galli, *Funzione del marchio e ampiezza …*, pp. 84-85. On the marks that create tastes and fashions, *see also* Gabriele Cuonzo, *Il caso 'Krizia': revirement della Corte di Appello di Milano sulla tutela dei marchi dei creatori del gusto e della moda*, Riv. Dir. Ind. 1991, II, pp. 44 et seq.

This approach was supported by several authors according to which the similarity between the goods should be assessed in a less restrictive way and trade mark law should condemn the likelihood of confusion in the broad sense.[136] Thus, the doctrine argued that there was no need to amend the trade mark law. It was sufficient to interpret the notion of similarity of the goods in a flexible way in order to condemn the use of reputed mark on the ground of trade mark infringement.[137]

The issue of the importance of subjective criteria in assessing the similarity of goods is a topical one. As we shall see, in the light of the jurisprudence of the Court of Justice, this criterion should be examined subjectively, even though this interpretation is not always adopted in case law of lower instances. It seems therefore that in many cases where the infringement of a reputed trade mark is claimed today, it should be sufficient to raise infringement for likelihood of confusion.

We will return to the question of the distinction between the fields of application of the two trade mark protection regimes and the consequences arising from them when we examine the relationship between the infringement of the reputed trade mark and the likelihood of confusion.[138]

24. Applications for registration: Germany, the Netherlands, Poland. To conclude the analysis on the evolution of the interpretation of trade mark law provisions with a view to strengthening the protection of reputed marks, it should be pointed out that, apart from the case of use of marks by non-competitors, in some countries, the general provisions of trade mark law were also used by owners to oppose the filing for registration of reputed marks by third parties. In Germany and the Netherlands, the refusal of such signs was possible on grounds of public policy, which led to effective protection of trade marks with a reputation against applications made by third parties.[139] In Poland, signs similar to famous trade marks were refused registration and cancelled, notwithstanding differences between the goods, in particular on the basis of grounds for refusal related to good morals.[140]

Nevertheless, the provisions related to the grounds for refusal of trade marks could not provide protection against the most harmful acts for owners – acts of effective use of reputed trade marks by third parties in the course of trade. The extensive interpretation of the principle of speciality made it possible to extend the protection of the reputed trade mark in a limited way. It was only the likelihood of confusion that could be condemned. As we have seen, however, it was also necessary to punish unfair

---

136. Giannantonio Guglielmetti, *La tutela di marchi di alta rinomanza*, Riv. Dir. Ind. 1980, I, pp. 292-294. The author did not consider the reputation of the trade mark as a value in itself worthy of protection against dilution in the absence of a likelihood of confusion. He argued for an extension of the protection of the reputed trade mark but only by means of a more flexible assessment of the similarity between the goods. Guglielmetti, *La tutela di marchi ...*, pp. 295-297.
137. *See* Caselli, *Il marchio che gode di rinomanza ...*, pp. 37-41.
138. *See* paras 110 et seq. *infra*.
139. *See* Brandt, *La protection élargie de la marque ...*, pp. 199-212.
140. Ryszard Skubisz, *Prawo znaków towarowych. Komentarz*, Wydawnictwa Prawnicze, Warsaw 1997, p. 73; Piotrowska, *Renomowane znaki ...*, p. 117.

acts made by non-competitors in the absence of any confusion. In order to condemn such acts, it was essential to rely on the rules of civil liability.

[b] General Provisions of Civil Liability

25. Grounds for tort liability. The main method of enhancing the protection of reputed trade marks outside the speciality in most European countries consisted in relying on tort liability, in some of them on general provisions provided by Civil Codes,[141] in others on the provisions of special laws on unfair competition based on tort liability. It should be noted that in some countries even the likelihood of confusion in the broad sense, assessed more flexibly with regard to the similarity of the goods, was often condemned on the basis of civil liability and not on the basis of the infringement of the exclusive trade mark right.[142] General civil liability was of course the only basis on which courts in Europe could condemn acts of usurpation of famous marks by third parties in the absence of a risk of confusion.

26. Germany. As we have established, the German jurisprudence is the origin of the theory of dilution which initially was based on the provisions of section 1 of the Law on Unfair Competition of 7 June 1909. The proprietor of a reputed trade mark could invoke them in order to oppose acts of third parties which might be generally detrimental to his trade mark. The implementation of the law required the existence of a competitive relationship between the injured party and his unfair rival; however, initially this requirement was interpreted rather broadly. For example, in the aforementioned decision of 11 September 1924, the use of the trade mark *Odol* was condemned on the basis of the Unfair Competition Act.[143] Over time, however, the courts preferred to condemn the use of famous trade marks under § 823, and sometimes also under § 1004, of the German Civil Code relating to tort liability and the right of traders to protect their commercial activities, which made it possible to escape the condition of a competitive relationship.[144] Under § 823 providing for tort liability, the degree of fame, as well as of inherent distinctive character, required from a mark in order to benefit from enhanced protection was however very high. Moreover, such a famous mark had to convey ideas of prestige or exclusive reputation. In the 1980s, German case law resumed the application of section 1 of the Law on Unfair Competition in cases of use of famous marks for dissimilar goods; hence in the absence of direct competition, which was

---

141. Besides the national legislations discussed below, in the Netherlands, owners of famous marks based their actions on Article 1401 of the Civil Code relating to general tort liability. Wichers Hoeth, *Étude comparative ...*, pp. 142 et seq.
142. In French jurisprudence *see* e.g. TGI Paris, 12 October 1967 and CA Paris, 19 October 1970, Ann. propr. ind. 1971, p. 1, comment of Raymond Dusolier, *Mazda*. *See* Portet, *Les marques notoirement connues ...*, pp. 169-170. Cf. also Wichers Hoeth, *Étude comparative ...*, pp. 144-145.
143. *See* Wolff, *Non-competing Goods ...*, p. 588.
144. *See* Baeumer, *La protection de la marque ...*, pp. 564 et seq.; Gerhard Schricker, *La tutela della Ausstattung e del marchio celebre nella Germania Federale*, Riv. Dir. Ind. 1980, I, p. 266; G.W. Seeling, *Protecting 'Famous Brands' in Germany*, EIPR 1989, vol. 11, No. 5, p. 158; Mathias Strasser, *The Rational Basis of Trademark Protection Revisited: Putting the Dilution Doctrine into Context*, Forham Intell. Prop., Media and Ent., L. J. 2000, vol. 10, No. 2, pp. 404-405.

advantageous for the right holders since, on this ground, the required level of consumer recognition was much lower. For example, in a judgment of 9 December 1982, the Federal Court of Justice condemned, on the basis of section 1, as an act contrary to good morals, the use of a famous trade mark of cars *Rolls Royce* by an advertising agency in an advertisement for whiskey.[145]

27. France. In France, the dominant position in case law consisted in condemning the use of reputed trade marks by third parties for dissimilar goods on the basis of general tort liability under the former Article 1382 of the Civil Code (the new Article 1240), requiring the establishment of a fault, damage and causal link.[146] The main difficulty consisted in characterising the fault of the alleged usurper. Since the trade mark right is limited by the rule of speciality, it is accepted that, in principle, the exploitation of a sign is lawful, in the absence of an exclusive right beyond the similarity.[147] The former Article 1382 already constituted the legal ground for an action that could be brought in the event of use of a sign by a third party, namely an action for unfair competition. The success of this action did not necessarily depend on the existence of a likelihood of confusion, in particular in the case of discrediting a competitor. However, unfair competition was traditionally perceived as an act committed against a competitor. The competitive relationship was sometimes assessed in a more flexible way by the courts.[148] French doctrine and case law were, however, generally hostile to a liberal interpretation of this requirement.[149] A new justification for condemning the use of famous trade marks for dissimilar goods, also on the grounds of the former Article 1382, was found in the theory of parasitism (freeriding). The idea was that undertakings using famous marks for different products benefited indirectly, but unfairly, from the reputation of others.[150] The concept of parasitism was further developed by Saint-Gal who, in his famous article published in 1956, pleaded for condemning parasitic practices even if they did not fall within the framework of classical unfair competition and, to that effect, recognising the notions of 'parasitic competition' (*concurrence parasitaire*), with respect to acts committed by competitors notwithstanding the absence of a risk of confusion, and of 'parasitic acts' (*agissements parasitaires*), with respect to acts committed by non-competitors, hence where there was no similarity of the goods, but the third party operated as a parasite, by taking advantage

145. Simon Fhima, *Exploring the Roots ...*, pp. 31-32. For a thorough study of the German jurisprudence on the protection of reputed trade marks prior to the implementation of Directive 89/104 *see* Annette Kur, *Borderline Cases of Trademark Protection: A Study in German Trademark Law on the Eve of Amendment*, IIC 1992, vol. 23, No. 4, p. 485.
146. *See* Dassas, *L'élargissement de la protection ...*, p. 180.
147. Cf. Joanna Schmidt-Szalewski, *Les relations entre contrefaçon et concurrence déloyale*, Propr. ind. 2008, No. 11, comment 91.
148. With respect to commercial names *see* Trib. comm. Paris, 1 September 1891, confirmed by CA Paris, 24 February 1892, Ann. propr. ind. 1893, p. 319, *Bureau Veritas*; Trib. com. Seine, 5 January 1940, Ann. propr. ind. 1940-1948, p. 289, *Waterman*; CA Bourges, 28 January 1958, PI 1959, p. 32, *Singer*. With respect to trade marks *see* CA Paris, 29 October 1951, PI 1953, p. 92, confirmed by Cass. com., 3 February 1959, JCP 1959, II, p. 11000, *Omega*. On the last judgment cf. Pérot-Morel, *L'extension de la protection ...*, p. 38.
149. Pérot-Morel, *L'extension de la protection ...*, p. 42; Chavanne, *Les marques notoirement connues ...*, p. 306.
150. Dusolier, *Note sous CA Paris 12 juill ...*, p. 137.

of the efforts and repute of others.[151] Notwithstanding some critics,[152] the works of Saint-Gal made a major contribution to the development of the theory of parasitism and had a significant impact on French case law. According to the above-mentioned judgment in the *Anne de Solène* case, the exploitation of the mark, for dissimilar products, represented a parasitic activity, which needed to be censored in the view of the morality of commerce.[153] Saint-Gal himself considered the said judgment as an important step in the recognition of an extended protection of famous trade marks.[154] French courts referred to the concept of parasitic acts in many further decisions.[155] Parasitism was also often justified by the concept of abuse of the right, or rather freedom, of fair competition, which in trade mark law manifests itself in the rule of speciality. Use of a famous mark could therefore be considered to constitute an abuse of that freedom.[156]

28. Italy. In Italy, because of the differences in the nature of the goods, some courts condemned the use of reputed trade marks on the basis of Article 2598, paragraph 1, of the Italian Civil Code, which punishes unfair competition and was considered to be more flexible than the provisions of trade mark law. Nevertheless, this approach was criticised by some authors who observed that the risk of confusion sanctioned in the field of this provision should be assessed in the same way, taking into account the risk of confusion between the products. In certain decisions, including the above-mentioned judgment of the Court of Turin of 11 March 1949 in the *Lucky Strike* case,

151. Yves Saint-Gal, *Concurrence déloyale et concurrence parasitaire (ou agissements parasitaires)*, RIPIA 1956, pp. 19 et seq.; Yves Saint-Gal, *Concurrence et agissements parasitaires en droit français et belge*, in: *La concurrence parasitaire en droit comparé. Actes du Colloque de Lausanne*, Libraire Droz, Geneva 1981, pp. 133-135.
152. Cf. Perent, *Marques notoirement connues* ..., p. 267; Brandt, *La protection élargie de la marque* ..., pp. 311-312.
153. CA Nancy, 26 June 1974, Ann. propr. ind. 1975, p. 161, JCP 1975, p. 18178, comment of Georges Bonet, *Anne de Solène*.
154. Saint-Gal, *Concurrence et agissements* ..., p. 140.
155. *See* e.g. CA Paris, 21 February 1989, PIBD 1989, No. 461, III, p. 450, *American Express*; CA Paris, 21 November 1991, PIBD 1992, No. 518, III, p. 174, *Orient-Express*; TGI Paris, 19 November 1992, PIBD 1993, No. 540, III, p. 208, *Porsche*; CA Paris, 18 February 1993, PIBD 1993, No. 546, III, p. 393, *Château d'Yquem*; Cass. com., 4 July 1995, PIBD 1995, No. 597, III, p. 497, *Orient-Express*. Cf. Pérot-Morel, *Notoriété et renommée* ..., pp. 469-470.
156. *See* Perent, *Marques notoirement connues* ..., p. 248; Desbois, *La protection des marques notoires* ..., p. 13; Chavanne, *Les marques notoirement connues* ..., p. 306; Dassas, *L'élargissement de la protection* ..., p. 18; Paul Mathély, *Note sous CA Paris 27 mai 1987*, Ann. propr. ind. 1987, p. 11; Bonet, *La protection des marques notoires* ..., p. 202; Nicolas Bouche, *L'objet spécifique du droit de marque*, D. 2000, No. 6, p. 103, para. 10. Cf. also Paul Roubier, *Le droit de la propriété industrielle*, t. II, Sirey, Paris 1954, p. 527. In case law *see* e.g. Cass. com., 27 May 1986, Ann. propr. ind. 1987, p. 3, D. 1986, p. 526, *Ritz*; CA Paris, 5 June 1986, Ann. propr. ind. 1987, p. 189, *Liberty*; TGI Paris, 17 March 1987, PIBD 1987, No. 419, III, p. 369, *American Express*; Cass com., 16 January 1990, case 88-10.856, *Bulgari*; TGI Paris, 22 May 1991, PIBD 1991, No. 511, III, p. 683, *Michelin*. That said, it should be noted that in French law, in the absence of a special provision relating to abuse of rights, such abuse is based directly on tort liability, nowadays under Article 1240 of the Civil Code. Cf. Pérot-Morel, *L'extension de la protection* ..., p. 40; Frédéric Pollaud-Dulian, *De quelques avatars de l'action en responsabilité civile dans le droit des affaires*, RTD com. 1997, No. 3, p. 352. Moreover, recourse to the concept of abuse is criticised with respect to freedoms which are very general prerogatives. Cf. Jérôme Passa, *Contrefaçon et concurrence déloyale*, Litec, Paris 1997, pp. 16, 150.

the judges referred to Article 2598, paragraph 3, of the Civil Code, which provides for a general clause of unfair competition condemning the use of means contrary to the principles of professional correctness and likely to harm the business of others. However, this approach was also criticised since its application presupposed a competitive relationship between the parties to the dispute.[157] Thus, the Italian courts rarely resorted to Article 2598, paragraph 3, of the Civil Code in order to condemn acts of use of famous trade marks, preferring to enhance their protection on the basis of trade mark law, thanks to a subjective interpretation of the concept of similarity of the goods.[158] Some Italian authors were also influenced by the theory of parasitism developed in France by Saint-Gal. In 1956, Franceschelli was the first in Italy to refer to parasitic acts as unlawful acts under Article 2598, paragraph 3, of the Italian Civil Code.[159] However, unlike Saint-Gal, Franceschelli and the Italian jurisprudence did not distinguish between parasitic competition and parasitic acts.[160]

29. Poland. In Poland, enhanced protection of trade marks outside the rule of speciality and in the absence of a likelihood of confusion was possible under the Law on Combatting Unfair Competition of 2 August 1926. Its Article 3 provided for a general clause condemning acts contrary to good morals (commercial probity) detrimental to another's business.[161] In the light of this provision, contrary to German law, the existence of a competitive relationship between the parties to the dispute was not necessary. Pursuant to Article 3, by a judgment of 3 July 1929, the Supreme Court held that acts likely to result in dishonestly usurping profits that should have been made by another undertaking, as the deserved fruit of the latter's efforts, creativity and energy, should be excluded from business life.[162] The doctrine considered that use of a mark for a dissimilar good could be contrary to professional probity, since it allowed to unfairly exploit another's repute, and could cause a harm, even where there was no confusion, consisting in depreciating the sign, hence undermining the value of intangible elements on which the attractive power of the business was based.[163] In a judgment of 30 November 1934, the use of the trade mark *Suchard*, renowned in relation to chocolates, by a manufacturer of soap was condemned by the Supreme Court on the basis of

157. Galli, *Funzione del marchio e ampiezza ...*, pp. 42-44. In judgments of 30 July 1955 and 25 May 1957, the Italian Court of Cassation expressly condemned the application of the provisions on unfair competition in the presence of different industries. Cited by Galli, *Funzione del marchio e ampiezza ...*, p. 44.
158. Cuonzo, *Il caso 'Krizia' ...*, p. 49. The proprietors also sometimes invoked Article 2043 of the Civil Code relating to general tort liability. Caselli, *Il marchio che gode di rinomanza ...*, pp. 44-45.
159. Remo Franceschelli, *Concorrenza parassitaria*, Riv. Dir. Ind. 1956, I, p. 265.
160. Remo Franceschelli, *La concurrence parasitaire en Italie*, in: *La concurrence parasitaire en droit comparé. Actes du Colloque de Lausanne*, Libraire Droz, Geneva 1981, pp. 9-12. That said, as we have seen, any recourse to Article 2598 of the Italian Civil Code failed to comply with the condition of a competitive relationship. Caselli, *Il marchio che gode di rinomanza ...*, pp. 44-45.
161. *See* Fryderyk Zoll, *À propos de la loi polonaise du 2 août 1926 concernant la répression de la concurrence déloyale*, PI 1927, p. 66.
162. SN, 3 July 1929, case R 469/29, OSP 1929, No. 513.
163. Alfred Kraus, Fryderyk Zoll, *Polska ustawa o zwalczaniu nieuczciwej konkurencji*, Poznan 1929, pp. 165-167, 223-224.

Article 3 of the Law on Combatting Unfair Competition.[164] Similarly, according to a judgment of 4 October 1938, concerning the use of an image of a coffee grinder by a manufacturer of sewing thread, the defendant committed an act of unfair competition under Article 3. According to the decision, the defendant chose the sign in order to benefit from the plaintiff's work and investments, and the appropriation of the fruits of the labour of others is contrary to good morals.[165] Article 3 of the Law of 1926 and a similar provision of Article 3 of the new Law on Combatting Unfair Competition of 16 April 1993 were considered possible to invoke in order to act against parasitic use of trade marks by non-competitors, qualified as contrary to good morals, until the implementation of Directive 89/104.[166]

[2] Special Provisions

30. Insufficiency of general grounds. The general legal grounds were insufficient to ensure a satisfactory level of protection for reputed trade marks. Moreover, invoking general civil liability or unfair competition in order to condemn acts qualified as parasitic was considered by some European scholars to be erroneous. Indeed, the theory of parasitism is a questionable concept, since the unlawfulness of the use of a trade mark enjoying protection that is by definition relative is open to discussion. Thus, some authors argued for the recognition of a special regime for protection of famous trade marks. Troller's works express well the critical approach towards basing enhanced protection on general civil liability or unfair competition and the need to adopt a special regime. The author observed that there is nothing unfair about promoting the development of one's company by using something that this person has not created himself and that it is normal for companies to take advantage of external factors to increase their commercial success. According to Troller, it should be possible to take advantage of the work of others as long as the law does not expressly prohibit it. This reasoning led the author to reject the protection of the reputed trade mark on the basis of general tort liability and to admit that it should be protected as an object in itself, an independent legal good, having its own value, on the basis of trade mark law.[167] This was also the conclusion of the study of Perent who noted that the commercial value of the famous mark allows to consider it as an independent legal asset, and consequently to grant it absolute protection against any practice that would threaten the value of this asset.[168]

Following critical opinions towards the use of the tort liability provisions, introduction of a special ground for enhanced protection of reputed trade marks that would recognise it expressly, so that the unlawfulness of their use would leave no room

164. SN, 30 November 1934, case C II 1744/34, OSN 1935, No. 5/218, p. 461, *Suchard*.
165. SO Nowy Sącz, 4 October 1938, case I C 180/28, PI 1939, p. 99.
166. Urszula Promińska, *Prawo z rejestracji znaku towarowego, treść i naruszenie*, thesis Lodz 1994, p. 139; Skubisz, *Prawo znaków* ..., p. 289. However, between 1945 and 1989, the question was rather theoretical since in the communist economic system trade marks had a very limited practical importance.
167. Alois Troller, *La marque de haute renommée*, PI 1953, pp. 81-82.
168. Perent, *Marques notoirement connues* ..., p. 280.

for doubt, was considered. Such initiatives were undertaken many times at the international level, with a view to amending the Paris Convention of 20 March 1883 for the Protection of Industrial Property, but never resulted in a concrete outcome (§1.01[B][2][a]). Some countries, however, succeeded in establishing special regimes that effectively strengthened the protection of reputed trade marks (§1.01[B][2][b]).

[a] Draft Amendments to the Paris Convention

31. Drafts proposed. Long before the introduction of the special regime for the protection of trade marks with a reputation by the first trade mark Directive 89/104, there were several attempts to adopt a regime of extended protection for famous signs at the international level. A concept for the protection of distinctive signs outside the principle of speciality was presented to the International Chamber of Commerce (ICC) already in the 1930s. A study on the 'well-known trade names' was then conducted. It was found that their protection should escape the regime of speciality, in order to be effectively protected against any unauthorised use, whatever the activity of the third party. This argumentation was then adopted for trade marks.[169]

After the Second World War, the works intensified and the question of extended protection of reputed trade marks was widely debated at several international conferences, particularly during the 1950s. Many lawyers agreed that it was necessary to introduce enhanced protection into the provisions of the Paris Convention. The debate focused on the modalities of such a special regime and, above all, on whether extended protection should be introduced in Article 6 bis or Article 10 bis of the Paris Convention. The first text already provided for special protection of 'well-known' trade marks on the basis of the trade mark right. The introduction, in 1925, of this concept similar to the reputed trade mark, which will be examined below, in the text of the Convention, was a first step in the extension movement in favour of the protection of reputed signs. Thanks to Article 6 bis, notoriety led to extend the territorial scope of the trade mark's validity beyond national borders. However, that provision only provided for an exception to the principle of territoriality and offered no remedy against the use of famous marks for goods or services unlikely to be confused.[170] Some authors considered that the privileged status of the reputed trade mark was not incompatible with the very notion of trade mark and, consequently, could defeat the rule of speciality and appear in the provisions related to trade mark rights. According to Bodenhausen, it was not reasonable to restrict the protection of the well-known trade mark to identical or similar goods since case law in many countries had to react to the use by third parties of well-known trade marks for completely different goods.[171] By contrast, Article 10 bis constitutes the conventional ground providing for protection against

169. Fernand Jacq, *Réflexions sur les marques notoires*, PI 1952, p. 190.
170. Brandt, *La protection élargie de la marque …*, pp. 22-23.
171. Georg Hendrik Christiaan Bodenhausen, *Problèmes actuels concernant la protection internationale de la propriété industrielle*, PI 1950, p. 87.

unfair competition. It was preferred by those who considered that abandoning the principle of speciality necessarily implied recourse to unfair competition.[172]

At the congress held in Quebec in 1949, the ICC recommended an amendment to Article 10 bis, proposing to extend the meaning of the notion of unfair competition and to include the use and registration of trade marks that had become symbols of another trader.[173] This wish was taken up by the International Law Association at a congress in Copenhagen in 1950. Then, however, the ICC suggested that extended protection should be provided in Article 6 bis.[174] At a congress in Lisbon in 1951, a new paragraph of Article 6 bis was proposed, aimed at condemning the use of well-known trade marks causing the likelihood of confusion in the broad sense.[175] Then, at congresses in Vienna in 1953 and Tokyo in 1955, the ICC expressed the wish to amend Article 6 bis of the Paris Convention, which would provide for extended protection applicable to dissimilar goods in case of confusion, unjustified enrichment of the applicant or user, or of a real weakening of the distinctive character or appeal of the well-known mark.[176]

The International Association for the Protection of Intellectual Property (AIPPI) adopted a resolution at a congress held in Vienna in 1952 under the terms of which the protection provided for in Article 6 bis shall apply, subject to rights acquired in good faith, to trade marks considered to have an exceptional reputation, even in respect of non-identical or similar goods, if this results in either a possibility of confusion or an unjustified advantage or a real weakening of the distinctive character or appeal of the exceptional reputation of the trade mark.[177] In addition, the resolution specified that this increased protection cannot be granted to all well-known trade marks benefiting from Article 6 bis, but shall be reserved for a particular category of more widely known trade marks, the definition of which was to be specified.[178] Also at the end of a congress held in Brussels in 1954, the AIPPI proposed to amend Article 6 bis.[179] The AIPPI subsequently discussed the question of extending the protection of the well-known trade mark, in particular at congresses held in Berlin in 1963 and Barcelona in 1990.[180]

The resolutions of the ICC and AIPPI were presented at a diplomatic conference held in Lisbon in 1958. The committee examining the issue found that it was agreed that anyone who takes advantage of the reputation of a well-known trade mark, even if he is not a competitor of the owner of that trade mark, is committing something illegal.[181] In addition to the ideas of amending Articles 6 bis and 10 bis, national delegations discussed the creation of a separate article. At the end of the proceedings,

172. Cf. Perent, *Marques notoirement connues …*, p. 284.
173. Ewa Wojcieszko-Głuszko, *Ochrona prawna znaków towarowych powszechnie znanych na tle prawnoporównawczym*, ZNUJ 1995, No. 65, p. 34.
174. Perent, *Marques notoirement connues …*, pp. 290-292.
175. Wojcieszko-Głuszko, *Ochrona prawna znaków …*, p. 34.
176. Cited by Perent, *Marques notoirement connues …*, p. 187.
177. Cited by Perent, *Marques notoirement connues …*, pp. 195-196.
178. Cited by Jacq, *Réflexions sur les marques …*, p. 189.
179. Perent, *Marques notoirement connues …*, p. 296.
180. Bonet, *La protection des marques notoires …*, p. 197.
181. Cited by Portet, *Les marques notoirement connues …*, p. 91; Giannantonio Guglielmetti, *Marques ordinaires, notoirement connues et de haute renommée: différences entre ces trois figures et la portée de leur protection*, ZNUJ 1981, No. 22, p. 74.

the drafting committee prepared a text to become the new Article 10 ter,[182] thus placing the problem on the ground of unfair competition.

32. Impact on the current regime. All these attempts never resulted in the inclusion of new provisions to the Paris Convention. Nevertheless, the works undertaken at those congresses and conferences made it possible to develop a model for the protection of reputed trade marks, and it is clear that the special regime adopted by the European legislator largely reflects the provisions proposed at the time.

It is interesting to note that, in all these projects, unlike the current regime, the likelihood of confusion is a form of infringement of the reputed trade mark. The risk of confusion was therefore considered to be possible in case of use of the mark for dissimilar goods. The abandonment of the likelihood of confusion as a form of infringement of the reputed trade mark by the European legislator may have an impact on the interpretation of the current provisions. We will come back to this question while examining the relationship between the likelihood of confusion and the special regime.[183]

Apart from the likelihood of confusion, it is clear that the provisions proposed at the time provided for three forms of infringement: unfair profit, without distinction for the benefit of reputation or distinctiveness, damage to the distinctive character and damage to the reputation of the mark, just as the Court of Justice does under the Trade Marks Directive and the EU Trade Mark Regulation.

It should be also noted that the old debate on the legal nature of the extended protection is still ongoing. As we will see, while under current EU legislation, the infringement of the mark with a reputation constitutes an infringement of trade mark rights, some national legislations placed the special protection of the reputed trade mark on the basis of tort liability.[184]

[b] Special Provisions Adopted in Some Countries

33. Criterion of similarity of the goods. The lack of a legal basis for condemning the use of trade marks with a reputation by third parties for dissimilar goods led several national legislators to amend trade mark law provisions in order to strengthen the protection of well-known trade marks. One method of achieving this end was to abandon the criterion of similarity of the goods in the assessment of the likelihood of confusion. The American trade mark law since 1947 only condemns the likelihood of confusion in general. The requirement provided by the previous law that the goods needed to have the same qualities was deleted from the new legislation. This made it possible to extend considerably the protection of well-known trade marks within the framework of trade mark law.[185] In the Netherlands, a tendency in the case law to give

182. Portet, *Les marques notoirement connues ...*, pp. 91 et seq.; Guglielmetti, *Marques ordinaires, notoirement connues ...*, p. 74.
183. *See* paras 117-118 *infra*.
184. *See* para. 124 *infra*.
185. Pérot-Morel, *L'extension de la protection ...*, p. 41. This new law seems to recognise Wolff's idea that well-known trade marks could be effectively protected without recourse to the theory

less importance to elements of similarity of the goods and to base trade mark protection on the likelihood of confusion led to an amendment of the trade mark law and the introduction of a new ground for invalidity. Cancellation could now be sought if the trade mark in question was similar to an earlier trade mark to such an extent that the public could be misled as to the origin of the goods. The condition of similarity of the products was abandoned and replaced by the criterion of confusion as to the origin. The criterion of similarity of the goods was still used by the judges to assess the likelihood of confusion but was no longer *a sine qua non* condition of the latter.[186]

It should be noted that, as we have pointed out, several of the first trade mark laws, such as the French law of 1857, did not expressly impose any condition of similarity of the goods in the assessment of the likelihood of confusion. The principle of speciality, from which it results, was originally a doctrinal and praetorian creation, firmly linked to the economic context of the time. Thus, a less rigorous assessment of the likelihood of confusion, giving less importance to the question of similarity between the goods, could have been made without amending the provisions in the light of which it was possible to interpret more flexibly the conditions for infringement of trade mark rights. However, this has never been the position of doctrine and jurisprudence in many countries.

34. First regime of enhanced protection against likelihood of confusion: Scandinavian countries. For the first time, extended protection of reputed trade marks was explicitly recognised at the legislative level by the Scandinavian countries. Denmark, Sweden, Norway and Finland jointly developed a regime of enhanced protection for well-known trade marks outside the speciality. According to Article 6 of the first of these laws, the Danish law of 11 June 1959, apart from the infringement of the trade mark in the speciality, in exceptional cases, trade marks may be considered liable to create confusion with other trade marks: (a) if a trade mark has acquired a particular reputation and is, in addition, so well known in Denmark that the use by another party of a similar mark, even with respect to goods of a different kind, would constitute an unjustifiable exploitation of the value (*achalandage*) of that trade mark; (b) if a trade mark has acquired a certain reputation and if the use by another party of a similar mark in respect of other goods would manifestly and substantially depreciate the *achalandage* of that trade mark because of the particular nature of those goods. The Danish law distinguished between trade marks with a 'particular reputation' – reputed trade marks – and trade marks with a 'certain reputation' which corresponded to well-known

of dilution, thanks to the concept of likelihood of confusion in the broad sense, and that very famous trade marks should be protected even when the goods are very different. Wolff, *Non-competing Goods* ..., p. 606.

186. However, some courts refused to grant protection in the absence of similarity of the goods. In a judgment of 19 October 1960, the Court of Appeal of The Hague rejected the claim of infringement of the trade mark *Kodak* by the use of a sign *Kopak* for potatoes because of the lack of similarity between the goods and, consequently, the likelihood of confusion. Cited by Wichers Hoeth, *Étude comparative* ..., pp. 145-151. On the *Kodak* case cf. Cohen Jehoram, *La protection des marques* ..., p. 226.

trade marks within the meaning of the Paris Convention.[187] Similar provisions were adopted by the other three countries with minor differences.[188]

The provisions adopted by the Scandinavian countries were a pioneering solution. At a time when the doctrine and jurisprudence in many countries either distorted the principle of speciality or constructed questionable theories on the basis of civil liability, the Scandinavian countries adopted modern and advanced provisions. Admittedly, the protection of the reputed trade mark depended on the likelihood of confusion, but its assessment was detached from the similarity between the goods, and the case law shows that they provided effective protection in the event of use of reputed trade marks by non-competitors.[189]

35. First regime of enhanced protection against parasitism: Benelux. Another special legislation had, however, a greater impact on the development of extended protection for reputed trade marks in Europe. Article 13A of the Benelux Uniform Law on Trade Marks, which entered into force on 1 January 1971, is considered to be the first legislative attempt to ensure special protection for famous trade marks against parasitic acts.[190] The Benelux system was described as a unique legislation in the world because it was the first to protect the advertising function of the trade mark[191] since the Benelux law ignored the criterion of likelihood of confusion. Indeed, under Article 13A(1) of the Law, the owner of a trade mark could object to any use of the mark, or a similar sign, for the goods for which the trade mark was registered or for similar goods. And under paragraph 2, the holder could object to any other use which, in the course of trade and without due cause, would be made of the mark or a similar sign, under conditions likely to cause prejudice to the owner of the mark. This provision made no reference to the likelihood of confusion.[192]

The Uniform Law and the jurisprudence of the Benelux Court of Justice influenced significantly the European legislation and the interpretation of the provisions of the trade mark Directives and Regulations. In a first judgment rendered pursuant to Article 13A(2) of the Uniform Law, of 1 March 1975, in the famous *Claeryn* case, the

187. *See* Portet, *Les marques notoirement connues* ..., p. 209; Guglielmetti, *La tutela di marchi* ..., pp. 289-290.
188. The Swedish law of 2 December 1960, in the second case of infringement, consisting in the depreciation of reputation, referred to well-known trade marks. The Finnish law of 1 June 1964, in its wording, curiously gave an example of a 'particularly well-established commercial symbol', namely 'the mark *Kodak*'. The Norwegian law of 3 March 1961, unlike the three aforementioned laws, provided for two distinct cases of infringement, but both were based on a depreciation of the reputation of the trade mark and did not condemn an unjustified exploitation. *See* Dassas, *L'élargissement de la protection* ..., pp. 211-213; Brandt, *La protection élargie de la marque* ..., pp. 228-230.
189. For example, in Sweden, the use of the sign *4712* in relation to condoms was condemned as an act of unjustified exploitation of the reputation of the trade mark *4711* of perfumes. In Finland, the owner of the trade mark *Omega*, famous for watches, successfully opposed to its registration by a third party for games, toys, vehicles and clothing. Nevertheless, in practice, these provisions were rarely applied. *See* Brandt, *La protection élargie de la marque* ..., pp. 230-231.
190. Saint-Gal, *Concurrence et agissements* ..., p. 145.
191. Brandt, *La protection élargie de la marque* ..., p. 226.
192. Cohen Jehoram, *La protection des marques* ..., pp. 226-227.

Benelux Court of Justice identified two forms of prejudice to a reputed trade mark which were subsequently recognised in Directive 89/104.[193] Moreover, we will come back to this point, the said decision, in which the Benelux Court of Justice gave a very narrow meaning to the exception of due cause, had a considerable influence on the interpretation of this negative condition for infringement of the trade mark with a reputation under the European provisions. A major difference between the Benelux legislation and the current provisions is that the Uniform Law did not reserve the protection outside the speciality to reputed trade marks only.[194] Moreover, the condition of use of the sign in the course of trade was interpreted very liberally, more broadly than it is nowadays by the Court of Justice of the European Union.[195]

36. Special regimes outside Europe. Finally, it should be noted that provisions providing for extended protection of reputed trade marks were also adopted outside Europe. For example, the Brazilian Code of Industrial Property of 21 December 1971 contained a special provision according to which trade marks considered as well known benefited from special protection in all classes, as soon as there was a possibility of confusion as to the origin of the goods, merchandises or services, or prejudice to the reputation of the trade mark in question.[196]

§1.02 CURRENT SPECIAL REGIME OF PROTECTION OF TRADE MARKS WITH A REPUTATION

37. Special ground for infringement. A regime of special protection of trade marks with a reputation beyond the speciality was first provided by the European legislator in Directive 89/104, further replaced by Directive 2008/95.[197] Article 5(2) of those acts

193. The mark *Claeryn* was famous in the Netherlands for juniper. A third company launched a cleaning product on the Dutch market under the name *Klarein*. The Benelux Court of Justice held that the exclusive right to the trade mark gave its proprietor the advantage of the trade mark's power to induce the purchase of marked goods. This power could be affected by the use of the mark even for dissimilar goods because, first, the mark could lose its exclusive and unique character so that it could no longer provoke in the mind of the public the immediate association with the goods for which it was registered and used, and, second, the attractive power of the mark could be affected. Cited by Cohen Jehoram, *La protection des marques* ..., pp. 227-228.
194. Cf. Cohen Jehoram, *La protection des marques* ..., p. 228.
195. According to a Dutch court, the qualification of use in the course of trade concerned any use of the trade mark related to a commercial activity. The Court applied Article 13 A(2) of the Uniform Law in order to condemn the infringement of the trade mark *Coca-Cola* by its use in a pornographic film in which an actress played with a bottle of Coca-Cola in such a way that, as observed, it could not characterise use in the function of the distinctive sign. Schricker, *La tutela della Ausstattung* ..., pp. 269-270; Brandt, *La protection élargie de la marque* ..., p. 225.
196. Cited by Dassas, *L'élargissement de la protection* ..., p. 213.
197. At the Community level, a special protection of the reputed trade mark was already envisaged in the Preliminary Draft of a Convention for a European Trade Mark of 1964. Article 14(1)(b) provided that the proprietor had the right to oppose any use in the course of trade of a trade mark or a similar sign undertaken without due cause under conditions liable to cause detriment to the proprietor of the Community trade mark. However, the Commission, in the Memorandum on the Creation of a Community Trade Mark of 6 July 1976, suggested that the protection of the trade mark outside the speciality should be regulated in the field of unfair competition. Guglielmetti, *La tutela di marchi* ..., pp. 291-292. In the Commission's view, the overly general

allowed to condemn use of signs in dispute with reputed trade marks. The provision was optional but almost all the Member States implemented it in their national legislations.[198] An analogous provision providing for enhanced protection with respect to the Community trade marks followed in Article 9(1)(c) of Regulation 40/94, replaced by Regulation 207/2009. As of today, special protection against infringing use of signs by third parties is provided by Article 10(2)(c) of Directive 2015/2436 and Article 9(2)(c) of Regulation 2017/1001, pursuant to which: the proprietor of a trade mark shall be entitled to prevent all third parties not having his consent from using in the course of trade, in relation to goods or services, any sign where the sign is identical with, or similar to, the trade mark irrespective of whether it is used in relation to goods or services which are identical with, similar to or not similar to those for which the trade mark is registered, where the latter has a reputation and where use of that sign without due cause takes unfair advantage of, or is detrimental to, the distinctive character or the repute of the trade mark. In the light of Directive 2015/2436, the implementation of the special regime in the national legislations is mandatory and all the Member States provide for enhanced protection.

38. Special ground for refusal or invalidity. A risk of infringement of a trade mark with a reputation is also a relative ground for refusal or invalidity of a later mark. In Directives 89/104 and 2008/95, this was provided by Article 4(3) concerning conflicts with Community trade marks and Article 4(4)(a) concerning conflicts with national trade marks. The transposition of the latter was optional. *De lege lata*, Article 5(3)(a) of Directive 2015/2436 provides that a trade mark shall not be registered or, if registered, shall be liable to be declared invalid where it is identical with, or similar to, an earlier trade mark irrespective of whether the goods or services for which it is applied or registered are identical with, similar to or not similar to those for which the earlier trade mark is registered, where the earlier trade mark has a reputation in the Member State in respect of which registration is applied for or in which the trade mark is registered or, in the case of an EU trade mark, has a reputation in the Union and the use of the later trade mark without due cause would take unfair advantage of, or be detrimental to, the distinctive character or the repute of the earlier trade mark. Pursuant to Article 8(5) of Regulation 2017/1001, corresponding to Article 8(5) of the former Regulations 40/94

---

wording of Article 14(1)(b) risked extending the trade mark proprietor's monopoly beyond the specific subject matter of the trade mark right. Consequently, the aforementioned provision was deleted from the text of the preliminary draft Regulation on the Community trade mark. Jehoram-Cohen considered this decision to be a serious step backwards in the protection of trade marks since, according to the author, the provisions of unfair competition law were difficult to apply in cases where there was no competitive relationship. Cohen Jehoram, *La protection des marques …*, p. 230. The Commission reintroduced a provision providing for special protection of the reputed trade mark in the Proposal for a Regulation on Community trade marks submitted on 25 November 1980. Brandt, *La protection élargie de la marque …*, p. 226. In the draft of the Directive, a provision on reputed trade marks appeared for the first time in 1986. Charles Gielen, *Harmonisation of Trade Mark Law in Europe: The First Trade Mark Harmonisation Directive of the European Council*, EIPR 1992, vol. 14, No. 9, p. 266. On the history of the introduction of extended protection in the first trade mark Directive and Regulation *see also* Kur, Senftleben, *European Trade Mark …*, pp. 9-10.

198. The exception was Cyprus, *see* Ilanah Simon Fhima, *Trade Mark Dilution in Europe and the United States*, Oxford University Press, Oxford 2011, p. 17.

and 207/2009, upon opposition by the proprietor of a registered earlier trade mark, the trade mark applied for shall not be registered where it is identical with, or similar to, an earlier trade mark, irrespective of whether the goods or services for which it is applied are identical with, similar to or not similar to those for which the earlier trade mark is registered, where, in the case of an earlier EU trade mark, the trade mark has a reputation in the Union or, in the case of an earlier national trade mark, the trade mark has a reputation in the Member State concerned, and where the use without due cause of the trade mark applied for would take unfair advantage of, or be detrimental to, the distinctive character or the repute of the earlier trade mark. A conflict with an earlier trade mark with a reputation is a ground for invalidity of an EU trade mark, in accordance with Articles 60(1)(a) and 8(2) and (5) combined of Regulation 2017/1001.

39. Special protection at the international level. In order to complete the presentation of the legal frameworks relating to the extended protection of trade marks with a reputation, it should be noted that, at the international level, Article 16(3) of the Agreement on Trade-Related Aspects of Intellectual Property Rights (TRIPS Agreement), relating to registered trade marks, recognises an enhanced protection of trade marks outside the speciality.[199] Indeed, pursuant to that provision: Article 6 bis of the Paris Convention shall apply, *mutatis mutandis*, to goods or services which are not similar to those in respect of which a trade mark is registered, provided that use of that trade mark in relation to those goods or services would indicate a connection between those goods or services and the owner of the registered trade mark and provided that the interests of the owner of the registered trade mark are likely to be damaged by such use.

40. Subject, scope and nature of protection. Having set out the legal provisions organising the regime of protection of trade marks with a reputation, I will examine the subject matter of the special protection (§1.02[A]), delimit the scope of its protection

199. *See* Charles Gielen, *Trademark Dilution under European Law*, TMR 2014, vol. 104, No. 3, p. 699; Marco Ricolfi, *Trattato dei marchi. Diritto europeo e nazionale*, Giappichelli, Turin 2015, p. 795. Cf. Martin Senftleben, *The Trademark Tower of Babel: Dilution Concepts in International, US and EC Trademark Law*, IIC 2009, vol. 40, No. 1, pp. 52-53. The author argues that this is not the only way to interpret Article 16(3) of TRIPS Agreement. According to the author, the wording of the said provision does not necessarily reflect a wish to establish a special regime for the protection of reputed trade marks, since the provision does not expressly refer to forms of infringement of the reputed trade mark, such as detriment to distinctiveness or unfair advantage, but rather to a complementary system of protection against confusion. However, the generality of the formula used by the TRIPS Agreement is rather explained by the desire to leave more freedom to the signatory States in the organisation of special protection. It should be noted that the solutions adopted in national legislations differ. For example, the US regime for the protection of famous trade marks does not consider taking of unfair advantage as a form of trade mark infringement beyond the speciality. *See* Ilanah Simon Fhima, *Protection of Well-Known and Famous Marks in the United States and United Kingdom*, in: Jacques de Werra (ed.), *Marques notoires et de haute renommée. Well-Known and Famous Trademarks*, Schulthess Verlag, Zurich 2011, p. 18; Simon Fhima, *Trade Mark Dilution ...*, pp. 189 et seq. Moreover, the language is far too general to limit the provision to the likelihood of confusion. Finally, if this had really been the intention of the authors of the TRIPS Agreement, it is difficult to understand why Article 16(3) does not expressly refer to the confusion contained in Article 16(1) of the Agreement.

with regard to the signs and the goods or services covered by them, which is broader than the subject of the trade mark right[200] (§1.02[B]), and finally examine the nature of the regime of special protection adopted by the European legislator (§1.02[C]).

[A] Subject of the Special Protection

41. Trade mark with a reputation and well-known trade mark. The subject of protection under the special regime is, of course, the trade mark with a reputation. It is necessary to define this notion which is crucial for this book (§1.02[A][1]). A distinction must then be made with the neighbouring concept of the well-known trade mark, within the meaning of Article 6 bis of the Paris Convention (§1.02[A][2]).

[1] Concept of the Trade Mark with a Reputation

42. Absence of legal definition. From the very beginning of the debates on the special protection of reputed trade marks, it was admitted that a satisfactory definition was the most urgent to formulate and the most difficult to find.[201] The doctrine raised the need to elaborate a common concept at the international level rather than leaving to the courts of every country to define it.[202] In the past, many terms were proposed, such as: 'mark of high reputation' (*marque de haute renommée*), 'famous mark' (*marque célèbre*), 'slogan mark' (*marque slogan*), 'more widely known mark' (*marque plus largement connue*), 'global mark' (*marque mondiale*),[203] 'mark known from the distance' (*marque connue au loin*), 'mark symbolising the company' (*marque symbolisant l'entreprise*),[204] 'supra notorious mark' (*marque supra notoire*) or 'mark with an exceptional reputation' (*marque de réputation exceptionnelle*).[205]

Neither Directive 2015/2436 nor Regulation 2017/1001 defines the trade mark with a reputation. This is also the case in most national legislations of the Member States. In this respect, the Spanish Trade Mark Law of 7 December 2001 is an exception. It defines the mark which benefits from enhanced protection, moreover distinguishing between two concepts: of a notorious mark (*marca notoria*)[206] and a reputed mark

200. Regarding protection of the mark in the speciality cf. Mathély, *Le droit français des signes …*, p. 317.
201. Jacq, *Réflexions sur les marques …*, p. 191.
202. Troller, *La marque de haute renommée …*, p. 76.
203. Troller, *La marque de haute renommée …*, p. 74.
204. Baeumer, *La protection de la marque …*, p. 551.
205. Brandt, *La protection élargie de la marque …*, p. 65.
206. Pursuant to Article 8(2) of the Spanish law, for the purposes of this law, notorious trade marks or trade names are those which, by reason of their volume of sales, duration of validity, intensity or geographical scope of use, value or prestige acquired on the market or for any other reason, are generally known to the segment of the public for which the goods, services or activities distinguishing that trade mark or trade name are intended. If all the conditions laid down in the first paragraph are met, the protection granted shall cover goods, services or activities of a nature that is all the more different in that the notorious trade mark or trade name is known in the relevant sector of the public or in other related sectors (*A los efectos de esta Ley, se entenderá por marca o nombre comercial notorios los que, por su volumen de ventas, duración, intensidad o alcance geográfico de su uso, valoración o prestigio alcanzado en el*

(*marca renombrada*),[207] both covered by the notion of trade mark with a reputation within the meaning of the Directive.[208] Should a normative definition of the trade mark with a reputation be introduced at the EU level? *Omnis definitio periculosa*, as the old saying goes.[209] The question of the definition gave rise to a great debate in the legal literature.

43. Criterion of uniqueness. A first criterion considered in the past to characterise the trade mark deserving enhanced protection was the 'uniqueness' of the mark.[210] As we have seen, the theorist of the concept of dilution, Schechter, argued in favour of extending the protection of 'coined, invented, arbitrary or fanciful' trade marks.[211] The criterion of uniqueness was used in the former German case law, which often required that the reputed trade mark be unique, that there cannot be therefore identical or similar marks on the market, even used for different goods or services.[212] In French doctrine, Dassas proposed to distinguish the reputed trade mark by reference not only to knowledge but also to the originality and uniqueness of the trade mark.[213] References to the originality of the trade mark which would justify extended protection can also be found in Polish doctrine.[214] The criterion of uniqueness was nevertheless rejected by many authors. Guglielmetti observed that there were certainly reputed marks on the market that deserved extended protection, such as *Fiat* or *Mercedes*, which were not unique because there were identical marks registered by third parties.[215] The concept of uniqueness was recently approved by an author who questions the principle of speciality and considers that the proprietor of each trade mark should be able to extend his protection to any good or service.[216] However, in the

mercado o por cualquier otra causa, sean generalmente conocidos por el sector pertinente del público al que se destinan los productos, servicios o actividades que distinguen dicha marca o nombre comercial. La protección otorgada en el apartado 1, cuando concurran los requisitos previstos en el mismo, alcanzará a productos, servicios o actividades de naturaleza tanto más diferente cuanto mayor sea el grado de conocimiento de la marca o nombre comercial notorios en el sector pertinente del público o en otros sectores relacionados).

207. Pursuant to Article 8(3) of the Spanish law, when the trade mark or trade name is known to the general public, it is considered to be reputed and the protection extends to all types of goods, services or activities (*Cuando la marca o nombre comercial sean conocidos por el público en general, se considerará que los mismos son renombrados y el alcance de la protección se extenderá a cualquier género de productos, servicios o actividades*).
208. In the light of their definitions, the first one, *marca notoria*, is known only by the relevant public, while the second one, *marca renombrada*, must be known by the general public. The difference between the two concepts is merely quantitative, not qualitative. Carlos González-Bueno, *Marcas notorias y renombradas en la ley y la jurisprudencia*, La Ley, Madrid 2005, p. 65.
209. Cf. the observations made by the national delegations at the Vienna Congress in 1952. Perent, *Marques notoirement connues* ..., pp. 80-81.
210. On the concept of uniqueness cf. para. 167 *infra*.
211. Schechter, *The Rational Basis* ..., p. 825.
212. Schricker, *La tutela della Ausstattung* ..., p. 267. However, the author notes that uniqueness should not be *a sine qua non* condition for the qualification of a reputed trade mark. For example, he noted, the reputation of the mark *Mercedes* in relation to automobiles has not been denied, although there were several marks consisting of the term *Mercedes*.
213. Dassas, *L'élargissement de la protection* ..., p. 91.
214. Cf. Promińska, *Prawo z rejestracji* ..., pp. 38-39.
215. Guglielmetti, *La tutela di marchi* ..., p. 287.
216. Friedmann, *The Uniqueness of the Trade Mark* ..., pp. 677 et seq.

view of the current legislation and case law, there is no doubt that uniqueness, or even originality, does not itself allow the trade mark to enjoy enhanced protection if the condition of knowledge of the sign by the public is not met. This is so because the advertising value of a mark is only affirmed by the use that is made of it and therefore its recognition.[217] As we will see, the question of uniqueness of the trade mark may be relevant, but at the stage of assessing the infringement, and in particular dilution.[218]

It is now almost unanimously accepted that a reputed trade mark is not a unique or original mark, but is a mark known to consumers. The reputation of a mark is therefore assessed on the basis of quantitative criteria (§1.02[A][1][b]). However, is the notion of reputation equivalent to the mere knowledge of the mark? Several authors argued that qualitative criteria should also be taken into consideration, hence that it should be examined whether the trade mark evokes particular associations in the public mind (§1.02[A][1][a]).

[a] Qualitative Definition of the Trade Mark with a Reputation

44. A 'qualitative' assessment of the trade mark with a reputation was proposed by European authors in many countries (§1.02[A][1][a][i]). However, this approach was condemned by the Court of Justice, which established a definition ignoring any qualitative criteria (§1.02[A][1][a][ii]). The solution must be approved, insofar as the qualitative definition would be inapplicable to all forms of infringement of the trade mark with a reputation (§1.02[A][1][a][iii]).

[i] Qualitative Definition Proposed by Scholars

45. Semantic approach. The semantic approach may imply two criteria of reputation: quantitative and qualitative. The trade mark with a reputation would then be a popular mark, i.e. known to a wide public and a mark enjoying a good repute.[219] References to the quality associated with the mark which should benefit from enhanced protection can be found in doctrine and jurisprudence of many European countries.

46. France. In French doctrine, qualitative criteria were important for Roubier.[220] References to criteria such as repute, prestige and high quality of goods were made by Pérot-Morel, who stressed that the reputed trade mark was not simply a well-known mark; a reputed mark was superior to the latter, since it implied good repute.[221] Portet also noted in her study that a trade mark was reputed when, in addition to its knowledge by the public, it was also appreciated, valued and recognised as 'a good mark'. According to the author, the reputed trade mark was a well-known trade mark whose fame was linked to excellent quality; hence it was a trade mark known and

217. *See* Dassas, *L'élargissement de la protection* ..., p. 89.
218. *See* para. 235 *infra*.
219. Marie-Eugénie Laporte-Legeais, *Clair-obscur sur la marque renommée: dix ans d'application de la loi du 4 janvier 1991*, JCP E 2001, No. 39, p. 1514, para. 10.
220. Roubier, *Le droit de la propriété* ..., t. II, p. 566.
221. Pérot-Morel, *Notoriété et renommée* ..., p. 475.

recognised as covering only products of exceptional quality, such as *Rolls Royce*, *Rolex*, *Piaget*, *Tiffany* and *Christian Dior*.[222] In the doctrine subsequent to the adoption of Directive 89/104, Laporte-Legeais observed that the qualitative criterion is in practice inseparable from the quantitative criterion, that the very important knowledge of the sign among the general public makes it possible to presume its good repute.[223] In this regard, it is worth mentioning the judgment in the case concerning the mark *Anne de Solène*,[224] in which the Court of Nancy insisted less on the knowledge of the mark than on its prestige when referring to 'luxury market', 'prestige among an informed clientele', 'advertisements in high quality magazines'.[225] Nevertheless, French case law never really considered good reputation to be a criterion for defining the reputed trade mark, either before or after the transposition of Directive 89/104.[226] The solution is thus closer to Jacq's opinion that the reputed trade mark expresses the need for special protection when it is exceptionally distinctive because of its celebrity,[227] or the conclusions of Perent, who stated in his study that the reputed trade mark, like the well-known trade mark, was a known mark. The celebrity of the mark can be due to several causes: intensive advertising, quality of the goods, long-lasting use, etc. Nevertheless, this does not matter; only the effect is relevant.[228]

47. Italy. Similarly, some Italian authors claimed that the reputed mark should convey a high prestige or excellent quality.[229] Guglielmetti considered that the quality of the designated good, together with a widespread knowledge of the mark, was a criterion for distinguishing the reputed mark. According to the author, it should be excluded that a trade mark designating poor quality products could have a reputation. Nevertheless, the author argued that this quality should not be superior or high, but only of such a nature as to satisfy the consumer and make him remember the mark favourably. He gave as examples the marks *Leica* and *Kodak* and noted that even if the latter was not considered by the public as designating goods of excellent quality, this would not prevent it from having a reputation.[230] Current Italian doctrine emphasises that, following the transposition of the Directive, there is no doubt that the definition of the reputed trade mark is neutral, thus associations with good quality are not necessary for a mark to have a reputation.[231]

48. Germany. The extended protection of reputed trade marks was strongly linked to the quality of the products bearing the mark in German case law in the 1950s.[232] The

222. Portet, *Les marques notoirement connues* ..., pp. 36, 40-42.
223. Laporte-Legeais, *Clair-obscur sur la marque renommée* ..., para. 10.
224. CA Nancy, 26 June 1974, Ann. propr. ind. 1975, p. 161, JCP 1975, p. 18178, comment of Georges Bonet, *Anne de Solène*.
225. Portet, *Les marques notoirement connues* ..., p. 192.
226. Cf. however TGI Paris, 7 March 2007, PIBD, No. 854, III, p. 404, *Cristal*.
227. Jacq, *Réflexions sur les marques* ..., p. 191.
228. Perent, *Marques notoirement connues* ..., p. 227.
229. Cf. Caselli, *Il marchio che gode di rinomanza* ..., pp. 31-32.
230. Guglielmetti, *La tutela di marchi* ..., pp. 285-286. *See also* Guglielmetti, *Marques ordinaires, notoirement connues* ..., p. 75.
231. Ricolfi, *Trattato dei marchi* ..., p. 729. *See also* Caselli, *Il marchio che gode di rinomanza* ..., p. 77.
232. Promińska, *Prawo z rejestracji* ..., p. 38.

qualitative criteria were eventually rejected by the courts.[233] Nevertheless, some German authors more recently seemed to favour the qualitative approach.[234]

49. The Netherlands. Nowadays, the qualitative approach finds supporters in Dutch doctrine.[235] Some authors note that the notion of reputation may indicate that the trade mark should be known in a positive sense, stressing however that the Court of Justice requires that account be taken only of knowledge of the sign and not of the effect it has on consumers.[236]

50. Spain. Similarly, some Spanish authors use two criteria of reputation, knowledge of the sign and a good reputation associated by the public with the products covered by the mark. In addition, it should be noted that the Spanish Trade Mark Law, in its Article 8(2), defining the notorious mark (*marca notoria*), which benefits from enhanced protection, expressly refers to 'prestige' as a factor in assessing the notorious character of a mark.[237] Nevertheless, scholars specify that this is only one of the factors of assessment which is not a necessary condition to establish that a mark is notorious or has a reputation.[238]

51. Poland. Polish doctrine traditionally approved the qualitative definition. Some authors linked the notion of the reputed trade mark to trade marks symbolising a good quality of the designated product,[239] stating that the reputed trade mark should evoke positive associations in the minds of consumers,[240] and opposing to reputed marks the marks of 'bad reputation' that discourage the public from acquiring the good or service designated by the sign.[241] Following the doctrine, Polish courts, including the Supreme Court and the Supreme Administrative Court, stated on many occasions that the trade mark with a reputation guarantees high quality, uniqueness and prestige of the goods

233. Wolfgang Büscher, in: Frederick W. Mostert et al. (ed.), *Famous and Well-Known Marks*, INTA, New York 2004, p. 4-174.
234. *See* Annette Kur, *Well-Known Marks, Highly Renowned Marks and Marks Having a (High) Reputation: What's It All About?*, IIC 1992, vol. 23, No. 2, pp. 226 et seq.
235. Senftleben, *The Trademark Tower of Babel ...*, p. 73.
236. Tobias Cohen Jehoram, Constant Van Nispen, Tony Huydecoper, *European Trademark Law: Community Trademark Law and Harmonized National Trademark Law*, Wolters Kluwer, Alphen aan den Rijn 2010, p. 299.
237. *See* Miguel Angel Baz, Alberto de Elzaburu, in: Frederick W. Mostert et al., *Famous and Well-Known Marks*, INTA, New York 2004, pp. 4-396 et seq. Cf. para. 42 *supra*.
238. González-Bueno, *Marcas notorias y renombradas ...*, p. 44.
239. Urszula Promińska, *Odpowiedzialność naruszającego prawo ochronne na znak towarowy*, in: *Odpowiedzialność cywilna. Księga pamiątkowa ku czci Profesora Adama Szpunara*, Wolters Kluwer, Cracow 2004, p. 690.
240. Ryszard Skubisz, *Naruszenie praw z rejestracji renomowanych znaków towarowych (w świetle dyrektywy o znakach towarowych)*, in: Adam Łazowski, Rudolf Ostrihansky (eds), *Współczesne wyzwania europejskiej przestrzeni prawnej. Księga pamiątkowa dla uczczenia 70. Urodzin Profesora Eugeniusza Piontka*, Zakamycze, Warsaw 2005, p. 437.
241. Piotrowska, *Renomowane znaki ...*, p. 25.

designated by the mark.[242] This approach is however less present in the most recent jurisprudence which applies only quantitative criteria.[243]

52. Switzerland. Outside the EU, references to quality appear relevant under Swiss trade mark law. In the older Swiss literature, Jaton was of the opinion that the reputed trade mark should arouse the idea of a good quality, but that it was a relative notion and that it should be a quality sufficient to avoid the risk of disappointment.[244] Also, Troller noted that the reputed mark is a 'general symbol of quality'.[245] Indeed, according to the author, the reputed trade mark was used to attest to the superior quality of the product and represented for the public a good of exceptional quality. However, the author noted that in the case of reputed marks that symbolise a company or its products in the eyes of the public, there was no need for them to arouse, in addition, the idea of exceptional quality.[246] As Blum observed, if Troller required that the mark should convey to the public a certain idea of quality, this condition appears in his opinion as an alternative and could be replaced by the fact that the public considers the mark as a symbol of the company.[247] By contrast, Brandt challenged the qualitative definition. The author gave the example of the mark *Coca-Cola* and noted that this mark, undeniably renowned, did not possess exceptional characteristics. According to the author, the prestigious sign is almost always famous, but the opposite is not true. Thus, the determination of reputation must not result from the quality of the good designated by the sign.[248] Swiss case law presently requires the reputed mark to constitute a symbol of quality and prestige. In the most recent work on the reputed trade marks, Alberini stresses the importance of qualitative criteria.[249] Some authors, including Gilliéron, consider however that the qualitative factors only help to assess the knowledge of the mark which should constitute the only and decisive criterion.[250]

242. NSA, 27 February 2008, case II GSK 359/07; SN, 12 October 2005, case III CK 160/05, *Braun*; SN, 21 October 2010, case IV CSK 231/10, *BP*.
243. *See* e.g. SO Warsaw, 22 December 2010, case XXII GWzt 25/10, *Red Bull*; SO Warsaw, 30 July 2012, case XXII GWzt 18/10, *My Little Pony*; SO Warsaw, 30 April 2013, case XXII GWzt 3/13, *Stop Shop*; SO Warsaw, 27 February 2015, case XXII GWzt 73/14, *Immergas*; NSA, 5 February 2013, case II GSK 2153/11, *L'Oréal*.
244. Jaton, *La protection des marques ...*, p. 28.
245. Alois Troller, *Précis du droit de la propriété immatérielle*, Helbing & Lichtenhahn, Basel 1978, p. 98.
246. Troller, *La marque de haute renommée ...*, pp. 75-76.
247. Rudolf E. Blum, *La marque de 'haute renommée'. Une réponse*, PI 1954, pp. 110-111. According to the latter, the notion of reputation was not necessarily linked to an idea of quality, it was fame alone that was decisive.
248. Brandt, *La protection élargie de la marque ...*, p. 90.
249. Alain Alberini, *L'exploitation de la renommée de la marque d'autrui. Du risque de confusion au risque d'association*, CEDIDAC, Lausanne 2015, pp. 62-63, 218-220.
250. Philippe Gilliéron, *Les marques notoirement connues et les marques de haute renommée en droit suisse*, in: Jacques de Werra (ed.), *Marques notoires et de haute renommée. Well-Known and Famous Trademarks*, Schulthess Verlag, Zurich 2011, pp. 52-53.

[ii] Qualitative Definition Rejected by the Court of Justice

53. Absence of reference to qualitative criteria in the jurisprudence. Due to the absence of a legal definition of the trade mark with a reputation in European provisions, it was left to the case law to define the scope of this concept. By a judgment of 14 September 1999 in the *Chevy* case,[251] the Court of Justice stated that the trade mark with a reputation is a mark 'known by a significant part of the public concerned by the products or services which it covers'.

It results clearly from the *Chevy* judgment that the qualitative criteria have no relevance to the assessment of the trade mark's reputation. No legal provision or case law requires, at the stage of examining the existence of reputation, that it be inspired by a particular positive image; the trade mark with a reputation is fame in the neutral sense of the term.[252] Indeed, since the *Chevy* judgment, the Court of Justice has never suggested that a reputed trade mark should enjoy a particular prestige.[253] Thus, the Court of Justice adopted the quantitative method of assessing the reputation of a trade mark at the stage of its qualification.[254] The solution takes into account, above all, these language versions of the Trade Marks Directive, in the light of which there is no doubt that the concept of the trade mark with a reputation refers only to knowledge of the sign, as it results in particular from its German, Dutch and Swedish versions.[255] The other language versions semantically also suggest a qualitative approach. However, in spite of the differences in the translation of the Directive, the concept of the trade mark with a reputation must be interpreted in the same way in all Member States.

Admittedly, very often a high public awareness of the trade mark, resulting from intensive use of the mark, is linked to a positive opinion of consumers and their associations with a good quality of the products designated by the mark. Thus, in most cases, in particular, luxury marks are undoubtedly likely to enjoy this special protection.[256] A reputed mark can therefore be associated in the minds of customers with high quality or prestige. However, the latter does not constitute components of this legal notion.[257] Indeed, marks that designate everyday consumer products, which are rarely associated with excellent quality, can also be qualified as reputed. The case law clarifies that the concept of the reputation of a mark should not be confused with its possible prestige or superior quality; 'it cannot be assumed that each mark with a

251. CJ, 14 September 1999, case C-375/97, *Chevy*.
252. Claude-Albéric Maetz, *Notoriété: essai sur l'appropriation d'une valeur économique*, Presses Universitaires, Aix-Marseille 2010, p. 93.
253. Simon Fhima, *Exploring the Roots ...*, p. 30.
254. Lionel Bently, Brad Sherman, *Intellectual Property Law*, Oxford University Press, Oxford 2009, p. 879. In favour of the quantitative approach before the *Chevy* judgment cf. Hazel Carty, *Les marques jouissant d'une renommée méritent-elles une protection particulière?*, PIBD 1998, No. 653, II, p. 79. The European legislation thus corresponds to the American approach protecting famous marks and is in line with the international provisions that only protect well-known trade marks. Senftleben, *The Trademark Tower of Babel ...*, p. 54.
255. *See* CJ, 14 September 1999, case C-375/97, *Chevy*, para. 22.
256. Cf. Emmanuelle Hoffmann, Laure Bouchard, *Les spécificités du luxe*, Propr. intell. 2015, No. 56, p. 232.
257. Ryszard Skubisz, *Glosa do wyroku NSA z dnia 27 lutego 2008 r. (II GSK 359/07)*, PS 2009, No. 4, p. 143; Maetz, *Notoriété: essai sur l'appropriation ...*, p. 93.

reputation conveys, by the mere fact of its reputation, an image of prestige or superior quality'.[258] Therefore, even if public knowledge of the mark and a good reputation often coexist, the reputed mark does not need to convey a particularly positive message about the good.[259] Moreover, it should be noted that the existence of a repute cannot compensate for the lack of knowledge of the mark by the customers.[260] In other words, proof of good image does not exempt the owner from demonstrating that the mark is known by a significant part of the public concerned.

[iii] Qualitative Definition Inapplicable to All Forms of Infringement

54. Forms of infringement related to the distinctive character. Unlike the qualitative definition, the quantitative definition is the only one that can be applied in all cases of infringement of trade marks with a reputation provided by the law. Its recognition by the Court of Justice must therefore be approved since it takes into account the various concepts of infringement condemned in the field of the special regime. The qualitative definition would only allow a reasonable interpretation of the conditions of trade mark infringement outside the speciality relating to the repute. A qualitative approach would be indeed justified if tarnishment and unfair advantage taken from the repute of the trade mark were the only forms of infringement of the trade mark with a reputation. Limiting the protection of reputed trade marks to the preservation of their image in no way results from the evolution of the protection of reputed trade marks and, above all, is not in conformity with the letter of the current legislation. Consequently, the qualitative definition is inapplicable to the other types of infringement, namely dilution and unfair advantage taken from the distinctive character.

As it will be established when exposing the subject matter of protection of the trade mark with a reputation against dilution, the fact that a trade mark is highly distinctive, known and memorised by the public gives it an important value, makes it an instrument of communication with customers. The mere knowledge of the mark represents a strong power of attraction that third parties have an interest in using. Thus, the economic value specially protected by the provisions relating to trade marks with a reputation does not necessarily translate into an exceptional image that the mark conveys, fame being in itself an appreciable advertising value.[261] The quantitative definition therefore reflects the need to protect the reputed trade mark also against the trivialisation of its distinctive power or against taking advantage of the distinctive character of the trade mark. For this reason, the question of the image, particular prestige or high quality of the goods designated by the sign is irrelevant for the concept

258. CFI, 22 March 2007, case T-215/03, *VIPS*, para. 58.
259. Ryszard Skubisz, *Znaki towarowe – ewolucja przedmiotu ochrony prawnej*, PPH 2008, No. 12, p. 17.
260. Krystyna Szczepanowska-Kozłowska, *Czy znak renomowany zawsze ma renomę?*, Glosa 2016, No. 2, p. 58.
261. *See* para. 212 *infra*.

of the trade mark with a reputation, defined in the *Chevy* judgment and confirmed on several occasions by the case law of the Court of Justice and the General Court.[262]

The qualitative approach must therefore be condemned, as not only incompatible with the definition imposed by the Court of Justice but also likely to call into question the recognition of dilution and unfair advantage taken of the distinctive character as specific forms of infringement provided in the field of the special regime. It is therefore not surprising that the authors who criticise the concept of dilution would prefer to subject the notion of the trade mark with a reputation to qualitative connotations.[263] However, this would circumvent the spirit of the legal provisions that expressly recognise the protection of the distinctive character of the trade mark. The high distinctiveness of the trade mark enjoys the same extended protection regime as the repute or image of the trade mark. Thus, it should be accepted that the concept of the trade mark with a reputation can and must be limited to the knowledge of the sign.

55. Distinct notions of reputation and repute. It is therefore possible to apply the special regime to highly distinctive marks and to marks with a particularly positive image among customers. In the latter case, the qualitative element becomes relevant when examining the existence of the infringement which occurs when an advantage is taken from the repute or a detriment caused to the repute, and therefore to the image of the mark.[264] The term of repute, used to characterise the infringement of the trade mark, does not have the same meaning as that of reputation. It does not refer to the knowledge or notoriety of the mark. The repute is assessed on the basis of qualitative criteria, and must therefore be interpreted in the stricter sense, which is synonymous with a positive image of the mark.[265] In the English versions, Directive 2015/2436 and of Regulation 2017/1001 use therefore two different terms which do not have the same meaning. However, it should be noted that in some language versions, one term is used in both cases and this polysemy is regrettable.[266]

[b] Quantitative Definition of the Trade Mark with a Reputation

56. Requirement of knowledge by the public. In the light of the *Chevy* judgment, a trade mark with a reputation is a mark 'known by a significant part of the public concerned by the products or services which it covers'. Thus, the Court of Justice established a broad definition of a reputed trade mark based on quantitative criteria,

262. *See* e.g. CFI, 22 March 2007, case T-215/03, *VIPS*, para. 57.
263. *See* Senftleben, *The Trademark Tower of Babel* ..., p. 73.
264. Irena Wiszniewska, *Znaki towarowe w prawie własności przemysłowej*, PPH 2001, No. 12, pp. 16-17; Maetz, *Notoriété: essai sur l'appropriation* ..., p. 93.
265. Cf. Adrien Bouvel, *Principe de spécialité et signes distinctifs*, Litec, Paris 2004, p. 368; Bently, Sherman, *Intellectual Property* ..., p. 879; Maetz, *Notoriété: essai sur l'appropriation* ..., p. 94; Ricolfi, *Trattato dei marchi* ..., pp. 729-730; Krystyna Szczepanowska-Kozłowska, in: Ewa Nowińska, Krystyna Szczepanowska-Kozłowska (ed.), *System prawa handlowego*, t. III, *Prawo własności przemysłowej*, C.H. Beck, Warsaw 2015, p. 345. *See* para. 241 *infra*.
266. For example, the following terms are used to refer to the mark which is the subject of the special regime and to tarnishment: in French, *renommée*; in Italian, *notorietà*; in Spanish, *renombre*; in Polish, *renoma*; in Portuguese, *prestígio*; in Czech, *dobré jméno*.

namely the knowledge of the mark by the public targeted by it.[267] This is a well-established definition in European case law which was never challenged by either the Court of Justice or the General Court.

The reputation of the trade mark is a preliminary condition that the owner is required to demonstrate in order to benefit from extended protection and that the Court needs to assess in the first place in order to rule whether the special regime is applicable.[268] In the view of the definition of the trade mark with a reputation, it must therefore be proven that the allegedly reputed trade mark is a mark known to the relevant public (§1.02[A][1][b][i]). There are several means of demonstrating reputation of a trade mark (§1.02[A][1][b][ii]).

[i] Subject of Proof of Reputation

57. Burden of proof. The knowledge of the trade mark must be demonstrated by the right holder who invokes the special protection, in accordance with the rule *actori incumbit probatio*. An exception to this principle may be allowed, in the view of the applicable procedural rules, where the reputation is not contested, *a fortiori* where it is admitted by the adverse party.[269]

58. Reputation as a well-known fact. In accordance with the applicable procedural rules, one might also argue that the proprietor does not need to establish reputation of a mark when it is a well-known fact.[270] However, it is often difficult to assess whether a circumstance is indeed well known. These are primarily historical or political events, natural phenomena, etc., which are commonly known to the public. As it was observed by a Swiss author, it is difficult to accept that the knowledge of a mark could be a well-known fact.[271] In any case, the Court should be very careful in implementing the rules related to the well-known facts, if only because it is always a question of demonstrating the reputation of the trade mark at the time of the disputed facts. In the proceedings before the EUIPO and EU courts, it is not possible to claim that the

267. Cf. Ewa Skrzydło-Tefelska, in: Gordian N. Hasselblatt (ed.), *Community Trade Mark Regulation. A Commentary*, C.H. Beck Hart Nomos, Munich-Oxford 2015, p. 280; Senftleben, *European Trade Mark ...*, p. 342.
268. Cf. GC, 28 September 2016, case T-362/15, *Henleys*, para. 22; GC, 1 June 2018, case T-900/16, *Dayaday*, para. 37; GC, 26 September 2018, case T-62/16, *Puma*, para. 67.
269. *See* e.g. in French jurisprudence, TGI Paris, 19 October 2012, case 11/04505, *Louis Vuitton*.
270. This opinion was expressed under Polish law. *See* Arkadiusz Michalak, Monika Witkowska, in: Arkadiusz Michalak (ed.), *Prawo własności przemysłowej. Komentarz*, C.H. Beck, Warsaw 2016, p. 435.
271. Gilliéron, *Les marques notoirement ...*, p. 55. However, as the author points out, Swiss jurisprudence admits that the right holder does not need to prove reputation when it is a well-known fact, as it was in the case of the mark *Nestlé*.

reputation of a mark is a well-known fact,[272] even though some facts taken into account in the assessment of reputation may be considered as universally known.[273]

59. Relevant date. In civil infringement proceedings, the claimant needs to establish reputation at the time of the use of the contested sign which is allegedly infringing.[274] By contrast, in order to establish infringement, the owner should not be required to prove that the trade mark still enjoys a reputation at the date on which the legal action is brought[275] or at the time the decision is rendered. The question is whether the trade mark had a reputation throughout its use by the third party, but its existence both prior and subsequent to the acts of disputed exploitation is irrelevant for an infringement to be established. Moreover, the trade mark right does not even need to longer exist at the time when the owner brings the action or when the Court rules on the merits. In such case, the owner may still seek liability for non-prescribed acts of use of his trade mark. In the event that the trade mark right no longer exists on one of these dates, the proprietor cannot request the cessation of use of the disputed sign; he is entitled, however, to request compensation for the damage suffered. The claimant should also establish that his mark still enjoys a reputation at the date of bringing the action and at the date of the decision so that a prohibition of its use beyond the speciality can be imposed.[276] In administrative proceedings, the proprietor should establish reputation on the filing date of the contested mark (or, where appropriate, on the priority date) and, in principle, that this reputation subsisted until the decision is taken.[277]

Consequently, the evidence filed in order to prove reputation should be dated, or at least indicate when the facts attested therein took place, and concern the relevant

272. Cf. GC, 2 October 2015, case T-624/13, *Darjeeling*, para. 82, according to which the application of the special regime under the Regulation 'necessarily requires a definitive conclusion regarding whether or not such a reputation exists, which, in principle, means that no analysis regarding the possible application of that provision can be carried out on the basis of a vague hypothesis, that is to say, a hypothesis which is not based on the acknowledgement of a reputation with a specific level of strength'. *See also* Guidelines for examination of European Union Trade Marks (2020), EUIPO, Part C, section 5, p. 28.

273. Cf. CFI, 22 June 2004, case T-185/02, *Picasso*, para. 29, according to which: 'the restriction of the factual basis of the examination by the Board of Appeal does not preclude it from taking into consideration, in addition to the facts expressly put forward by the parties to the opposition proceedings, facts which are well known, that is, which are likely to be known by anyone or which may be learnt from generally accessible sources'. On that finding *see* Bertrand Geoffray, *La protection des marques renommées en droit communautaire*, Propr. ind. 2008, No. 5, étude 11, paras 65 et seq.

274. Passa, *Traité de droit* ..., p. 512. Regarding likelihood of confusion cf. CJ, 27 April 2006, case C-145/05, *Levi Strauss*, para. 20. Reputation should exist from the beginning of the disputed use.

275. Cf. Bouvel, *Principe de spécialité* ..., p. 352.

276. Cf. Bouvel, *Principe de spécialité* ..., p. 352. That being said, a situation in which the judge admits the existence of a reputation of a trade mark at the time of the acts of exploitation of the disputed sign and finds that it has lost its reputation before the date on which the action was brought or the date of the decision will be very rare to see in practice.

277. *See* Skrzydło-Tefelska, *Community Trade Mark* ..., p. 281. Likewise, in practice, the loss of reputation during the proceedings might happen exceptionally since it presupposes a dramatic change of market conditions over a relatively short period of time. Therefore, in most cases, it will be sufficient for the right holder to show that its mark had a reputation on the filing date. *See* Guidelines for examination of European Union Trade Marks (2020), EUIPO, Part C, section 5, p. 14.

time.[278] An important part of documents should bear dates relatively close to the relevant date, although it cannot be ruled out that a 'historical' mark might still enjoy a certain surviving reputation.[279] In principle, the date of the documents submitted should be prior to the disputed use or application, including much earlier period since the reputation is in general acquired progressively and the duration of use may be an important factor of assessment. However, documents bearing a later date cannot be denied evidential value if they enable conclusions to be drawn with regard to the situation as it was on that date.[280]

60. Perception of the sign, relevant public and territory. In order to benefit from the special protection, the trade mark owner must demonstrate the reputation, hence that the sign is known as a trade mark, among the public concerned by the goods or services designated by it, in the relevant territory.

Reputation of the sign perceived as a trade mark

61. Other distinctive signs. The proprietor should establish that this is the 'trade mark', i.e. the sign perceived by the public as an indicator of the commercial origin of a good or service, which has a reputation. It is not therefore sufficient for the right holder to prove reputation of one of his other distinctive signs, such as his company name, trade name or shop name since their purpose is to identify a legal person, a business or a place of exploitation and not the commercial origin of a good or service. Doubts may arise when the trade mark also constitutes one of these signs. In this respect, the General Court ruled that 'even if the name of a company is known, that recognition is not capable of establishing that the mark of which it is the proprietor, even if it is a "house mark" which is identical to the name of the company, is known to a significant part of the public in respect of the goods and services which it covers'.[281] The decision seems harsh.[282] It must be admitted that very often these signs indirectly fulfil the distinctive function of the mark.[283] Indeed, when they are used in relations with customers, they are likely to have the effect of designating the goods or services constituting the subject matter of the activity carried out by their user.[284] The Court of Justice accepts that a distinctive sign such as a company name or a trade name may be

278. *See* Guidelines for examination of European Union Trade Marks (2020), EUIPO, Part C, section 5, p. 15.
279. GC, 3 May 2018, case T-2/17, *Masi*, para. 58. Cf. GC, 8 May 2014, case T-327/12, *Simca*, para. 49.
280. GC, 18 October 2018, case T-548/17, *Kipling*, paras 103-104. Cf. CJ, 17 April 2008, case C-108/07 P, *Ferrero*, para. 53. Regarding establishment of genuine use cf. also CJ, 27 January 2004, case C-259/02, *Laboratoires de la mer*, para. 31.
281. GC, 28 October 2016, case T-123/15, *Unicorn*, para. 57.
282. In this direction, in relation to a similar judgment of TGI Paris, 19 September 2007, case 06/09465, cf. Passa, *Traité de droit ...*, p. 513.
283. Jérôme Passa, *L'usage de marque dans la jurisprudence récente de la CJCE*, RJDA 2003, No. 3, p. 199. Cf. Mathély, *Le droit français des signes ...*, p. 629.
284. Passa, *Traité de droit ...*, p. 305.

used 'in relation to goods or services' and therefore be perceived as a trade mark[285] and the legislator currently admits this *expressis verbis* in Article 10(3)(d) of Directive 2015/2436 and in Article 9(3)(d) of Regulation 2017/1001. That being said, the Court or trade mark office appreciating reputation should always examine whether the acts of use of another distinctive sign were such as to establish knowledge of it as an indicator of the commercial origin of a good or service. Moreover, the trade mark and the other sign should be, in principle, identical,[286] at least in their distinctive elements. Thus, the right holder wishing to benefit from the special protection may invoke the reputation of other distinctive signs used in the course of trade provided that they are perceived as indirectly indicating the commercial origin of a good or service. The judge should always consider whether the use of another distinctive sign can also be qualified as use as a trade mark. However, it seems that when the sign in question is identical to the mark whose reputation is claimed and used in relation to a good or service, this should usually be the case.

62. Surnames, geographical names, common names. Uncertainty as to the reputation of the sign as a trade mark may also appear in the case of trade marks composed of family names or names of musical groups, such as *Beatles*,[287] or inspired by geographical locations, as was the case with the mark *Dakar*.[288] The assessment of the existence of a trade mark's reputation is also problematic when it consists of commonly used terms. It is important to establish the reputation of the trade mark in relation to the designated good or service and not recognition of the word constituting the sign in common language. Admittedly, following significant exploitation of such names as trade marks, they may detach themselves from their original perception and acquire an independent reputation as indicators of the commercial origin of a good or service. Nevertheless, the only evidence likely to establish the reputation of a trade mark is that which demonstrates its use for goods or services.

63. Recognition of goods or services. By contrast, proof of recognition of goods or services under the trade mark can be used to demonstrate the reputation of the trade mark itself. A trade mark is always used in connection with a good or service and cannot be detached from it. Proving the recognition of a good or service under the mark implies demonstrating its reputation. It was, for instance, rightly decided, with regard to the mark *Playboy*, that it has a reputation, thanks to the success of the eponymous magazine.[289]

64. Use of the mark with or within other trade marks. A difficulty may also arise when the mark needs to be isolated, this time not from another distinctive sign or its original meaning, but from other marks belonging to the right holder. It often happens

285. CJ, 11 September 2007, case C-17/06, *Céline*, paras 22-23. *See* Jacques Azéma, *Marques et signes distinctifs traditionnels: Enseigne, nom commercial, dénomination sociale*, in: *Les défis du droit des marques au XXIe siècle. Actes du colloque en l'honneur du professeur Yves Reboul*, LexisNexis, Paris 2011, pp. 23-24.

286. Szczepanowska-Kozłowska, *Czy znak renomowany zawsze ...*, pp. 58-59.

287. *See* GC, 29 March 2012, case T-369/10, *Beatles*, paras 55-58.

288. In the Polish jurisprudence NSA, 25 May 2011, case II GSK 578/10, *Dakar*.

289. TGI Paris, 14 October 2008, case 06/16051, *Playboy*.

that a mark is part of another composite mark, or it is always used with another mark. Naturally, when the proprietor invokes several trade marks, the evidence submitted must refer to each of them. Proof of the reputation of one trade mark shall not entail recognition of the reputation of the trade marks that may be attached to it.[290] However, if the proprietor always uses two marks together, for example, a word mark next to a figurative mark or a word mark applied to the product whose shape itself constitutes a mark, he cannot be obliged to communicate proof of use and reputation of each of these marks in isolation. Provided that all marks affixed to the product are perceived as such by the public, all documents relating to this product are likely to establish the reputation of each of them.[291] When the right holder exploits two trade marks simultaneously and one of them is the 'main' mark, it does not exclude that the second sign, for instance designating a line of products, will not also fulfil the origin function.[292] For instance, the reputation of a trade mark consisting of the shape of a product, always used with a word sign affixed to it, may be admitted if the shape itself indicates to the consumer the commercial origin of the good.[293]

The acquisition of reputation may also result from the use as part of another registered trade mark.[294] The fact that the owner always uses the composite trade mark does not prevent one of its elements from being qualified as a reputed mark. It is therefore possible to establish reputation of a trade mark on the basis of evidence relating to the use of another registered trade mark provided that the mark whose reputation is claimed fulfils the distinctive function. To this end, the mark should continue to be perceived as an indication of the origin of the good or service in question,[295] in other words 'have an independent distinctive role' within the complex mark.[296] This question was discussed by the General Court, for example, in a case concerning a composite trade mark combining the term *Longines* with a graphic element. It was established that the composite mark had a reputation in relation to watches. However, the right holder failed to demonstrate the reputation of the graphic element independently. According to the Court, the acquisition of reputation by the latter could not be deduced from the evidence relating to the complex mark if the

290. *See* GC, 15 March 2016, case T-645/13, *Etam*, para. 128.
291. Cf. GC, 17 October 2018, case T-8/17, *Ballon d'or*, paras 99-101.
292. Regarding the assessment of genuine use cf. Jérôme Passa, *Contrefaçon de marque: condition d'usage à titre de marque dans l'hypothèse de l'emploi du signe litigieux en complément de la marque principale du défendeur*, RTD com. 2019, No. 2, p. 377.
293. In Polish jurisprudence *see* SN, 10 February 2011, case IV CSK 393/10, *skopek*. In Belgian jurisprudence cf. CA Bruxelles, 16 September 2016, case 2011/AR/1184, *Spa*. Regarding the assessment of genuine use cf. CJ, 23 January 2019, case C-698/17 P, paras 41-49, 57-65. On the last judgment *see* Jérôme Passa, *Déchéance pour défaut d'usage sérieux: usage sous une forme modifiée dans l'hypothèse de l'emploi d'un signe verbal sur le produit dont la forme seule est enregistrée comme marque*, RTD com. 2019, No. 2, p. 372.
294. Regarding the acquisition of the distinctive character cf. CJ, 7 July 2005, case C-353/03, *Have a break*, para. 30.
295. *See* CJ, 17 July 2008, case C-488/06 P, *Arbre magique*, paras 49-53; GC, 1 March 2018, case T-629/16, *Adidas*, paras 28, 76; GC, 29 November 2018, case T-372/17, *LV*, para. 94; GC, 27 June 2019, case T-334/18, *Anna*, para. 45. Regarding the assessment of genuine use cf. CJ, 18 April 2013, case C-12/12, *Levi's*, para. 35; GC, 24 September 2015, case T-211/14, paras 30-31.
296. Regarding the assessment of the likelihood of confusion cf. CJ, 6 October 2005, case C-120/04, *Life*.

graphic element did not occupy a 'visually important position' in the composite sign. Indeed, it was the verbal element that was larger than the figurative element and remained easily legible, so that the latter remained 'clearly ancillary and in the background' in the overall impression which consumers perceiving that mark would have since the verbal element *Longines* was 'dominant' in the overall impression created by that composite sign.[297] However, it should be stressed that the only relevant criterion should be the ability of the trade mark to perform the function of indicating the commercial origin of a good or service. The fact that a mark occupies a less visually important position does not mean that it no longer produces this effect. Nevertheless, if a trade mark is only a minor element of a composite mark, which loses its distinctive position within it and is perceived only as an element of the composite sign, its reputation cannot be deduced from the evidence relating to the composite mark.[298]

Reputation of the sign within the relevant public

65. Public concerned by the mark. In the light of the jurisprudence of the Court of Justice, the reputation of a trade mark needs to be established among the relevant public. According to the *Chevy* judgment, 'the degree of knowledge required must be considered to be reached when the earlier mark is known by a significant part of the public concerned by the products or services covered by that trade mark'.[299] The Court specified that 'the public amongst which the earlier trade mark must have acquired a reputation is that concerned by that trade mark, that is to say, depending on the product or service marketed, either the public at large or a more specialised public, for example traders in a specific sector'.[300] Thus, recognition of the trade mark is assessed in a flexible way since the Court is satisfied with the recognition of the mark by the public targeted by it and not by the general public. This concept is sometimes referred to as the 'niche reputation approach'.[301]

The solution is contrary to the position traditionally adopted by many authors and national courts that considered that the reputed mark should be known by the general public,[302] and criticised for questioning the principle of speciality.[303] Indeed, in

297. GC, 12 February 2015, case T-76/13, *Longines*, paras 91-108.
298. Cf. GC, 18 November 2015, case T-606/13, *Mustang*, para. 39.
299. CJ, 14 September 1999, case C-375/97, *Chevy*, para. 26.
300. CJ, 14 September 1999, case C-375/97, *Chevy*, para. 24.
301. Cf. Senftleben, *European Trade Mark ...*, p. 342.
302. *See* Brandt, *La protection élargie de la marque ...*, pp. 83-85; Albert Chavanne, in: Jean-Jacques Burst, Albert Chavanne, *Droit de la propriété industrielle*, 5th ed., Dalloz, Paris 1998, p. 587; Maetz, *Notoriété: essai sur l'appropriation ...*, p. 87; Frédéric Pollaud-Dulian, *Propriété intellectuelle. La propriété industrielle*, Economica, Paris 2011, p. 1072.
303. *See* Frédéric Pollaud-Dulian, *Marque de renommée. Histoire de la dénaturation d'un concept*, Propr. intell. 2001, No. 1, pp. 48 et seq. It is interesting to note that a solution contrary to the one adopted by the Court of Justice was adopted by the American legislator, which expressly requires the general public to be familiar with the trade mark. As a result, in Europe, access to the extended protection is easier. *See* Senftleben, *The Trademark Tower of Babel ...*, pp. 54-55. Cf. also Joanna Sitko, *Trade Marks with a Reputation and Famous Marks: Differences in Approach Between the European Union, Poland and the United States in Relation to the Principle of Speciality*, Queen Mary Journal of Intellectual Property 2017, vol. 7, No. 3, pp. 331 et seq.

the past, the reputed mark was linked to a recognition going outside the public concerned.[304] However, even at that time, some authors considered that it was not necessary for a reputed trade mark to be known beyond the buyers of the goods designated by the mark.[305]

66. Justified solution. There is no decisive reason why the trade mark with a reputation should be known outside its clientele. Requiring that the reputed trade mark be known to the general public would favour marks designating consumer products over marks covering goods aimed at narrower, specialised public, which would hardly be justified.[306] It is, for example, easier for a sign to be known if it is used for beverage products than for a sign designating musical instruments. Nevertheless, both can be equally subject to infringement under the special regime, particularly in the form of detriment. For example, a trade mark designating musical instruments of excellent quality may be tarnished in the eyes of the musicians who use them if it is exploited for detergents. It is hard to understand why a manufacturer of musical instruments would not deserve the same protection as a manufacturer of beverage products. Hence, the rule according to which the clientele concerned by the trade mark constitutes the reference public appears to be the most justified. Moreover, it does not seem reasonable to allow undertakings to take advantage of the reputation of a mark already known by professionals.[307] In addition, it should be noted that some highly prestigious trade marks may be ignored by the general public, while they should be granted extended protection. We can see to what extent the more restrictive criterion could deprive several trade marks of the enhanced protection if we read that, in 1975, the trade marks such as *Lamborghini*, *Rolex* or *Tiffany* were recognised only by a small fraction of the French population.[308]

67. Solution compliant with the TRIPS Agreement. The solution adopted by the Court of Justice is in full compliance with Article 16 of the TRIPS Agreement on the well-known trade mark and the extension of protection beyond the speciality of registered trade marks. Article 16(2) of the TRIPS Agreement provides that in determining whether a mark is well known, account should be taken 'of the knowledge of the trademark in the relevant sector of the public'. And Article 16(3), as we have seen, provides for a special regime for the benefit of registered trade marks. Baeumer observed that it follows from Article 16(3) of the TRIPS Agreement that the protection outside the speciality cannot depend on a degree of notoriety that goes beyond what is

304. Troller, *La marque de haute renommée …*, p. 75.
305. In this direction Guglielmetti, *Marques ordinaires, notoirement connues …*, p. 75; Dassas, *Conditions et effets …*, p. 30.
306. *Contra* Robert Burrell, Michael Handler, *Reputation in European Trade Mark Law: A Re-examination*, ERA Forum 2016, vol. 17, No. 1, p. 91. Cf. also Martin Senftleben, *Adapting EU Trademark Law to New Technologies: Back to Basics?*, in: Christophe Geiger (ed.), *Constructing European Intellectual Property Achievements and New Perspectives*, Edward Elgar Publishing, Cheltenham-Northampton 2013, p. 150.
307. Cf. Joan Anfossi-Divol, *L'usage et l'enregistrement, éléments essentiels de l'harmonisation du droit des marques*, Presses Universitaires, Strasbourg 2003, p. 179.
308. Portet, *Les marques notoirement connues …*, p. 296.

sufficient under Article 6 bis of the Paris Convention.[309] Thus, a reputed trade mark, a registered mark referred to in Article 16(3), should not be known more widely than the well-known trade mark assessed, in accordance with Article 16(2) of the TRIPS Agreement, within the targeted public.

68. Determination of the relevant public. In the light of the case law, the reference to the public should be therefore modulated according to the destination of the objects covered by the reputed trade mark. If the goods or services for which the mark is used are intended for the general public, the reputation must extend to the public at large, and it cannot be limited to a specialised public;[310] if they are intended for a narrower public, it is then sufficient for the reputation to extend to this clientele.[311] In each case, it is therefore necessary to determine the public concerned by the goods or services covered by the trade mark, which is not always easy.[312] In the assessment, account must be taken of the sector of activity to which the goods covered by the mark belong. In addition, it is necessary to take into consideration the goods or services for which the trade mark is actually used and to determine the public concerned on a product-by-product basis. The trade mark may be reputed for some but not all of the goods or services for which it is used.[313] If the mark is exploited for different goods which target different segments of the public, the reputation will have to be assessed separately for each category of goods or services involved.[314]

The Court of Justice, stating that the public concerned is to be assessed 'depending on the product or service marketed',[315] seems to be in favour of the idea that the public targeted by the mark is the one that acquires the goods or services in question and not, more broadly, the one that is interested in them or knows them but does not acquire them.[316] The public concerned refers to potential buyers, who are not specialists in the field in which the product falls or amateurs of the product.[317] Thus, certain goods or services by their nature will only target a more limited, specialised public, in particular the professionals in a field. In such cases, the public concerned will not always be the final consumers of the product. For example, a mark of medical equipment must be known to physicians and not patients.[318] It is therefore always the public interested in purchasing products or services under the mark that is the reference.

309. Ludwig Baeumer, in: Frederick W. Mostert et al., *Famous and Well-Known Marks*, INTA, New York 2004, p. 3-24.
310. Cf. GC, 19 September 2017, case T-315/16, *Butterfly*, para. 55.
311. Dassas, *Conditions et effets* ..., p. 30. Cf. Anfossi-Divol, *L'usage et l'enregistrement* ..., p. 180.
312. *See* e.g. GC, 6 July 2012, case T-60/10, *Shakespeare*, paras 31-32, where there was a discussion whether the public among which the mark had a reputation for theatre productions and related services was the public at large or 'theatre goers' who have an average interest in culture and theatre and a higher level of education and who are able to 'access' productions.
313. Passa, *Traité de droit* ..., pp. 507-508.
314. Guidelines for examination of European Union Trade Marks (2020), EUIPO, Part C, section 5, p. 12.
315. CJ, 14 September 1999, case C-375/97, *Chevy*, para. 24.
316. Passa, *Traité de droit* ..., p. 508.
317. Promińska, *Prawo z rejestracji* ..., p. 36.
318. Cf. Frederick W. Mostert, in: Frederick W. Mostert et al., *Famous and Well-Known Marks*, INTA, New York 2004, p. 1-37.

Moreover, in order to determine the public concerned by a good or service, it is necessary to take into consideration not only its nature but also its characteristics and in particular the price which is likely to restrict the public targeted by the mark to a wealthy clientele. Thus, the determination of the public concerned often poses a problem in case of luxury products or services.[319] In the light of the jurisprudence of the General Court, when the access to a product is available to all, thanks to affordable prices, it can be considered that, in principle, the mark targets the public at large.[320] *A contrario*, marks designating luxury products should therefore not be aimed at the general public. The solution seems reasonable. Nevertheless, the national case law is divided. There are decisions in which judges consider that luxury products may target a smaller audience than the general public, a 'prestigious clientele',[321] or that the relevant audience for high-end luxury products is not the average consumer but 'a wealthy and enlightened amateur'.[322] In another case, it was decided that, in relation to products intended for all consumers, such as watches, even if they are luxury products, knowledge of the mark must be established among the general public.[323] We will return to the question of the determination of the public concerned because it is also relevant to the condition of overlap of the publics covered by the signs in dispute in the context of assessing the existence of a link.[324]

69. Need for stricter assessment of other conditions for infringement. Finally, it should be noted that the comprehensive definition of the trade mark with a reputation imposed by the *Chevy* judgment should be counterbalanced by strict conditions for the implementation of its protection.[325] The less rigorous definition of a reputed trade mark adopted by the Court of Justice thus makes it more demanding to prove that the disputed use is detrimental or allows to take unfair advantage, which cannot result from the sole reputation of the mark.[326] Therefore, it is more likely that the conditions for infringement will not be met if the earlier trade mark is known only to customers in a narrow area and the later mark is used in another area, especially if that area is also narrow.[327] The Court of Justice's choice to adopt a broad definition therefore made it more important to assess the conditions for infringement of the reputed trade mark, which will be studied in the next chapters. As we will see, particularly in the case of unfair advantage, infringement of a mark that is not known outside the public

319. *See* Sylviane Durrande, *La définition d'une marque renommée*, D. 2002, No. 13, p. 1132.
320. GC, 6 July 2012, case T-60/10, *Shakespeare*, para. 34.
321. In French jurisprudence *see* Cass com., 20 November 2012, case 12-11.753, Bull. civ. IV, No. 209, *Diptyque*. In Polish jurisprudence cf. WSA Warsaw, 8 December 2014, case VI SA/Wa 1359/14, *Montblanc*.
322. Cf. while referring to the likelihood of confusion and the level of attention of the public, CA Paris, 4 October 2016, case 15/04193, *Goyard*.
323. Cass. com., 7 June 2006, case 04-16.908, Bull. civ. IV, No. 138, *Ebel*.
324. *See* 150 et seq. *infra*.
325. Adrien Bouvel, *Marques et renommée. À propos de l'arrêt 'Intel', rendu par la Cour de justice des communautés européennes le 27 novembre 2008 (aff. C-252/07)*, in: *Les défis du droit des marques au XXIe siècle. Actes du colloque en l'honneur du professeur Yves Reboul*, LexisNexis, Paris 2011, p. 126.
326. Laporte-Legeais, *Clair-obscur sur la marque renommée …*, para. 35.
327. Passa, *Traité de droit …*, p. 509.

concerned, if the latter is a highly specialised public, can be easily ruled out at the stage of assessing the existence of a link between the signs, because there is no overlap between the publics.

Reputation of the sign in the relevant territory

70. Relevant territory (national trade mark). The reputation of a mark must be demonstrated at least in 'a substantial part' of the relevant territory,[328] with respect to national trade marks, of the Member State at issue. However, it is necessary to demonstrate a reputation at the national level. A purely local knowledge is not sufficient, which the Court of Justice clearly held regarding well-known trade marks.[329] The same reasoning can be applied to the reputed trade mark.[330] The determination of a substantial part of a country is not always straightforward.[331] It is therefore up to the Court or trade mark office to determine it in each individual case.

71. Relevant territory (EU trade mark). Regarding the EU trade marks, in the light of the *Pago* judgment, in order to benefit from the special protection, an EU trade mark must be known in a substantial part of the territory of the Community, today of the EU, and the territory of one Member State, in the case at issue of Austria, may be considered to constitute a substantial part of the territory of the EU.[332] Proof of reputation in a single Member State may therefore suffice for the special regime to apply.[333] Relying on the *Pago* decision, the General Court considered, for example, sufficient the reputation of EU trade marks established in the United Kingdom[334] and in Germany.[335] It should be pointed out that, according to the *Impulse* judgment, it is not necessary to establish reputation of an EU trade mark in the country where the extended protection is invoked.[336] However, in order to prove infringement, the trade mark cannot be completely unknown to the public in the relevant country. According to the Court of Justice, it must be known to a 'commercially significant part' of the public that will be able to make a connection between the signs in dispute.[337]

328. CJ, 14 September 1999, case C-375/97, *Chevy*, para. 29.
329. CJ, 22 November 2007, case C-328/06, *Fincas Tarragona*.
330. Tristan Azzi, *Étendue géographique de la notoriété d'une marque*, D. 2008, No. 5, p. 322, para. 12.
331. On this issue cf. Azzi, *Étendue géographique de la notoriété* ..., para. 13.
332. CJ, 6 October 2009, case C-301/07, *Pago*, pt 30.
333. The *Pago* decision is, however, open to discussion since the area of Austria represents 2% of the territory and its population less than 1.7% of the total population of the European Union. Thus, one may have doubts as to whether its territory really constitutes a substantial part of the EU. Thibault Lancrenon, *La marque communautaire renommée*, Légicom 2010/1, No. 44, p. 56.
334. GC, 30 November 2016, case T-2/16, *Prêt à manger*, para. 73.
335. GC, 1 March 2018, case T-629/26, Adidas, paras 80-81.
336. CJ, 3 September 2015, case C-125/14, *Impulse*.
337. CJ, 3 September 2015, case C-125/14, *Impulse*, para. 30. I do not agree with the interpretation of the judgment made by Senftleben who considers that enhanced protection is only available in the territory where the requisite reputation exists. Cf. Senftleben, *European Trade Mark* ..., p. 344. This opinion is contrary to the *Impulse* ruling, including its operative part.

72. Territorial scope of prohibition (EU trade mark). Another question is what is the territorial scope of a prohibition against further infringement of an EU trade mark with a reputation which has been proven in only part of the territory of the EU. In the light of the *DHL* judgment of the Court of Justice, given the unitary character of the EU trade mark, the scope of a prohibition extends, as a rule, to the entire area of the EU.[338] However, according to the decision, in some cases, the prohibition can be territorially restricted if, in the circumstances of the case, the acts of infringement or threatened infringement are limited to part of the territory of the EU. Apart from the situation where the application for a prohibition is restricted by the claimant himself, this can happen in particular where 'the defendant proves that the use of the sign at issue does not affect or is not liable to affect the functions of the trade mark, for example on linguistic grounds'.[339] Indeed, a sign or its element may be purely descriptive in one language while it is considered distinctive in another one,[340] and this is likely to have an impact on the assessment of similarity between the signs in dispute. In the field of the protection against the likelihood of confusion, such a prohibition cannot cover the territories where, in particular for linguistic reasons, the disputed use does not create a likelihood of confusion.[341] It seems that, *mutatis mutandis*, the prohibition against further infringement of a trade mark with a reputation should be restricted if, due to linguistic differences, a link between the signs in dispute does not exist in part of the EU. It does not seem, however, that the proprietor should establish reputation in all the Member States in order to obtain a territorially unlimited prohibition based on the special regime.[342] This view seems in accordance with the *Pago* ruling[343] and may be further deduced from the *Impulse* judgment. Since it is not necessary to prove reputation in the country where enhanced protection is sought, it would not make any sense to require it for other territories. It does not seem either necessary to prove the presence of the mark in all the Member States, thanks to which the sign would be known to a 'commercially significant part' of the public, within the meaning of the *Impulse* judgment. The rule resulting from the *DHL* decision is that the prohibition extends to the entire area of the EU, in accordance with the unitary character of the EU trade mark. The exception to that rule should not be interpreted too broadly. The reasoning for restricting the scope of the prohibition applicable to the likelihood of confusion is not relevant under the special regime beyond the question of assessing the existence of a link which can be excluded, in particular for linguistic reasons. In such case, there is indeed no risk that the use of the sign by the third party would be detrimental to the mark or would allow to take an unfair advantage of it if the public could not associate both signs. If a link can be established, even when the mark is not

338. CJ, 12 April 2011, case C-235/09, *DHL*, para. 44.
339. CJ, 12 April 2011, case C-235/09, *DHL*, paras 46-48.
340. Cf. CJ, 25 October 2007, case C-238/06 P, *Develey Holding*, para. 58.
341. CJ, 22 September 2016, case C-223/15, *Combit Software*, paras 31-32.
342. *Contra* Senftleben, *European Trade Mark* ..., p. 344. Cf. also Łukasz Żelechowski, *Infringement of a Community Trade Mark: Between EU-Wide and Non EU-Wide Scope of Prohibitive Injunctions*, EIPR 2013, vol. 5, p. 293.
343. The question appeared in the *Pago* case but the Court did not address it. *See* CJ, 6 October 2009, case C-301/07, *Pago*, paras 14 and 31. Cf. opinion of Advocate General Eleanor Sharpston in case C-301/07, *Pago*, paras 53-57.

sufficiently known in another territory, such a risk, however, potentially exists since the proprietor may intensify or extend the use of its mark in this territory.

73. Irrelevance of actual use in the relevant territory. It should be stressed that the law only considers the knowledge of the trade mark by the public. As in the case of the well-known trade mark, the reputed trade mark must be known in the territory where the special protection is claimed, but not necessarily actually used there.[344] In particular cases, reputation may therefore result from the use of the trade mark made abroad,[345] for example due to cross-border shopping, or from prior use that stopped. Knowledge of a mark may also be generated by intensive advertising prior to the launching of a new product.[346] Hence, a simple promotion of the mark may be sufficient to demonstrate its reputation. Thus, the right holder does not need to present proof of marketing of goods or services under the trade mark. Indeed, the justification for the special protection shall be sought in the existence of reputation and not in the cause of that reputation.[347] Having said that, the exclusive right to a non-used trade mark with a reputation is vulnerable to revocation due to lack of genuine use. The reputation itself does not prevent from revoking such a mark.

[ii] Means of Proving Reputation

74. Factors of reputation and public opinion surveys. The right holder claiming special protection may submit documents demonstrating several factors likely to characterise the reputation of a trade mark. In addition, he may use opinion polls and consumer surveys.

Factors of reputation

75. Non-exhaustive list of factors. The *Chevy* judgment contains a non-exhaustive list of factors for assessing the reputation of a trade mark, including: the market share held by the trade mark; the intensity, geographical extent and duration of its use; and the size of the investment made by the undertaking in promoting it.[348] There is no doubt that the list is merely illustrative, and it cannot be required that proof of the reputation of a mark pertains to all those elements.[349] In principle, the right holder is free to choose the form of evidence which he considers useful to submit; no type of evidence should be rejected out of hand on the basis of its form.[350] The different elements of evidence need to be assessed globally; an accumulation of items of evidence may allow

344. *Contra* Gielen, *Trademark Dilution under European Law* ..., p. 702. Cf. also Giulio E. Sironi, in: Adriano Vanzetti (ed.), *Codice della proprietà industriale*, Giuffrè, Milan 2013, p. 369.
345. Cf. Chavanne, *Droit de la propriété* ..., p. 587.
346. *See* Guidelines for examination of European Union Trade Marks (2020), EUIPO, Part C, section 5, p. 23.
347. In relation to well-known marks cf. Anfossi-Divol, *L'usage et l'enregistrement* ..., p. 186.
348. CJ, 14 September 1999, case C-375/97, *Chevy*, para. 27.
349. GC, 16 October 2018, case T-548/17, *Kipling*, para. 95.
350. CJ, 19 April 2018, case C-478/16 P, *Group Company*, para. 58; CJ, 28 June 2018, case C-564/16 P, *Puma*, para. 58.

establishing reputation of a mark, even though each of those items, taken individually, may be insufficient to prove it.[351]

The examination of reputation will depend on the circumstances of the case. It needs to be made taking into account the nature of the goods or services designated. The Court must therefore determine and take into consideration the criteria of assessment appropriate to the methods of marketing the products in question. For example, trade marks designating goods or services offered occasionally shall not be assessed in the same way as trade marks covering everyday consumer goods.[352]

76. Duration of use. The duration of use of the trade mark is one of the classic factors in establishing reputation;[353] even though it has little impact when assessed alone, it needs indeed to be accompanied by additional types of evidence.[354] The older the mark is, especially when it is subject to a continuous and intense use, the more likely it is to be anchored in the public's mind. However, a long period of use is not *a sine qua non* condition for reputation. A recent trade mark may very well be considered to have a reputation.[355] It is perfectly possible for a sign used for a short period of time to acquire reputation; for example, when this use is linked to a sport event, its exploitation is very intensive and takes place through several means of communication.[356] Sometimes, thanks to advertising, a mark becomes known even before the goods or services designated are present on the market.[357]

77. Position of the trade mark on the market (turnover, investment, market share). The proprietor may submit evidence of a good market position of the trade mark, such as turnover and investments made for the promotion of the mark or the market share enjoyed by the goods or services designated by the mark. They appear to be verifiable objective evidence which makes it possible to assess the market share held by the mark.[358] The proof can take the form of invoices, annual reports on economic results, company profiles and other commercial documents.[359] What amounts of turnover, investment and market share will be considered sufficient? This will depend on the circumstances of the case, and in particular on the nature of the goods or services designated by the trade mark and the specificities of the market in

351. GC, 16 October 2018, case T-548/17, *Kipling*, para. 96; GC, 27 June 2019, case T-334/18, *Anna*, para. 35.
352. Cf., for instance, regarding the mark *Dakar* designating the Dakar Rally in Polish case law NSA, 25 May 2011, case II GSK 578/10, *Dakar*.
353. *See* e.g. GC, 27 November 2014, case T-173/11, *Carrera*, para. 63.
354. Cf. Skrzydło-Tefelska, *Community Trade Mark* ..., pp. 282-283.
355. Chavanne, *Droit de la propriété* ..., p. 586; Jacques Azéma, in: Jacques Azéma, Jean-Christophe Galloux, *Droit de la propriété industrielle*, 6th ed., Dalloz, Paris 2006, p. 796; Passa, *Traité de droit* ..., p. 512.
356. As it could be, for instance, in the case of the sign *Euro 2012* designating the European Football Championship in 2012. In Polish case law cf. SA Gdańsk, 13 March 2013, case V ACa 1059/12, *Euro 2012*.
357. Mostert, *Famous and Well-Known Marks* ..., p. 1-1.
358. Cf. CFI, 13 December 2004, case T-8/03, *Emidio Tucci*, paras 71-73.
359. Skrzydło-Tefelska, *Community Trade Mark* ..., p. 282.

question.[360] The characteristics of the market at issue must therefore always be taken into account. As regards the market share, contrary to what was held by the General Court,[361] the fact that there are a large number of operators on a market should imply that market share is a secondary criterion for assessing the reputation of a trade mark, which is the case, for example, of the clothing market. As Folliard-Monguiral observed, it is difficult to understand why the acquisition of market share, in a sector as competitive as clothing, would be a prerequisite for an excellent reputation. Moreover, there are marks which owe the strength of their reputation to an image of exclusivity, which is incompatible with a dominant position on the overall market for the goods concerned.[362] Likewise, the intensity of use will depend on the kind of product concerned. It goes without saying that it is easier to achieve high sales volume for everyday mass consumption goods than for luxury products.[363] Hence, a trade mark of luxury goods or services may be exploited only in limited quantities and this cannot be an indication against reputation. Commercial success is therefore not always decisive for the assessment.[364]

Regarding investments, all investments are targeted, direct promotion of the goods or services under the mark, as well as patronage and sponsorship operations are likely to demonstrate the reputation of a mark.[365] The judge could take into account, by way of example, the presence of the trade mark in question in the international press, sponsorship of prestigious events or press campaigns with celebrities.[366]

78. Advertisements. The advertisements themselves are undoubtedly of such a nature as to establish reputation of a trade mark. Moreover, as we have pointed out, since the proprietor only has to demonstrate knowledge of his mark, reputation is likely to be established through advertising, even in the absence of proof of marketing of the goods or services designated by the trade mark.[367]

79. Value of the trade mark (evaluations, rankings). The reputation of the trade mark influences its value. From the value of the trade mark, it can be deduced that, in principle, it is a mark known to the public. Therefore, any evidence likely to demonstrate a significant value of the trade mark can be submitted. The proprietor may

360. For instance, a market share of 23.6% on the market for mineral water in the Benelux, accompanied by significant advertising investments and sponsorship a number of events, allowed to demonstrate a reputation 'at the very least, very significant' in the territory concerned. CFI, 18 June 2008, case T-93/06, *Spa*, para. 34.
361. GC, 18 November 2015, case T-606/13, *Mustang*, para. 34.
362. Arnaud Folliard-Monguiral, *Arrêt Mustang: ternissement de la renommée et tabac*, Propr. ind. 2016, No. 1, comment 3, para. 2. Cf. also Guidelines for examination of European Union Trade Marks (2020), EUIPO, Part C, section 5, p. 20.
363. Guidelines for examination of European Union Trade Marks (2020), EUIPO, Part C, section 5, p. 21.
364. *See* Bouvel, *Principe de spécialité ...*, p. 353; Passa, *Traité de droit ...*, p. 512.
365. CFI, 18 June 2008, case T-93/06, *Spa*, para. 34; GC, 1 March 2018, case T-629/16, *Adidas*, para. 73. On the *Adidas* judgment *see* Arnaud Folliard-Monguiral, *Arrêt Adidas: trompettes de la renommée ou trompettes de Jericho?*, Propr. ind. 2018, No. 5, comment 34.
366. Cf. Cass. com., 7 June 2006, case 04-16.908, *Ebel*.
367. *See* para. 73 *supra*.

use evaluations made by financial experts and institutions.[368] It can also present rankings of the most valuable marks published each year by several institutions, or press articles indicating high value of the mark.[369]

80. Geographical extent. The geographical extent of the use of the trade mark is another classic factor in the assessment of reputation. In particular, a wide geographical distribution of the goods bearing the trade mark makes it easier to establish reputation.[370] The proprietor must of course establish reputation of a trade mark in the relevant territory.[371] Nevertheless, it cannot be excluded that the worldwide presence of a trade mark can be a factor to be taken into account. Indeed, a cross-border reputation is likely to corroborate the national or regional reputation. Thus, the proprietor may submit evidence likely to establish the international or even worldwide presence of the mark.[372] The fact that the mark is intensively exploited abroad may strengthen the reputation of the mark if the national public is able to get to know it while travelling,[373] or through Internet.

81. Evidence of good quality associated with the mark. As we have seen, a good quality associated with the trade mark is not necessary for a mark to be qualified as having a reputation. However, the proprietor may submit evidence likely to establish the excellence of the goods or services designated by the trade mark, such as certificates, prizes, awards, distinctions, etc., in order to establish reputation of the trade mark. Such evidence shows the presence of the mark on the market and is thus likely to indirectly indicate its knowledge by the public.[374]

82. Previous decisions. Previous decisions admitting the reputation of the mark in the relevant territory can also be important.[375] Although they are not binding for the Court or trade mark office assessing each case individually[376] and the right holder shall not substantiate his claim merely on prior judgments, they constitute a strong indicator of reputation, in particular when such decisions are relatively recent. In this respect, it has been ruled that when, in proceedings before the EUIPO, the right holder relies on earlier EUIPO decisions relating to the reputation of a mark, in a precise manner, as evidence of reputation, it is incumbent to take into account the decisions already adopted and to consider with especial care whether it should be decided in the same way. Where the EUIPO decides to take a different view from the one adopted in those

368. Piotrowska, *Renomowane znaki* ..., p. 16.
369. Cf. GC, 4 October 2017, case T-411/15, *Gap*, para. 170.
370. *See* e.g. GC, 27 November 2014, case T-173/11, *Carrera*, para. 63.
371. Regarding the relevant territory cf. paras 70 et seq. *supra*.
372. To this effect, foreign court decisions admitting reputation may be of relevance. Cf. GC, 1 March 2018, case T-629/16, *Adidas*, para. 72.
373. Cf. TGI Paris, 14 November 2000, case 99/08810, *Hilton*.
374. Cf. Thibault Lachacinski, Fabienne Fajgenbaum, *Quelle marque notoire ou renommée au XXIe siècle?*, Légicom 2010/1, No. 44, p. 44.
375. Cf. CJ, 10 May 2012, case C-100/11 P, *Botox*, para. 78.
376. Cf. GC, 17 December 2010, case T-192/09, *Seve Trophy*, para. 79.

previous decisions, it should provide an explicit statement of the reasoning for departing from those decisions.[377]

83. Other factors. A number of other elements can be used to demonstrate the reputation of a trade mark. The fact that the proprietor uses several distribution channels,[378] that the trade mark is cited in the press[379] or books, included in a dictionary[380] may be relevant. Statements or certificates of reputation issued by regional chambers of commerce and industry or other professional associations may also be submitted;[381] this practice exists for example in Spain.

Public opinion surveys

84. Optional and supportive evidence of reputation. In addition to the various factors set out above, proprietors also make use of opinion polls and surveys aimed at demonstrating the public's knowledge of the trade mark. It is a type of evidence preferred by some authors as well as judicial and administrative authorities.[382]

It should be stressed that, for reasons of legal certainty, it is essential that the survey meets the requirements of objectivity and neutrality. Thus, the survey must be carefully prepared and carried out by a specialised institution. The data should be accurately reported and all interviews should be duly analysed.[383] Suggestive questions which could distort the results must be avoided, and the wording of the questions must be adapted to each individual case.[384] The survey needs to be performed on a representative and sufficient sample, the number of samples varying according to the goods or services designated by the mark.[385] In addition, the reputation must be examined within the public concerned, including from a geographical point of view.[386] Last but not least, the questions asked must be relevant, in the sense that they make it possible to establish knowledge of the sign as an indicator of the commercial origin of a good or service.[387]

---

377. CJ, 28 June 2018, case C-564/16 P, *Puma*, para. 66; GC, 22 May 2019, case T-161/16, *Puma*, para. 34; GC, 27 June 2019, case T-334/18, *Anna*, para. 54.
378. Mostert, *Famous and Well-Known Marks ...*, p. 1-20.
379. GC, 27 November 2014, case T-173/11, *Carrera*, para. 63.
380. Cf. CJ, 10 May 2012, case C-100/11 P, *Botox*, para. 70. This circumstance can be dangerous for the mark as it is likely to lead to degeneration. This will however depend on the definition given. Degeneration is only possible when the trade mark is used as a generic term to designate a product and dictionaries of course do not contain only such names.
381. Cf. CJ, 22 June 1999, case C-342/96, *Lloyd*, para. 23.
382. Cf. Mathély, *Le droit français des signes ...*, p. 619. The EUIPO considers opinion polls and market surveys that fulfil the requirements of reliability a strong indication of reputation. *See* Guidelines for examination of European Union Trade Marks (2020), EUIPO, Part C, section 5, p. 34.
383. Skrzydło-Tefelska, *Community Trade Mark ...*, p. 283.
384. Brandt, *La protection élargie de la marque ...*, p. 96.
385. In French jurisprudence cf. CA Paris, 26 September 2014, case 13/21712, where the sample of 1,000 people was not considered sufficient.
386. Cohen Jehoram, Van Nispen, Huydecoper, *European Trademark Law ...*, p. 302.
387. According to Brandt, the survey should consist of a single question: *Which products does the XYZ trade mark designate?*. Brandt, *La protection élargie de la marque ...*, p. 101.

Surveys are often questionable. The parties to the proceedings argue that the terms used are imprecise, criticise their reliability, methods of presentation of signs, inappropriate or biased questions to show that respondents have been influenced in their answers, the panel chosen was not representative, etc. As a result, courts (or trade mark offices) often have to examine the relevance and representativeness of the survey conducted.[388] Indeed, the judge must remain relatively vigilant to the probative value of surveys. In addition, each party may communicate its own study and their results may be contradictory.[389]

Furthermore, it should be emphasised that the reputation of the trade mark must be established at the time of the allegedly infringing use. The Court or trade mark office may not take into account reputation subsequent to the use in dispute regardless of the degree of the mark's reputation.[390] However, in principle, it is not possible to require the right holder to submit a survey conducted at the time of the disputed facts. A certain time lag is inevitable,[391] which, in some cases, may distort the results.

In the view of all this criticism, one should not overestimate surveys that are not binding for the Court (or the administrative authority) that has the sovereign power to assess their probative value.[392] The results of opinion polls cannot be decisive and are no substitute for the judge's assessment.[393] In this respect, a recognition rate of 80% was not considered to be sufficient to qualify a trade mark as enjoying an exceptionally high reputation.[394] Thus, the results of market research are of limited importance and can only be one of the criteria to be taken into account. Indeed, they should rather corroborate the other elements of evidence;[395] in other words, surveys should always be supported by other evidence. There is no doubt that consumer surveys are not a mandatory type of evidence.[396] Thus, the absence of a survey cannot exclude the demonstration of reputation, which can be done by any other means. The main method of assessment remains that of the bundle of factors of overall assessment.[397] Hence, even if the survey is questionable, because of the way it was conducted, the other factors may support the claim, so that all of the elements can lead to the recognition of the reputation.[398]

85. Importance of surveys in particular cases. That said, sometimes surveys can be particularly useful in demonstrating the reputation of a trade mark, especially in the cases that we have mentioned above, where there may be doubts about the perception

388. In French jurisprudence cf. CA Paris, 4 April 2014, case 12/20559.
389. Cohen Jehoram, Van Nispen, Huydecoper, *European Trademark Law* ..., p. 292.
390. Cf. CA Paris, 18 December 1998, PIBD 1998, No. 675, III, p. 198, *Windows*.
391. Cf. CJ, 17 April 2008, case C-108/07 P, *Ferrero*, para. 53.
392. Pollaud-Dulian, *Propriété intellectuelle. La propriété industrielle* ..., p. 1073. Cf. Bouvel, *Principe de spécialité* ..., pp. 355-356.
393. In French jurisprudence *see* CA Paris, 23 October 2015, case 14/06720.
394. GC, 18 November 2015, case T-606/13, *Mustang*, paras 32-33. Since the documents submitted by the proprietor did not adequately set out the method used to collect and evaluate the data in question.
395. Passa, *Traité de droit* ..., p. 513.
396. Skrzydło-Tefelska, *Community Trade Mark* ..., p. 283.
397. Lachacinski, Fajgenbaum, *Quelle marque notoire* ..., p. 45.
398. In French jurisprudence *see* TGI Paris, 23 May 2014, case 13/11915, *Red Bull*.

of the sign as a trade mark. By way of example, where the allegedly infringed mark is a figurative mark which the proprietor always exploits together with a word mark, so that the public perceives the whole as a complex mark in which the word is predominant and the graphics are merely incidental, it should be established that consumers perceive the figurative element itself as an indication of the origin of a good or service. In the above-mentioned judgment concerning the *Longines* trade mark, the General Court stressed the usefulness of presenting opinion surveys conducted among the relevant public.[399] Likewise, a survey may help to establish that the shape of the product itself is perceived as a trade mark.[400]

Furthermore, as we have pointed out, reputation, as well as notoriety of the well-known mark, means knowledge, which does not always have to result from the actual use of a trade mark in the territory concerned.[401] In certain cases, it should be possible to establish the reputation of a trade mark that is not actually used in the territory where the special protection is invoked. Since it is impossible to submit documents of such a nature as to establish knowledge resulting from use, a survey may be the only means of proving reputation.

86. No minimum percentage required. Survey results indicate a percentage based on the responses given by the respondents. The assessment of these results is a matter for the judge's sovereign assessment. It should be stressed that one cannot arbitrarily and a priori quantify the 'significant part of the public'.[402] Indeed, in the light of the *Chevy* judgment, it cannot be inferred from either the letter or the spirit of the provisions on enhanced protection that the trade mark must be known by a given percentage of the public concerned.[403] Thus, the Court of Justice condemned all tests involving a minimum threshold of knowledge.[404]

[2] Distinction of the Concept of the Well-Known Trade Mark

87. Close concepts. Long before the introduction by the European legislator of the concept of the trade mark with a reputation, a similar concept of the well-known trade mark was already provided by the Paris Convention in Article 6 bis, adopted following a diplomatic conference for its revision held in The Hague in 1925, then amended by

399. GC, 12 February 2015, case T-76/13, *Longines*, para. 91. The Court stated that surveys should include the public's perception of the marks used by the public, which elements of the marks were memorised or, at the very least, recognised by the public when faced with various marks in the course of shopping. According to the judgment, the right holder should submit opinion polls in which the target persons were shown only the figurative sign, should state whether they knew the sign and, if so, what they associated it with.
400. Cf. CFI, 15 December 2005, case T-262/04, *Briquet à pierre*, paras 82-88.
401. *See* para. 73 *supra*.
402. Pollaud-Dulian, *Propriété intellectuelle. La propriété industrielle ...*, p. 1072.
403. CJ, 14 September 1999, case C-375/97, *Chevy*, para. 25.
404. Several thresholds were proposed by the doctrine. Almost all the figures were given, from 20% to 80%. Cf. e.g. Christine Zanella, *Les marques nominatives*, Litec, Paris 1995, p. 238; Brandt, *La protection élargie de la marque ...*, p. 99; Schricker, *La tutela della Ausstattung ...*, p. 267; André R. Bertrand, *Droit des marques. Signes distinctifs, Noms de domaine*, Dalloz, Paris 2005, p. 106.

revision conferences in London in 1934 and Lisbon in 1958.[405] Pursuant to Article 6 bis, the countries of the Union undertake 'to refuse or to cancel the registration, and to prohibit the use, of a trademark which constitutes a reproduction, an imitation, or a translation, liable to create confusion, of a mark considered by the competent authority of the country of registration or use to be well known in that country as being already the mark of a person entitled to the benefits of this Convention and used for identical or similar goods'. Thus, the well-known trade mark allows for a derogation from the registration requirement. Under the Paris Convention, however, its protection is limited by the rule of speciality.

The trade mark with a reputation and the well-known trade mark are very close to each other, in the sense that the two concepts express fame,[406] and for that reason, although they do not comply with fundamental principles to which trade mark law is subject, they benefit from derogatory regimes. The notion of the well-known trade mark should be defined in order to distinguish it from the trade mark with a reputation (§1.02[A][2][a]). Both were established for different reasons and their purposes under trade mark law remain distinct. However, their proximity had some impact on the protection regime of the well-known trade mark (§1.02[A][2][b]). Finally, it is worth assessing the usefulness of invoking the concept of a well-known trade mark today when most marks exploited on the market are registered (§1.02[A][2][c]).

[a] Definition of the Well-Known Trade Mark

88. Degree of knowledge required. The question of the distinction between the trade mark with a reputation and the well-known trade mark has caused some debates in doctrine. Indeed, their proximity creates confusion. Since, under certain national laws, the well-known trade mark is subject to the extended protection alongside the reputed trade mark, some authors use both concepts as synonyms.[407] However, this is precisely because the legal provisions distinguish between the two concepts, the reputed mark and the well known cannot be considered equivalent.[408]

The question of the distinction between the two concepts led to the development of two theories that can be referred to as 'hierarchical' and 'egalitarian'.[409] Hierarchical theories presuppose the superiority, in terms of public knowledge of the sign, of one of

405. Georg Hendrik Christiaan Bodenhausen, *Guide to the Application of the Paris Convention for the Protection of Industrial Property*, BIRPI, Geneva 1968, p. 89; Dassas, *L'élargissement de la protection ...*, pp. 36-39; Portet, *Les marques notoirement connues ...*, pp. 73 et seq.; Brandt, *La protection élargie de la marque ...*, pp. 14-15.
406. David Lefranc, *La renommée en droit privé*, Defrénois, Paris 2004, pp. 160 et seq.
407. With respect to French law *see* Bonet, *La protection des marques notoires ...*, p. 189; Chavanne, *Droit de la propriété ...*, p. 585; Charles de Haas, *La 'contrefaçon' de la marque notoire en droit compare américain, européen et français: une leçon américaine encore mal comprise*, Propr. intell. 2003, No. 7, p. 145; Joanna Schmidt-Szalewski, in: Joanna Schmidt-Szalewski, Jean-Luc Pierre, *Droit de la propriété industrielle*, 7th ed., LexisNexis, Paris 2007, p. 227; Nicolas Binctin, *Droit de la propriété intellectuelle*, LGDJ, Paris 2010, pp. 465-466.
408. Pérot-Morel, *Notoriété et renommée ...*, p. 473. *See also* Bouvel, *Principe de spécialité ...*, p. 336.
409. Bouvel, *Principe de spécialité ...*, pp. 336 et seq. Cf. also Anfossi-Divol, *L'usage et l'enregistrement ...*, pp. 260 et seq.

the two marks. According to several authors, it is the trade mark with a reputation that should be better known because of the exceptional nature of its protection which goes beyond the speciality.[410] Others consider that it is the well-known mark that should enjoy a higher degree of knowledge.[411] This was proposed by Advocate General Jacobs in his opinion in the *Chevy* case.[412] The idea was shared by the General Court.[413] By contrast, according to egalitarian theories, there is no difference in the degree of knowledge between the well-known trade mark and the trade mark with a reputation. The difference is due to the existence of registration for reputed trade marks or its absence for well-known trade marks.[414]

89. Quantitative concept of the well-known mark. There is no doubt that the well-known trade mark is to be assessed only on the basis of quantitative criteria. This is clearly reflected in Article 16(2) of the TRIPS Agreement. Thus, the authors who approve the qualitative definition of the trade mark with a reputation point out a difference in nature between the two concepts. The well-known trade mark would be defined in relation to the quantitative criterion, while the reputed trade mark in relation to the quality associated with the mark.[415] Consequently, a well-known trade mark could also have a reputation. The reputed trade mark would be a well-known mark whose fame is linked to an exceptional quality.[416]

---

410. Dassas, *Conditions et effets ...*, p. 35; André R. Bertrand, *De la marque notoire à la marque renommée*, RDPI 1992, No. 44, p. 11; Pérot-Morel, *Notoriété et renommée ...*, pp. 474-475. *See also* Brandt, *La protection élargie de la marque ...*, p. 72; Laporte-Legeais, *Clair-obscur sur la marque renommée ...*, para. 35; Pierre Vivant, *Marque notoire et marque renommée: une distinction conforme au droit des marques*, D. 2010, No. 37, p. 2496. Such propositions can be found in the previous draft amendments to the Paris Convention. For example, the resolution adopted at the Vienna Congress in 1952 provided that a reputed trade mark should be even better known than a well-known trade mark, stating that the increased protection cannot be granted to all well-known trade marks benefiting from Article 6 bis, but should be reserved for a category of more widely known marks. *See* Perent, *Marques notoirement connues ...*, p. 200.
411. Azéma, *Droit de la propriété ...*, p. 797; Ricolfi, *Trattato dei marchi ...*, p. 794; Skrzydło-Tefelska, *Community Trade Mark ...*, p. 280. The superiority of the well-known trade mark is admitted by several Polish authors, *see* Ryszard Skubisz, in: Ryszard Skubisz (ed.), *System prawa prywatnego*, t. 14 B, *Prawo własności przemysłowej*, 2nd ed., C.H. Beck, Warsaw 2017, p. 722; Ewa Wojcieszko-Głuszko, in: Ryszard Skubisz (ed.), *System prawa prywatnego*, t. XIV B, *Prawo własności przemysłowej*, 2nd ed., C.H. Beck, Warsaw 2017, p. 490; Łukasz Żelechowski, in: Piotr Kostański, Łukasz Żelechowski, *Prawo własności przemysłowej*, C.H. Beck, Warsaw 2014, p. 406.
412. Opinion of Advocate General Francis Geoffrey Jacobs in case C-375/97, *Chevy*, paras 30 et seq. Cf. Irene Calboli, *'Marchio che gode di notorietà': una discutabile pronuncia della Corte di Giustizia delle Communità Europee*, Riv. Dir. Ind. 2000, II, p. 267.
413. CFI, 17 June 2008, case T-420/03, *Boomerang*, para. 110; GC, 3 May 2018, case T-2/17, *Masi*, para. 75. According to the judgments, the degree of recognition to be proved regarding marks possessing a reputation is not as high as that in the case of well-known marks within the meaning of Article 6 bis of the Paris Convention.
414. Pollaud-Dulian, *Marque de renommée. Histoire ...*, p. 46. In favour of the egalitarian theory *see* Canlorbe, *L'usage de la marque ...*, p. 114; Jacques Azéma, *Marques renommées et marques notoirement connues en droit européen et en droit français*, in: Jacques de Werra (ed.), *Marques notoires et de haute renommée. Well-Known and Famous Trademarks*, Schulthess Verlag, Zurich 2011, pp. 27-28; Basire, *Les fonctions de la marque ...*, p. 283.
415. Piotrowska, *Renomowane znaki ...*, p. 24.
416. Portet, *Les marques notoirement connues ...*, pp. 40-42. Cf. also Pérot-Morel, *Notoriété et renommée ...*, p. 475.

In addition, as a result of this distinction, it was proposed that a further category of trade marks, which could be referred to as 'famous' or 'of high renown', should be recognised, which would be particularly well known to the general public and associated with an excellent quality. Each 'famous' mark would at the same time be both reputed and well known.[417] Certainly, in reality, some marks meet the criteria of knowledge and recognition more than others. However, it is difficult to see the point of distinguishing another category of trade mark which would be subject to the same protection regime provided for all well-known and reputed trade marks. A 'celebrity' may be of major importance at the stage of assessing the infringement, but, in the light of the provisions, in the absence of a special regime, the distinction between a new concept of a famous trade mark or a 'supernotorious' trade mark[418] is useless.

90. Relevant criterion of distinction: registration. As explained above, the quantitative definition of the trade mark with a reputation is the only one that complies with the case law of the Court of Justice. The two concepts are therefore assessed according to the same criteria. Both are known marks for which the relevant public is the public concerned by the goods or services designated by the mark.[419] Indeed, pursuant to Article 16(2) of the TRIPS Agreement, 'In determining whether a trademark is well-known, Members shall take account of the knowledge of the trademark in the relevant sector of the public, including knowledge in the Member concerned which has been obtained as a result of the promotion of the trademark.' The said provision imperatively imposes the criterion of the public targeted by the mark.[420] Moreover, it has always been accepted that a well-known trade mark, since it is protected only against use for goods or services of the same kind, does not need to be known outside the circle of buyers who may be interested in the product or service. The concept only allowed territorial extension of protection of the reputation, outside the country of origin.[421]

This does not yet prejudge that one of the two should not be better known than the other, in the sense that a higher degree of knowledge could be required, as some authors have suggested, for example 25% for the reputed trade mark and 50% for the well-known trade mark.[422] However, this argument does not seem plausible to defend in the light of the provisions and case law of the Court of Justice. As we have seen, it is not possible to determine a minimum threshold of knowledge of the trade mark with a reputation. The same applies to the well-known trade marks. It is therefore not possible to require that the well-known trade mark be known to a specific part of the public.[423] This opinion was confirmed in the jurisprudence of the General Court.[424]

417. Cf. Piotrowska, *Renomowane znaki* ..., pp. 25-27.
418. Cf. Pollaud-Dulian, *Propriété intellectuelle. Propriété industrielle* ..., pp. 1069-1070.
419. *See* Passa, *Traité de droit* ..., p. 507.
420. Pérot-Morel, *Notoriété et renommée* ..., pp. 464-465.
421. Troller, *La marque de haute renommée* ..., p. 77.
422. Skubisz, *Naruszenie praw z rejestracji* ..., p. 437.
423. Szczepanowska-Kozłowska, *System prawa handlowego* ..., p. 336.
424. GC, 2 February 2016, case T-169/13, *Motobi*, paras 58-59; GC, 3 May 2018, case T-2/17, *Masi*, paras 52-53.

The trade mark with a reputation should not be better known than the well-known trade mark in the light of Article 16(3) of the TRIPS Agreement, from which it follows that the protection of trade marks registered outside the speciality may not depend on a degree of knowledge that goes beyond what is sufficient under Article 6 bis of the Paris Convention. The legislator of each unionist country could possibly require a lower level of knowledge for trade marks with a reputation.[425] Nevertheless, unlike the Advocate General in the *Chevy* case, the Court of Justice has not in any way ruled in favour of the idea that the well-known trade mark should enjoy a higher degree of knowledge. Although the Court of Justice has not ruled on the concept of the well-known trade mark, having regard to Article 16(2) of the TRIPS Agreement, which imposes the same criterion of the public concerned, and the fact that, in the *Fincas Tarragona* judgment,[426] the Court of Justice seems to transpose to the well-known trade mark the solutions of the *Chevy* judgment,[427] it should be admitted that the degree of knowledge required is the same for both categories of marks.[428] This is the only solution in line with the spirit of trade mark law.[429] The idea that one of the categories of mark should be known to a wider public would be even more difficult to accept in those national legislations where the special regime of extended protection applies also to the well-known trade marks.[430]

It should also be noted that the Paris Union and World Intellectual Property Organization (WIPO), at a series of meetings of assemblies of 20-29 September 1999, adopted a joint recommendation indicating, in a non-exhaustive manner, the factors that can be taken into account in determining whether a trade mark is well known.[431] The General Court expressly refers to those criteria in its jurisprudence.[432] All those factors may serve to examine the knowledge of a sign by the relevant public. They are therefore also perfectly applicable to assess the reputation of a mark within the

425. In this direction Baeumer, *Famous and Well-Known Marks* ..., p. 3-24.
426. CJ, 22 November 2007, case C-328/06, *Fincas Tarragona*.
427. Cf. GC, 2 February 2016, case T-169/13, *Motobi*, para. 58; GC, 3 May 2018, case T-2/17, *Masi*, para. 52.
428. *See* Passa, *Traité de droit* ..., p. 507. Cf. also Joanna Schmidt-Szalewski, *Régime de la marque notoire ou renommée*, RTD eur. 2008, No. 4, p. 938; Verena von Bomhard, Artur Geier, *Unregistered Trademarks in EU Trademark Law*, TMR 2017, vol. 107, No. 3, p. 684.
429. Pollaud-Dulian, *Propriété intellectuelle. La propriété industrielle* ..., p. 844.
430. Under French law, cf. Passa, *Traité de droit* ..., p. 510; Pollaud-Dulian, *Propriété intellectuelle. La propriété industrielle* ..., p. 1070.
431. Under Article 2 of the joint recommendation, in determining whether a mark is a well-known mark within the meaning of the Paris Convention, the competent authority can take into account any circumstances from which it may be inferred that the mark is well known, including: the degree of knowledge or recognition of the mark in the relevant sector of the public; the duration, extent and geographical area of any use of the mark; the duration, extent and geographical area of any promotion of the mark, including advertising or publicity and the presentation, at fairs or exhibitions, of the goods and/or services to which the mark applies; the duration and geographical area of any registrations, and/or any applications for registration, of the mark, to the extent to which they reflect use or recognition of the mark; the record of successful enforcement of rights in the mark, in particular, the extent to which the mark has been recognised as well known by competent authorities; the value associated with the mark.
432. CFI, 17 June 2008, case T-420/03, *Boomerang*, paras 79-80; GC, 2 February 2016, case T-169/13, *Motobi*, paras 55-57; GC, 3 May 2018, case T-2/17, *Masi*, paras 49-51.

meaning of the EU trade mark law.[433] Likewise, the factors for examining the reputation analysed here above should also be helpful in implementing the provisions on the well-known marks.[434]

Therefore, and taking into account the fact that in both cases knowledge of the sign is assessed among the targeted public, any hierarchy of the two concepts seems impossible. Moreover, the practical interest of such a gradation of the two notions is very doubtful.[435] Indeed, we have difficulty seeing under which circumstances the judge would be obliged to confront them. It is always for the Court only to decide whether the plaintiff bringing the infringement action of a reputed or well-known trade mark has succeeded in proving that his mark is known to a significant part of the public concerned.

I join therefore the supporters of the egalitarian theories. The formal criterion of registration is the only one which should be used to distinguish the well-known trade mark from the trade mark with a reputation. Indeed, under Directive 2015/2436 and Regulation 2017/1001, registration is a component of the definition of the trade mark with a reputation. The *Chevy* judgment and the case law of the General Court confirm this approach.[436] By contrast, according to Article 6 bis of the Paris Convention, the well-known trade mark is by definition an unregistered sign.[437] A trade mark cannot therefore be both reputed and well known at the same time; the two concepts are mutually exclusive.[438]

91. Irrelevance of actual use. Finally, it should be noted that the majority of authors agree that the well-known trade mark does not necessarily have to be used in the country where protection is claimed, as long as it is well known in that country,[439] as

433. In that direction also Kur, *European Trade Mark* ..., p. 258.
434. Cf. paras 75 et seq. *supra*.
435. Cf. Kur, *European Trade Mark* ..., p. 258. The author points out that in practice it hardly makes much sense to establish a gradation between both notions.
436. *See* CFI, 11 July 2007, case T-150/04, *Tosca Blu*, para. 55.
437. It should be stressed that in order to invoke protection of a well-known trade mark, the sign does not need to be registered in another country. The opposite approach dominates in Swiss jurisprudence and is supported by an important part of Swiss scholars. *See* e.g. Ralph Schlosser, Claudia Maradan, in: Jacques de Werra, Philippe Gilliéron (ed.), *Propriété intellectuelle. Commentaire romand*, Helbing Lichtenhahn Verlag, Basel 2013, pp. 781-783. This opinion is however criticised by several authors. *See* Gilliéron, *Les marques notoirement* ..., pp. 42-43; Alberini, *L'exploitation de la renommée*, pp. 177-179. The requirement of a foreign registration does not result from Article 6 bis of the Paris Convention and is contrary to the joint recommendation of the Paris Union and WIPO of 1999 concerning the provisions on the protection of well-known trade marks.
438. The Paris Grand Instance Court highlighted this nuance in a judgment of 8 October 2010, observing that the marks relied on were registered; thus, although the plaintiff invoked well-known marks, they were in fact marks with a reputation. TGI Paris, 8 October 2010, case 07/01247, *Paris Match*. In this respect, the observation of the General Court that a well-known mark enjoys protection 'irrespective of whether proof of registration is provided' is wrong. GC, 3 May 2018, case T-2/17, *Masi*, para. 48.
439. Perent, *Marques notoirement connues* ..., pp. 51-52; Bodenhausen, *Guide to the Application* ..., p. 91; Mathély, *Le droit français des signes* ..., p. 253; Pollaud-Dulian, *Propriété intellectuelle. La propriété industrielle* ..., p. 842; Skubisz, *System prawa prywatnego* ..., p. 740.

it was rightly held by the General Court.[440] The text of Article 6 bis of the Paris Convention is not explicit in this respect.[441] This interpretation is nevertheless in accordance with its spirit.[442] It must be admitted that the requirement of actual use would add an additional condition that is not provided for in the provision.[443] Moreover, Article 16(2) of the TRIPS Agreement provides that in determining whether a trade mark is well known, account should be taken 'of the knowledge of the trademark in the relevant sector of the public, including knowledge in the Member concerned which has been obtained as a result of the promotion of the trademark'. Thus, the expression 'well-known' refers to the acquisition of knowledge by any means. In other words, it is in the existence of notoriety that the justification for all the protection granted must be sought and not in the causes of that notoriety.[444] The Court of Justice seems to have endorsed this approach.[445] A foreign mark can become famous in a country even if it is not used there, in particular through its advertising, including advertisements in other countries.[446] Nowadays, when the means of communication make it possible to make a trade mark famous before it reaches the market, the criterion of effective use in the country where protection is claimed should not apply.[447]

[b] Regime of Protection of the Well-Known Trade Mark

92. Paris Convention and TRIPS Agreement. Pursuant to Article 6 bis of the Paris Convention, the well-known trade mark is protected in accordance with the principle of speciality against registration or use[448] of identical or similar signs by third parties for goods identical or similar to those for which the mark claimed was well known in the event of a likelihood of confusion. Article 6 bis of the Paris Convention refers only to

440. GC, 2 February 2016, case T-169/13, *Motobi*, para. 60; GC, 3 May 2018, case T-2/17, *Masi*, para. 54.
441. *See* Perent, *Marques notoirement connues* ..., pp. 87-89.
442. Dassas, *L'élargissement de la protection* ..., p. 45.
443. Marie-Angèle Pérot-Morel, *Les difficultés d'application de l'article 6 bis de la Convention d'Union de Paris relatif à la protection internationale des marques notoires*, Riv. Dir. Ind. 1981, I, p. 46. It should be noted that during the Congress of Vienna in 1952 and the Lisbon Conference in 1958, it was proposed to clarify Article 6 bis of the Paris Convention by specifying that use of a well-known mark in the country in which its protection is claimed would not be necessary for such protection. Perent, *Marques notoirement connues* ..., pp. 91-94; Bodenhausen, *Guide to the Application* ..., p. 91.
444. Anfossi-Divol, *L'usage et l'enregistrement* ..., p. 186; Urszula Promińska, in: Alicja Adamczak, Andrzej Szewc (ed.), *Konwencja paryska o ochronie własności przemysłowej. Komentarz*, Wolters Kluwer, Warsaw 2008, p. 201.
445. *See* CJ, 22 November 2007, case C-328/06, *Fincas Tarragona*. In this direction Ryszard Skubisz, *Wielkość terytorium używania znaku jako przesłanka powstania prawa do znaku towarowego powszechnie znanego*, EPS 2008, No. 1, p. 41.
446. Bodenhausen, *Guide to the Application* ..., p. 91.
447. Promińska, *Konwencja paryska* ..., p. 201.
448. In its initial version of 1925, Article 6 bis did not refer to use without registration. The drafters of the text considered that in this case it was up to the owner of the well-known trade mark to apply for registration and to bring an action for cessation of use on this basis. The amendment to prohibit the use of well-known trade marks was adopted at the Lisbon Conference in 1958. Perent, *Marques notoirement connues* ..., pp. 36-45.

goods, but Article 16(2) of the TRIPS Agreement extends its scope of application to services.

93. EU law. At the EU level, the well-known trade mark is protected only within the limits of the principle of speciality.[449] According to Article 8(2)(c) of Regulation 2017/1001, a trade mark is refused registration when it is identical or similar to a well-known trade mark and filed for identical or similar goods or services. The extended protection provided for in Article 8(5) of Regulation No. 2017/1001 applies only to registered trade marks.[450] By contrast, an action for infringement of an EU trade mark can only be based on a registered trade mark since the EU is not a contracting party to the Paris Convention. Consequently, Article 6 bis of the Paris Convention does not apply to it. The EU trade mark system is indeed register-based; hence there are no unregistered EU trade marks even if the mark is well known in the EU.[451] Directive 2015/2436 refers to well-known trade marks in Article 5(2)(d) among the relative grounds for refusal of registration in the speciality.

94. Self-executing character of Article 6 bis and protection under national laws. Article 6 bis of the Paris Convention is 'self-executing', which means that interested parties may directly claim its application by the administrative or judicial authorities of the country concerned, even if the national law does not provide for the protection of well-known trade marks. Indeed, the provision contains an undertaking also on behalf of those authorities, and not only an obligation for the Member States to legislate on the subject concerned.[452]

Nevertheless, many national legislators provide for special texts expressly protecting well-known trade marks in the speciality.[453] This protection may be covered by the exclusive trade mark right or based on tort liability rules. The conditions for infringement of the well-known trade mark should be the same as for registered trade marks. The disputed sign must be used as a trade mark and in the course of trade. The infringement of the trade mark should be assessed according to the same criteria as the infringement of any trade mark registered in the speciality.[454]

95. Minimum level of protection. It should be stressed that the protection of well-known trade marks in national legislation cannot be less advantageous than that provided for by the Paris Convention and the TRIPS Agreement. For example, national law should not provide for a condition of actual use of the mark in the country where the protection is claimed, since as we have seen, the Paris Convention and the TRIPS

449. *See* CFI, 11 July 2007, case T-150/04, *Tosca Blu*, paras 49 et seq.
450. CJ, 12 June 2014, case C-285/13 P, *Bimbo*, paras 27-28. On this issue cf. Skrzydło-Tefelska, *Community Trade Mark* ..., p. 279.
451. von Bomhard, Geier, *Unregistered Trademarks* ..., p. 679.
452. Perent, *Marques notoirement connues* ..., p. 126; Bodenhausen, *Guide to the Application* ..., pp. 89-90. However, it should be noted that the wording of Article 6 bis UPC, referring to 'the countries of the Union undertake', is somewhat ambiguous. Bodenhausen, *Guide to the Application* ..., p. 90; Dassas, *L'élargissement de la protection* ..., pp. 39-40.
453. Cf. Kur, *European Trade Mark* ..., p. 254.
454. Under Polish law cf. Michał Mazurek, in: Ryszard Skubisz (ed.), *System prawa prywatnego*, t. 14B, *Prawo własności przemysłowej*, 2nd ed., C.H. Beck, Warsaw 2017, pp. 1140-1141.

Agreement, in the light of which national laws must be interpreted, do not require that the mark be used but only known. This is also confirmed by Article 5(2)(d) of Directive 2015/2436, pursuant to which the Court of Justice does not link well-known character of a mark to its actual use.

96. Possible extended protection under national laws. Article 16(3) of the TRIPS Agreement provides for an extension of the protection of well-known trade marks *mutatis mutandis* beyond the speciality, but only in respect of registered marks.[455] Thus, the provision refers to trade marks with a reputation within the meaning of the EU legislation. As the Paris Convention and the TRIPS Agreement require only a minimum of protection, the Member States are free to extend special protection also to well-known trade marks, marks that are not registered.[456] Some national trade mark laws provide for such an extended protection in favour of well-known trade marks.[457] In other jurisdictions, protection of well-known trade marks beyond the speciality may only be possible pursuant to the provisions related to unfair (parasitic) competition.[458] It seems, however, that the interpretation of those provisions should have an account of the conditions of infringement of trade marks with a reputation developed in trade mark law. Otherwise, non-registered famous marks would benefit from a wider protection than registered marks, and this would be difficult to accept.

[c] Practical Importance of Well-Known Trade Marks

97. Limited practical importance. It is often pointed out that well-known trade marks are presently of little practical importance.[459] However, in some situations invoking the status of a well-known mark can be of interest.

98. Marks vulnerable to revocation due to non-use. The protection of a mark as well known may come to the rescue of non-used marks that can be referred to as 'vintage' marks.[460] As we have established, a well-known trade mark does not need to be effectively used in the country where the protection is sought. Therefore, invoking a

455. Pursuant to Article 16(3) of the TRIPS Agreement: 'Article 6*bis* of the Paris Convention (1967) shall apply, *mutatis mutandis*, to goods or services which are not similar to those in respect of which a trademark is registered, provided that use of that trademark in relation to those goods or services would indicate a connection between those goods or services and the owner of the registered trademark and provided that the interests of the owner of the registered trademark are likely to be damaged by such use.'
456. Baeumer, *Famous and Well-Known Marks* ..., p. 3-23.
457. For instance, well-known trade marks benefit from extended protection under French law. *See* Article L.713-5 of the French Intellectual Property Code (they are, however, nowadays expressly protected under the regime of tort liability, not covered by the trade mark exclusive right). In Germany, well-known marks enjoy the same kind of protection as registered marks, including extended protection. *See* Kur, *European Trade Mark* ..., p. 254.
458. This is the case of Poland. On the protection of well-known trade marks beyond the speciality in other EU Member States *see* Danguolė Klimkevičiutė, *The Legal Protection of Well-Known Trademarks and Trademarks with a Reputation: The Trends of the Legal Regulation in the EU Member States*, University of Wroclaw, Social Sciences Studies 2010, vol. 7, No. 3, pp. 236-242.
459. Cf. Kur, *European Trade Mark* ..., p. 256.
460. von Bomhard, Geier, *Unregistered Trademarks* ..., p. 680.

well-known trade mark can be of interest in the event where a registered mark is revoked due to lack of genuine use. In the countries where the well-known mark enjoys extended protection beyond the speciality, this can also apply to trade marks with a reputation vulnerable to revocation due to non-use. Indeed, although the knowledge of the sign should be also the only relevant criterion of assessing whether a mark has a reputation, if it has not been put to an actual use, the exclusive right over such a reputed mark is subject to revocation.

99. Non-conventional trade marks. Apart from the situation of non-used marks, in the case of so-called conventional trade marks, in particular word, figurative and semi-figurative trade marks, which have an inherent distinctive character, the observation on a limited practical importance is undoubtedly true. In most cases, owners register the names and images that they use or wish to use in the course of trade. However, relying on the provisions relating to well-known trade marks may be important for the users of less ordinary 'non-conventional' signs, such as three-dimensional signs, sound, smell, colours as such, etc., which are often devoid of *ab initio* distinctiveness and therefore are not registered, but are likely to acquire distinctive character through use.

100. Marks consisting of the shape of the product. The shape of a product is, for example, likely to become so famous that it indicates to the public the commercial origin of the good. As a result, it may itself enjoy protection as a well-known trade mark. In this context, it is worth mentioning two French decisions concerning Cartier's famous *Tank* watch. Its design had fallen into the public domain; however its reproductions were condemned on the basis of general civil liability. By a judgment of 22 October 2002,[461] the Court of Cassation considered that it was a watch of high reputation, having an attractive and prestigious power, a well-known product whose reproduction was faulty, even if it was no longer covered by an exclusive right. In the second decision, a judgment of 14 June 2006,[462] the Paris Court of Appeal condemned, in the field of parasitism, a reproduction of this watch, the appearance of which, according to the decision, is known throughout the world and is associated in the minds of the public with the Cartier company, of which it is an emblem. According to the Court, the consumer identifies the shape and appearance of the well-known *Tank* watch, of this legendary and emblematic model.[463] Indeed, it seems that the model of the *Tank* watch had become so famous that its very shape allowed the public to

461. Cass. com., 22 October 2002, case 00-12.914, Bull. civ. IV, No. 152, JCP E 2003, p. 493, comment of Daniel Mainguy, *Tank*.
462. CA Paris, 14 June 2006, case 05/08030, Propr. ind. 2006, comment 81, of Jean-Pierre Gasnier, Comm. com. électr, 2006, comment 153, of Christophe Caron, *Tank*.
463. The judgments were criticised in doctrine for overprotection of objects being in public domain because of the expiration of the intellectual property rights to them. *See* Jacques Azéma, *L'incidence des dérives du parasitisme sur le régime des droits de propriété industrielle (à propos de quelques décisions récentes)*, in: *Études de droit privé. Mélanges offerts à Paul Didier*, Economica, Paris 2008, pp. 5-6; Christian Le Stanc, *Le domaine public, le libre accès, incluant la liberté d'imiter comme un principe légal ou un concept oublié?*, ATRIP, Munich 2008, pp. 1 et seq.; Pascale Tréfigny, *Action en contrefaçon et action en concurrence déloyale. L'évolution de la jurisprudence la plus récente face au parasitisme*, in: *Le droit de la propriété intellectuelle dans*

distinguish its commercial origin. It became in fact a well-known mark.[464] The shape of the product can be therefore protected because it is so well known that it fulfils the primary function of the trade mark to indicate the commercial origin.

In such cases, protection may be sought on the basis of the regime of well-known trade marks under trade mark law. It should be a more certain basis for protection than parasitism (freeriding), invoked under general tort liability or special provisions on unfair competition. Parasitism is a questionable concept since, in principle, the reproduction of objects not protected by exclusive rights is not unlawful. In practice, however, it should be more frequent to see actions brought on the basis of the infringement of the well-known trade mark if the sign is registered as a trade mark, but the owner's claims also concern facts prior to the filing, as was the case with the famous bottle of perfume *No. 5* of Chanel.[465] That being said, parasitism, whose conditions of implementation are more vague and therefore can be assessed in a less rigorous way, may be preferred by claimants. It could seem that a person who invokes parasitism would not have to demonstrate that his sign does indeed constitute a trade mark and establish its knowledge within the relevant public. However, it should be noted that, first, in the absence of an exclusive right, the claim may be rejected if the act is not found to be unlawful.[466] Second, the infringement of the well-known trade mark must be assessed under the same conditions as the infringement of a registered trade mark with a reputation. In the speciality, it is then necessary to compare the signs and the goods or services in question. It is often easier to establish the likelihood of confusion in the field of trade mark law, as long as it is assessed in an abstract manner and not *in concreto* as in the case of unfair competition.[467] Outside the speciality, all the conditions for infringement of the reputed trade mark should be met. It cannot be accepted that invoking parasitism could allow to circumvent the special regime or that the non-application of those conditions could give preference to the owners of unregistered distinctive signs.

101. Marks consisting of the shape excluded from registration. With regard to trade marks consisting of the shape of the product, it should also be noted that recourse to the protection of well-known trade marks can be useful since those marks may be refused registration if the shape is considered to result from the nature of the goods themselves, necessary to obtain a technical result or to give substantial value to the good.[468] In the latter case in particular, thanks to its originality, the shape may be

---

un monde globalisé. Mélanges en l'honneur du Professeur Joanna Schmidt-Szalewski, LexisNexis, Paris 2014, p. 350. Cf. less critical Christophe Caron, *Les nouvelles frontières du parasitisme*, Comm. com. électr. 2006, No. 12, comment 153.

464. For an alternative interpretation of the judgments *see* Maetz, *Notoriété: essai sur l'appropriation …*, p. 403. The author pleads for the recognition of a property right over notoriety which contains an autonomous value.

465. TGI Paris, 26 November 1997, PIBD 1998, No. 650, III, p. 177, *Chanel*.

466. Cf. Joanna Schmidt-Szalewski, *La commercialisation d'un produit non protégé n'est pas une faute*, Propr. ind. 2004, No. 1, comment 10.

467. Indeed, if, e.g., the affixing of a word or another distinctive sign on the product by the third party is likely to exclude the likelihood of confusion on the ground of unfair competition, the same cannot be said on the basis of trade mark law.

468. *See* Articles 4(1)(e) of Directive 2015/2436; 7(1)(e) of Regulation 2017/1001.

perfectly distinctive, but it is excluded from protection as a registered trade mark.[469] The provisions on absolute grounds for refusal of registration cannot, however, deprive of protection, as a well-known trade mark, i.e. an unregistered mark, a form likely to indicate to the public the commercial origin of a product.

[B] Scope of the Special Protection

102. Delimitation and distinction of the likelihood of confusion. I will delimit the scope of the regime of extended protection related to the signs and goods or services covered (§1.02[B][1]), and then distinguish the classical case of trade mark infringement consisting in causing a likelihood of confusion as to the commercial origin of goods and services (§1.02[B][2]).

[1] Delimitation of the Scope of Protection

103. Covered signs and goods or services. It is necessary to characterise the scope of the extended protection of the trade mark with a reputation, insofar as this concerns the signs whose use may infringe a reputed trade mark (§1.02[B][1][a]) and the goods or services that fall under the special regime (§1.02[B][1][b]). However, it should be admitted that the notion of scope of protection may have a broader meaning and encompass all the conditions for infringement of the reputed mark that will be examined in the next chapters of this study.

[a] Protection Against Use of Identical or Similar Signs

104. Absence of distinction between reproduction and imitation. Directive 2015/2436 and Regulation 2017/1001, as well as the texts preceding them, explicitly provide that the trade mark with a reputation may be infringed in the event of use by a third party of an identical or similar sign. In the past, some national provisions literally limited enhanced protection to the use against identical signs.[470] The approach of the European legislator merits approval. Limitation of the special protection exclusively to cases of exact reproductions would be difficult to explain. As Desbois said as early as 1963, if the trade mark law is to ensure exclusivity even with respect to completely dissimilar products, there is no reason to make the distinction between reproduction and mere imitation.[471]

105. Practical importance. I will analyse the question of similarity between the signs when examining the condition of a link between the mark and the disputed sign at

469. *See* Albert Chavanne, Jacques Azéma, *Réflexions sur les marques figuratives*, in: *Mélanges offerts à Jean-Jacques Burst*, LexisNexis, Paris 1997, pp. 43-45; Passa, *Contrefaçon et concurrence ...*, p. 159.

470. *See* the former wording of Article L.713-5 of the French Intellectual Property Code. On this issue cf. Bouvel, *Principe de spécialité ...*, pp. 358 et seq.; Passa, *Traité de droit ...*, pp. 514 et seq.

471. Desbois, *Note sous CA Paris 8 déc. 1962 ...*, p. 408.

issue.[472] Here it should be only pointed out that invoking the special regime may be more useful in the case of imitations of reputed trade marks. As it has been observed, in the case of slavish reproduction of a famous trade mark, even for goods that are different in their intrinsic nature, it is often difficult to exclude a risk of confusion, unless the goods designated by the signs at issue have no common features. The public is normally led to believe that the use has been authorised by the right holder. In such cases, it is not necessary to rely on the special protection offered to trade marks with a reputation. The act of use which creates a likelihood of confusion may be condemned under the provisions related to the infringement in the speciality.[473] Indeed, in cases where the signs are identical, it is often possible that the owner may succeed in demonstrating the infringement of his trade mark in the form of a likelihood of confusion that may be condemned as an infringement. As we shall see, the likelihood of confusion must be assessed globally and the special regime should apply in cases where no risk of misleading the public as to the commercial origin can be established.[474] In cases of slavish reproductions, the public often risks associating the origin of the goods or services of the third party with the proprietor, at least believing in the existence of economic relations between them, particularly where the reputed mark has a strong inherent distinctiveness, unless the goods or services are completely different, such as to rule out any confusion.

[b] Protection Against Use for Any Goods or Services

106. Functional interpretation. The provisions of former Directives and Regulations referred, respectively in Articles 5(2) and 9(1)(c), only to 'goods or services which are not similar' to those for which the earlier trade mark is registered. Thus, literally, special protection only applied in cases of use of reputed trade marks beyond the speciality. However, in the *Davidoff* judgment, the Court of Justice ruled that, where a sign is used for identical or similar goods or services, a trade mark with a reputation must enjoy protection at least as extensive as where a sign is used for non-similar goods or services.[475] The solution was explicitly reaffirmed in the *Adidas* judgment.[476] The literal interpretation of the former provisions has thus yielded to the functional interpretation advocated by certain authors who considered that, *a fortiori*, the trade mark with a reputation should be protected against its use for similar goods or services.[477]

At present, this is *expressis verbis* admitted by Directive 2015/2436. Pursuant to Article 10(2)(c) of Directive 2015/2436, the special regime is intended to apply in the case of use of a third-party sign 'irrespective of whether it is used for goods or services

472. *See* paras 141 et seq. *infra*.
473. Luigi Mansani, *La nozione di rischio di associazione fra segni nel diritto comunitario dei marchi*, Riv. Dir. Ind. 1997, I, pp. 143-144.
474. *See* paras 110 et seq. *infra*.
475. CJ, 9 January 2003, case C-292/00, *Davidoff*, paras 25-26.
476. CJ, 23 October 2003, case C-408/01, *Adidas*.
477. Wiliam R. Cornish, *Intellectual Property*, 3rd ed., Sweet & Maxwell, London 1996, p. 600. In favour of this solution *see also* Gielen, *Trademark Dilution under European Law* ..., p. 711.

which are identical, similar or dissimilar to those for which the trade mark is registered'. This is also the wording of Article 9(2)(c) of Regulation 2017/1001.

107. Practical importance. The solution of the *Davidoff* ruling, currently enshrined in Directive 2015/2436 and Regulation 2017/1001, was criticised by part of the scholars.[478] Some authors consider that the idea that the special protection granted to owners of trade marks with a reputation can also be enforced against a competitor is only theoretical.[479] A situation in which the use of a similar sign for similar goods does not give rise to a likelihood of confusion, while allowing such use to be condemned on the basis of the special regime, would be highly unlikely in practice. Thus, the solution would be entirely redundant.[480]

Admittedly, in most cases, the likelihood of confusion is easily demonstrated when the earlier mark is reputed, the sign at issue is identical or similar to it and their specialities are identical or similar. This is all the more likely since, according to the overall method of assessing the likelihood of confusion, reputation is a factor to be taken into account, which facilitates the admission of its existence. However, the use of a sign similar to a mark with a reputation for similar goods does not necessarily have to cause a likelihood of confusion, even if this would only rarely occur in practice.[481] Moreover, it cannot be accepted that the absence of a risk of confusion always implies the absence of a link between the signs in the public mind, which is required in the field of the special regime. If the right holder acting on the basis of the extended protection must demonstrate the existence of a link, it should be pointed out that the degree of similarity between the conflicting signs may be less. Access to the special protection may therefore be easier as regards the degree of similarity between the signs in dispute, even though the borderline between similarity that is insufficient to establish a likelihood of confusion and at the same time allowing to characterise a link is very delicate and subject to subjective assessment by the Court.

Once the link between the signs in dispute has been established, it is still necessary to demonstrate the existence of unfair advantage or a form of detriment, which, according to some authors, is very difficult in the absence of a likelihood of confusion.[482] However, it must be noted that the likelihood of confusion is by no means a condition for infringement of a trade mark with a reputation and, as a rule, the purpose of the special regime is to ensure protection when there is no danger of misleading the public as to the commercial origin. Furthermore, the case law shows

478. *See* Georges Bonet, *Protection de la marque renommée contre l'usage d'un signe identique ou similaire pour des produits ou services non identiques ou similaires*, RTD eur. 2004, No. 1, p. 110; Pollaud-Dulian, *Propriété intellectuelle. La propriété industrielle* ..., p. 1075.
479. Adrien Bouvel, *La protection des marques renommées*, Fascicule 7320, JurisClasseur 2016, para. 73. The *Davidoff* judgment was also criticised by McCarthy, *Dilution of a Trade Mark* ..., p. 1178. In favour of the ruling *see* Christine Vilmart, *La CJCE arbitre le match en faveur de la marque renommée*, Gaz. Pal. 2003, No. 135, p. 6.
480. Adrien Bouvel, *Étendue de la protection des marques renommées en droit communautaire*, JCP E 2003, No. 36, p. 1249, para. 12. *See also* Urszula Promińska, in: Ewa Nowińska, Urszula Promińska, Krystyna Szczepanowska-Kozłowska, *Własność przemysłowa i jej ochrona*, LexisNexis, Warsaw 2014, p. 522.
481. Skubisz, *Naruszenie praw z rejestracji* ..., p. 444.
482. Bouvel, *La protection des marques* ..., para. 75.

that it is easier to establish infringement where the conflicting signs are used in the same specialities but are not sufficiently similar for a likelihood of confusion to be established. For example, according to the Dutch court which referred the question for a preliminary ruling in a case concerning the trade mark *Red Bull*, the signs *Red Bull* and *Bulldog*, used for identical goods, were similar in so far as the public could establish a link without confusing them.[483] Thus, it is clear that the situation is not only theoretical.

108. Conceptual differences between the signs in dispute. The proprietors of trade marks with a reputation may have recourse to the extended protection in particular when there are visual and phonetic similarities between the signs, but the likelihood of confusion is excluded due to conceptual differences. This is the case when one of the conflicting signs has a particular meaning, for example, consists of the name of a person or a place, while the other has no such meaning or has an entirely different meaning.[484] This will also be the case when a competitor alters the sign constituting the mark or adds expressions to it, in particular with the aim of ridiculing the mark or suggesting that the competing product is better, so that the information contained in the third-party sign excludes confusion. In such cases, in particular because of obvious conceptual differences, the public is not likely to associate the same commercial origin with the goods or services designated by the two signs. However, it would be unjustified to deprive the right holders of the extended protection. Thus, the solution is far from being entirely useless.

In this context, we can cite an old matter decided in the Benelux in 1981, in which the judge held that the trade marks *Mama Mia's*, *Yam-Yam's*, *Wokkels* and *Super Chips*, renowned in the field of chips, were infringed by the use of the slogan: *What then now? Hyper Chips? Papa Pia's? Pokkels? Yak-Yaks? Foei-Foei's? No! New salt crackers without the usual nonsense. Simply: Potato Slices.*[485] The defendant clearly wanted to make the public think of the plaintiff's marks and to ridicule them in its eyes, without there being any danger of confusion. This was also the case in the matter opposing the trade mark *Ricard*, registered, *inter alia*, for clothing, to several signs making fun of it, such as *Smicard* or *Ringard* affixed to T-shirts.[486] According to the Paris Court, despite visual and phonetic similarities, the intellectual differences, linked to the connotation of the terms used, were such that the average attentive consumer could not attribute the origin of the T-shirts designated by the disputed signs to the owner of the *Ricard* mark. However, the public could establish a link by association of ideas, which allowed the judge to condemn the use of the signs at issue on the basis of the special regime.[487] There are also two cases in which competitors of the proprietor of the trade mark *Botox* sought to suggest to customers that they offered products

483. CJ, 6 February 2014, case C-65/12, *Red Bull*, para. 12.
484. Passa, *Traité de droit ...*, p. 524. Cf. also Ricolfi, *Trattato dei marchi ...*, p. 751.
485. Cited by D.W. Feer Verkade, *Unfair Use of and Damage to the Reputation of Well-Known Trademarks, Trade Names and Indications of Source – A Contribution from Benelux*, IIC 1986, vol. 17, No. 6, p. 774. The use of this slogan was condemned on the basis of the extended protection provided for in Article 13 A(2) of the Uniform Benelux Law.
486. CA Paris, 11 May 2007, case 05/21446, *Ricard*.
487. Cf. also CA Rennes, 27 April 2010, case 09/00413, *Petit Navire*.

equivalent to or better performing than those designated by that trade mark. The Warsaw Court considered that the differences between the mark *Botox* and the sign *Alternative to Botox* precluded the public from attaching the same commercial origin to them. The judgment condemning the contested use was based on the special regime since the use of the disputed sign took an unfair advantage of the reputed trade mark because of the transfer of positive associations as regards the characteristics attached to the goods bearing the trade mark *Botox*.[488] Likewise, the Paris Court dismissed the claim of infringement for likelihood of confusion between the trade mark *Botox* and, among others, the sign *Better than Botox?*. According to the decision, the consumer was informed from the very first words that the second product was not *Botox* and had to be compared to it.[489]

109. Practical consequences. One of the consequences of this solution is that where the degree of similarity between the conflicting signs is rather low, proprietors of reputed trade marks sometimes base their claims, even in the case of use of their marks for identical goods, only on the special regime.[490] However, most of the time, the owners cumulate their actions and base their claims on the infringement for likelihood of confusion and on the infringement of the reputed trade mark. The invocation of the two grounds as complementary seems questionable since no distinct harm shall result from the infringement of the reputed trade mark;[491] the damage caused to the reputation of the trade mark can be compensated on the basis of the infringement for likelihood of confusion.[492] By contrast, claiming extended protection of the trade mark with a reputation as a subsidiary ground is perfectly justified. As we shall see, if the Court dismisses the action due to the lack of likelihood of confusion, it may very well condemn the disputed use as an infringement of a trade mark with a reputation.

It is sometimes also considered that bringing together an action based on both grounds is detrimental to legal certainty since it does not facilitate the adoption of a distinctive sign. Referring to the position of the British government in the *Davidoff* case, Bouvel stresses that competitors wishing to use similar marks for similar goods are obliged to make sure not only that they have avoided any likelihood of confusion but also that no action can be brought against them on the basis of the special regime.[493] However, it is difficult to see why a third party wishing to use a sign similar to a reputed

488. SO Warsaw, 14 July 2015, case XXII GWzt 17/15, *Botox*.
489. TGI Paris, 1 February 2006, case 05/09092, *Botox*. In this case, the disputed use was condemned on the basis of provisions related to consumers' protection, as unlawful comparative advertising, because it took unfair advantage of the reputation attached to the *Botox* trade mark and caused its degradation. If the right holder had invoked the special regime, the decision would probably have been pronounced also on this basis since, as we shall see, the conditions for assessing unfair advantage and discrediting or degradation should be the same under the trade mark law and the provisions on comparative advertising. *See* para. 181 *infra*.
490. *See* e.g. GC, 12 November 2014, aff. T-524/11, *Volvo*, para. 15. However, it must be admitted that the conflicting signs, *Volvo* and *Lovol*, were found dissimilar. Consequently, the claim of any infringement was dismissed.
491. Bouvel, *Étendue de la protection ...*, para. 7. In this direction also Promińska, *Własność przemysłowa ...*, p. 523. *See* para. 119 *infra*.
492. *See* Passa, *Contrefaçon et concurrence ...*, p. 185.
493. Bouvel, *Étendue de la protection ...*, para. 8.

trade mark for dissimilar products would be subject to the obligation to examine the risk on the ground of extended protection, whereas a competitor would be exempt from it. *A fortiori*, greater diligence should be required from competitors.

[2] Distinction of the Likelihood of Confusion

110. Likelihood of confusion under the special regime. Prior to the adoption of Directive 89/104, it was often raised in doctrine that a likelihood of confusion was possible outside the speciality and that it should be condemned under general civil liability law or under the special provisions relating to unfair competition.[494] As it has been established, almost all of the draft amendments to the Paris Convention aimed at introducing extended protection for well-known trade marks provided for the risk of confusion among forms of trade mark infringement outside the field of speciality.[495]

Nowadays, many authors consider that the likelihood of confusion can be condemned on the ground of the special regime.[496] Some scholars even believe that the use of the mark outside the speciality must be punished in particular when it leads the public to believe in a community of origin of the goods designated by the conflicting signs,[497] and that it would be difficult to prove unfair advantage or detriment to the distinctive character or repute of a trade mark with a reputation in the absence of a likelihood of confusion.[498] Moreover, it follows from the case law of the Court of Justice that a likelihood of confusion is likely to arise in the field of extended protection. Although the likelihood of confusion is not a condition for the success of an action for infringement of a trade mark with a reputation,[499] the Court of Justice refers to it as a factor aggravating the existence of a link between the signs in question which may also be taken into account at the stage of the assessment of the infringement.[500] In national case law, the courts sometimes cumulatively find infringement for likelihood of confusion and infringement of the reputed trade mark.[501]

In accordance with Recital 16 of Directive 2015/2436 and Recital 11 of Regulation 2017/1001, within the limits of speciality, apart from the case of double identity in

494. *See* e.g. Jaton, *La protection des marques ...*, pp. 41-42. Moreover, the author considered that damage to reputation was only possible if the public succumbed to confusion.
495. *See* para. 31 *supra*.
496. *See* Laporte-Legeais, *Clair-obscur sur la marque renommée ...*, para. 12; Cohen Jehoram, Van Nispen, Huydecoper, *European Trademark Law ...*, p. 316; Maetz, *Notoriété: essai sur l'appropriation ...*, pp. 114-115; Szczepanowska-Kozłowska, *System prawa handlowego ...*, p. 343.
497. Bouvel, *Principe de spécialité ...*, p. 325. *See also* Bouvel, *La protection des marques ...*, para. 101.
498. Bouvel, *Étendue de la protection ...*, para. 16. Cf. also Gustavo Ghidini, Giovanni Cavani, *On the Scope of Protection of Renowned Trade Marks*, Queen Mary Journal of Intellectual Property 2018, vol. 8, No. 4, pp. 273 et seq.
499. CJ, 22 June 2000, case C-425/98, *Marca Mode*, para. 36. In order to invoke infringement of a trade mark with a reputation, 'it is sufficient for the degree of similarity between the mark with a reputation and the sign to have the effect that the relevant section of the public establishes a link between the sign and the mark'. CJ, 23 October 2003, case C-408/01, *Adidas*, para. 31.
500. CJ, 27 November 2008, case C-252/07, *Intel*, para. 42.
501. In Polish jurisprudence *see* e.g. NSA, 23 April 2013, case II GSK 191/12, *Cartier*. In French jurisprudence *see* TGI Paris, 2 March 2012, case 10/14345, *Louis Vuitton*.

which the mark enjoys 'absolute' protection, the likelihood of confusion constitutes the 'specific condition' of protection. The mark is then protected as a designation of origin, in its distinctive function, and the likelihood of confusion must be assessed by reference to the function of guaranteeing the identity of origin.[502] In the field of the special regime, however, it is not the essential function that is protected but the economic (accessory[503]) functions of the trade mark which are then protected as advertising value, a means of conveying to the public messages which go beyond the indication of the commercial origin. This observation is fully in line with the spirit of the Directive and Regulation and with the aims of the regimes of protection of trade marks, within and outside the speciality. The legal provisions which repress the likelihood of confusion only within the speciality and at the same time completely disregard it in the field of extended protection indicate that no likelihood of confusion is possible outside the speciality; the risk of confusion is in principle conceivable provided that there is a certain degree, albeit a small one, of similarity between the goods or services in question. The special regime should therefore be reserved for cases in which the public is not misled as to the origin. I will set out below the reasoning that should enable to justify this opinion, which appears to be in line with the rule of overall assessment of the likelihood of confusion (§1.02[B][2][a]), and which leads to consider the special regime as complementary (§1.02[B][2][b]).

[a] Global Assessment of the Likelihood of Confusion Within the Speciality

111. Rule of global assessment. Directive 2015/2436 and Regulation 2017/1001 allow to condemn any danger of confusion in the speciality, thanks to the global method of assessing the likelihood of confusion. According to Recital 16 of Directive 2015/2436 and Recital 11 of Regulation 2017/1001, the appreciation of the likelihood of confusion 'depends on numerous elements and, in particular, on the recognition of the trade mark on the market, the association which can be made with the used or registered sign, the degree of similarity between the trade mark and the sign and between the goods or services identified'. Indeed, in the light of the jurisprudence of the Court of Justice, 'the likelihood of confusion must therefore be appreciated globally, taking into account all factors relevant to the circumstances of the case'.[504] Moreover, 'a global assessment of the likelihood of confusion implies some interdependence between the relevant factors'.[505] This method consists of simultaneously taking into account all the relevant factors which thus appear to be interdependent. The overall method is justified as being in line with the intellectual approach of the average consumer, who does not compare signs and goods or services separately, but has an overall perception of the marked products.[506] Indeed, the consumer always carries out an overall examination of the trade mark in relation to the product. The likelihood of confusion is thus the

502. Passa, *Traité de droit ...*, p. 386.
503. This term is used by Kur, Senftleben, *European Trade Mark ...*, p. 9.
504. CJ, 11 November 1997, case C-251/95, *Sabel v. Puma*, para. 22.
505. CJ, 29 September 1998, case C-39/97, *Canon*, para. 17.
506. Passa, *Traité de droit ...*, pp. 412-413.

essential condition for infringement of the mark, which is demonstrated by the similarity of the signs combined with other relevant elements.[507]

112. Relevance of reputation. According to Recital 16 of Directive 2015/2436 and Recital 11 of Regulation 2017/1001, the likelihood of confusion is assessed on the basis of 'the recognition of the trade mark on the market'. Therefore, there is no doubt that reputation must be taken into account when examining the likelihood of confusion. The solution was reaffirmed by the Court of Justice.[508] In the light of its case law, the distinctive character of the mark, and in particular its reputation, can compensate a lesser degree of similarity between the goods or services covered.[509] The legislator has thus approved the idea that knowledge of the mark increases the likelihood of confusion.[510]

113. Impact of reputation on the assessment of similarity of the goods or services. The idea that similarity between the goods should be assessed more flexibly in the presence of a trade mark known to the public was clearly enshrined by the Court of Justice.[511] Indeed, according to the *Canon* judgment, 'the distinctive character of the earlier trade mark, and in particular its reputation, must be taken into account when determining whether the similarity between the goods or services covered by the two

507. Pollaud-Dulian, *Propriété intellectuelle. La propriété industrielle* ..., p. 981. On the rule of overall assessment *see also* Matthieu Dhenne, *Appréciation comparée du risque de confusion entre marques en jurisprudence française et communautaire*, Propr. ind. 2007, No. 4, étude 10.
508. *See* CJ, 11 November 1997, case C-251/95, *Sabel v. Puma*, para. 24.
509. CJ, 29 September 1998, case C-39/97, *Canon*, para. 19. For a critical opinion on taking into account reputation in assessing the likelihood of confusion *see* Canlorbe, *L'usage de la marque* ..., pp. 104 et seq.
510. The reputation of the mark aggravates the risk of confusion since a famous mark leaves a certain and persistent memory in the mind of the clientele. Mathély, *Le droit français des signes* ..., p. 568. At the same time, the contrary approach, according to which reputation makes it easier to avoid confusion, was condemned. Cf. on this approach Baeumer, *La protection de la marque* ..., p. 561; de Haas, *La 'contrefaçon' de la marque notoire* ..., p. 142; Sabine Casparie-Kerdel, *Dilution Disguised: Has the Concept of Trade Mark Dilution Made Its Way into the Laws of Europe?*, EIPR 2001, vol. 23, No. 4, p. 192; Benoît Humblot, *Droit des marques: de l'influence ou non du risque de confusion sur la similitude et vice versa*, RLDI 2011, No. 72, para. 20; Lotte Anemaet, *The Many Faces of the Average Consumer: Is It Really So Difficult to Assess Whether Two Stripes Are Similar to Three?*, IIC 2020, vol. 51, No. 2, pp. 193-198. The solution adopted by the Court of Justice deserves approval since the likelihood of confusion must be interpreted broadly and it includes the likelihood of association between the conflicting signs. In the latter case, the public distinguishes between the two signs but, as a result of the association, is likely to think that they are exploited by the same undertaking. *See* Passa, *Traité de droit* ..., p. 404. While it is certainly true that reputed trade marks can hardly be subject to a direct likelihood of confusion, the indirect likelihood is undoubtedly reinforced when the trade mark invoked is a mark known to consumers. *See* Jaton, *La protection des marques* ..., pp. 34-38; Portet, *Les marques notoirement connues* ..., pp. 49-51. It should also be noted that a consumer seeing an imitation of a reputed trade mark may think that the proprietor himself has modified his mark to 'refresh' its image, in other words that the second mark is a new mark of a family belonging to the same company. Cf. Chavanne, *Droit de la propriété* ..., p. 591. Moreover, it has to be said that the idea that the public will be less likely to confuse a mark that is known to them leads to rather illogical results: it is not the unknown mark that deserves the greatest protection, but the famous and valuable mark. Perent, *Marques notoirement connues* ..., p. 147. Cf. also Senftleben, *European Trade Mark* ..., p. 326.
511. Bouvel, *Principe de spécialité* ..., p. 319.

trade marks is sufficient to give rise to the likelihood of confusion'.[512] Consequently, in the case of trade marks with a reputation, it is possible to extend the concept of similarity between goods and services.[513] French courts rightly pointed out, even before the *Canon* ruling, that the similarity between the goods should not be considered in the absolute but must take into account what they represent in the eyes of the public precisely because of the reputation of the mark.[514] It was observed that, in the event of the use of a famous trade mark, in order to assess the likelihood of confusion, the nature of the goods concerned will be neither a decisive nor a preponderant element. By contrast, the reputation of the mark itself will be taken into consideration because the likelihood of confusion resulting from the use of a famous mark corresponds to the reputation of that mark.[515] Consequently, the likelihood of confusion, depending on the strength of the trade mark's reputation, may exist even for goods of a very different nature.[516] The reputation of the trade mark therefore has an impact on the assessment of the similarity between the goods and services.[517] Hence, the overall method of examining the risk of confusion has a major influence on the appreciation of that similarity.[518]

That being said, there is no doubt that similarity between the goods or services is *a sine qua non* precondition for a likelihood of confusion. However, the overall method has a great influence on its assessment. Even where the goods are objectively different, the identity or strong similarity of the signs may, especially where the mark relied on is highly distinctive, lead the public to attribute them to the same origin. Consequently,

512. CJ, 29 September 1998, case C-39/97, *Canon*, para. 24.
513. Guglielmetti, *La tutela di marchi* ..., p. 294.
514. CA Paris, 1 June 1987, PIBD 1987, No. 423, III, p. 467, *Coca-Cola*. *See also* CA Paris, 16 February 1972, Ann. propr. ind. 1972, p. 182.
515. Perent, *Marques notoirement connues* ..., pp. 108-109.
516. *See* Pérot-Morel, *L'extension de la protection* ..., p. 22.
517. Sironi, *Codice della proprietà* ..., p. 360.
518. *See* Passa, *Traité de droit* ..., pp. 386-387. Following the case law of the Court of Justice, the French Court of Cassation now requires that the distinctive character and reputation of the trade mark be taken into account when assessing the similarity of the goods or services designated by the signs in dispute. Cass. com., 5 April 2005, case 03-11.318, *Bistrot du sommelier*. It should be pointed out that the approach adopted by the Court of Justice is not interpreted in the same way by all the authors. Some consider that the distinctive character of the mark has no impact on the assessment of the existence of similarity between the goods or services; this criterion should be taken into account only in the context of the overall examination of the likelihood of confusion, but the condition of similarity should be assessed independently. Skubisz, *System prawa prywatnego* ..., pp. 685 and 1107. For a strict assessment of the similarity of the goods or services in the case of reputed trade marks cf. also Bonet, *Protection de la marque renommée contre l'usage* ..., pp. 110 et seq. This reasoning does not appear to be entirely consistent with the *Canon* judgment and the rule of a global assessment of the likelihood of confusion. As Passa points out, the only evidence incumbent on the proprietor of the mark is the existence of a likelihood of confusion. The similarity between the signs or between the goods or services does not have to be demonstrated beforehand. The condition of similarity is not separate from but inherent in the condition of likelihood of confusion. That idea finds a very clear translation in the overall method of assessing the likelihood of confusion enshrined by the Court of Justice. Passa, *Traité de droit* ..., p. 379. Indeed, as one author observed more than fifty years ago, the notion of similarity of the goods, and therefore the rule of speciality, is not a criterion in itself but constitutes one of the means to determine whether the use of similar marks is likely to create confusion. Wichers Hoeth, *Étude comparative* ..., p. 140.

the Court may easily conclude that there is a likelihood of confusion if the mark relied on enjoys a high reputation.[519] Hence, the use of a reputed trade mark is often liable to be condemned on the ground of infringement for likelihood of confusion.

114. Subjective assessment of similarity of the goods or services. The overall method of assessing the likelihood of confusion involves a subjective examination of the similarity between the goods or services in question. Indeed, if, under Recital 16 of Directive 2015/2436 and Recital 11 of Regulation No. 2017/1001, it is the likelihood of confusion which constitutes the 'specific condition' for the protection and 'it is indispensable to give an interpretation of the concept of similarity in relation to the likelihood of confusion', it goes without saying that the assessment of the similarity of goods or services cannot be limited to the comparison of the objective nature of the products. The principle of an overall assessment and the search for the likelihood of confusion, as a specific condition of protection, requires an examination of the criterion of similarity between the goods or services in the light of all the relevant factors and not only the intrinsic nature of the products.

As we have seen, in the past, judges generally relied on an objective assessment of similarity between the goods based on their intrinsic nature.[520] Case law often preferred the objective method, insisting on the principle of freedom of trade and industry, or for reasons of legal certainty.[521] However, the objective method could be implemented at a time when technological processes and methods of manufacturing and marketing products were poorly developed.[522] By the end of the 19th century, the economic context began to change, so that the objective method of assessing the similarities between the products ceased to correspond to the reality of the trade.[523] Indeed, companies began to extend their activities to new, sometimes very distant areas. As a result, the likelihood of confusion had to be assessed more broadly,[524] since the trends in business expansion by large companies were not without influence on expectations and behaviour of the consumers.[525] Many authors pointed out that it was therefore necessary to examine whether the public could think of an extension of the trade mark owner's activity, that this circumstance should be taken into account when assessing the likelihood of confusion, and consequently the similarity of the goods should be assessed more flexibly.[526] Moreover, the doctrine stated that it was not the individual conduct of the right holder in question that was relevant, but that it was a

519. Passa, *Traité de droit* ..., pp. 386 and 417.
520. *See* para. 7 *supra*.
521. Cf. Baeumer, *La protection de la marque* ..., p. 562. In favour of this strict approach *see* Durrande, *Note sous CA Paris 27 mai 1987* ..., p. 528. More recently cf. Bouvel, *Principe de spécialité* ..., p. 316.
522. Urszula Promińska, *Ustawa o znakach towarowych. Komentarz*, PWN, Warsaw 1998, pp. 38-39.
523. *See* para. 7 *supra*.
524. *See* Pérot-Morel, *L'extension de la protection* ..., p. 22.
525. Galli, *Funzione del marchio e ampiezza* ..., p. 82.
526. *See* Portet, *Les marques notoirement connues* ..., p. 52; Guglielmetti, *La tutela di marchi* ..., pp. 292-294; Giovanni Guglielmetti, *Il caso Camel: une correzione del trend?*, Riv. Dir. Ind. 1995, II, p. 309. Cf. also Chavanne, *Les marques notoirement connues* ..., p. 306.

question of establishing a trend of expansion of the undertakings active on the market at issue.[527]

Consequently, in more recent case law, the criterion of similarity of the goods or services is interpreted more subjectively. A very good example of this trend is a judgment rendered by the French Court of Cassation in a case concerning the use of the trade mark *Bulgari*, famous in the field of jewellery, by a manufacturer of clothing, perfumes, glasses, etc. The Court noted that a general trend towards diversification led leading fashion designers to create jewellery and perfumes, while famous jewellers marketed perfumes and accessories.[528] The trend towards the expansion of activities and diversification, often in the field of luxury goods, was adopted in other cases in order to assess the similarity of the goods in a flexible manner and to qualify products such as clothing, perfumes, watches and fashion accessories as similar.[529] Thus, it is accepted that similarity between the goods can result from circumstances external to their nature. The criterion of the diversification of the activities of undertakings may therefore be taken into consideration in order to infer similarity between the goods, since, because of the trend towards diversification of activities, the public is likely to believe in an 'attempt to despecialise' on the part of the proprietor of the trade mark.[530] This trend of expansion of activity, if it is common and hence constitutes an established trade customs known to the public, is nowadays a criterion for assessing similarity of the goods or services.[531]

115. Overall assessment of similarity of the goods or services. In the jurisprudence of the Court of Justices, the subjective assessment of similarity between the goods or services results from the rule of its overall examination. According to the *Canon* judgment, 'in assessing the similarity of the goods or services concerned ... all the

527. *See* E. Tomassini, *Il nome Camel come marchio celebre, protezione allargata e principio di specialità*, Riv. Dir. Ind. 1990, II, p. 214. In Italian doctrine and jurisprudence, as we have seen, taking into account the economic expansion of companies led to the development of a theory known as 'marks that create taste and fashions' ('*marchi creatori del gusto e della moda*'). *See* para. 23 *supra*. According to this conception, all goods were similar which, although different in nature, were related to each other in such a way that, in the opinion of the public, they could have a common origin. The theory was likely to apply in particular to luxury goods, perfumes, clothing, accessories, etc. Sotriffer, *Protezione allargata del marchio di rinomanza ...*, p. 116. *See also* Galli, *Funzione del marchio e ampiezza ...*, pp. 84-85. The image of luxury associated with the mark was sometimes the only element taken into account to assess the similarity between the goods. This approach has not avoided criticism. Cf. Caselli, *Il marchio che gode di rinomanza ...*, pp. 47-48. Moreover, the theory is still being implemented by some Italian judges to condemn use of reputed trade marks. Agata Sobol, *Marchio notorio e decadenza*, Riv. Dir. Ind. 2009, II, pp. 219-221. By contrast, it was observed that this concept was inapplicable to highly specialised companies, often manufacturing a single product or type of product, or operating in very specific sectors. Lorenzo Biglia, *Alcuni problemi sull'affinità dei prodotti e sul giudizio di confondibilità fra marchi*, Riv. Dir. Ind. 1982, II, pp. 44 et seq. Indeed, it was often held that the '*monoproduttività*' of the trade mark owner's business made the extension of his activity less likely and therefore reduced the risk of confusion. *See* Guglielmetti, *La tutela di marchi ...*, p. 295; Caselli, *Il marchio che gode di rinomanza ...*, pp. 153 et seq.
528. Cass. com., 16 January 1990, case 88-10.856, *Bulgari*.
529. *See* e.g. CA Paris, 2 December 2005, PIBD 2006, No. 824, III, p. 123.
530. Canlorbe, *L'usage de la marque ...*, pp. 101-102.
531. *See* Guidelines for examination of European Union Trade Marks (2020), EUIPO, Part C, section 2, Chapter 2, p. 35.

relevant factors relating to those goods or services themselves should be taken into account. Those factors include, *inter alia*, their nature, their end users *[should read "intended purpose"]* and their method of use and whether they are in competition with each other or are complementary'.[532] Other factors may also be taken into account, such as the distribution channels for the products in question.[533] In addition, in the overall assessment, trade usages, such as those relating to the way of marketing of the products, must be taken into account.[534] Thus, generally speaking, consideration should be given to the business practices of companies in a sector of activity with which the public is familiar.[535] It is indeed necessary to consider the reality of the relevant market and customs in the sector of industry or commerce in question.[536] As noted above, if the average consumer has become accustomed to attributing the same origin to products, even if they are intrinsically different, the similarity should be accepted.[537] In other words, an established trade custom known to the public allows to conclude that goods or services of different nature have the same origin, hence are similar.[538] Therefore, if, for instance, the right holder demonstrates that the licensing of the third party's products is a general practice in the relevant sector of the market, the goods or services being compared may be considered similar, notwithstanding the differences in their nature.[539] Indeed, where licensing between two products has become a commercial usage, this can lead to a familiarisation of the public with such practices which needs to be taken into account in the appreciation of similarity.[540]

Thus, there should be no doubt that the absence of intrinsic similarities between two products does not exclude that the average consumer is tempted to believe in a community of origin. This may be the case in the presence of products which, although clearly different, are commonly manufactured, distributed or sold together by the same companies, such as clothing and perfumes. The similarity is then extrinsic since it does not result from an objective comparison of the goods or services, but from the

532. CJ, 29 September 1998, case C-39/97, *Canon*, para. 23.
533. GC, 8 September 2010, case T-152/08, para. 41; GC, 28 June 2011, case T-480/09, para. 26. Cf. also Kur, *European Trade Mark* ..., p. 221.
534. *See* e.g. CFI, 21 April 2005, case T-164/03, *bebe*, para. 53; CFI, 11 July 2007, case T-443/05, *Piranha*, para. 45. Cf. CFI, 13 December 2004, case T-8/03, *Emidio Tucci*, para. 43.
535. Sotriffer, *Protezione allargata del marchio di rinomanza* ..., p. 116.
536. Andrea Jaeger-Lenz, in: Gordian N. Hasselblatt (ed.), *Community Trade Mark Regulation. A Commentary*, C.H. Beck Hart Nomos, Munich-Oxford 2015, p. 219.
537. In French case law admitting similarity *see* Cass. com. 16 January 1990, case 88-10.856, *Bulgari* – on the one hand, articles of jewellery and, on the other hand, clothing, glasses, perfumes; Cass. com., 6 April 1993, PIBD 1993, No. 549, III, p. 486 – on the one hand, hotel and restaurant services, on the other hand, food products; CA Paris, 3 March 1999, PIBD 1999, No. 681, III, p. 330 – on the one hand, clothing and, on the other hand, perfumes marketed by haute couture houses; CA Paris, 6 September 2000, PIBD 2000, No. 707, III, p. 514 – on the one hand, clothing and, on the other hand, perfumes and cosmetics marketed by ready-to-wear houses; Cass. com., 7 June 2006, case 04-16.908, *Ebel* – on the one hand, luxury watches and, on the other hand, cosmetics and perfumery products.
538. Guidelines for examination of European Union Trade Marks (2020), EUIPO, Part C, section 2, Chapter 2, p. 35.
539. Cf. GC, 18 November 2015, case T-606/13, *Mustang*, para. 54. On this judgment cf. para. 148 *supra*.
540. Jaeger-Lenz, *Community Trade Mark* ..., p. 220.

consideration of an external factor – the commercial practice.[541] Inherently different products shall therefore be considered similar if there is a relationship between them which, according to the public, can justify the same commercial origin.[542] The assessment is then considered more realistic.[543] The concept of similarity of goods must indeed be interpreted in relation to the distinctive function and purpose of the protection of the trade mark, which is to protect against the likelihood of confusion as to the commercial origin.[544] The term 'similar goods or services' should therefore be understood as referring to any good or service which is likely to cause confusion in the mind of the public.[545] In other words, goods are similar when, irrespective of the signs which identify them, the relevant public is likely to believe that they come from the same undertaking.[546] Consequently, since the assessment must be based on consumer reactions, the similarity of the goods or services must be assessed on the basis of the public's perception.[547] Thus, it is necessary to qualify the goods or services as similar not in the abstract but in light of the public's perception in assessing whether there is a relationship between the goods or services in question that may make them 'similar' within the meaning of the legal provisions.[548] Indeed, it should not be a question of searching for an intrinsic similarity, but a similarity in terms of trade mark law.[549]

Therefore, similarity of the goods or services is a flexible criterion and the Court enjoys a broad power of assessing it.[550] According to the subjective approach, two articles, qualified as similar in one case, may be considered different in another matter.[551] This is likely to depend on the level of reputation of the mark at issue. The EUIPO seems, for instance, to consider that extension of activity of fashion designers to the perfume industry is an established trade custom which applies however only to

541. Bouvel, *Principe de spécialité* ..., pp. 312-312.
542. *See* Durrande, *Note sous CA Paris 27 mai 1987* ..., p. 528; Adriano Vanzetti, Vincenzo Di Cataldo, *Manuale di diritto industriale*, 4th ed., Giuffrè, Milan 2003, pp. 205-206.
543. *See* Dassas, *L'élargissement de la protection* ..., p. 106.
544. Vanzetti, Di Cataldo, *Manuale di diritto* ..., p. 205.
545. Perent, *Marques notoirement connues* ..., p. 149. *See also* Canlorbe, *L'usage de la marque* ..., p. 100.
546. Passa, *Traité de droit* ..., p. 380. *See also* Bouvel, *Principe de spécialité* ..., p. 312. The definition according to which goods or services are similar when they can be traced by customers to the same origin is quite correct. *See* e.g. Cass. com., 7 April 1992, case 90-11.273, Bull. civ., IV, No. 152.
547. *See* Pérot-Morel, *L'extension de la protection* ..., p. 22; Passa, *Traité de droit* ..., p. 386; Sironi, *Codice della proprietà* ..., p. 360; Pollaud-Dulian, *Propriété intellectuelle. La propriété industrielle* ..., p. 988.
548. Vanzetti, Di Cataldo, *Manuale di diritto* ..., pp. 205-206.
549. Mathély, *Le droit français des signes* ..., p. 602.
550. Pérot-Morel, *L'extension de la protection* ..., p. 22; Passa, *Traité de droit* ..., p. 380. Cf. also Kur, *European Trade Mark* ..., p. 222. Extending the concept of similarity of the goods is sometimes criticised for calling into question the principle of speciality and hence the freedom of commerce and industry. Cf. Bouvel, *Principe de spécialité* ..., pp. 329-330. However, the third party cannot invoke the freedom of trade and industry if he distorts the market by causing a risk of confusion. The principle of speciality interpreted rigorously, too dogmatically, would lead to a perverse effect.
551. Brandt, *La protection élargie de la marque* ..., p. 218. *Contra* Skubisz, *System prawa prywatnego* ..., pp. 685 and 1107. The author considers that the assessment of similarity should be constant, that in each case the same goods or services should be qualified as similar or different.

economically successful designers.[552] In other words, the proprietor of a mark of clothing enjoying an important reputation may establish a likelihood of confusion when a similar sign is used in relation to perfumes, and the goods can then be qualified as similar. In other cases, when the earlier mark does not enjoy such a reputation, they may be considered dissimilar. Furthermore, it needs to be noted that the similarity of the goods or services should not be assessed by reference to the date of registration of the trade mark but at the time of bringing the infringement action,[553] or rather at the time of the disputed use.[554]

116. Abstract assessment of the likelihood of confusion. It is important to stress that the principle of an overall assessment of the likelihood of confusion and the rule of subjective assessment of the similarity of goods which derives from it in no way call into question the rule of an abstract assessment of the likelihood of confusion in trade mark law. The examination of the likelihood of confusion is always carried out solely by reference to the content of the registration of the allegedly infringed trade mark.[555]

---

552. Guidelines for examination of European Union Trade Marks (2020), EUIPO, Part C, section 2, Chapter 2, p. 35.
553. Pollaud-Dulian, *Propriété intellectuelle. La propriété industrielle* ..., p. 989.
554. Thus, it must be recognised that the assessment of the likelihood of confusion may change over time as a result of changes in the relevant market sector and the commercial behaviour to which the public is accustomed. In extreme cases, the initially lawful use of a sign by the third party could subsequently become unlawful. The situation becomes even more complicated when the third party files its own trade mark for goods considered different at the filing date and obtains its registration. Since the availability of the trade mark is assessed at the filing date, it cannot be subsequently invalidated. Guglielmetti, *Il caso Camel* ..., pp. 309-310. Prima facie, this may create legal uncertainty. Nevertheless, this risk appears to be limited. In such cases, it seems that the peaceful coexistence of the signs on the market should allow to rule out confusion. Cf. CJ, 3 September 2009, case C-498/07 P, *Carbonnel*, para. 82. On taking into account the peaceful coexistence of signs in assessing the likelihood of confusion *see* Arnaud Folliard-Monguiral, *Conditions et effets de la coexistence de marques en droit communautaire*, Propr. ind. 2006, No. 9, étude 24.
555. Giuseppe Sena, *Confondibilità fra segni e confondibilità fra prodotti o servizi nella giurisprudenza comunitaria: alcune considerazioni pertinenti e impertinenti*, Riv. Dir. Ind. 2004, I, p. 202; Jérôme Passa, *L'appréciation abstraite du risque de confusion en matière de contrefaçon de marque*, in: *Le droit de la propriété intellectuelle dans un monde globalisé. Mélanges en l'honneur du Professeur Joanna Schmidt-Szalewski*, LexisNexis, Paris 2014, p. 240. Cf. CJ, 21 December 2016, case C-654/15, *Matek*, para. 27. While the Court of Justice requires that all relevant factors of the case be taken into account, these are always factors relating to the signs and goods or services. The overall method does not allow account to be taken of elements external to the trade mark itself linked to its exploitation and to the product for which it is used, such as the distribution arrangements or channels, the price, the quality or the appearance or packaging of the product. *See* Sena, *Confondibilità fra segni* ..., p. 211; Passa, *Traité de droit* ..., p. 421; Skubisz, *System prawa prywatnego* ..., p. 1114. Thus, the goods or services must be considered in a generic or abstract way, without focusing on the particular characteristics of the goods or services that the proprietor offers specifically under the trade mark. Passa, *L'appréciation abstraite du risque de confusion* ..., p. 242. If the ways in which the products are used or distributed can be taken into account in assessing the likelihood of confusion, it is only with a view to assessing the abstract similarity of the goods. In other words, those circumstances may make inherently different goods similar within the meaning of trade mark law. However, this is always an abstract assessment. It is necessary to demonstrate the conduct of the market players in general and not the behaviour of the parties to the dispute. Consequently, the reasoning does not amount to taking account of the concrete ways in which the products in question are marketed. Regarding assessment of the similarity between the signs cf. Passa,

117. Similarity of the goods or services specific to the likelihood of confusion. Where the Court finds a likelihood of confusion which is assessed globally and not separately for the signs and goods, it shall always be possible to condemn such a danger of confusion in the field of the general regime of protection within the speciality.[556] There is no point in assessing the risk of confusion between the signs alone, which could then be condemned on the basis of the special regime. The consumer may confuse signs in relation to goods or services, never signs per se, detached from any products. Moreover, as we have seen, the similarity between the signs as well as the reputation and distinctiveness of the infringed mark are likely to compensate the differences between the goods or services. If, therefore, the Court finds that there is a likelihood of confusion, that necessarily means that it has accepted a certain similarity between the goods or services. It is important to stress that 'the likelihood of confusion presupposes that the goods or services covered are identical or similar'.[557] Indeed, *de lege lata*, a certain degree of similarity between the goods or services in question appears to be a necessary condition for any likelihood of confusion. Consequently, it is only possible to appear within the subjectively assessed speciality. The literal and historical interpretation of the current legislation supports this finding. Under the legislation in force, in the absence of similarity between the goods or services, it is impossible to accept that a likelihood of confusion can be established in the public mind.[558] The current provisions, unlike the draft amendments to the Paris Convention discussed in the past,[559] in no way provide that the likelihood of confusion can be condemned on the ground of the special regime. If the legislator accepted that a danger of confusion is possible outside the speciality, it should *a fortiori* have referred to it in the articles on the extended protection. This is clearly not the case. It must be admitted that the legislator, aware of the former drafts intended to establish a regime of enhanced protection for reputed trade marks, consciously decided not to mention the likelihood of confusion as a form of infringement of the trade mark with a reputation. It should be inferred from this that the likelihood of confusion is impossible in the absence of any similarity of the goods or services.

L'appréciation abstraite du risque de confusion ..., pp. 244-245. Finally, reputation is also not an element external to the trade mark, it is linked only to the perception that the relevant public has of the sign such as registered. Passa, *Traité de droit* ..., p. 421; Passa, *L'appréciation abstraite du risque de confusion* ..., p. 245. Exceptionally, however, the colour in which a mark is used can be taken into account in the assessment. *See* CJ, 18 July 2013, case C-252/12, *Specsavers*, para. 50; GC, 7 May 2015, case T-599/13, para. 40. It needs to be stressed that it can only strengthen, never weaken, the likelihood of confusion. *Contra* Senftleben, *European Trade Mark* ..., p. 316. A trade mark which is not yet vulnerable to revocation is protected notwithstanding the absence of its use. On this issue cf. Jérôme Passa, *Précisions sur la protection de la marque non exploitée et non encore sujette à déchéance*, JCP 2017, No. 10, p. 253. If the circumstances of use of the conflicting signs, including the colour in which the earlier mark is used, could allow to rule out the likelihood of confusion, the non-used marks would benefit from a broader protection than the used marks. Such a solution would be unacceptable. This goes without saying.

556. In this direction Mansani, *La nozione di rischio* ..., pp. 143-144.
557. CJ, 29 September 1998, case C-39/97, *Canon*, para. 22.
558. *See* Canlorbe, *L'usage de la marque* ..., p. 124.
559. *See* para. 31 *supra*.

Consequently, if there is no connection between the goods or services designated by the signs in question, the likelihood of confusion is not likely to arise. This interpretation of the texts corresponds to the economic reality. Notwithstanding the tendency of undertakings to diversify their activities and the practice of licensing their marks in different sectors of industry to which the public is accustomed, the likelihood of confusion is not possible in all cases. It is still true to say that too much diversity excludes the likelihood of a common origin.[560] Thus, customers cannot believe in the existence of a common commercial origin without any similarity between the products. In certain cases, it is obvious that the consumer will not be able to associate, even in the case of identical reproduction, the conflicting signs with a single commercial origin.[561] Using the example of an old Dutch case of the usurpation of the trade mark *Kodak* for potatoes,[562] it appears unlikely that the public would believe that the potatoes come from a company with any connection to the manufacturer of cameras. This would also be the case if a famous mark of toys was used by a manufacturer or sprinklers.[563] Likewise, it seems very unlikely that a manufacturer of high-quality wines would expand its activities in the field of cleaning preparations and leaching substances.[564] Indeed, there is no similarity between the products in question; as a consequence, there is no danger of confusion. In such cases, proof of the reputation of the trade mark cannot suffice to characterise the existence of a likelihood of confusion. The Court may therefore conclude that there is no likelihood of confusion even where it has found similarity between the signs and a high degree of distinctiveness of the mark relied on.[565]

[b] Complementary Role of the Special Regime

118. Question of coexistence of the regimes of trade mark protection. The overall assessment of the likelihood of confusion, carried out in the light of consumer perception, makes it possible to regard the special regime for the protection of trade marks with a reputation as complementary to the traditional protection of the mark against the likelihood of confusion. Thus, it should always be possible to condemn the use of a reputed trade mark which gives rise to a risk of confusion on the ground of infringement within the speciality.

First of all, it should be borne in mind that the likelihood of confusion is not such as to coexist with one of the forms of infringement of a trade mark with a reputation, namely dilution.[566] The question of a possible coexistence of the likelihood of confusion and infringement of the reputed trade mark could appear more nuanced with regard to tarnishment or unfair advantage. Indeed, the danger of confusion may influence the perception which the public, misled into believing that there is a

560. Desbois, *Note sous CA Paris 8 déc. 1962 ...*, p. 409.
561. *See* Cuonzo, *Il caso 'Krizia' ...*, p. 48.
562. Cited by Wichers Hoeth, *Étude comparative ...*, pp. 145-151. The disputed sign was *Kopak*.
563. Example given by Durrande, *Note sous CA Paris 27 mai 1987 ...*, p. 528.
564. Cf. however CA Paris, 18 February 1993, PIBD 1993, No. 546, III, p. 393, *Château d'Yquem*.
565. *See* Passa, *Traité de droit ...*, p. 417; Skubisz, *System prawa prywatnego ...*, p. 685.
566. *See* 215 *infra*.

commercial relationship between the proprietor of the trade mark and the third party, has of the trade mark with a reputation, in particular because of the poor quality of the goods designated by the sign of the third party.[567] This situation would be likely to characterise a kind of degradation of the mark's image. Likewise, use of a mark which causes a danger of confusion could be considered as allowing a transfer of reputation,[568] even though it could be argued that this transfer of image which characterises the unfair advantage derived from the repute does not really occur. It seems that such a transfer of image presupposes a mental process due to the fact that the public distinguishes the commercial origin of the goods in question. Assuming that a likelihood of confusion exists, in such case, there is in fact no 'transfer' of the image to the goods designated by the sign at issue. In any event, the aim of protection against unfair advantage is clearly not to condemn the likelihood of confusion.[569] The distinction between unfair advantage and the risk of confusion was stressed by the General Court.[570]

That being said, the possibility of condemning any likelihood of confusion on the ground of infringement of the trade mark in the speciality leads to the admission that invoking extended protection becomes relevant only where there is no danger of misleading the public as to the commercial origin of a good or service, in other words, where the essential function of the trade mark as a guarantee of identity of origin is not affected. That finding is consistent with the idea that, under the special regime, the economic functions of the mark are protected, that is to say, the advertising effect of the mark and its power to attract consumers, beyond its role of indicating the commercial origin.

Indeed, it is rightly accepted that the protection of a reputed trade mark is intended to apply in cases in which there is no likelihood of confusion.[571] It is when there is no longer any risk of confusion between the goods or services in question, that the extended protection may take over in order to strengthen the protection of the trade marks with a reputation.[572] Therefore, the protection of the trade mark in the field of speciality and the special protection of the trade mark with a reputation are independent and autonomous, since the two regimes are subject to different conditions of application and have different purposes. Consequently, these regimes do not cumulate but complement each other.[573]

As we have seen, this interpretation of the current legislation is literally the most correct and, moreover, it is supported by the historical interpretation. Indeed, the

567. Simon Fhima, *Trade Mark Dilution* ..., pp. 159-160.
568. On the unfair advantage consisting in the transfer of trade mark image (repute) *see* paras 273 et seq. *infra*.
569. *Contra* Bonet, *La protection des marques notoires* ..., p. 202.
570. *See* CFI, 22 March 2007, case T-215/03, *VIPS*, para. 42.
571. Cohen Jehoram, *La protection des marques* ..., p. 225.
572. Yves Reboul, *L'arrêt 'Davidoff' de la Cour de justice des Communautés européennes du 9 janvier 2003: Schisme ... ou 'Yalta' de la protection des marques renommées?*, Propr. ind. 2003, No. 3, comment 17.
573. Promińska, *Własność przemysłowa* ..., pp. 523-523. *See also* Simon Fhima, *Trade Mark Dilution* ..., p. 102. The author argues that it is very doubtful that the likelihood of confusion could prove any form of infringement of the reputed trade mark.

provisions in force in no way provide that the likelihood of confusion can be condemned in the field of the special regime. By contrast, all the draft amendments to the Paris Convention drawn up in the past provided for the likelihood of confusion as a separate case of infringement of the trade mark outside the speciality. The European legislator had to therefore consciously omit to refer to the likelihood of confusion in the field of extended protection. Indeed, if the current legislator admitted the possibility of condemning the likelihood of confusion beyond the speciality, it is difficult to see why this is not expressly mentioned in the provisions.

119. Redundancy. Thus, once the proprietor demonstrates the existence of a likelihood of confusion, his action is justified on the ground of infringement in the speciality and he does not need to have recourse to the special regime for the protection of reputed trade marks. It should be emphasised that a possible accumulation of the grounds on which the decision is pronounced has no influence on the scope of protection of trade marks with a reputation. In civil infringement cases, the right holder can always seek the same sanctions, namely the prohibition of the disputed use and the award of damages. And the amount of the latter may not be higher in the event that the Court upholds the infringement of the reputed trade mark cumulatively with the likelihood of confusion.

In that regard, it should be pointed out that the fact that the likelihood of confusion is not likely to coexist with dilution, as a form of infringement of the trade mark with a reputation enshrined in the special regime, cannot mean that the likelihood of confusion cannot imply a kind of 'trivialisation' or 'vulgarisation' of the trade mark, which is then an element to be taken into account in assessing the damage caused to the proprietor.[574] In particular, where the mark is a mark conveying ideas of exclusivity and its proprietor tends to keep it as a rare sign, the omnipresence of the sign which gives rise to the likelihood of confusion surely harms the exceptional character of the mark. That is what may be characterised as trivialisation or vulgarisation resulting from the likelihood of confusion, which does not then constitute dilution within the meaning of the provisions on extended protection. Similarly, the damage to the image conveyed by the mark may be due to the likelihood of confusion. The depreciation of the mark resulting from the damage to its repute due to the likelihood of confusion is then one of the poles of the damage suffered by the proprietor and must be taken into account for the calculation of compensation for infringement.[575]

The damage to the value of the trade mark can be therefore compensated in the field of infringement within the speciality.[576] The solution is likely to apply both to reputed marks and to ordinary marks which do not enjoy special protection. It is obvious that the latter may have a repute, an image for which the public's error as to the commercial origin is detrimental. They can even be marks of great prestige which

574. In French jurisprudence cf. e.g. CA Paris, 6 October 2004, case 03/09292, *Desperados*; TGI Paris, 14 October 2008, case 06/16051, *Playboy*.

575. Passa, *Contrefaçon et concurrence …*, p. 185.

576. In French jurisprudence cf. Cass. com., 9 February 1999, case 96-19.660, *Conquest*; Cass. com., 18 December 2001, case 99-13.384, *Galway*. *See also* Caroline Rodà, *Les conséquences civiles de la contrefaçon des droits de propriété industrielle*, LexisNexis, Paris 2011, p. 231.

escape the qualification of a trade mark with a reputation because of a low degree of public knowledge. Consequently, the invocation of a trade mark infringement action for likelihood of confusion and an action for infringement of a trade mark with a reputation as a complementary ground is open to criticism. In practice, some right holders may do so in the hope that the courts will allow both and that consequently higher damages will be awarded. The compensation awarded under the first would seek to indemnify the affection of the function of guarantee of origin, due to the likelihood of confusion, while the other would compensate the right holder for the damage to the reputation of his mark. Nevertheless, awarding additional damages on the basis of the special regime would be tantamount to compensating twice for the same damage.[577]

Thus, in the light of Directive 2015/2436 and Regulation 2017/1001, according to which the protection of the trade mark with a reputation is based on the exclusive right,[578] there is no point in introducing the question of the likelihood of confusion into the field of extended protection.

120. Risk of blurring the regimes of trade mark protection. Apart from the risk of double compensation for the same damage in civil infringement cases, it should be noted that condemning an act of trade mark use on the basis of the infringement of the trade mark for likelihood of confusion and the infringement of the reputed trade mark[579] tarnishes the true role and purpose of the special regime. The motivations of some judgments which link the establishment of the various forms of infringement of the reputed trade mark to the existence of a likelihood of confusion are not only redundant. The danger lies in the fact that they may give the impression that the likelihood of confusion, even if it is not necessary in order to establish infringement of the mark with a reputation, would be the main case for benefiting from extended protection, which it is clearly not. The special regime was created in order to strengthen the protection of trade marks in cases where there is no infringement of the trade mark in the speciality.[580] Therefore, case law accepting the accumulation of bases should be abandoned. This approach only makes less clear the protective frameworks and complicates the matters unnecessarily by blurring the two protective regimes.

That being said, the action based on the special regime may be brought on a subsidiary basis. If the Court dismisses the infringement action for lack of likelihood of confusion, it may very well allow the action for usurpation of the reputed trade mark. Thus, we should approve court decisions that do not consider the claim made under the special regime where the action based on the likelihood of confusion is upheld,[581] or decisions granting the action based on the infringement of the reputed trade mark when it is complementary, in cases where the sign at issue has been used for several goods. In such cases, as regards the similar goods, the disputed use is subject to

577. Bouvel, *Étendue de la protection ...*, para. 7.
578. Cf. para. 123 *infra*.
579. Cf. e.g. GC, 7 December 2010, case T-59/08, *La Perla*, paras 50-58.
580. Under American law cf. Casparie-Kerdel, *Dilution Disguised ...*, p. 188.
581. *See* e.g. GC, 5 February 2015, case T-78/13, *Redbull*, para. 61; GC, 17 March 2015, case T-611/11, *Spa*, para. 91.

sanctions on the ground of likelihood of confusion and, outside the speciality, the Court can condemn usurpation of the mark with a reputation.[582]

[C] Legal Nature of the Special Protection

121. Several legal grounds proposed in the past. In the past, several grounds of law were proposed by scholars and implemented by courts in order to ensure a reinforced protection of reputed trade marks, and in particular, as we have seen, the general principles of civil liability or special provisions related to unfair competition but also unjust enrichment,[583] or personality rights.[584]

122. Two mechanisms of protection. In the national legislations of the Member States of the EU, two legal mechanisms on which the special regime is based can be distinguished. One is the exclusive right mechanism, where the infringement of the reputed trade mark constitutes an infringement of the trade mark right enforceable *erga omnes*. The other places the special regime on the basis of tort liability rules. The two mechanisms correspond to the two solutions historically envisaged with a view to amending the Paris Convention. As we have seen, while some authors proposed situating the extended protection within the trade mark rights on the basis of Article 6 bis, others preferred to place it in the field of unfair competition, in Article 10 bis.[585]

123. Exclusive right. Under Directive 2015/2436 and Regulation 2017/1001, the special protection is undoubtedly situated within the scope of the exclusive right. Thus, the European legislature extends the scope of the trade mark right in accordance with the assumptions expressed in the past by, *inter alia*, Troller,[586] Callmann[587] or Perent,[588] to frame special protection by the trade mark exclusive right. The European legislation is therefore more in line with the draft amendments to the Paris Convention aimed at recognising enhanced protection in Article 6 bis, as a component of the trade mark right, and not in Article 10 bis. This being the case, it can be indeed admitted that the European legislator has operated a partial harmonisation of unfair competition rules,[589] in the sense that, in the field of trade mark law, acts classically falling within the scope of tort liability may be condemned. However, the solution is in no way shocking. In the past, national European legislators did the same, like the French

582. Cf. GC, 13 May 2015, case T-363/13, *Clinique*.
583. The theory of unjust enrichment was usually considered insufficient since it did not make it possible to seek prohibition of the disputed use of the mark by the third party. Troller, *La marque de haute renommée* ..., pp. 73 et seq.; Pérot-Morel, *L'extension de la protection* ..., p. 39; Georges Bonet, *Note sous CA Nancy 26 juin 1974*, JCP 1975, p. 18178.
584. In particular under Swiss law, the reputed trade mark was protected on the basis of personality rights. *See* Troller, *Précis du droit de la propriété* ..., p. 98.
585. *See* para. 31 *supra*.
586. Troller, *La marque de haute renommée* ..., pp. 81-82.
587. Callmann, *Unfair Competition* ..., pp. 460 et seq.
588. Perent, *Marques notoirement connues* ..., p. 281.
589. Cf. Laure Marino, *L'affaire l'Oréal: le droit des marques et la publicité comparative sous le sceau du parasitisme*, JCP 2009, No. 31, p. 180. The author considers that the trade mark with a reputation is the Trojan horse of unfair competition in EU law.

legislator in 1857, when they enshrined the exclusive right to a trade mark, which made it possible to condemn, as violating exclusive rights, acts that gave rise to a likelihood of confusion, and thus acts previously punishable on the basis of tort liability.[590] Indeed, under Article 10(1) of Directive 2015/2436 and Article 9(1) of Regulation 2017/1001, the registration of a trade mark shall confer on the proprietor exclusive rights therein. And the infringement of the trade mark with a reputation constitutes one of the three forms of infringement of that exclusive right, pursuant to Article 10(2)(c) of the Directive and Article 9(2)(c) of Regulation 2017/1001.

Placing the protection of the trade mark with a reputation within the exclusive right means that all the provisions of trade mark law are applicable thereto. The right holders may seek compensation for their damage in accordance with the rules provided for in Directive 2004/48,[591] which allows for a derogation from the principle of full compensation since unfair profits made by the infringer are taken into account in calculating damages, have an infringement seizure carried out, invoke the right of information, etc. The limitation period for trade mark infringement actions is the same within and outside the speciality. These actions are also subject to the rule of acquiescence.

In practice, there is a tendency for trade mark owners to regularly rely on extended protection in situations where the common regime could apply and would be perfectly sufficient. This is so because the demonstration of infringement of the reputed trade mark may appear easier than the establishment of infringement for likelihood of confusion. The proprietors sometimes invoke, primarily, the infringement of a mark with a reputation and, in the alternative, the likelihood of confusion, even in the presence of a strong likelihood of similarity between the goods or services in question, or even evidence of actual confusion on the market,[592] or the right holders claim only the infringement of the reputed trade mark in the presence of a likelihood of confusion.[593] This practice is regrettable, as it reverses the logic of the special protection granted to the trade mark with a reputation, which is intended to be complementary to the protection confined within the limits of the principle of speciality.[594] Indeed, the special regime is subsidiary and becomes redundant once the likelihood of confusion is established.[595] In civil infringement proceedings, as observed above, a decision based on two grounds brought in a complementary manner may entail a risk of double compensation for the same act. The claim based on the special regime should therefore be made on a subsidiary basis.[596] Moreover, it seems more prudent to always invoke infringement in the speciality since it is then impossible for the defendant to raise the existence of a due cause, since it may allow to avoid liability

590. *See* para. 7 *supra*.
591. Directive 2004/48/EC of the European Parliament and of the Council of 29 April 2004 on the enforcement of intellectual property rights, Official Journal L 157 of 30 April 2004.
592. GC, 7 December 2010, case T-59/08, *La Perla*, paras 21, 38 and 50.
593. *See* GC, 30 November 2016, case T-2/16, *Prêt à manger*, para. 111.
594. *See* paras 118-120 *supra*.
595. Cf. GC, 1 February 2018, case T-102/17, *Sangre de Toro*, paras 62-63. *See also* CA Bruxelles, 11 March 2016, case 2013/AR/2244, *Kodak*.
596. Cf. Passa, *Traité de droit* ..., p. 521.

on the ground of the special regime, even if, as we shall see, the implementation of this limitation to the trade mark right is not easy in practice.

124. Tort liability. The classical approach was until recently different in particular in France where enhanced protection was traditionally considered to be a specific form of tort liability, uncovered by the exclusive trade mark right.[597] The previous solution of the French legislator to place the protection of the trade mark with a reputation under the regime of tort liability had important consequences. The proprietors of reputed trade marks were a priori deprived of the benefits of the trade mark right regime. Even if the case law applied some rules related to the trade mark exclusive rights in the field of enhanced protection,[598] the implementation of several provisions was problematic. As a consequence, in France, there were differences, difficult to explain, in the protection of national and EU trade marks covered by the trade mark right, pursuant to Regulation 2017/1001.[599]

The idea of situating enhanced protection on the grounds of tort liability could be justified under Directives 89/104 and 2008/95. First, Article 5(2) of those acts was optional for the Member States. Hence, since the Directives provided for a complete harmonisation of the scope of the trade mark right,[600] it could be reasonably argued that the extended protection should not remain within the exclusive rights. If some of the Member States could not implement this provision, this would prevent the scope of the trade mark right from being the same in the national legislations in accordance with the rule of complete harmonisation. Second, Article 5(2) did not refer to the 'exclusive right', contrary to Article 5(1) relating to the protection of the trade mark in the speciality.[601] However, the approach to the special protection adopted by Directive 2015/2436 clearly demonstrates that the trade mark with a reputation must be protected on the basis of the trade mark right.[602] One could argue whether the European legislator has made a real change in the approach to the enhanced protection. In the view of the interpretation of Article 5(2) of Directives 89/104 and 2008/95 in most Member States, it could be considered that it is only the character of the provision on the special regime, which is now mandatory, that changed. In any event, it should

597. *See* Passa, *Traité de droit* ..., p. 504; Pollaud-Dulian, *Propriété intellectuelle. La propriété industrielle* ..., p. 1073. Cf. previous wording of Article L.713-5 of the French Intellectual Property Code.

598. Cf. Cass. com., 20 February 2007, case 04-16.712, *Brasserie de Tahiti*, accepting application of the provisions related to the seizure of goods (*saisie-contrefaçon*) in the field of enhanced protection. On the judgment *see* Pascale Tréfigny, *La saisie-contrefaçon offerte aux marques renommées* ..., Propr. ind. 2007, No. 5, comment 39; Jacques Larrieu, *La saisie-contrefaçon et l'action spéciale en responsabilité civile de l'article L. 713-5 du Code de la propriété intellectuelle*, Propr. ind. 2007, No. 6, comment 58; Passa, *Traité de droit* ..., p. 550. Regarding the rule of acquiescence cf. Cass. com., 6 January 2015, case 13-21.940, *Paris-Match*. On the judgment *see* Jacques Azéma, *Protection des marques renommées*, RTD com. 2015, No. 2, p. 270; Julien Canlorbe, in: *Droit des marques et autres signes distinctifs. Chroniques*, Propr. intell. 2015, No. 57, p. 438.

599. *See* Passa, *Traité de droit* ..., p. 552.

600. Cf. CJ, 20 November 2001, cases C-414/99 to C-416/99, para. 39.

601. Passa, *Traité de droit* ..., p. 553.

602. *See* Basire, *Les fonctions de la marque* ..., p. 275; Yann Basire, *La réforme du droit des marques en Europe: quid novi?*, Europe 2016, No. 5, étude 4, para. 10.

be pointed out that the Court of Justice never suggested that the protection of the trade mark with a reputation is outside the exclusive right. It should be concluded that, in the light of the clear wording of Directive 2015/2436, the trade mark with a reputation must be protected by the trade mark right, which implies the application of all rules relating thereto. Thus, the recourse to tort liability mechanism, incompatible with Directive 2015/2436, was rightly abandoned by the French legislator, which currently places the special protection within the exclusive trade mark right.[603]

603. *See* new wording of Article L.713-3 of the French Intellectual Property Code.

CHAPTER 2

Conditions for Infringement Common to All Forms of Infringement of Trade Marks with a Reputation

125. Positive and negative conditions. There are conditions common to all forms of infringement of trade marks with a reputation. Among these, a distinction shall be made between positive conditions, the existence of which is necessary for the establishment of the infringement (§2.01) and negative conditions, the existence of which excludes the infringement (§2.02). The former are preliminary conditions that precede the demonstration of the types of infringement of the reputed trade mark. They must be established by the right holder who invokes the special protection. The negative conditions are taken into account once an infringement is established a priori. The burden of proof then lies with the defendant.

§2.01 POSITIVE CONDITIONS FOR INFRINGEMENT OF TRADE MARKS WITH A REPUTATION

126. General and specific conditions. In order to condemn a use of a sign under the special regime, it must be an act of use likely to characterise trade mark infringement in general (§2.01[A]). In the case of trade marks with a reputation, there is an additional prerequisite. It is necessary to establish the existence of a 'link' between the reputed trade mark relied on and the contested sign at issue (§2.01[B]).

[A] Use of the Disputed Sign Likely to Cause Trade Mark Infringement

127. Use in the course of trade, use as a trade mark, trade mark functions. The disputed use must meet certain general conditions for trade mark infringement. First, such use must be made without the consent of the trade mark proprietor, as expressly provided for in Article 10(2) of Directive 2015/2436 and Article 9(2) of Regulation

2017/1001. Second, this use must be performed in the course of trade (§2.01[A][1]) and as a trade mark (§2.01[A][2]). After examining those conditions for trade mark infringement resulting from the legal provisions, I will address the question of whether the infringement of a trade mark with a reputation requires the affection of a trade mark function, in the light of the jurisprudence of the Court of Justice recognising several functions of the mark (§2.01[A][3]).

[1] Use of the Disputed Sign in the Course of Trade

128. Concept of use in the course of trade. Pursuant to Article 10(2) of Directive 2015/2436 and Article 9(2) of Regulation 2017/1001, the scope of trade mark rights is limited to acts of use performed 'in the course of trade'. The solution is justified because a mark that is not commercially exploited cannot fulfil its functions[604] and the role assigned to the mark is exclusively of an economic nature.[605] According to the *Arsenal* judgment, 'the use of the sign identical to the mark is indeed use in the course of trade, since it takes place in the context of commercial activity with a view to economic advantage and not as a private matter'.[606] The Court of Justice referred to this definition on several occasions in its subsequent case law.[607] Thus, the act of use must be performed in an economic context. It should be noted that the interpretation of the notion of use in the course of trade must be broad.[608] The search for profit is not decisive for the qualification of use in the course of trade.[609]

By contrast, the demonstration of an economic damage is not sufficient to consider that the act was committed in the course of trade. It should be specified that trade mark use in the course of trade must be related to the marketing of a good or the provision of a service.[610] There are cases in which use of a mark is clearly not related

604. Jérôme Passa, *Les conditions générales d'une atteinte au droit sur une marque*, Propr. ind. 2005, No. 2, étude 2, para. 3.
605. Julien Canlorbe, *L'usage dans la vie des affaires, condition nécessaire de la contrefaçon des marques*, Légicom 2010/1, No. 44, p. 109.
606. CJ, 12 November 2002, case C-206/01, *Arsenal*, para. 40. On this formula *see* Jérôme Passa, in: Michel Vivant (ed.), *Les grands arrêts de la propriété intellectuelle*, 2nd ed., Dalloz, Paris 2015, p. 595.
607. *See* CJ, 16 November 2004, case C-245/02, *Anheuser-Busch*, para. 62; CJ, 25 January 2007, case C-48/05, *Opel*, para. 18; CJ, 11 September 2007, case C-17/06, *Céline*, para. 17; CJ, 12 June 2008, case C-533/06, *02 Holdings*, para. 60. According to the Court of Justice, the condition laid down in Article 16 of the TRIPS Agreement, pursuant to which the use must be made 'in the course of trade' (in the other authentic language versions in French and Spanish – '*au cours d'opérations commerciales*', '*en el curso de operaciones comerciales*') appears to correspond to that laid down in the Directive. CJ, 16 November 2004, case C-245/02, *Anheuser-Busch*, para. 73. One might argue that the formula used in the French version of the TRIPS Agreement (*au cours d'opérations commerciales*) is literally narrower. Passa, *Les conditions générales* ..., para. 4; José Monteiro, Vincent Ruzek, *L'usage du signe à des fins autres que celle de distinguer les produits et services d'un opérateur économique*, Propr. ind. 2007, No. 4, étude 9, para. 9.
608. The test of use in the course of trade is therefore a low threshold. Senftleben, *European Trade Mark* ..., p. 279.
609. A non-profit association may commit trade mark infringement. Passa, *Les grands arrêts* ..., p. 596; Szczepanowska-Kozłowska, *System prawa handlowego* ..., p. 688. Cf. Canlorbe, *L'usage dans la vie des affaires* ..., p. 111.
610. Skubisz, *System prawa prywatnego* ..., p. 1068.

to the marketing of a good or the provision of a service. Infringement is then excluded even if the right holder suffers an economic damage.[611] That being said, it is not necessary for the disputed act to consist in putting the sign in contact with the clientele, to exploit it outside the private sphere of the company, in order to be accomplished in the course of trade. Acts of reproduction or imitation performed in the phase of manufacturing or promotion of the disputed goods before their offer to the public, or the preparation of services, are already performed in the course of trade, as is the use of the sign in a relationship between two professionals without a public offer of goods or services under this sign.[612] Acts preparatory to the placing of a good on the market may constitute acts of trade mark infringement. Article 10(3) of Directive 2015/2436 and Article 9(3) of Regulation 2017/1001 that provide an illustrative list of prohibited acts likely to amount to infringement[613] show that this general condition for bringing an action for trade mark infringement applies both to acts involving contact between the trade mark and customers and to acts which do not involve any communication of the sign to the public, such as the mere affixing of the sign or stocking of the goods bearing the mark.[614] There is, however, no doubt that the use likely to be qualified as infringement refers exclusively to active behaviour on the part of the third party.[615]

129. Filing an application for trade mark registration. With regard to the acts preceding the marketing of marked products, attention should be drawn to the possibility of committing trade mark infringement by filing an application for registration. This is a controversial issue which is assessed differently by doctrine and case law in different Member States. In France, the courts traditionally qualify the mere application for registration as an act of use made in the course of trade with a view of deriving an economic advantage from the mark.[616] This approach was approved by many authors.[617] The question is however disputed nowadays since some courts consider that in the light of the case law of the Court of Justice, the mere filing of a trade mark does not constitute use of a trade mark in the course of trade.[618] It seems that in

611. *See* Canlorbe, *L'usage dans la vie des affaires ...*, pp. 111-112. Cf. opinion of Advocate General Ruiz-Jarabo Colomer in case C-206/01, *Arsenal*, para. 62, according to which: 'The use which the proprietor of the trade mark may prevent is not any that might constitute a material advantage for the user, or even a use which is capable of being expressed in economic terms, but only ... use which occurs in the world of business, in trade, the subject of which is, precisely, the distribution of goods and services in the market.'
612. Passa, *Les conditions générales ...*, para. 7.
613. Cf. Senftleben, *European Trade Mark ...*, pp. 368 et seq. There is no doubt that the list is not exhaustive. CJ, 12 November 2002, case C-206/01, *Arsenal*, para. 38.
614. Canlorbe, *L'usage dans la vie des affaires ...*, p. 110. Cf. also Jérôme Passa, *La contrefaçon de marque et l'exigence d'une mise dans le commerce*, Propr. ind. 2008, No. 5, étude 10, para. 1.
615. CJ, 3 March 2016, case C-179/15, *Mercedes-Benz*, para. 40.
616. Recently *see* Cass. com., 24 May 2016, case 14-17.533, Propr. intell. 2016, No. 60, p. 357, comment of Julien Canlorbe, RTD com. 2016, No. 4, p. 729, comment of Jacques Azéma, *I-Message*.
617. Mathély, *Le droit français des signes ...*, p. 628; Paul Mathély, *La protection de la marque renommée*, Ann. propr. ind. 1996, p. 32. *See also* Azéma, *Droit de la propriété ...*, p. 850; Passa, *Traité de droit ...*, pp. 532-533; Michel Vivant, *Prendre la contrefaçon au sérieux*, D. 2009, No. 25, p. 1839, para. 6; Canlorbe, *L'usage dans la vie des affaires ...*, p. 111.
618. For the first time TGI Paris, 20 September 2011, case 10/10320, *Aventis*. The judgment was annulled by the Court of Appeal, CA Paris, 30 November 2012, case 11/22840. The opinion was

most countries, including Italy[619] and Poland,[620] filing a trade mark application is not considered to be an act of use made in the course of trade. The harmonisation of trade mark law resulting from the Directive rules out such a divergence. Having regard to the objective of complete harmonisation of the exclusive trade mark right, it is unacceptable that one act could be regarded as infringing in one Member State and not in another one. It is of course for the Court of Justice to rule and decide on the matter.

It seems that filing an application for registration is not an act of use made in the course of trade in the light of Directive 2015/2436 and Regulation 2017/1001. It should be noted that all the acts referred to in Article 10(3) of Directive 2015/2436 and Article 9(3) of Regulation 2017/1001 either involve bringing the sign designating a good or service into contact with customers, such as offering, placing on the market, using the sign in business papers or advertising, or are non-public acts concerning a particular product which precede the marketing of the latter, such as affixing the sign, holding, importing or exporting marked goods. Admittedly, as we have seen, the list of acts of trade mark use is not exhaustive. However, it does allow to characterise what types of acts are covered by the notion of use of a trade mark in the course of trade. These are acts which involve bringing the sign into contact with the public or acts preceding the marketing of a product designated by the sign. The act of filing a trade mark application is neither. When the mark does not appear in the eyes of the public, all the acts preceding marketing referred to in Article 10(3) of Directive 2015/2436 and Article 9(3) of Regulation 2017/1001 are linked to the future marketing of an existing physical product bearing the trade mark. By contrast, in the case of a mere filing, there is no physical product. It cannot therefore be an act preceding its actual marketing. Moreover, the filing of a trade mark application does not seem to constitute an act of use made as a trade mark, as long as the mere filing is not made in order to distinguish goods or services.[621] As we shall see, a sign is used as a trade mark when it individualises goods or services by linking them to a commercial origin and when it is used in connection with the current or future offer of those goods or services to customers.[622] A simple filing is not likely to indicate to the public the origin of any good or service. The designation of a good or service in the application for registration in no way implies that the sign will actually be used for that good or service.[623] Indeed, the use of a trade mark is entirely independent of its registration. It must be noted that, in the event of registration, there is no offer, even potential, for a good or service bearing the trade mark. The above reasoning seems confirmed by the case law of the General

however repeated in TGI Paris, 5 November 2015, case 13/18435. Cf. Jacques Azéma, *Portée du droit de marque*, RTD com. 2015, No. 2, p. 267; Jacques Azéma, *Existence de la contrefaçon de marque*, RTD com. 2016, No. 4, p. 729. The author agrees with the final outcome of the decisions.

619. *See* Sironi, *Codice della proprietà* ..., p. 301. Cf. Ricolfi, *Trattato dei marchi* ..., pp. 1119-1120.
620. *See* Skubisz, *System prawa prywatnego* ..., p. 1092; Szczepanowska-Kozłowska, *System prawa handlowego* ..., p. 720.
621. Szczepanowska-Kozłowska, *System prawa handlowego* ..., p. 720.
622. Passa, *Traité de droit* ..., p. 295. *See* paras 131 et seq. *infra*.
623. Cf. regarding registration of a company name, Passa, *Traité de droit* ..., p. 308.

Court which made a clear distinction between an application for registration and use of the mark.[624]

130. Removal of the trade mark from the goods. Another controversial situation which is not mentioned by the provisions of Directive 2015/2436 and Regulation 2017/1001 is the case of removing the trade mark from the goods by the third party, often referred to as 'de-branding'. It is uncertain whether such an action is an act of use of the mark in the course of trade, or even an act of 'use' of the mark as such likely to be qualified as infringement. Unlike Directive and Regulation, some national legislations expressly provide that removing a mark is an act of infringement.[625] However, such national provisions could be considered contrary to Directive 2015/2436 if de-branding should not be qualified as use within the meaning of its provisions. Admittedly, the list of the types of use considered as infringement indicated in the Directive is not exhaustive.[626] However, the Directive 'carries out a complete harmonisation and defines the exclusive rights of trade mark proprietors' in the EU; its objective is to ensure 'that the trade mark proprietor enjoys the same protection under the legal systems of all the Member States'.[627] Therefore, national legislators do not have the freedom of broadening the concept of use infringing exclusive trade mark rights.[628] If removing a mark is not an act of use in the light of the Directive, such national provisions of trade mark laws are contrary to the EU law.[629]

The Court of Justice has already decided in the *Mitsubishi* judgment that an operation consisting, on the part of the third party, of removing signs identical to the trade mark in order to affix its own signs may be regarded as a use in the course of trade.[630] However, this ruling expressly concerns cases where de-branding regards products placed in the customs warehouse with a view to importing them or trading them in the European Economic Area (EEA) where they have never yet been marketed. Therefore, some authors believe that this judgment applies only to this very specific situation and does not prevent from considering that removing a mark is not an act of infringing use.[631] One could argue that the reasoning of the *Mitsubishi* judgment regarding the affection of the trade mark functions could also apply in cases of removal

---

624. GC, 7 May 2013, case T-579/10, *Makro*, para. 86.
625. *See* in particular Article L.713-3-1, pt. 7 of the French Intellectual Property Code.
626. CJ, 12 November 2002, case C-206/01, *Arsenal*, para. 38; CJ, 3 March 2016, case C-179/15, *Mercedes-Benz*, para. 40.
627. CJ, 12 November 2002, case C-206/01, *Arsenal*, paras 43-44.
628. *Contra* Fabio Angelini, Simone Verducci Galletti, *If You Remove It, You Use It: The Court of Justice of the European Union on Debranding – On the Mitsubishi v. Duma Judgment by the Court of Justice of the European Union*, TMR 2019, vol. 109, No. 5, p. 876. The authors consider that the absence of provisions in the Directive allows the Member States to provide rules not harmonised with the rest of the other Member States. This can be deduced from the opinion of Advocate General Campos Sánchez Bordona in case C-129/17, *Mitsubishi*, paras 61-66.
629. Cf. Passa, *Traité de droit …*, pp. 370-371. The author considers that the French provisions are therefore contrary to the Directive.
630. CJ, 25 July 2018, case C-129/17, *Mitsubishi*, para. 48. Cf. critics of the decision by Annette Kur, *Trademark Functions in European Union Law: Also Containing a Comment on CJEU case C-129/17, Mitsubishi v. Duma*, Max Planck Institute for Innovation & Competition Research Paper 2019, No. 19-06, pp. 18-22.
631. Jérôme Passa, *Contrefaçon de marque par suppression?*, RTD com. 2019, No. 2, p. 379.

of trade marks per se, although the Court of Justice expressly links it with the right of the proprietor to control the initial marketing in the EEA of goods bearing the mark.[632] Furthermore, the jurisprudence of the Court of Justice could seem somewhat inconsistent if the removal of the mark was not considered to be an act of infringement in case of goods already marketed in the EEA whereas, in the *Mitsubishi* judgment, an operation consisting of removing the mark was expressly qualified as use in the course of trade within the meaning of the Directive.[633] However, when the goods have been put on the market in the EEA under the trade mark by the proprietor or with his consent, the issue of qualifying de-branding as use might become irrelevant if the removal of the trade mark constitutes a 'legitimate reason' preventing the effect of exhaustion, within the meaning of Article 15(2) of Directive 2015/2436 and Article 15(2) of Regulation 2017/1001, assuming that this would make it possible to base the action for infringement on those provisions. The solution seems legitimate.[634] The jurisprudence of the Court of Justice does not preclude it,[635] but de-branding as such has not yet been expressly recognised as a legitimate reason.[636] Therefore, if the removal of the mark did not allow bringing an action for infringement on the ground of the provisions limiting exhaustion, the Court of Justice should rule whether by further marketing de-branded products, already put on the market in the EEA by the right holder or with his consent, the third party commits an act of trade mark use in the course of trade.

[2] Use of the Disputed Sign as a Trade Mark

131. Concept of use as a trade mark. In the light of Article 10(2) of Directive 2015/2436 and Article 9(2) of Regulation 2017/1001, even when used in the course of trade, a sign is only likely to infringe a trade mark right if it is used 'in relation to goods or services', hence 'as a trade mark'. This means that the sign must be used to designate goods or services and to link them to a commercial origin by distinguishing them from other goods or services.[637] Indeed, in some situations, the sign is used in an

632. *See* CJ, 25 July 2018, case C-129/17, *Mitsubishi*, paras 42-47.
633. In favour, as it seems, of the idea that removal of a mark from a good already marketed in the EEA should constitute an act of infringement cf. Angelini, Verducci Galletti, *If You Remove* ..., p. 885.
634. In favour of the idea that de-branding is a legitimate reason limiting the effect of exhaustion *see* Krystyna Szczepanowska-Kozłowska, *Wyczerpanie praw własności przemysłowej. Patent i prawo ochronne na znak towarowy*, C.H. Beck, Warsaw 2003, p. 317.
635. Cf. CJ, 26 April 2007, case C-348/04, *Boehringer II*, para. 45; CJ, 8 July 2010, case C-558/08, *Portakabin*, para. 86. On de-branding in the light of the *Portakabin* ruling cf. Senftleben, *European Trade Mark* ..., pp. 277-278.
636. It may be, however, deduced from the *Viking Gas* judgment which suggests that masking the origin is likely to alter the condition of the good, which constitutes a legitimate reason. CJ, 14 July 2011, case C-46/10, *Viking Gas*, para. 41.
637. *See* Schmidt-Szalewski, *Droit de la propriété* ..., p. 243; Passa, *Les conditions générales* ..., para. 11; Passa, *Traité de droit* ..., pp. 531-532; Pollaud-Dulian, *Propriété intellectuelle. La propriété industrielle* ..., p. 948; Skubisz, *System prawa prywatnego* ..., p. 1073; Szczepanowska-Kozłowska, *System prawa handlowego* ..., p. 683.

economic context but is not perceived by the public as a sign indicating the commercial origin of a good or service.[638]

For the first time, this condition for trade mark infringement was formulated by the Court of Justice in a judgment delivered on 23 February 1999 in the *BMW* case, according to which the use of a sign likely to infringe a trade mark, pursuant to Article 5(1) and (2) of Directive 89/104, must be made 'for the purpose of distinguishing the goods or services in question as originating from a particular undertaking, that is to say, as a trade mark as such, or whether it is used for other purposes'.[639] The Court of Justice reaffirmed that use as a trade mark is a condition of infringement in several subsequent decisions.[640]

It should be stressed that use as a trade mark does not need to result in public use of the sign. Indeed, as we have seen, Article 10(3) of Directive 2015/2436 and Article 9(3) of Regulation 2017/1001 expressly prohibit acts that are not of a public nature, such as acts preceding the marketing of marked goods.[641] What matters is that the sign can later be perceived as a trade mark.[642] It should also be noted that trade mark infringement may consist of an act that is not related to the marketing of concrete copies of a product, such as use in advertising or business papers.[643] Nevertheless, any use must be made in connection with a good or service that allows the public to perceive the sign as indicating the commercial origin of that good or service.

The sign is therefore used as a trade mark when it identifies goods or services by linking them to a commercial origin and when it is used in connection with their current or future offer to customers.[644] Although, in principle, most authors and courts agree that use as a trade mark is *a sine qua non* condition for infringement, the interpretation of this condition varies and therefore its implementation may pose difficulties.

132. Excessively broad interpretations. The condition of use as a trade mark is sometimes interpreted very broadly. Some authors suggest that it would be sufficient for the sign to be perceived as an 'allusion' to a trade mark of another undertaking.[645]

---

638. *See* Passa, *Traité de droit* ..., p. 534. This is the case, e.g., when the mark is used exclusively: as decoration (CA Paris, 17 May 2013, case 11/22637, *Moulin rouge*); as the title of a work (CA Paris, 28 May 2010, case 08/15425, *Lui*); in its current sense (TGI Strasbourg, 15 December 2003, case 02/03781, *Maman je t'aime*); or as a trade name if such use is not likely to characterise at the same time a use as a trade mark (TGI Paris, 25 September 2014, case 14/00145, *Vip Room*), etc.
639. CJ, 23 February 1999, case C-63/97, *BMW*, para. 38. *See* Schmidt-Szalewski, *Droit de la propriété* ..., p. 243.
640. *See* in particular CJ, 16 November 2004, case C-245/02, *Anheuser-Busch*, para. 60; CJ, 11 September 2007, case C-17/06, *Céline*, para. 27; CJ, 19 February 2009, case C-62/08, *UDV North America*, para. 42.
641. Cf. para. 128 *supra*.
642. Cf. Canlorbe, *L'usage de la marque* ..., p. 142.
643. Szczepanowska-Kozłowska, *System prawa handlowego* ..., p. 682.
644. Passa, *Traité de droit* ..., p. 295.
645. *See* Patrice de Candé, *Amélioration de la protection des marques renommées depuis les arrêts 'Davidoff' et 'Adidas' de la Cour de justice des Communautés européennes*, Propr. ind. 2004, No. 4, chron. 7. The author made this remark with respect to the infringement of the reputed trade mark, but, as we shall see, the condition of use as a trade mark applies in the field of the special regime in the same way.

It was observed that, in the view of the *Céline* judgment, according to which use is made in relation to goods or services where the third party uses the sign in such a way that a link is established between the sign and the goods marketed or the services provided by the third party,[646] a sign is used as a trade mark when the public associates the sign with the owner's good or service. In most cases, the mark would remind customers of the goods or services designated by them. Consequently, the use of signs which would not be made in relation to goods or services, within the meaning of the Directive, would be very rare.[647] This interpretation of the *Céline* decision seems too liberal. The link referred to by the Court of Justice in this decision means that a sign can be perceived by the consumer as a trade mark even if it is not affixed to the good. However, it is explicitly stated in the judgment that this needs to be a link between the sign and 'the goods marketed or the services provided by the third party'.[648] The public must therefore perceive the disputed sign as designating the commercial origin of the good marketed or the service provided by the infringer.[649] This interpretation was recently reaffirmed by the Court of Justice which stated that the wording 'in relation to goods or services' relates, in principle, to goods or services of a third party who uses a sign identical (or similar) with the mark.[650] Thus, it is not sufficient that the sign simply reminds the consumer of the good or service of the trade mark's proprietor or that it is perceived by the public as an 'allusion' to the trade mark.

That said, it should be noted that in the light of the *O2 Holdings* decision, the disputed sign may be used to designate a good or service of the trade mark owner. Such use then characterises use as a trade mark.[651] However, this is a particular solution adopted in the field of comparative advertising.[652] The particularity of this form of trade mark exploitation is that the third party uses another's trade mark to designate the owner's good but at the same time, indirectly, also to promote his own product, an identical good, marketed by himself.[653] It is therefore not a question of establishing a simple association between the trade mark and the good of the owner designated by that trade mark in the minds of the public. Another particular situation was the subject of the *BMW* judgment, according to which the use of a mark designating goods to identify their source by an advertiser providing services related to those goods, characterises use as a trade mark. The Court of Justice noted that the use of the trade mark in question was 'undoubtedly intended to distinguish the subject of the services

646. CJ, 11 September 2007, case C-17/06, *Céline*, para. 23.
647. Krystyna Szczepanowska-Kozłowska, *Swoboda wypowiedzi a prawo ochronne na znak towarowy*, ZNUJ 2013, No. 119, p. 12. In this respect cf. also Senftleben, *European Trade Mark ...*, pp. 290-291, who seems to adopt a broad interpretation of the condition of link resulting from the *Céline* decision.
648. CJ, 11 September 2007, case C-17/06, *Céline*, para. 23.
649. In this direction Passa, *Les grands arrêts ...*, p. 597.
650. CJ, 11 April 2019, case C-690/17, *ÖKO-Test*, para. 29. *See also* para. 35 of the judgment.
651. Cf. also regarding the judgment CJ, 14 May 2002, case C-2/00, *Hölterhoff*, Jérôme Passa, *L'usage de la marque d'un tiers pour décrire les caractéristiques de produits concurrents*, D. 2002, No. 41, p. 3137, para. 4.
652. CJ, 12 June 2008, case C-533/06, *O2 Holdings*, para. 33.
653. In this direction also Passa, *Les grands arrêts ...*, p. 597. Cf. also Ricolfi, *Trattato dei marchi ...*, pp. 1152-1155, and further Albert Chavanne, *Le délit d'usage de marque et son évolution*, in: *Mélanges dédiés à Paul Mathély*, Litec, Paris 1990, p. 106.

provided'.[654] In such case, there is a specific link between the service provided by the third party and the holder's good which is the subject of that service, what the Court of Justice specified in the *Opel* judgment.[655] Thus, as the Court recently reaffirmed in the *ÖKO-Test* decision, use of the sign by the third party to identify the goods of the trade mark proprietor can only 'exceptionally' constitute infringement.[656] Other specific situations can be found in the case law relating to the use of marks on the Internet as keywords.[657]

Therefore, it can certainly be considered that the Court of Justice established a broader approach than that adopted traditionally in some European countries with regard to the condition of use as a trade mark.[658] Nevertheless, apart from the specific cases mentioned above, in which there is a particular relationship between the goods or services of the proprietor and the third party, in accordance with the *Opel* and *Céline* judgments, the use of a sign likely to infringe a trade mark must be made for 'the goods marketed or the services provided by the third party'.[659] In principle, the condition of use as a trade mark is therefore met when the infringer uses a sign reproducing or imitating another person's trade mark to distinguish a good marketed or a service provided by himself.

133. Excessively narrow interpretations. The requirement of use as a trade mark is sometimes interpreted too restrictively, which leads to questionable solutions. An illustration can be found in a decision of the Paris Court of Appeal of 21 November 2012.[660] In the case in question, the trade mark *Galliano*, registered in relation to clothing, was used by a manufacturer of bags, as the name of one of the models of bag marketed on its website. It seems that the mark was used to designate a good, in this case a bag of the third party, as coming from a specific company.[661] It should be pointed out that the fact that the third party uses its own mark to indicate the commercial origin

654. CJ, 23 February 1999, case C-63/97, *BMW*, para. 39.

655. CJ, 25 January 2007, case C-48/05, *Opel*, para. 27: 'the vehicles marketed under the BMW trade mark by the proprietor of that mark constituted the subject-matter of the services – the repairing of vehicles – supplied by the third party, so that it was essential to identify the origin of the BMW cars, the subject-matter of those services. It was having regard to that specific and indissociable link between the products bearing the trade mark and the services provided by the third party that the Court of Justice held that, in the specific circumstances of the BMW case, use by the third party of the sign identical to the trade mark in respect of goods marketed not by the third party but by the holder of the trade mark fell within Article 5(1)(a) of the directive'.

656. CJ, 11 April 2019, case C-690/17, *ÖKO-Test*, para. 31.

657. *See* e.g. CJ, 19 February 2009, case C-62/08, *UDV North America*.

658. Cf. Krystyna Szczepanowska-Kozłowska, *Używanie firmy jako naruszenie prawa ochronnego na znak towarowy*, PPH 2008, No. 10, p. 10.

659. CJ, 25 January 2007, case C-48/05, *Opel*, para. 28; CJ, 11 September 2007, case C-17/06, *Céline*, para. 23.

660. CA Paris, 21 November 2012, case 11/11544, *Galliano*.

661. Cf. Julien Canlorbe, *Contrefaçon de marque. Usage illicite de la marque*, Fascicule 7513, JurisClasseur 2016, para. 63. The author considers that the name *Galliano* was not used as a trade mark but also criticises the decision. Similarly, Azéma finds it harsh and wonders whether the use in question did not affect one of the new functions of the trade mark, communication, investment and advertising, recognised by the Court of Justice. Jacques Azéma, *Défaut de distinctivité de la marque*, RTD com. 2013, No. 4, p. 693.

of its goods or services in no way implies that another sign used cannot also be perceived by the public as a trade mark. While, in principle, it can be assumed that it is the mark of the third party that will identify the origin of its goods,[662] it cannot be excluded that the public may not perceive the other mark as such at the same time and therefore not believe that the third party and the right holder claiming the infringement are economically linked. Indeed, in the *Galliano* case, it seems, the third party's customers could believe in the existence of commercial relations between the third party and the proprietor of the *Galliano* trade mark that the third party's good was manufactured with the consent of the right holder, that it therefore came from the proprietor of the mark in the broad sense of the term. It seems reasonable to accept that, where a sign is used to promote a good marketed by the third party, it is used as a trade mark.[663]

134. Application under the special regime. It should be stressed that the requirement of use as a trade mark applies perfectly in the field of the special regime. Several authors point out that use as a trade mark is *a sine qua non* condition for any infringement of the trade mark rights, including the infringement of reputed trade marks.[664]

Indeed, pursuant to Article 10(6) of Directive 2015/2436, to which Article 5(5) of Directives 89/104 and 2008/95 corresponded, 'Paragraphs 1, 2, 3 and 5 shall not affect provisions in any Member State relating to the protection against the use of a sign other than use for the purposes of distinguishing goods or services, where use of that sign without due cause takes unfair advantage of, or is detrimental to, the distinctive character or the repute of the trade mark.' Article 10(6) therefore makes it possible to protect a reputed trade mark against its use for purposes other than to distinguish goods or services.[665] It thus clearly follows from Article 10(6) that the acts infringing the trade mark rights referred to in the Directive in Article 10(2) must be carried out in order to distinguish goods or services, hence as a trade mark.[666]

---

662. Cf. Passa, *Traité de droit ...*, p. 313.
663. In this direction in French jurisprudence CA Paris, 11 December 2015, case 14/23109, *Ricard*.
664. Po Jen Yap, *Making Sense of Trade Mark Use*, EIPR 2007, vol. 29, No. 10, p. 425; Canlorbe, *L'usage de la marque ...*, pp. 136, 143; Passa, *Traité de droit ...*, p. 531; Pollaud-Dulian, *Propriété intellectuelle. La propriété industrielle ...*, p. 1076; Skubisz, *System prawa prywatnego ...*, pp. 1076-1077; Basire, *Les fonctions de la marque ...*, p. 285; Szczepanowska-Kozłowska, *System prawa handlowego ...*, p. 683. On the condition of use as a trade mark in relation to famous marks in American and Australian law cf. Mark Davison, Frank Di Giantomasso, *Use as a Trade Mark: Avoiding Confusion when Considering Dilution*, EIPR 2009, vol. 31, No. 9, p. 443.
665. Joanna Schmidt-Szalewski, *Notion d'usage contrefaisant d'une marque*, RTD eur. 2007, No. 4, p. 689. *See also* Georges Bonet, *Protection d'un signe constituant une marque renommée contre l'usage qui en est fait par un tiers non autorisé à des fins autres que la distinction de produits ou services*, RTD eur. 2004, No. 1, p. 119. This provision was, in particular, transposed in Benelux law. *See* Article 2.20(2)(d) of the Benelux Convention on Intellectual Property. Under Italian law cf. Ricolfi, *Trattato dei marchi ...*, p. 1143.
666. Cesare Galli, *I limiti di protezione dei marchi rinomati nella giurisprudenza della Corte di Giustizia C.E.*, Riv. Dir. Ind. 2004, II, p. 140; Monteiro, Ruzek, *L'usage du signe à des fins ...*, para. 57; Yap, *Making Sense ...*, p. 425; Łukasz Żelechowski, *Funkcje znaku towarowego a naruszenie prawa ochronnego na znak towarowy (cz. I)*, PPH 2015, No. 5, p. 7.

The importance of the condition of use as a trade mark in the field of enhanced protection is confirmed by an abundant jurisprudence of the Court of Justice. Already in the *BMW* judgment, the Court noted that the infringing use must be made 'for the purpose of distinguishing the goods or services in question as originating from a particular undertaking, that is to say, as a trade mark as such' and that this allows to distinguish the scope of application of Article 5(1) and (2) of Directive 89/104, on the one hand, and Article 5(5), on the other.[667] Moreover, in the *Adidas* judgment, rendered precisely under Article 5(2) of Directive 89/104, the Court of Justice ruled that it is only when the relevant section of the public views the sign purely as an embellishment that the infringement cannot be established.[668] A sign may nevertheless be considered at the same time as indicating the commercial origin of a good or service. This means that the regime of protection is applicable even though the disputed sign is perceived as a decoration if it is also perceived as an indication of a commercial origin.[669] Thus, it follows from the judgment that use as a trade mark is indeed a condition of infringement of a trade mark with a reputation.[670]

It should be noted that some authors dispute the application of the condition of use of the sign as a trade mark in the field of the special regime, in particular, arguing that, in part of its decisions, starting with the famous *Arsenal* judgment,[671] the Court of Justice emphasises the need to affect one of the functions of the trade mark. Since the functions of the trade mark are not limited to the origin function, the perception of the

667. CJ, 23 February 1999, case C-63/97, *BMW*, para. 38. *See also* CJ, 11 September 2007, case C-17/06, *Céline*, para. 20.
668. CJ, 23 October 2003, case C-408/01, *Adidas*, para. 40. Cf. CJ, 10 April 2008, case C-102/07, *Adidas*.
669. Passa, *Traité de droit ...*, p. 535. Cf. Georges Bonet, *Du risque de confusion par l'utilisation d'un signe ressemblant à celui d'une marque renommée*, RTD eur. 2004, No. 4, p. 706.
670. Yap, *Making Sense ...*, p. 425; Po Jen Yap, *Essential Function of a Trade Mark: From BMW to O2*, EIPR 2009, vol. 31, No. 2, p. 84. *Contra* Ilanah Simon, *Embellishment: Trade Mark Use Triumph or Decorative Disaster?*, EIPR 2006, vol. 28, No. 6, pp. 324-328; Gielen, *Trademark Dilution under European Law ...*, p. 709. The authors point out that the Court does not make explicit reference to the use of the sign as a trade mark as a condition of trade mark infringement. Cf. also Sironi, *Codice della proprietà ...*, p. 307. The requirement of use as a trade mark under the regime of enhanced protection of reputed trade marks is applied, in accordance with the jurisprudence of the Court of Justice, by the French Court of Cassation. Cass. com., 20 February 2007, case 05-10.319, Comm. com. électr. 2007, comment 93, of Christophe Caron, *Décathlon*; Cass. com., 11 March 2008, case 06-15.594, Bull. civ. IV, No. 60, D. 2008, p. 917, comment of Jeanne Daleau, Propr. intell. 2008, No. 28, p. 360, comment of Jérome Passa, Propr. ind. 2008, comment 39, of Pascale Tréfigny-Goy, *Louis Vuitton*. *See also* CA Lyon, 17 June 2014, case 13/03461, *Poste*. Cf. Jacques Azéma, *Usage de la dénomination dans son sens commun*, RTD com. 2014, No. 4, p. 795.
671. CJ, 12 November 2002, case C-206/01. The judgment, being imprecise, raised several doubts and was the subject of much criticism in doctrine. *See* Passa, *L'usage de marque dans la jurisprudence récente ...*, p. 197; Patrice de Candé, *L'usage d'un signe à titre de marque*, D. 2003, No. 11, p. 755; Canlorbe, *L'usage de la marque ...*, p. 166; Andrew Griffiths, *The Trade Mark Monopoly: An Analysis of the Core Zone of Absolute Protection under Art.5(1)(a)*, IPQ 2007, No. 3, p. 343; Szczepanowska-Kozłowska, *Używanie firmy jako naruszenie ...*, p. 8. In addition, the judgment led to divergences in the case law. Two different British courts have drawn completely different conclusions from this decision regarding the use of the sign as a trade mark as a condition of trade mark infringement. *See* Yap, *Making Sense ...*, pp. 422-423.

sign as an indication of source would not be essential in order to establish infringement of the reputed trade mark.[672]

However, it is important to note that the requirement of use as a trade mark, as the primary condition of any infringement, does not mean that the origin function needs to be affected in order to find such use unlawful. In other words, a distinction must be made between the prerequisite of use as a trade mark and the protection of the function of indication of origin. An act performed by the third party for the purpose of distinguishing a good or service needs to be distinguished from the impact of that act on the protected trade mark in the form of a negative influence on its functions. They appear to be two distinct criteria of assessment. First, it must be examined whether the sign was used to designate the origin of a good or service, i.e. whether it was used as a trade mark. Second, the affection of one of the functions of the mark can be examined.[673] Consequently, the requirement of use of the sign as a trade mark does indeed apply to the marks with a reputation, even though the function of indication of origin is not the one to be protected in the field of enhanced protection.

[3] Question of Affection of Trade Mark Functions

135. Role of the trade mark functions. It should now be examined whether affecting one of the trade mark functions is indeed a subsequent precondition for the application of the special regime. According to some opinions, this criterion should also apply in the field of extended protection. Hence, the affection of one of the functions of the trade mark would be a general condition of any form of infringement of the trade mark right, within and outside the speciality, hence applicable in the event of double identity, likelihood of confusion and under the special regime.[674]

There is no doubt that the so-called economic or accessory trade mark functions constitute a theoretical ground for enhancing the protection of trade marks with a reputation.[675] Thanks to the special regime, the law liberates the trade mark with a reputation from the limits of the rule of speciality in order to preserve, no longer the function of guaranteeing the identity of origin, but other economic functions of the trade mark, in particular the traditionally admitted advertising function, hence the

672. Cf. Galli, *I limiti di protezione ...*, p. 141; Wojciech Włodarczyk, *Użycie oznaczenia 'w charakterze znaku towarowego' (w orzecznictwie ETS)*, PiP 2009, No. 11, p. 104; Monika Żuraw, *Znak towarowy jako przedmiot ochrony – uwagi o użyciu oznaczenia 'w charakterze znaku towarowego'*, Studia Iuridica 2010, No. 52, p. 175; Caselli, *Il marchio che gode di rinomanza ...*, pp. 26-27. Cf. also Daniel R. Bereskin, *Anti-dilution/Anti-free-Riding Laws in the United States, Canada, and the EU: Bridges Too Far?*, TMR 2011, vol. 101, No. 6, p. 1747.

673. Skubisz, *System prawa prywatnego ...*, pp. 1076-1077.

674. *See* Tobias Cohen Jehoram, *The Function Theory in Trade Mark Law and the Holistic Approach of the ECJ*, in: *Verbindend recht, liber amicorum K. F. Haak*, Kluwer, Alphen aan den Rijn 2012, p. 177; Ewa Skrzydło-Tefelska, Mateusz Żuk, in: Gordian N. Hasselblatt (ed.), *Community Trade Mark Regulation. A Commentary*, C.H. Beck Hart Nomos, Munich-Oxford 2015, p. 365; Senftleben, *European Trade Mark ...*, pp. 291-294; Skubisz, *System prawa prywatnego ...*, p. 1082. Nevertheless, some authors note that it is of real importance only in the case of reproduction of the mark for identical goods or services. Żelechowski, *Prawo własności ...*, p. 360.

675. Cf. para. 3 *supra*.

value of the trade mark, its attractive power and its image.[676] Thus, the extension of protection can be regarded as the legal recognition of those functions of the trade mark and in particular of the advertising function,[677] as it was traditionally defined,[678] considered to be the most important function of the mark,[679] which, in the field of enhanced protection, prevails over the distinctive function.[680] The case law expressly recognises that the special regime protects the trade mark beyond its function of indication of origin, as an 'inherent economic value which is independent of and separate from that of the goods and services for which it is registered'.[681]

136. Trade mark functions recognised by the Court of Justice. In its jurisprudence, the Court of Justice refers to the trade mark functions not only to justify the rationale of the trade mark protection but also as criteria for assessment of the infringement. The Court of Justice recognised the protection of new functions with respect to the infringement consisting in a double identity.[682] Those functions include advertising function, which is however interpreted more restrictively, one could say more technically, than it was traditionally,[683] investment, quality and communication functions. As a result, some authors consider that the special regime serves to protect the

676. Frédéric Pollaud-Dulian, *Les atteintes à la marque de renommée. À propos de l'arrêt Intel de la Cour de justice des Communautés européennes du 27 novembre 2008*, Gaz. Pal. 2009, No. 90, p. 7.
677. *See* Calboli, *'Marchio che gode di notorietà'* ..., p. 264; Anfossi-Divol, *L'usage et l'enregistrement* ..., pp. 166, 207-208; Szczepanowska-Kozłowska, *Wyczerpanie praw własności* ..., p. 86; Antoine Braun, Emmanuel Cornu, *Précis des marques*, 4th ed., Larcier, Bruxelles 2004, p. 452; Bently, Sherman, *Intellectual Property* ..., p. 877; Pollaud-Dulian, *Propriété intellectuelle. La propriété* ..., p. 1075; Caselli, *Il marchio che gode di rinomanza* ..., pp. 21, 66; Ricolfi, *Trattato dei marchi* ..., p. 53; Senftleben, *European Trade Mark* ..., pp. 337-339. Cf. Cohen Jehoram, *La protection des marques* ..., p. 225; Brandt, *La protection élargie de la marque* ..., p. 37.
678. *See* para. 3 *supra*.
679. *See* Basire, *Les fonctions de la marque* ..., p. 140.
680. Bertrand, *De la marque notoire* ..., p. 13; Anfossi-Divol, *L'usage et l'enregistrement* ..., p. 166.
681. CFI, 22 March 2007, case T-215/03, *VIPS*, para. 35; GC, 28 October 2010, case T-131/09, *Botox*, para. 90.
682. *See* CJ, 18 June 2009, case C-487/07, *L'Oréal*, para. 58; CJ, 23 March 2010, cases C-236/08 to C-238/08, *Louis Vuitton*, para. 77; CJ, 22 September 2011, case C-323/09, *Interflora*, para. 38. On the new functions recognised by the Court of Justice *see* Jérôme Passa, *Caractérisation de la contrefaçon par référence aux fonctions de la marque: la Cour de justice sur une fausse piste*, Propr. ind. 2011, No. 1, étude 1; Jérôme Passa, *Les nouvelles fonctions de la marque dans la jurisprudence de la Cour de justice: portée? Utilité?*, Cah. dr. entr. 2012, No. 1, dossier 5, paras 1 et seq.; Georges Bonet, *Les trois âges de la fonction de la marque. Selon la jurisprudence de la Cour de justice*, Propr. intell. 2012, No. 43, pp. 154 et seq.; Cohen Jehoram, *The Function Theory* ..., p. 177; Adrien Bouvel, *La construction du droit des marques par la Cour de justice à la lumière contentieux relatif au référencement payant des sites*, in: Christophe Geiger (ed.), *La contribution de la jurisprudence à la construction de la propriété intellectuelle en Europe*, LexisNexis, Paris 2013, pp. 81-83; Charles de Haas, *La fonction d'identification de la marque, la bonne fonction essentielle qui éclipse toutes les autres*, Propr. intell. 2013, No. 46, p. 4; Annette Kur, *Trade Marks Function, Don't They? CJUE Jurisprudence and Unfair Competition Principles*, IIC 2014, vol. 45, No. 4, pp. 434 et seq.; Kur, *Trademark Functions in European Union Law* ..., pp. 1 et seq.
683. In the light of the *Louis Vuitton* judgment, the advertising function is affected where the use made by the third party 'adversely affects the proprietor's use of its mark as a factor in sales promotion or as an instrument of commercial strategy'. CJ, 23 March 2010, cases C-236/08 to C-238/08, *Louis Vuitton*, para. 92. *See also* CJ, 22 September 2011, case C-323/09, *Interflora*, paras 57-59. Cf. Passa, *Les nouvelles fonctions* ..., paras 47-48.

accessory functions recognised by the Court,[684] including in particular the investment function, hence the investments made for the promotion of the mark.[685] This function is however difficult to characterise in the light of the jurisprudence of the Court of Justice.[686] It shows a clear overlap with the advertising function;[687] in fact, it seems to be covered by the concept of advertising function in its traditional sense.[688] Some authors mention also a so-called goodwill function, which has not been however recognised by the Court of Justice.[689]

137. Inapplicability under the special regime. Thus, a priori one could regard the infringement of a reputed trade mark in particular as a form of affection of the advertising function, as it was traditionally understood, and consider that affection of trade mark functions is a precondition for infringement also in the field of enhanced protection. This opinion, however, is not convincing.[690] Admittedly, as we have seen, the advertising function, or more broadly the economic or accessory functions of the trade mark, justifies the extended protection. Nevertheless, in the light of the case law of the Court of Justice, recourse to the concept of affection of the functions of the trade mark appears to be appropriate only to the infringement in the speciality, to the situations of double identity and to the likelihood of confusion, the latter resulting in the affection of the function of indication of origin. The Court of Justice never ruled on a need to establish a risk for one of the functions of the trade mark in order to characterise the infringement in the field of extended protection. On the contrary, the Court clearly distinguishes between the cases of infringement of the trade mark in the speciality, where an affection of one of the functions is required, and the special protection of the trade mark with a reputation. According to the *Red Bull* judgment, rendered pursuant to Directive 89/104, the exclusive right under Article 5(1): 'was conferred in order to enable the trade mark proprietor to protect his specific interests as proprietor of that mark, that is, to ensure that the trade mark can fulfil its functions. Therefore, the exercise of that right must be reserved to cases in which another party's

684. *See* Senftleben, *European Trade Mark* ..., p. 339.
685. *See* Cohen Jehoram, Van Nispen, Huydecoper, *European Trademark Law* ..., pp. 14-15. Cf. Basire, *Les fonctions de la marque* ..., pp. 145, 271.
686. *See* Passa, *Les nouvelles fonctions de la marque* ..., para. 54; de Haas, *La fonction d'identification* ..., p. 21; Kur, Senftleben, *European Trade Mark* ..., 14. Moreover, the aim of trade mark law is not to protect investment. *See* Basire, *Les fonctions de la marque* ..., p. 143. In general, the industrial property rights do not preserve investment as such. Cf. Pollaud-Dulian, *Propriété intellectuelle. La propriété industrielle* ..., p. 6.
687. *See* Cohen Jehoram, *The Function Theory* ..., p. 184. This was admitted by the Court. *See* CJ, 22 September 2011, case C-323/09, *Interflora*, para. 61.
688. In the light of the *Interflora* judgment, the investment function is protected since 'a trade mark may also be used by its proprietor to acquire or preserve a reputation capable of attracting consumers and retaining their loyalty'. It is distinct from the advertising function because 'when the trade mark is used to acquire or preserve a reputation, not only advertising is employed, but also various commercial techniques'. CJ, 22 September 2011, case C-323/09, *Interflora*, paras 60-62. However, according to its traditional interpretation, the advertising function is not limited to the use of a trade mark in advertising as such. It should thus encompass the investment function.
689. Cohen Jehoram, *The Function Theory* ..., pp. 184 et seq.
690. Cf. also Passa, *Les grands arrêts* ..., p. 608. The author considers that in the field of extended protection, no function newly recognised by the Court of Justice needs to be affected.

use of the sign adversely affects or is liable adversely to affect one of the functions of the trade mark'.[691] By contrast, Article 5(2): 'establishes, for the benefit of trade marks with a reputation, a wider form of protection than that laid down in Article 5(1). The specific condition of that protection consists of a use without due cause of a sign identical with or similar to a registered mark which takes, or would take, unfair advantage of, or is or would be detrimental to, the distinctive character or the repute of the earlier mark'.[692] Thus, the affection of the functions of the trade mark is specific to the infringement of the trade mark in the speciality, while the conditions of infringement of the reputed trade mark constitute 'specific conditions' that are not related to the trade mark functions. Invoking the affection of trade mark functions is in this context redundant since there should be no doubt that affection of one of the functions could not be an autonomous condition of infringement of the trade mark with a reputation.

Moreover, even if it is possible to justify the extended protection of the trade mark with a reputation by the need to take into consideration the advertising effect of the trade mark, and therefore the advertising function in its traditional sense, if the affection of one of the functions is to be considered as a general condition for infringement of the trade mark right in the light of the case law of the Court of Justice, it is to this case law that reference should be made. However, as we have pointed out, the Court of Justice imposed a much more restrictive, technical, definition of the advertising function and, in addition, distinguished the investment function. The latter seems to be covered by the advertising function according to its classical understanding. The jurisprudence of the Court of Justice remains particularly vague on this point, and the definitions given in the context of infringement in the case of double identity seem difficult to transpose to the special regime. Consequently, it is unclear which of the functions recognised by the Court of Justice would characterise the infringement of the trade mark with a reputation.

Finally, one could possibly consider a real affection of the advertising function, in its traditional sense, only in the event of detriment to the repute or distinctive character of the mark, since dilution or tarnishment weakens the mark's ability to attract customers. However, in the light of the jurisprudence of the Court of Justice, there is no doubt that the mere fact of taking an unfair advantage constitutes a form of infringement of the trade mark with a reputation.[693] Thus, in the event of unfair advantage, which is independent of any idea of detriment, none of the functions of the trade mark is affected. Protection in this case can only be considered related to the advertising function, in its traditional sense, but would then be characterised by taking an unfair advantage of this function and not by causing it a damage. Thus, the mere fact of taking unfair advantage is a 'specific condition' of the infringement of a reputed trade mark to

691. CJ, 6 February 2014, case C-65/12, *Red Bull*, para. 30.
692. CJ, 6 February 2014, case C-65/12, *Red Bull*, para. 33.
693. CJ, 6 February 2014, case C-65/12, *Red Bull*, para. 40: 'In particular, the proprietor of a mark with a reputation is not required, in order to claim the protection provided for in Article 5(2) of Directive 89/104, to prove detriment to the distinctive character or repute of that mark, where a third party, by using a sign identical or similar to that mark, takes unfair advantage of its reputation.' *See also* CJ, 18 June 2009, case C-487/07, *L'Oréal*, paras 42-43.

which the idea of an affection of one of the functions is inapplicable. As a consequence, the role of the concept of affection of trade mark functions should be limited to the infringement of the trade mark in the speciality.

[B] Establishment of a Link Between the Signs in Dispute

138. *A sine qua non* condition resulting from the jurisprudence. In the light of the case law of the Court of Justice, the establishment of a link between the conflicting signs is a necessary condition for infringement of a trade mark with a reputation.[694] Indeed, the later sign must evoke the reputed mark in the mind of the public for an infringement to be possible. The solution is not questionable, it goes without saying, although the condition is not included in the provisions of Directive 2015/2436 and Regulation 2017/1001.[695] By contrast, it is stated *expressis verbis* in Article 16(3) of the TRIPS Agreement, according to which: Article 6 bis of the Paris Convention shall apply, *mutatis mutandis,* to goods or services which are not similar to those in respect of which a trade mark is registered, provided that use of that trade mark in relation to those goods or services 'would indicate a connection' between those goods or services and the owner of the registered trade mark.

It must be noted that the establishment of a link, such as the establishment of a likelihood of confusion, is not a question of fact. The Court of Justice presents a normative approach to the requirement of a link.[696] In addition, it should be specified that the notion of link used in the field of the special regime must be distinguished from the notion of 'association', within the meaning of Articles 10(2)(b) of Directive 2015/2436 and 9(2)(b) of Regulation 2017/1001, which characterises the likelihood of confusion in the broad sense.[697]

139. Non-exhaustive list of factors. Several factors must be taken into account when assessing the existence of a link. The examination is not limited to comparing the signs in question. Indeed, in the *Intel* judgment, the Court of Justice ruled on the assessment of the link between the signs, providing for a non-exhaustive list of indications allowing to establish a link.[698] In trying to systematise these, it should be noted that some of the factors for assessing the existence of a link refer to the comparison of the signs and the goods or services in question (§2.01[B][1]), while others concern the distinctive power of the allegedly infringed trade mark (§2.01[B][2]). Since the list of factors for assessing the link given by the Court of Justice in the *Intel* judgment is not exhaustive, other elements may be taken into account by the Court. Like in the case of the likelihood of confusion, these may include other factors of 'overall assessment'. For

694. CJ, 23 October 2003, case C-408/01, *Adidas*, para. 29.
695. *See* Bouvel, *Marque et renommée ...*, p. 125.
696. Gielen, *Trademark Dilution under European Law ...*, p. 712.
697. On the likelihood of confusion *lato sensu* Passa, *Traité de droit ...*, p. 404. On the distinction of both terms cf. Charles Gielen, *The Relevance of 'Association' for Trade Mark Conflicts*, in: Verena von Bomhard, Jochen Pagenberg, Detlef Schennen (eds), *Harmonisierung des Markenrechts: Festschrift für Alexander von Mühlendahl*, Carl Heymanns Verlag, Cologne 2005, p. 212, and in French jurisprudence Cass. com., 7 June 2016, case 14-16.885, *Visa*.
698. CJ, 27 November 2008, case C-252/07, *Intel*.

example, in the light of the *Specsavers* judgment of the Court of Justice, the colours in which the earlier trade mark and the sign at issue have been used may be taken into account in order to assess the unfair advantage.[699] *A fortiori* this factor can be taken into account already at the stage of the assessment of the link. In general, in administrative proceedings where, in principle, only the application is examined, evidence of actual use of the mark applied for may be presented and be taken as an indication of the existence of a link, and also of the alleged injury.[700] By contrast, a 'peaceful coexistence' of the signs in dispute on the market may contribute to diminishing the likelihood of a link between them.[701]

[1] Factors for Assessment Related to the Comparison of the Signs and of the Goods and Services

140. Factors related to the comparison of signs and goods or services include: similarity of signs (§2.01[B][1][a]), closeness of goods or services and of the relevant sections of the targeted public (§2.01[B][1][b]) and likelihood of confusion (§2.01[B][1][c]).

[a] Similarity of the Signs

141. *A sine qua non* condition resulting from the law. A certain degree of similarity between the signs in dispute is necessary in order to establish infringement of the reputed trade mark.[702] The Court of Justice repeatedly noted that a link is unlikely to be established in the absence of any similarity between the signs in conflict.[703] Similarly, in the light of the case law of the General Court, where the signs are not similar, no link can be established between them.[704] Thus, the existence of other factors for assessing the link cannot compensate for the lack of similarity between the signs. In particular, the reputation, which is taken into account when assessing the existence of the link and the infringement, has no impact on the assessment of the similarity between the signs

---

699. CJ, 18 July 2013, case C-252/12, *Specsavers*, paras 39-40 and 48.
700. GC, 1 March 2018, case T-85/16, *Adidas*, para. 44.
701. GC, 1 March 2018, case T-629/16, *Adidas*, paras 32-34; GC, 1 March 2018, case T-85/16, *Adidas*, paras 37-39.
702. It should be noted that the similarity of the signs is not only an element taken into account in assessing the existence of a link. Indeed, it can be considered as an autonomous condition for infringement of a trade mark with a reputation, which is expressly provided for in the provisions.
703. CJ, 2 September 2010, case C-254/09 P, *Calvin Klein*, para. 53; CJ, 24 March 2011, case C-552/09 P, *Kinder*, paras 65-66; CJ, 20 November 2014, case C-581/13 P and C-582/13 P, *Ballon d'or*, para. 73. On the *Ballon d'or* judgment *see* Alberto Bellan, *Different Degrees of Similarity Between Normal and Reputed Trade Marks Lead to Separate Assessment*, JIPLP 2015, vol. 10, No. 6, p. 393.
704. GC, 17 February 2011, case T-10/09, *F1*, para. 67; GC, 12 November 2014, case T-524/11, *Volvo*, paras 56-57; GC, 15 October 2014, case T-515/12, *El Corte Inglés*, para. 39; GC, 21 May 2015, case T-55/13, *F1*, para. 67; GC, 31 May 2017, case T-637/15, *Sol*, para. 78.

in question; hence it does not allow to question the lack of similarity.[705] Likewise, the fact that the relevant section of the public targeted by the conflicting signs overlaps does not imply the existence of a link if the signs are so dissimilar that the later sign is unlikely to bring the earlier sign to the mind of the relevant public.[706]

142. Degree of similarity required. The degree of similarity required on the grounds of the extended protection is, however, lower than in the field of infringement for likelihood of confusion. It is settled case law of the Court of Justice that the infringements covered by the special regime 'may be the consequence of a lesser degree of similarity between the earlier and the later marks, provided that it is sufficient for the relevant section of the public to make a connection between those marks, that is to say, to establish a link between them'.[707] Indeed, the degree of similarity between the signs can be even faint.[708] The jurisprudence of the General Court is fully consistent with this approach.[709]

Consequently, it is quite conceivable that the judge may decide that the similarity between the compared signs is insufficient to retain a likelihood of confusion, but sufficient to establish a link in the mind of the public.[710] Indeed, it is admitted that, since the degree of similarity between the signs at issue is different on both grounds, from the lack of similarity sufficient to establish likelihood of confusion it cannot be deduced that the application of the special regime is precluded.[711] This may happen, for example, as we have seen, when the conflicting signs are not considered sufficiently similar to cause a risk of confusion because of conceptual differences, which are not such as to rule out the existence of a link.[712] Of course, the Court (or trade mark office) may find that the signs in conflict are by no means similar, which allows it to dismiss both the claim of likelihood of confusion and infringement of the reputed trade mark, but certain decisions according to which the lack of similarity between the signs in conflict, found when examining the likelihood of confusion, implies the absence of

705. CJ, 24 March 2011, case C-552/09 P, *Kinder*, para. 68. Regarding likelihood of confusion cf. GC, 11 December 2014, case T-618/13, *Java*, para. 65.
706. *See* CJ, 27 November 2008, case C-252/07, *Intel*, para. 49.
707. CJ, 20 November 2014, case C-581/13 P and C-582/13 P, *Ballon d'or*, para. 72. *See also* CJ, 2 September 2010, case C-254/09 P, *Calvin Klein*, para. 53.
708. CJ, 20 November 2014, case C-581/13 P and C-582/13 P, *Ballon d'or*, para. 73.
709. CFI, 16 May 2007, case T-137/05, *La Perla*, para. 34; GC, 28 October 2010, case T-131/09, *Botox*, para. 74; GC, 21 May 2015, case T-145/14, *Adidas*, para. 52; GC, 16 January 2018, case T-398/16, *Starbucks*, para. 78; GC, 24 September 2019, case T-356/18, *Volvo*, para. 55.
710. *See* CJ, 10 December 2015, case C-603/14 P, *El Corte Inglés*, paras 45-50.
711. GC, 16 January 2018, case T-398/16, *Starbucks*, para. 77.
712. *See* para. 108 *supra*. *See* CA Paris, 11 May 2007, case 05/21446, *Ricard*. According to the Court, despite the visual and phonetic similarities between the mark *Ricard* and several signs making fun of it, in particular *Smicard* and *Ringard*, used for identical goods, the intellectual differences, linked to the connotation of the terms used, were such that the consumer of average attention could not attribute the origin of the goods designated by the signs in question to the owner of the mark *Ricard*. However, the public could establish a link by association of ideas, which allowed the judge to condemn the use of the signs in question on the basis of the special regime. *See also* SO Warsaw, 14 July 2015, case XXII GWzt 17/15, *Botox*. The Warsaw District Court noted that the differences between the mark *Botox* and the sign *Alternative to Botox* precluded the public from attaching the same commercial origin to them, but retained the existence of a link.

similarity, such as to establish a link between the signs,[713] appear questionable. For the sake of precision, the judge should always specify that the signs are not sufficiently similar even in the field of the regime of enhanced protection of reputed trade marks where the degree of similarity required is lower.

143. Method of assessing similarity. It should be noted that similarity is assessed in the same way with regard to the provisions relating to infringement in the speciality and to infringement of the reputed trade mark.[714] The condition of similarity between the mark and the sign at issue presupposes the existence of elements of visual, aural or conceptual similarity.[715] According to the case law, 'two marks are similar where, from the point of view of the relevant public, they are at least partially identical as regards one or more relevant aspects'.[716] The criteria for assessing similarity therefore remain the same; it is only the degree of similarity required that is lower.[717]

It is important to note that the comparison of the signs must be made taking into account their distinctive elements.[718] The case opposing an earlier trade mark *La Perla*, registered for women's clothing, and a later mark *Nimei La Perla Modern Classic*, filed for pearls,[719] is a good example. In this case, the General Court upheld the application for invalidity. However, it is indeed questionable whether the term *La Perla*, particularly for the Italian public, would not be considered generic for pearls, so as to exclude the establishment of a link between the signs.[720] When in a complex trade mark composed of several terms some of them are generic or descriptive, it is appropriate to focus on those that are distinctive and therefore allow the public to perceive the sign as a trade mark.[721] The similarity cannot concern only the terms which are generic or descriptive.[722]

144. Importance of the degree of similarity. Although the degree of similarity may be lower in the field of the special protection, the more similar the signs are, the more likely it is that the disputed sign will evoke in the minds of the relevant public the reputed mark. This is the case, *a fortiori*, when the signs are identical. It is easier for the public to make an intellectual association between the reputed trade mark and the

713. Cf. GC, 27 September 2011, case T-207/09, *Nike*, para. 32; GC, 27 June 2019, case T-334/18, *Anna*, para. 27.
714. GC, 11 December 2014, case T-480/12, *Coca-Cola*, para. 32.
715. CJ, 24 March 2011, case C-552/09 P, *Kinder*, para. 52.
716. GC, 5 February 2015, case T-78/13, *Redbull*, para. 27.
717. Gielen, *The Relevance ...*, p. 213; Charles Gielen, *Trademark Dilution in the European Union*, in: Daniel R. Bereskin (ed.), *International Trademark Dilution*, Thomson Reuters, New York 2013, pp. 219-220. *Contra* Arnaud Folliard-Monguiral, *CJCE, arrêt Intel: que reste-t-il de la dilution?*, Propr. ind. 2009, No. 1, comment 3, para. 4. The author points out that the same degree of similarity must be required both in the field of the special regime and within the speciality. However, the fact that the similarity of the signs is assessed in the same way does not mean that its degree should be the same.
718. Cf. GC, 25 February 2016, case T-402/14, *Aqualia*, paras 97-99.
719. GC, 7 December 2010, case T-59/08, *La Perla*.
720. *See* Bertrand Geoffray, in: *Droit des marques et autres signes distinctifs. Chroniques*, Propr. intell. 2009, No. 38, p. 130.
721. Cf. GC, 16 February 2017, case T-71/15, *Land Rover*, paras 67-78.
722. Cf. GC, 20 February 2018, case T-118/16, *Post*, para. 115.

disputed sign when the latter reproduces the mark identically. Moreover, the identity reinforces not only the existence of a link but also the infringement itself.[723]

145. Particular practical importance in case of imitations. That being said, as we have pointed out, the special regime may be more important in practice with respect to trade mark imitations.[724] In the case of servile reproductions, even for goods that are different in nature, it is often difficult to exclude a likelihood of confusion, since the public is likely to believe that the use has been authorised by the owner. Since the goods or services should be compared subjectively, hence by reference to their perception by the public, it is possible that products which are different in their intrinsic characteristics may be qualified as similar within the meaning of trade mark law. In such cases, it should not be necessary to claim the special protection offered to reputed trade marks. The use that creates a likelihood of confusion may be condemned in the speciality. Indeed, the likelihood of confusion must be assessed globally and the special regime should apply in cases where no likelihood can be established.[725]

146. One of the factors of assessment. Finally, it should be stressed that the existence of a link is not a substitute for the criterion of similarity of the signs. The identity between the conflicting signs, *a fortiori* their mere similarity, is not sufficient to conclude that there is a link between these signs.[726] In particular, when the signs in dispute are exploited in different, narrow sectors, to the point that the specialised clientele of the trade mark owner has no reason to know the disputed sign, the public should not establish a link between the two signs, even though they are similar, which excludes the infringement of the reputed trade mark.[727]

[b] Existence of Relations Between the Goods or Services and Between the Relevant Groups of Public

147. Two distinct factors. In the light of the *Intel* judgment, another factor for assessment of the link is 'the nature of the goods or services for which the conflicting marks were registered, including the degree of closeness or dissimilarity between those goods or services, and the relevant section of the public'.[728] Thus, in fact, we can distinguish two distinct factors. First, the closeness of the goods or services designated by the signs in dispute should be taken into consideration (§2.01[B][1][b][i]). Second, it is necessary to compare the sectors of public concerned by them (§2.01[B][1][b][ii]).

723. Cf. Bouvel, *La protection des marques ...*, para. 91.
724. *See* para. 105 *supra*.
725. On the relationship between the likelihood of confusion and the special regime *see* paras 110 et seq. *supra*.
726. CJ, 27 November 2008, case C-252/07, *Intel*, paras 44-45.
727. *See* Passa, *Traité de droit ...*, p. 539; Ryszard Skubisz, *Kolizja późniejszego znaku towarowego z wcześniejszym renomowanym znakiem towarowym*, EPS 2009, No. 2, pp. 35-36.
728. CJ, 27 November 2008, case C-252/07, *Intel*, para. 42.

[i] Closeness of the Goods or Services

148. Importance of the factor. In accordance with the *Intel* decision, the nature of the goods or services designated by the conflicting signs must be taken into account in assessing the existence of a link between these signs.[729] Like the Court of Justice, the General Court notes that the proximity of the goods or services designated by the signs in dispute may reinforce the existence of a link.[730] *A fortiori*, when the goods or services are identical, the public will make it all the easier to link the disputed sign to the earlier trade mark.

Thus, a 'dose of speciality' was reintroduced to the regime of protection of reputed trade marks.[731] There is a tendency to give major importance to the comparison of the goods or services. Unless the mark has an 'exceptionally high' reputation,[732] the General Court often rules out the risk of infringement of a reputed trade mark due to the lack of similarities between the goods or services.[733] It seems that the courts, as well as trade mark offices, sometimes attach too much importance to the similarity of the goods or services, seeking in fact the existence of a likelihood of confusion in the broad sense.[734]

149. Optional factor. However, the absence of similarities between the goods or services in question cannot exclude infringement. The special protection is designed to

729. CJ, 27 November 2008, case C-252/07, *Intel*, paras 49-50.
730. *See* CFI, 16 May 2007, case T-137/05, *La Perla*, para. 51; GC, 28 October 2010, case T-131/09, *Botox*, paras 83-86.
731. Lancrenon, *La marque communautaire ...*, p. 59.
732. *See* CFI, 22 March 2007, case T-215/03, *VIPS*, para. 48.
733. GC, 26 September 2014, case T-490/12, para. 74, confirmed by CJ, 17 September 2015, case C-548/14 P, *Grazia*; GC, 19 May 2015, case T-71/14, *Swatch*, paras 30-31; GC, 30 September 2016, case T-430/15, *Sylvania*, para. 49; GC, 5 June 2018, case T-111/16, *Prada*, para. 50.
734. For example, by a judgment of 18 November 2015, the General Court ruled out the existence of a link because of differences in nature between the goods in dispute, clothing and tobacco, despite the fact that the owner had shown that the owners of several marks, such as *Marlboro* and *Camel*, sold clothing under these marks and that some owners granted licences for cigarettes. According to the judgment, the holder did not establish that the granting of a licence for clothing constituted a general practice in the tobacco sector. GC, 18 November 2015, case T-606/13, *Mustang*, paras 54-55. Thus, the Court of Justice has in fact sought to establish the existence of a likelihood of confusion *lato sensu* on the ground of the special regime. As we have seen, the notion of similarity between the goods or services can no longer be assessed solely in the view of their intrinsic nature. It is necessary to take into account the perception of the customers. *See* paras 114-115 *supra* and cf. paras 36-37 *supra*. The public is used to the fact that, e.g., clothing and perfumes can be manufactured by the same company. Consequently, these products can be considered similar. Cf. Cass com., 16 January 1990, case 88-10.856, *Bulgari*. In a case such as that in the *Mustang* judgment, if the public considered the granting of licences as a general practice, it would believe in the existence of commercial links between the two, then would attribute the same commercial origin to the goods designated by the two signs, which characterises the likelihood of confusion in the broad sense. In this case, the claimant was under no obligation to demonstrate that licences were granted between both sectors. If, however, he succeeded in proving that such a practice existed, even if it was not a general practice, which excluded the likelihood of confusion, this circumstance could have strengthened the existence of a link.

be applied to non-similar goods or services.[735] The General Court sometimes points out that the degree of closeness between the goods covered by the signs at issue does not imply that the goods in question must be identical or similar.[736] Nevertheless, a certain proximity between goods or services is often required to establish a link and it is difficult to understand how the judge must distinguish between 'similar' and only 'close' products since the similarity should be assessed subjectively and not taking into account the intrinsic nature of the goods or services.

Therefore, the proximity between the goods or services should not be overemphasised. The extended protection is intended to apply, above all, in cases where a third party uses a reputed trade mark for dissimilar products.[737] Although similarities between the goods or services are likely to facilitate the establishment of a link,[738] completely different characteristics of the goods or services in question can in no way exclude it, since the purpose of the special regime is to ensure extended protection against the use of trade marks with a reputation for any goods or services,[739] and the law expressly provides that the reputed trade mark is protected against its use for dissimilar goods or services. Indeed, attaching too much importance to the nature of the goods or services covered by the conflicting marks is likely to call into question the extended protection. As Folliard-Monguiral observed, it cannot be excluded that, in the case of a trade mark with a high reputation, the risk of infringement can be established even where the sectors covered by the signs in dispute are as distinct as, for example, tea and underwear.[740] There is no reason why a consumer who knows a reputed trade mark, seeing a similar, and *a fortiori* identical, sign, should not think of that mark.

Moreover, it should be noted that the existence of one of the forms of damage to a reputed trade mark, namely the detriment to the repute, is often assessed in relation to the incompatible nature of the goods or services of the right holder and the third party.[741] For instance, the use of a mark of perfume for garbage cans is likely to damage its image. However, the goods in question are by no means similar. Consequently, although the similarities between the goods or services should be taken into account, the absence of proximity between the products cannot imply the absence of a link and therefore the infringement of the trade mark.

---

735. GC, 18 November 2015, case T-606/13, *Mustang*, para. 23 (as we have seen, this observation did not prevent the Court from excluding the existence of a link because of the differences between the goods, *see* para. 55 of the judgment); GC, 8 June 2017, case T-341/13 RENV, *SO ...?*, para. 89.
736. GC, 16 March 2016, case T-201/14, *Spa*, para. 45.
737. Simon Fhima, *Trade Mark Dilution ...*, p. 153.
738. Cf. CJ, 26 July 2017, case C-471/16 P, *Meissen*, paras 54-55.
739. *Contra* Célia Zolynski, *La protection étendue de la marque renommée en droit de l'Union européenne*, D. IP/IT 2016, No. 2, p. 94. The author excludes the link, and hence the infringement of the reputed trade mark, as soon as the economic fields covered by the goods appear very distant. Otherwise, she believes, the freedom of trade and industry would be unduly compromised by the too wide unavailability of the sign.
740. Arnaud Folliard-Monguiral, *Arrêt Puma: preuve de la renommée et pratique décisionnelle*, Propr. ind. 2016, No. 11, comment 75, para. 5. Cf. GC, 2 October 2015, case T-624/13, *Darjeeling*, para. 107.
741. *See* paras 252-253 *infra*. Regarding dilution cf. para. 213 *infra*.

The nature of the goods or services themselves should therefore not have a significant impact on the existence of a link, what can be deduced from several recent rulings of the General Court which stressed that the dissimilarity between the goods or services designated by the signs at issue is not a sufficient factor for excluding the existence of a link,[742] especially when the mark has an important reputation, the signs in dispute are similar and the publics overlap.[743] Therefore, as regards the goods or services, what needs to be essentially assessed are the relevant sections of the public targeted by the goods or services designated by each of the signs. The goods or services may be similar but intended for specialised and very distant sectors. The existence of a link is then unlikely, as long as the sections of the public do not overlap.[744] By contrast, the goods or services may be completely different but their publics may overlap, so that they will be confronted with the other sign. As Advocate General Sharpston rightly indicated in her opinion in the *Intel* case, the problem is rather at the level of the relevant public and not simply at the level of comparison of the goods or services.[745] The real criterion to be taken into account is therefore that of overlapping publics.

[ii] Overlapping Groups of the Relevant Public

150. Necessity of an overlap. In the light of the *Intel* judgment, the relevant sections of the public as regards the goods or services covered by the respective signs need to overlap. It is therefore conceivable that the public targeted by the good or service designated by the earlier reputed mark is completely distinct from the relevant section of the public as regards the goods or services covered by the sign in dispute. In such case, the public targeted by each of the two signs may never be confronted with the other sign, so that it will not establish any link between those signs.[746] The solution is logical and deserves approval since a trade mark with a reputation does not need to be known to the general public. Indeed, this additional requirement of overlapping publics can be explained by the fact that reputation is assessed in a non-restrictive way and that, consequently, the access to the special protection is relatively easy. Thus, the Court of Justice seeks to balance the regime of enhanced protection by making it more exceptional. That being said, it is sufficient if one of the conflicting signs designates a

742. GC, 26 September 2018, case T-62/16, *Puma*, para. 100; GC, 29 November 2018, case T-372/17, *LV*, para. 110.
743. *See* GC, 8 May 2018, case T-721/16, *Ray-Ban*, para. 87.
744. *See* CJ, 27 November 2008, case C-252/07, *Intel*, para. 46.
745. Opinion of Advocate General Eleanor Sharpston in case C-252/07, *Intel*, para. 60. 'There is, however, a way in which the nature of the goods or services covered by the respective marks may be relevant when determining the existence of a link in the mind of the public. If two marks are similar, yet used in widely separated product areas, the fact that the earlier mark has a reputation in one area … might not lead to the establishment of a mental link with the later mark if it were used in a quite different area … since there might be very little overlap between the two relevant publics. Where either mark is used for goods or services familiar to the general public, or where both are used for similar products, the likelihood of overlap and of the establishment of a link is correspondingly much stronger.'
746. CJ, 27 November 2008, case C-252/07, *Intel*, para. 48.

good or service intended for the public at large and the link is likely to be established. By contrast, if the two signs concern specialised and distinct sections of the public, it is possible that the link does not exist since the public targeted by each of the two signs may never be confronted with the other.

151. Importance of the relevant public at different stages of the assessment of infringement. It needs to be noted that the public concerned taken into account for the assessment of the reputation of the trade mark is not necessarily the same as the public concerned which must be taken into consideration for the assessment of the existence of the infringement of that trade mark.[747] It seems that the role of the public concerned by the trade mark is double. First, it serves to qualify the sign as a trade mark with a reputation, and second, to examine the existence of a link and the infringement itself. A priori, both are intimately linked. If the public concerned is assessed in a way that is more favourable to the right holder at the stage of assessing the character of the sign, the existence of a link may be more difficult to demonstrate. By contrast, if initially a more strictly appreciated public is taken into account, in particular by requiring knowledge by the general public, the establishment of a link is easier. Nevertheless, it is possible to assess the public concerned in a different way depending on the stage of the examination of the infringement. At the stage of qualifying the sign, it is necessary to determine the public concerned as the public targeted by the trade mark owner, to whom the latter directs his offer, as follows from the *Chevy* judgment, and therefore in a less rigorous manner.[748] It is however conceivable that the trade mark may become known beyond the public targeted by the proprietor. The existence of a link could therefore be examined in relation to a public appreciated more broadly.

The Court of Justice prima facie does not distinguish between the public concerned according to the stage of the assessment of the infringement of a reputed trade mark. However, it does so implicitly by imposing the requirement to take into account 'the strength of the earlier mark's reputation in order to determine whether that reputation extends beyond the public targeted by that mark'.[749] The Court ruled: 'It must also be pointed out that certain marks may have acquired such a reputation that it goes beyond the relevant public as regards the goods or services for which those marks were registered. In such a case, it is possible that the relevant section of the public as regards the goods or services for which the later mark is registered will make a connection between the conflicting marks, even though that public is wholly distinct from the relevant section of the public as regards goods or services for which the earlier mark was registered.'[750]

The General Court clarified that the reputation of a trade mark depends not only on the persons who buy and use the goods or services in respect of which the mark in question is protected and used but also on the knowledge by the public at large. Indeed, the reputation of a mark may go beyond the relevant public as regards the goods or

747. Passa, *Traité de droit ...*, p. 508.
748. *See* para. 65 *supra*.
749. CJ, 27 November 2008, case C-252/07, *Intel*, para. 53.
750. CJ, 27 November 2008, case C-252/07, *Intel*, paras 51-52. *See also* GC, 26 September 2018, case T-62/16, *Puma*, paras 87-88.

services covered by that mark. Thus, even if the mark was registered for goods and services aimed at a limited public, it can be known to a wider public, namely the public at large, precisely by reason of its reputation.[751] It is therefore necessary to distinguish between the reputation that the trade mark has in relation to the potential clientele of the goods or services covered by it and the reputation beyond the relevant public of the trade mark, appreciated in relation to the customers who only know the sign, the 'external' public.[752] For example, as the General Court noted, the public of the mark *Viagra* is made up only of men, yet its reputation extends to the entire population and not only to the average consumers of the products covered by this mark.[753]

It should also be noted that the assessment of the existence of a link in relation to a wider public than the public targeted by the trade mark will only be relevant in the case of unfair advantage. Indeed, the public to be taken into account varies depending on the type of injury alleged by the proprietor of the mark.[754] In case of the detriment to the distinctive character and to the repute, the relevant public is the clientele targeted by the goods or services designated by the mark. The existence of dilution and tarnishment must therefore be assessed by reference to the perception of the relevant public, which consists of average consumers of the goods or services for which that mark is registered.[755] This is further confirmed by the requirement of proof of a change in the economic behaviour of the consumer concerned which, in the light of case law, is specific to dilution, but which, as we shall see, is also theoretically applicable to degradation.[756] There is no risk that a consumer who knows a trade mark, without being interested in the product on which it is affixed, will change his behaviour and lose interest in the product covered by the mark that he never had. As far as dilution and degradation are concerned, the distinction between the relevant sections of the public is therefore useless. If a sign of a third party in conflict with the trade mark *Viagra* was aimed exclusively at the female public, men should not be likely to change their economic behaviour, i.e. lose interest in the product of the proprietor of the mark, since they should not even know the sign of the third party.

By contrast, in the case of unfair advantage, the infringement is assessed by reference to the clientele concerned by the disputed sign.[757] It is therefore relevant to take into account the reputation that extends beyond the public targeted by the earlier trade mark. By using our example of the mark *Viagra*, the female public could be attracted by a sign reproducing or imitating it, so that unfair advantage could be envisaged. Thus, the observation that the fact that reputation extends beyond the specialised professional public targeted by the trade mark strengthens the possibility of

751. GC, 6 July 2012, case T-60/10, *Shakespeare*, para. 34. *See also* GC, 26 September 2018, case T-62/16, *Puma*, paras 89 et seq.
752. *See* Susie Middlemiss, Steven Warner, *The Protection of Marks with a Reputation: Intel c CPM*, EIPR 2009, vol. 31, No. 6, p. 331.
753. GC, 25 January 2012, case T-332/10, *Viagra*, para. 48.
754. CJ, 27 November 2008, case C-252/07, *Intel*, para. 33.
755. CJ, 27 November 2008, case C-252/07, *Intel*, paras 34-35.
756. *See* para. 248 *infra*.
757. This dichotomy is considered logical in theory but difficult to implement by the Court. Bouvel, *Marque et renommée* ..., p. 129. In addition, in many cases, the two types of violations are actually cumulative. Pollaud-Dulian, *Les atteintes à la marque de renommée* ..., p. 7.

existence of an infringement[758] is relevant only for the purpose of establishing an unfair advantage and not a detriment.

In conclusion, either the publics overlap, which makes it possible to establish both detriment and unfair advantages, or a priori they do not overlap, but the reputation of the mark goes beyond the public targeted by it, so that the public concerned by the disputed sign will know the mark, which makes it possible to establish an unfair advantage. Consequently, since the detriment is assessed in relation to the public targeted and in the view of the requirement of a change of the consumer's economic behaviour, it should be accepted that, as regards dilution and degradation, the public concerned by the reputed trade mark should be assessed according to the same criterion of the public targeted by the mark. A wider public, theoretically possible for the assessment of the link, is not relevant in the final appreciation of the infringement.

152. Determination of the relevant public. As it has been established, the determination of the public concerned often poses difficulties.[759] It is necessary to consider whether the good or service is directed to the general public or to a limited group of consumers. The general public logically includes narrower sections of the public, including specialised publics composed of professionals. If a trade mark is known to the public at large, it is presumed to be known to restricted publics. Of course, one mark that designates several goods or services can target the general public and more specialised consumers.[760] Moreover, one type of good can be directed to both the public at large and a more specialised public.[761] As we have seen, the determination of the public concerned is particularly problematic in the case of luxury or prestige goods or services.[762] In the jurisprudence of the General Court, a tendency to distinguish the public of luxury products can be observed.[763] National case law varies.[764]

153. Level of attention of the relevant public. The determination of the relevant public also allows to define the level of attention of the public targeted by the mark. Logically, when the mark is directed to a professional public, its level of attention is higher.[765] Nevertheless, the level of attention of the relevant public should be of minor importance in the field of extended protection. Unlike the general protection of the trade mark in the speciality, the special regime does serve to condemn the likelihood of confusion between the signs. The fact that the relevant public has a higher level of

758. *See* CFI, 10 May 2007, case T-47/06, *Nasdaq*, para. 58.
759. *See* para. 68 *supra*. Cf. GC, 6 July 2012, case T-60/10, *Shakespeare*, para. 31.
760. Cf. CJ, 10 May 2012, case C-100/11 P, *Botox*, paras 66 and 68.
761. Cf. GC, 8 May 2018, case T-721/16, *Ray-Ban*, para. 44.
762. *See* para. 68 *supra*.
763. *See* GC, 6 July 2012, case T-60/10, *Shakespeare*, para. 34; GC, 22 January 2015, case T-322/13, *Kenzo*, para. 42.
764. For example, some French and Polish courts suggest that luxury products target a 'prestigious clientele' (Cass com., 20 November 2012, case 12-11.753, Bull. civ. IV, No. 209, *Diptyque*), a narrower public of wealthy consumers who appreciate high-quality products (WSA Warsaw, 8 December 2014, case VI SA/Wa 1359/14, *Montblanc*). Others consider that goods which are aimed at all consumers, even if they are luxury products, concern the general public, Cass. com., 7 June 2006, case 04-16.908, *Ebel*.
765. Cf. GC, 8 May 2018, case T-721/16, *Ray-Ban*, para. 42.

attention cannot diminish the risk that it will establish a link between two similar signs, without being misled by associating them with one commercial origin.

154. Overlap in case of general public. In principle, there should be an overlap of the publics concerned when at least one of the signs is aimed at the general public,[766] *a fortiori* when the latter is concerned by both signs.[767] However, in the view of the case law, an overlap of publics is not always sufficient to establish the existence of a link, particularly where the goods or services in question are very different. For example, according to the General Court, there is no link between two almost identical signs designating, for one, synthetic materials intended for a specialised public and, for the other, electrical vehicles and appliances intended for non-professionals, i.e. the general public.[768] In some decisions, the Court is less severe in the assessment of the link, relying more on the issue of overlap of the publics than on the comparison of goods or services.[769] That approach can only be approved.

Moreover, it should be noted that the assessment of the link should vary according to the public for which it is examined and therefore the type of alleged infringement. When the reputed trade mark is known to the general public and the disputed sign to a specialised public, the link is probably more easily established by the public targeted by the disputed sign. Therefore, in such a case, it would be more likely to demonstrate an unfair advantage. However, in the event that the reputed trade mark is known to a narrower public and the disputed sign to the general public, it should be easier to establish a link among the public concerned by the reputed trade mark, thus proving dilution or tarnishment.

[c] Likelihood of Confusion

155. Redundant factor. The *Intel* judgment refers to the likelihood of confusion as a factor in establishing a link between the signs in dispute and then the existence of an infringement.[770] Indeed, in the light of the case law, the existence of a likelihood of confusion in the mind of the public, even though it is not a necessary criterion of the link, is an aggravating factor.[771] Although the existence of a likelihood of confusion implies the existence of a link between the signs, the point of referring to this criterion is questionable. A link between the signs made by the public is not an objective in itself;[772] it can only allow to initiate the assessment of the infringement which requires from the plaintiff to establish a form of injury to the trade mark. As we shall see, the coexistence of dilution and of the likelihood of confusion is doubtful. Indeed, the risk

766. Cf., however, GC, 19 May 2015, case T-71/14, *Swatch*, paras 32-33.
767. GC, 26 September 2014, case T-490/12, *Grazia*, para. 75.
768. GC, 9 April 2014, case T-288/12, *Zytel*, paras 71-74. Cf. GC, 26 September 2014, case T-490/12, *Grazia*, paras 73-80.
769. GC, 29 March 2012, case T-369/10, *Beatles*, paras 50-53.
770. CJ, 27 November 2008, case C-252/07, *Intel*, para. 42.
771. CFI, 6 February 2007, case T-477/04, *TDK*, para. 67.
772. Simon Fhima, *Trade Mark Dilution* ..., p. 104.

of confusion seems to exclude the existence of detriment to the distinctive character.[773] In general, the existence of a likelihood of confusion should make it possible to establish the infringement in the speciality. In the view of the principle of an overall assessment of the likelihood of confusion *lato sensu* and the subjective appreciation of the criterion of similarity of the goods or services which results from it, invoking extended protection is unnecessary in the event of a danger of misleading customers, unless the goods or services are completely different, so as to avoid any confusion.[774] The jurisprudence of the General Court which notes that the implementation of the special protection 'does not require the existence of a likelihood of confusion'[775] confirms the uselessness of taking into account the risk of confusion. Therefore, this last factor for assessing the link is in fact of no importance.

[2] Factors for Assessment Related to the Distinctive Power of the Trade Mark

156. Reputation, distinctiveness, uniqueness. A second group of factors for assessing the link consists of factors related to the distinctive power of the trade mark, namely: reputation (§2.01[B][2][a]), distinctiveness (§2.01[B][2][b]), insofar as it does not result from reputation, and the uniqueness of the mark (§2.01[B][2][c]). It should be noted that all these factors remain relevant at the final stage of assessing the infringement, related to the appreciation of the forms of injury. Thus, they will also be analysed in this regard.

[a] Reputation of the Trade Mark

157. Importance to the assessment of the link. The strength of the reputation is one of the main factors in assessing the existence of a link. The stronger the earlier mark's reputation, the easier it will be to accept that there is a link and that detriment has been caused to it.[776] Indeed, the reputation of the mark reinforces its distinctive power in the eyes of customers.[777] Taking into account the knowledge of the mark is also common for all types of infringements, including the likelihood of confusion.[778]

773. *See* para. 215 *infra*.
774. On the relationship between the special regime and the likelihood of confusion *see* paras 110 et seq. *supra*.
775. *See* e.g. GC, 29 March 2012, case T-369/10, *Beatles*, para. 59; GC, 8 June 2017, case T-341/13 RENV, *SO ...?*, para. 76; GC, 29 November 2018, case T-372/17, *LV*, para. 107.
776. CJ, 27 November 2008, case C-252/07, *Intel*, para. 69. *See also* CJ, 14 September 1999, case C-375/97, *Chevy*, para. 30; CFI, 25 May 2005, case T-67/04, *Spa*, para. 41; CFI, 22 March 2007, case T-215/03, *VIPS*, para. 47.
777. Cf. CJ, 27 November 2008, case C-252/07, *Intel*, para. 73.
778. As it has been established, the Court of Justice considers that the more the mark is known to the public, the greater the risk that it will be confused with another sign. *See* CJ, 29 September 1998, case C-39/97, *Canon*, para. 19. On the old debate whether reputation of the earlier mark increases or decreases the danger of misleading the public as to its commercial origin. *See* Baeumer, *La protection de la marque ...*, p. 561. Some authors continue to argue that the more the mark is known, the more likely it is that the consumers will be able to distinguish it from

158. Importance to the assessment of the infringement itself. The reputation of the earlier trade mark is an essential criterion for assessing the infringement of the reputed mark itself. A particularly important reputation is sometimes considered sufficient to establish infringement. In particular, according to the General Court, in the case of a mark 'with an exceptionally high reputation', the probability of a future risk of detriment to or unfair advantage can be 'so obvious' that the proprietor of the mark does not need to put forward and prove any other fact to that end.[779] This solution, very favourable to the owners of reputed trade marks, was criticised by the Advocate General in the *Intel* case, who considered that the Court had gone too far in making this assumption.[780] However, this observation was repeated by the General Court in judgments subsequent to the *Intel* decision. The General Court considers that 'it is possible that an extremely strong reputation may, exceptionally, constitute in itself an indication of the future, non-hypothetical risk of the mark applied for [disputed mark] as such taking unfair advantage in relation to each of the goods and services which are not similar to the goods and services in respect of which the earlier trade mark is registered'.[781] In the view of the specific conditions of each form of infringement of a reputed trade mark, such as the requirement to prove a change in the economic behaviour of the average consumer in the case of dilution or of transfer of reputation in the case of unfair advantage, this approach is unlikely to be approved by the Court of Justice. Thus, the courts (or trade mark offices) should avoid considering the reputation alone as sufficient to establish infringement, but should further develop the motivations, linking significant reputation to, depending on the case, the risk of a change in the behaviour of consumers, of a transfer of reputation, etc., even though this method may seem somewhat artificial.

159. Types of infringement. The factor relating to the strength of reputation may play a different role depending on the form of infringement invoked. As we have seen, the reputation of the trade mark which goes beyond the public targeted by it makes it possible for the public concerned by the disputed sign to make a connection between the signs.[782] Thereafter, an unfair advantage may be established, since it is assessed among the public targeted by the disputed sign that knows the earlier mark, notwithstanding the absence of an a priori existing overlap between the publics concerned. However, as regards the detriment, a high reputation can facilitate the establishment of a link and injury with the public for whom the earlier trade mark is intended. Indeed, it is the public concerned, and not the entire public knowing the sign, who may change their behaviour in relation to the earlier mark. The intensity of reputation in the eyes of

a sign imitating it, because they will be more attentive to the differences between the signs. Cf. Casparie-Kerdel, *Dilution Disguised* ..., p. 192; de Haas, *La 'contrefaçon' de la marque notoire* ..., p. 142; Anemaet, *The Many Faces* ..., pp. 193-198. Cf. para. 113 *supra*.

779. CFI, 22 March 2007, case T-215/03, *VIPS*, para. 48.

780. Opinion of Advocate General Eleanor Sharpston in case C-252/07, *Intel*, para. 70.

781. GC, 14 December 2012, case T-357/11, *Bimbo*, para. 43; GC, 2 October 2015, case T-624/13, *Darjeeling*, para. 134; GC, 1 March 2018, case T-85/16, *Adidas*, para. 46. Cf. GC, 17 March 2010, case T-63/07, *Maurer*, para. 40.

782. *See* CJ, 24 March 2011, case C-552/09 P, *Kinder*, para. 57. Cf. para. 151 *supra*.

the public targeted by the trade mark can therefore be used to assess the infringement in the form of dilution or degradation.

In addition, more particularly concerning dilution, Simon Fhima pointed out that a strong reputation, likely to strengthen the distinctiveness of the mark, should not necessarily facilitate the detriment to the distinctive character but that, on the contrary, a mark enjoying a high level of distinctiveness could better resist attacks and therefore more easily retain its distinctiveness. According to the author, it might be more difficult to undermine a trade mark's ability to create immediate associations in the public mind if it has a very strong distinctive character.[783] Nevertheless, as we shall see, in order to establish dilution, it must be found that the use by a third party of a sign reproducing or imitating the mark is likely to deprive it of its ability to evoke instant associations in the mind of the public with the goods or services covered by the latter as originating from its proprietor.[784] Not all reputed trade marks need to evoke such an immediate association. In other words, any reputed trade mark is not by definition capable of being diluted by the use of an identical or similar sign by a third party. Otherwise, the monopoly granted to the owners of trade marks with a reputation would be unlimited. Therefore the finding of the Court of Justice appears logical and useful. The more the trade mark is known, the more likely it is to lead to immediate associations with its owner and, therefore, the higher the risk of unlawful dilution. In addition, the adoption of a reverse rule would lead to the admission of a perverse effect consisting in a limitation of the protection of the most reputed trade marks. This is undoubtedly not the objective of the legislator. A highly distinctive sign is particularly suitable for capturing the attention of customers[785] and that is what the legislator intends to protect.

[b] Distinctiveness of the Trade Mark

160. Importance of the factor. According to the Court of Justice, 'the stronger the distinctive character of the earlier mark, whether inherent or acquired through the use which has been made of it, the more likely it is that, confronted with a later identical or similar mark, the relevant public will call that earlier mark to mind'.[786] In assessing whether a mark is highly distinctive, the Court 'must make an overall assessment of the greater or lesser capacity of the mark to identify the goods or services for which it has been registered as coming from a particular undertaking'.[787]

It should be pointed out that, since the distinctive character can arise and grow, thanks to the use and reputation of the mark, this factor for assessing the link is often inseparable from that relating to reputation. It can be distinguished from reputation in the case of inherent distinctiveness of the mark (§2.01[B][2][b][i]). In addition,

783. Simon Fhima, *Trade Mark Dilution ...*, pp. 143-145.
784. *See* paras 213 and 234 et seq. *infra*.
785. *See* Passa, *Traité de droit ...*, p. 416.
786. CJ, 27 November 2008, case C-252/07, *Intel*, para. 54.
787. CJ, 22 June 1999, case C-342/97, *Lloyd*, para. 22.

distinctiveness can be enhanced by the existence of a 'family' of trade marks (§2.01[B][2][b][ii]).

[i] Inherent Distinctiveness

161. Relationship between reputation and distinctiveness. A trade mark can have 'a particularly distinctive character, either per se or because of the reputation it enjoys with the public'.[788] As I have mentioned, the relationship between reputation and distinctiveness is very strong. It is well established in doctrine and case law that knowledge of the trade mark has a particular influence on the assessment of the distinctive character.[789] The reputation is even likely to create the distinctive power of a mark that is inherently devoid of it. However, the existence of distinctive character does not necessarily depend on reputation, since, under European trade mark law, the distinctive character, within the meaning of the condition of the validity of the trade mark, does not depend on the exploitation of the sign.[790] Reputation can reinforce the distinctive character of a trade mark, but the opposite is not possible. In cases of reputed marks, the two are often inseparable.[791] The Court imposed two separate factors for assessing the infringement, observing nevertheless that a trade mark with a reputation 'necessarily has distinctive character, at the very least acquired through use'.[792] Indeed, it is difficult to identify the relevance of the distinctiveness factor if the reputation is taken into account upstream. There is unquestionably a certain redundancy in taking into consideration both the degree of distinctiveness of the trade mark and that of its reputation as factors in assessing the link.[793]

162. Degree of inherent distinctiveness. The factor related to distinctiveness becomes however important when the mark is initially, before any use, highly distinctive. An inherently distinctive mark is normally a mark devoid of generic or descriptive elements,[794] or at least a mark in which such elements have a minor importance. The degree of inherent distinctiveness depends on the meaning of the sign and the nature of the designated goods or services. It must be assessed solely by reference to the goods or services in respect of which that mark was registered; it is of no relevance that the mark may be perceived as descriptive in respect of other goods.[795] The inherent distinctiveness is weak when the meaning of the sign refers to associations with the good or service itself, such as the word 'grazia', meaning 'grace', 'elegance', which, according to the General Court, refers to the image that fashion magazines put

788. CJ, 11 November 1997, case C-251/95, *Sabel v. Puma*, para. 24.
789. Marie-Angèle Pérot-Morel, *Dégénérescence de la marque par excès de notoriété*, in: *Mélanges en l'honneur de Daniel Bastian*, t. II, Librairies techniques, Paris 1974, p. 51.
790. Cf. de Haas, *La 'contrefaçon' de la marque notoire* ..., p. 142, who makes reference to American law to claim the opposite.
791. Cf. Simon Fhima, *Trade Mark Dilution* ..., p. 99.
792. CJ, 27 November 2008, case C-252/07, *Intel*, para. 73. *See also* GC, 26 September 2014, case T-490/12, *Grazia*, para. 76.
793. Regarding the likelihood of confusion cf. Canlorbe, *L'usage de la marque* ..., p. 108.
794. *See* Passa, *Traité de droit* ..., p. 416.
795. GC, 26 September 2018, case T-62/16, *Puma*, para. 75.

forward.[796] In the case law, the factor relating to inherent distinctiveness, in the field of the special regime, is sometimes close to originality.[797] However, an inherently distinctive mark does not need to be original. Originality is an objective criterion, while the distinctive character of the trade mark is always assessed in the light of the nature of the designated goods or services. Indeed, a banal mark may have a high degree of distinctiveness in relation to a particular good or service. Nevertheless, in the field of the special regime, the importance of the distinctiveness factor is limited. Even in the case of trade marks with a high inherent distinctive character, it is the distinctiveness acquired through use, covered by reputation, that plays a crucial role.[798]

Thus, when a trade mark is not inherently distinctive, in principle, this criterion for assessing the link and the infringement will be inextricably linked to the factor relating to reputation. An exception may occur when there exists a 'family' of trade marks that is likely to strengthen the distinctive character of a mark through the existence of other marks owned by the right holder.

[ii] Increased Distinctiveness in Case of Families of Trade Marks

163. Concept of a family of trade marks. Another factor that can be taken into account in assessing the link is the existence of a 'family' or 'series' of trade marks, a concept which appeared in EU case law for the first time in the judgments of the General Court and the Court of Justice in the *Bainbridge* case.[799] A family of marks exists when the right holder owns several marks which 'reproduce in full a single distinctive element with the addition of a graphic or word element differentiating them from one another, or when they are characterised by the repetition of a single prefix or suffix taken from an original mark'.[800] All those marks need to be present on the market.[801] According to this concept, the existence of a family of marks justifies an extension of the protection of marks, since it allows to establish a likelihood of confusion even though the comparison of the disputed sign and the earlier mark, each taken individually, does not make it possible to prove a danger of confusion. It is, however, irrelevant in assessing whether there is a similarity between the marks.[802]

164. Role of the concept under the special regime. As regards the likelihood of confusion, the question is whether the consumer can consider that the sign at issue is

796. GC, 26 September 2014, case T-490/12, *Grazia*, para. 76.
797. *See* GC, 29 March 2012, case T-369/10, *Beatles*, para. 57. Which, moreover, could also be taken into account in assessing the existence of the uniqueness of the mark. Cf. para. 167 *infra*.
798. Cf. GC, 29 March 2012, case T-369/10, *Beatles*, paras 57-58.
799. CFI, 23 February 2006, case T-194/03; CJ, 13 September 2007, case C-234/06 P, *Bainbridge*.
800. CFI, 23 February 2006, case T-194/03, *Bainbridge*, para. 123; GC, 5 July 2016, case T-518/13, *McDonald's*, para. 43.
801. CFI, 23 February 2006, case T-194/03, *Bainbridge*, para. 126; GC, 5 July 2016, case T-518/13, *McDonald's*, para. 44; GC, 10 October 2019, case T-428/18, *McDonald's*, para. 67.
802. *See* Jérôme Passa, *Les 'familles' de marques dans la jurisprudence européenne: surcroît de protection ou trompe-l'œil?*, Propr. intell. 2015, No. 54, pp. 16-22. Cf. CJ, 24 March 2011, case C-522/09 P, *Kinder*; CJ, 16 June 2011, case C-317/10 P, *Uniweb*; GC, 26 September 2012, case T-301/09, *Citi*.

part of the same series of trade marks.[803] This is of course not the case under the special regime where the family of trade marks can only be another factor reinforcing the existence of a link. Indeed, in the light of a judgment of the General Court, 'the existence of a family of trade marks may be regarded, for the purpose of the application of Article 8(5) of Regulation No 207/2009,[804] as merely one of the factors to be taken into account in establishing whether there is connection between the mark applied for and one of the earlier marks forming part of that family, in so far as that earlier mark enjoys a reputation'.[805] It is not necessary that the other marks constituting the family have a reputation, nor that the family be reputed.[806] The solution is justified because, unlike the case of infringement for likelihood of confusion, the concept of family of marks is not applied here to assess the existence of the infringement but only of a link, the latter being a prerequisite for the search for the appreciation of the injury.[807]

The role of this concept in the field of the special regime is therefore different and results in the strengthening of the distinctive character of the trade mark. The General Court pointed out that 'recognition of the existence of a family of trade marks increases the distinctive character of the marks belonging to that family'.[808] The distinction between reputation and extrinsic distinctiveness then makes sense. The existence of a family of marks is irrelevant to the reputation of the marks considered individually, but it is likely to strengthen the distinctive character of each of them, so that the public will more easily establish a link between the disputed sign and these marks, thanks to their common structure.[809]

165. Practical importance. As Passa observed, the influence of the existence of a family of trade marks on trade mark protection, including the special regime, seems marginal. Where the disputed sign and the marks constituting the family are similar, an association will normally be established with these marks considered individually, so that invoking the concept of family of marks is redundant. Indeed, in the decisions in which the benefit of the increased protection attached to a family of marks has been obtained, a likelihood of confusion by connection to the family was assessed from the outset, without prior examination with the earlier marks taken in isolation.[810] By contrast, in the judgments in which the sign at issue was found not to be similar to the marks taken separately, the Court did not take account of the fact that all those marks belonged to a family.[811] That said, this concept, as a means of demonstrating the distinctive character of the mark, perhaps has more potential precisely in the field of the special regime, where it should not be taken into account in the absence of a link

803. CJ, 13 September 2007, case C-234/06 P, *Bainbridge*, para. 63; CJ, 24 March 2011, case C-522/09 P, *Kinder*, para. 97.
804. Presently, of Article 8(5) of Regulation 2017/1001.
805. GC, 26 September 2012, case T-301/09, *Citi*, para. 22.
806. GC, 26 September 2012, case T-301/09, *Citi*, paras 105-107.
807. Passa, *Les 'familles' de marques* ..., p. 27.
808. GC, 26 September 2012, case T-301/09, *Citi*, para. 119.
809. *See* GC, 10 October 2019, case T-428/18, *McDonald's*, para. 75.
810. Passa, *Les 'familles' de marques* ..., pp. 26-27.
811. In French jurisprudence *see* Cass. com., 18 October 2016, case 15-14.523, Propr. ind. 2017, No. 1, comment 2, of Pascale Tréfigny, *Puma*.

between the sign at issue and the earlier reputed mark taken individually, but would be assessed from the outset and taken into consideration as one of the factors allowing to establish the existence of a link.[812]

166. Assessment of the infringement. Finally, it should be mentioned that, according to the General Court, the risk of unfair advantage is aggravated by the existence of a family of trade marks,[813] therefore, that it influences the assessment of the infringement itself.

[c] Uniqueness of the Trade Mark

167. Concept of uniqueness. According to the Court of Justice, the link is easier to establish when the trade mark is 'unique'.[814] Prima facie, similarly, as in the case of reputation and distinctiveness, there is some redundancy. Indeed, there exists a close relationship between inherent distinctiveness and uniqueness. However, it seems that uniqueness of the trade mark goes even further than distinctiveness because the uniqueness is not examined in relation to the goods or services for which the trade mark is registered. As Simon Fhima noted, unlike distinctiveness, which is assessed in the view of public perception, uniqueness requires an objective examination of the marks present on the market.[815]

This term, which has long been used by the doctrine, is far from clear and several interpretations have been proposed over the years. According to an extensive concept, uniqueness means that a word mark has not been used by a third party for goods or services covered by that mark.[816] The approach seems too liberal since many marks would then be unique, so that the sense of this criterion would be difficult to identify. In addition, it should be noted that the concept of uniqueness is not reserved for word marks.

Several authors present a narrower approach. Guglielmetti argued that a trade mark is unique when there are no goods or services of others on the market designated by an identical mark.[817] Simon Fhima considers that a trade mark can be qualified as unique if its owner is the only one to exploit the sign in the course of trade.[818] This approach was indeed adopted by the Court of Justice. In the light of the *Intel* judgment, a mark is unique if the sign it consists of 'has not been used by anyone for any goods or services other than by the proprietor of the mark for the goods and services it markets'.[819] Hence, a mark is not unique if, even though it is purely fanciful in relation to the good or service, and therefore inherently distinctive, it has been exploited in other, even remote, sectors of the market. With regard to figurative marks, a mark is

812. Cf. GC, 5 July 2016, case T-518/13, *McDonald's*, paras 69-73.
813. GC, 26 September 2012, case T-301/09, *Citi*, para. 122.
814. CJ, 27 November 2008, case C-252/07, *Intel*, para. 56.
815. Simon Fhima, *Trade Mark Dilution ...*, p. 146.
816. Gielen, *Trademark Dilution under European Law ...*, p. 713.
817. Guglielmetti, *Marques ordinaires, notoirement connues ...*, p. 76.
818. Simon Fhima, *Trade Mark Dilution ...*, p. 146. *See also* Skrzydło-Tefelska, *Community Trade Mark ...*, p. 290.
819. CJ, 27 November 2008, case C-252/07, *Intel*, para. 56.

not unique if the figurative element of the mark has been used in other marks, such as the image of the camel, which is used to designate several products of oriental origin.[820] Of course, not all reputed marks need to be unique.[821] A reputed trade mark may coexist with a similar sign used in a different economic sector. Moreover, it is not unlikely that two identical marks could enjoy a reputation. As an example we can cite the mark *Mont Blanc*, renowned in France in relation to food products, whose reputation was recognised in French case law,[822] and an identical mark reputed for writing instruments. The two signs coexist harmoniously in France without harming each other.[823]

A third and more restrictive approach involves assessing uniqueness not only in relation to other marks on the market but also in relation to the meaning of the term used in the sign. It was retained by Wichers Hoeth who considered that in order to be unique, a mark must have no other meaning; it must not suggest any other association than with the specific product.[824] This idea is reflected in the case law. According to a judgment of the General Court, a trade mark is not unique if it uses a term from everyday language, such as the term *VIPS*, which is widely and frequently used both internationally and nationally to describe famous personalities.[825] In Polish case law, a court refused to qualify the mark *Mont Blanc* as unique, since there were other trade marks containing this name and, in addition, the term constitutes a geographical designation.[826]

The median approach seems the most justified, insofar as it is the most appropriate for assessing trade mark infringement. The concept of uniqueness assessed in the light of the meaning of the sign seems to correspond to the originality of the sign, which is not relevant in trade mark law. *De lege lata*, fanciful marks do not enjoy any particular protection. The law only recognises reputation.[827] Indeed, very often marks are inspired by terms coming from everyday language, culture, geography, etc., for example, *Nike*, *Ajax*, *Cadillac*, *Mercedes* or *Tiffany*,[828] which therefore already have a meaning. It is, however, important to note that uniqueness is likely to be taken into account at the stage of assessing the link, i.e. once the reputation of the sign perceived by the public as a trade mark has been established.[829]

168. Importance to the assessment of dilution. In order for the uniqueness criterion to have its own role, it could be linked to the immediate association that the sign arouses in the public mind. Indeed, this criterion appears particularly relevant at the stage of assessing the infringement itself in the form of dilution, which consists in

820. CFI, 30 January 2008, case T-128/06, *Camel*, para. 58.
821. *See* before Directive 89/104, Guglielmetti, *Marques ordinaires, notoirement connues ...*, p. 76.
822. TGI Valence, 2 November 2004, case 00/00953, *Mont Blanc*.
823. *See* Pollaud-Dulian, *Propriété intellectuelle. La propriété industrielle ...*, p. 1067.
824. Wichers Hoeth, *Étude comparative ...*, p. 190. *See also* Bouvel, *La protection des marques ...*, para. 110. Cf. Schechter, *The Rational Basis ...*, pp. 828-830.
825. CFI, 22 March 2007, case T-215/03, *VIPS*, para. 62.
826. WSA Warsaw, 8 December 2014, case VI SA/Wa 1359/14, *Mont Blanc*.
827. Cf. in older doctrine Stephen P. Ladas, *Lettre des États-Unis*, PI 1951, p. 157.
828. *See* Katya Assaf, *Protection of Trade Marks Against Dilution: A Semiotic Perspective*, JIPLP 2009, vol. 4, No. 9, pp. 644-645.
829. Cf. paras 61 et seq. *supra*.

weakening an immediate association that the mark arouses in the public mind, or in the unfair advantage taken of the distinctive character of the mark. According to the *Intel* judgment, 'the more "unique" the earlier mark appears, the greater the likelihood that the use of a later identical or similar mark will be detrimental to its distinctive character'.[830] The immediate association which is the subject of the assessment of dilution refers to the perception of the sign in the course of trade as a trade mark and not to all the associations that the sign may give rise to in the mind of the consumer. For example, supposing that there is only one mark *Mercedes*, owned by the famous car manufacturer, it is likely to be diluted if it is used by other companies to designate different products. Given the degree of reputation of this mark, the fact that the term has a meaning, that it is also a female first name, should not affect the perception of this term as a mark.

It seems that at the stage of examining the existence of a link, the role of this factor should be secondary. The fact that a mark is unique is certainly likely to strengthen the association between the signs in the public mind, but its absence should not weaken it. The uniqueness criterion will become relevant, particularly at the stage of assessing dilution. That being said, a non-unique trade mark may be diluted, particularly when its reputation is exceptionally high, which may lead to immediate association with the right holder. Even if, in fact, there are several marks as *Mercedes*,[831] it seems that the public always instantly associates it with the car manufacturer. Immediate association in the minds of the public is therefore possible, thanks to the mere exceptional reputation. I will come back to this question when I examine dilution.[832]

§2.02 NEGATIVE CONDITIONS FOR INFRINGEMENT OF TRADE MARKS WITH A REPUTATION

169. General and specific limitations. The legislator also provides for negative conditions for trade mark infringement, i.e. conditions whose absence makes it possible to establish liability. The burden of proof lies on the alleged infringer. Pursuant to Article 10(2)(c) of Directive 2015/2436 and Article 9(2)(c) of Regulation 2017/1001, a negative condition for infringement specific to the special regime is the existence of a 'due cause'. In addition, there are several exceptions to trade mark protection that are common to all forms of infringement, whether within or outside the speciality, including the limitations provided for in Article 14 of Directive 2015/2436 and Article 14 of Regulation 2017/1001. They are perfectly applicable to trade marks with a reputation protected under the special regime.[833] According to some authors,

830. CJ, 27 November 2008, case C-252/07, *Intel*, para. 74.
831. Cf. Schricker, *La tutela della Ausstattung* ..., p. 267.
832. *See* paras 234 et seq. *infra*.
833. Vincenzo Di Cataldo, *The Trade Mark with a Reputation in EU Law: Some Remarks on the Negative Condition 'Without Due Cause'*, IIC 2011, vol. 42, No. 7, p. 839; Andreas Ebert-Weidenfeller, in: Gordian N. Hasselblatt (ed.), *Community Trade Mark Regulation. A Commentary*, C.H. Beck Hart Nomos, Munich-Oxford 2015, p. 383.

due cause may fall within one of these exceptions,[834] or rather the latter are examples of due cause.[835] Moreover, in the past, due cause was invoked in particular in the cases covered by those exceptions.[836] Thus, it can be considered that the general limitations of trade mark rights, in the context of the special regime, characterise due cause.[837] However, the situations covered by due cause should not be limited to these exceptions. Otherwise, the negative condition of due cause would be superfluous and fully redundant.[838] Since the general exceptions make it possible to avoid liability on the basis of the provisions common to all trade marks (§2.02[A]), invoking due cause provided for by the provisions on extended protection seems excessive.[839] It is preferable to analyse which special situations, not covered by the exceptions common to all trade marks, fall within the condition of due cause (§2.02[B]).

It should be noted that the provisions concerning exceptions are generally difficult to implement. This is even more true when it comes to the trade marks with a reputation. In the light of the case law of the Court of Justice, to quote Bonet, the idea is that the third party, only exceptionally authorised by law to use another's mark, must be particularly cautious.[840]

[A] Limitations Common to All Trade Marks

170. Sources of limitations. Among the exceptions that may be invoked by the alleged infringer of each trade mark, whether in or beyond the speciality, a distinction must be made between the limitations provided for by trade mark law (§2.02[A][1]) and a special exception related to comparative advertising (§2.02[A][2]). I do not intend to examine these limitations to trade mark protection as a whole, as the issue is not specific to the special regime. I will study them insofar as they are likely to legitimise the infringement of a reputed trade mark that is a priori established. Moreover, I will not address the limitation to the trade mark right constituted by the exhaustion of rights, which refers to cases in which the trade mark is lawfully affixed to the product by the owner and does not concern the extended protection.

834. Passa, *Traité de droit ...*, p. 541.
835. Cohen Jehoram, Van Nispen, Huydecoper, *European Trademark Law ...*, p. 317; Elżbieta Traple, *Reklama internetowa (adwords) jako uzasadniona przyczyna użycia cudzego znaku towarowego*, in: *Problemy polskiego i europejskiego prawa prywatnego. Księga pamiątkowa Profesora Mariana Kępińskiego*, Wolters Kluwer, Warsaw 2012, p. 419; Caselli, *Il marchio che gode di rinomanza ...*, p. 132.
836. *See* Braun, Cornu, *Précis des marques ...*, pp. 454-458.
837. Cf. in French jurisprudence CA Paris, 13 January 2015, case 13/13126, *SNCF*.
838. Caselli, *Il marchio che gode di rinomanza ...*, p. 140; Ricolfi, *Trattato dei marchi ...*, p. 758.
839. Cf. Łukasz Żelechowski, *'Uzasadniony powód' używania oznaczenia kolidującego z renomowanym znakiem towarowym*, Glosa 2014, No. 3, p. 81.
840. Georges Bonet, *Les conditions strictes de l'usage autorisé de la marque d'autrui selon la CJCE*, Propr. intell. 2005, No. 16, p. 283.

[1] *Limitations Provided by Trade Mark Law*

171. List of limitations. The exceptions provided for by trade mark law are referred to in Article 14 of Directive 2015/2436 and analogous Article 14 of Regulation 2017/1001, entitled: 'Limitation of the effects of a trade mark'. Under Article 14(1) of these provisions, a trade mark shall not entitle its proprietor to prohibit a third party from using: its name or address, non-distinctive indications and the trade mark as a reference, in particular in order to indicate the purpose of a product or service,[841] provided that such use is made 'in accordance with honest practices in industrial or commercial matters'.[842] In addition, Article 14(3) of Directive 2015/2436 provides for an exception in favour of holders of prior rights of local scope,[843] which can also be invoked against EU trade marks.[844]

It should be stressed that invoking limitations is only relevant in cases where a trade mark infringement is a priori established, whether in the field of double identity, likelihood of confusion or special protection of trade marks with a reputation. The sign of the third party must therefore be used in the course of trade and as a trade mark. Consequently, the role of these exceptions is in practice limited.

172. Name limitation. Among the exceptions mentioned above, it is worth considering in particular the one relating to the name of the third party exploiting a sign which constitutes a reproduction or imitation of a trade mark, which is sometimes referred to under the usual term 'homonymy'. Indeed, according to some authors, the main justification for exploiting the reputation of a mark is the case of homonymy.[845] The importance of this exception results in particular from the fact that other distinctive signs used in commerce, such as the company name or trade name, are likely to be perceived by the public as a trade mark and therefore to infringe the trade mark rights of others.[846]

In this respect, it should be noted that Article 14(1)(a) of Directive 2015/2436 and Article 14(1)(a) of Regulation 2017/1001 have a more limited scope than Article 6(1)(a)

841. Pursuant to Article 14(1): 'A trade mark shall not entitle the proprietor to prohibit a third party from using, in the course of trade: (a) the name or address of the third party, where that third party is a natural person; (b) signs or indications which are not distinctive or which concern the kind, quality, quantity, intended purpose, value, geographical origin, the time of production of goods or of rendering of the service, or other characteristics of goods or services; (c) the trade mark for the purpose of identifying or referring to goods or services as those of the proprietor of that trade mark, in particular, where the use of the trade mark is necessary to indicate the intended purpose of a product or service, in particular as accessories or spare parts.'

842. Article 14(2) of Directive 2015/2436 and of Regulation 2017/1001.

843. Pursuant to Article 14(3): 'A trade mark shall not entitle the proprietor to prohibit a third party from using, in the course of trade, an earlier right which only applies in a particular locality, if that right is recognised by the law of the Member State in question and the use of that right is within the limits of the territory in which it is recognised.'

844. *See* Article 138 of Regulation 2017/1001.

845. *See* Maetz, *Notoriété: essai sur l'appropriation ...*, p. 116.

846. *See* Mathély, *Le droit français des signes ...*, p. 629; Skubisz, *Prawo znaków ...*, pp. 137-138; Passa, *Traité de droit ...*, p. 305; Michal Bohaczewski, *Usage de nom comme contrefaçon de marque en droit de l'Union européenne*, Les cahiers de propriété intellectuelle 2015, vol. 27, No. 1, pp. 79-82.

of the previous Directives and Article 12(1)(a) of the previous Regulations. Under the former Article 6(1)(a) of Directive 89/104, the Court of Justice noted that the term 'name' was not limited to the names of natural persons but also covered trade names.[847] However, Article 14(1)(a) of Directive 2015/2436 and Article 14(1)(a) of Regulation 2017/1001 expressly reserve the benefit of this limitation to natural persons. Thus, a legal person can no longer invoke its right to the name in order to avoid liability for trade mark infringement, even if the name of a natural person, and in particular of a partner (shareholder), is included in the company name.

One can wonder whether this amendment adopted by the European legislator is accurate.[848] In practice, in most cases, relying on the exception in question by legal persons was justified when a partner's name was used in the company name.[849] Consequently, pursuant to the old provisions, it could be assumed that the use of a company name, which in principle infringed a trade mark, was justified where the insertion of a natural person's name was the result of a desire to highlight a relationship between the person (partner, shareholder, etc.) and the company, in particular where the holder of the name was personally and genuinely engaged in the company's activity.[850]

This limitation of the trade mark right could also be claimed where the insertion of a surname was mandatory under the relevant national legislation.[851] For instance, Polish law imposes a mandatory requirement to include the surname of at least one partner (shareholder) of some types of commercial companies. If, for example, a certain Mr Dior wished to manufacture clothing in Poland, he could be required to insert his name in the corporate name of the company. Since the use of a company name is likely to qualify as trade mark use, such use may lead to an infringement.[852] It seems that the former provisions of the Directives and Regulations could apply in such cases where the use of the disputed sign was required by a legal provision. However, in the light of Article 14(1)(a) of Directive 2015/2436 and of Regulation 2017/1001, only a natural person may invoke his right to a name.

---

847. CJ, 16 November 2004, case C-245/02, *Anheuser-Busch*, para. 81.

848. Even though it seems consistent with the original idea adopted by the European legislature in the former Directives. Cf. Charles Gielen, *On the Limitations of Rights under European Trade Mark Law*, in: Dietrich Beier, Laurence Brüning-Petit, Christopher Heath (eds), *Festschrift für Jochen Pagenberg*, Carl Heymanns Verlag, Cologne 2006, p. 131.

849. *See* Zanella, *Les marques nominatives* ..., pp. 183-184. In French case law *see* TGI Paris, 22 May 1991, PIBD 1991, No. 511, III, p. 683, *Michelin*; Cass. com., 21 June 2011, case 10-23.262, *Henriot*. In the latter judgment, the Court of Cassation ruled that the use of a surname in the corporate name of the company in which the owner of the surname exercised, as manager, control and management functions, so that the company identified itself with him, justified an exception.

850. Cf. Zanella, *Les marques nominatives* ..., p. 199; Passa, *Traité de droit* ..., p. 433.

851. Bohaczewski, *Usage de nom* ..., p. 93.

852. Even if he added other distinctive verbal elements in order to justify the honesty of his practices, having regard to the criteria for assessing the likelihood of confusion in trade mark law, an element such as *Dior*, with strong distinctive power, would undoubtedly be capable of having an autonomous distinctive position within the sign of the third party. Consequently, given the identity of the goods and the similarity of the signs, in such case it would be difficult to rule out the existence of a likelihood of confusion. In the absence of a likelihood of confusion such use could of course characterise an infringement of the reputed trade mark.

Natural persons will however rarely need to rely on this exception. A name used as such does not infringe the trade mark right.[853] The use of names by natural persons is in principle unrelated to the conduct of business and does not constitute use as a trade mark. Thus, the solution will only continue to apply to those entrepreneurs who are natural persons and who use their names in the course of trade to designate their business.[854] In addition, Article 14(1)(a) of Directive 2015/2436 and Article 14(1)(a) of Regulation 2017/1001 are likely to cover a specific case in which a natural person, in particular an artist, a fashion designer, etc., registers his name as a trade mark, then assigns the trade mark rights to a third party, but continues to create and his name is applied to his works in order to indicate the name of the creator. Admittedly, the question of use of the name as a trade mark arises at first, but, in the view of its broad assessment, it cannot be ruled out that such use may be qualified as use made in the function of indicating the commercial origin of a good. This situation is illustrated in a case that gave rise to the judgments of the Paris Court of Appeal of 10 October 2014 and the Court of Cassation of 8 February 2017.[855] As a result, the scope of application of Article 14(1)(a) of Directive 2015/2436 and Article 14(1)(a) of Regulation 2017/1001 appears to be very limited.[856]

That being said, in the case of trade marks with a reputation, legal persons will be able to invoke homonymy as due cause. If, therefore, in our invented hypothesis of a company founded by a Mr Dior in Poland, because of differences between the signs, the likelihood of confusion was ruled out but the infringement of the reputed trade mark was retained, the company could claim due cause. This question will be discussed further.[857]

173. Other limitations. The other limitations referred to in Article 14(1) of Directive 2015/2436 and Article 14(1)(a) of Regulation 2017/1001 are also perfectly applicable in

853. Patrice de Candé, Alix Phiquepal d'Arusmont, *Article 6 de la directive 89/104: la notion d'usage honnête, le cheval de Troie de la concurrence déloyale du droit communautaire*, Propr. intell. 2008, No. 28, p. 292; Bohaczewski, *Usage de nom ...*, p. 84.
854. Cf. Gielen, *On the Limitations ...*, p. 130.
855. CA Paris, 10 October 2014, case 14/01577; Cass. com., 8 February 2017, case 14-28.232, Propr. ind. 2017, No. 4, comment 24, of Pascale Tréfigny, *Christian Lacroix*. Mr Christian Lacroix, who had assigned the rights to the trade mark consisting of his name (registered in particular for clothing, fabrics, etc.), began to use a designation 'designed by Mr Christian Lacroix' on furniture made of luxury upholstery fabrics. The assignee of the trade mark objected to this exploitation of Mr Lacroix's surname. According to the judgment of the Court of Appeal, the sign was used not only to indicate the artistic origin but also as a trade mark. It should be noted that if, as in the case in question, the name holder always used terms such as 'designed by', reflecting a descriptive reference, and added another sign intended to indicate the commercial origin, compliance with the requirement of honest practices in commercial and industrial matters could have been demonstrated. Therefore, it seems that in the present case the exception could have been successfully invoked. The question was not decided because the exception was not raised in the last pleadings. The likelihood of confusion was ruled out because of differences between the conflicting goods and the infringement of the reputed trade mark due to the failure to establish the reputation of the claimed trade mark.
856. Moreover, the interpretation of the limitation in question is generally restrictive. The right to commercial use of a name registered by a third party as a trade mark is reserved solely for the owners of patronymic names. Other names, such as first names, pseudonyms and nicknames, are excluded from the scope of the article. Zanella, *Les marques nominatives ...*, p. 178.
857. *See* para. 189 *infra*.

the case of trade marks with a reputation. It should nevertheless be noted that their recognition by the legislator can be questioned, as it is not certain that the situations covered by these exceptions are likely to characterise use as an indication of the commercial origin.[858] In particular, the purpose of the address exception is difficult to identify, since the use of a sign in an address does not constitute use as a trade mark.[859] Similarly, the use of a non-distinctive, for instance exclusively descriptive, sign cannot characterise use in the distinctive function of a trade mark. Indeed, the use of an element not performing the origin function is not capable of constituting an infringement of the trade mark right.[860] The exception relating to the referential use of the mark, especially where it is necessary to indicate the purpose of a good or service, in particular as accessories or spare parts, could also be called into question, since it could be a use made for information purposes, and therefore not use as a trade mark.[861] Indeed, even in the old doctrine, supported by part of the case law, some authors admitted that the use of a trade mark as a mere reference, therefore to indicate no longer the origin, but the destination of a product, did not constitute an unlawful act of infringement.[862] Consequently, the limitation to the trade mark right might appear questionable. However, as we have seen, the condition of use as a trade mark is now widely interpreted, not necessarily limited to the use of a trade mark for a good or service of the infringer. In accordance with the *BMW* judgment, where the third party provides services relating to a product, the use of the mark designating the product to indicate its origin constitutes use liable to infringe the trade mark right. Thus, the use of a mark as a reference may fall a priori within the scope of the exclusivity conferred by the trade mark.[863] That being said, the *BMW* decision was criticised precisely because of the absence of use as a trade mark, understood as use to designate a good or service of the infringer.[864] The *O2 Holdings* judgment[865] of the Court of Justice and the current wording of the provision, modified as a result of that decision,[866] confirm that use of a sign to indicate goods as coming from the right holder may lead to trade mark infringement.

858. *See* Szczepanowska-Kozłowska, *Wyczerpanie praw własności ...*, p. 90.
859. Passa, *Traité de droit ...*, p. 429; de Candé, Phiquepal d'Arusmont, *Article 6 de la directive 89/104: la notion d'usage ...*, p. 292; Basire, *Les fonctions de la marque ...*, p. 214. *See* CFI, 13 July 2005, case T-40/03, *Murua*.
860. Passa, *Traité de droit ...*, pp. 314 and 446; Ebert-Weidenfeller, *Community Trade Mark ...*, p. 383; Szczepanowska-Kozłowska, *System prawa handlowego ...*, p. 705. *See* CJ, 18 June 2009, case C-487/07, *L'Oréal*, para. 61. Cf. Cohen Jehoram, Van Nispen, Huydecoper, *European Trademark Law ...*, pp. 245, 265.
861. de Candé, Phiquepal d'Arusmont, *Article 6 de la directive 89/104: la notion d'usage ...*, p. 292.
862. Fernand Jacq, *La référence à un nom commercial ou à une marque déposée, pour désigner des pièces détachées, est-elle licite?*, Ann. propr. ind. 1928, pp. 121 et seq.; Fernand Jacq, *Pièces détachées, marques et noms commerciaux*, PI 1930, pp. 39 et seq.
863. *See* CJ, 23 February 1999, case C-63/97, *BMW*, para. 59.
864. *See* Szczepanowska-Kozłowska, *Wyczerpanie praw własności ...*, p. 105; Yap, *Essential Function ...*, p. 82.
865. CJ, 12 June 2008, case C-533/06, *O2 Holdings*, para. 33. *See* para. 172 *supra*.
866. Article 14(1)(c) of Directive 2015/2436 and of Article 14(1) of Regulation 2017/1001 now specify that the use must be made in relation to goods or services 'as those of the proprietor' of the trade mark. At the same time, they do not limit the application of this provision to the cases where the use of the mark is necessary to indicate the intended purpose of a product or service.

174. Honest practices in industrial or commercial matters. In order for all the limitations of trade mark rights referred to in Article 14(1) of Directive 2015/2436 and Article 14(1) of Regulation 2017/1001 to be such as to legitimise the use of a reputed trade mark by a third party, the use in question must be made 'in accordance with honest practices in industrial or commercial matters'. The burden of proof is on the third party raising the defence.[867] The interpretation of this condition is complicated.[868] According to the *BMW* judgment, 'the condition requiring use of the trade mark to be made in accordance with honest practices in industrial or commercial matters must be regarded as constituting in substance the expression of a duty to act fairly in relation to the legitimate interests of the trade mark owner'.[869] The formula is vague and not very informative.[870] The subsequent case law of the Court of Justice provides more guidance for interpreting the condition of honest practices. According to the *Gillette* judgment, use of the trade mark will not be in accordance with honest practices in industrial and commercial matters in particular if: (1) it is done in such a manner as to give the impression that there is a commercial connection between the third party and the trade mark owner;[871] (2) it affects the value of the trade mark by taking unfair advantage of its distinctive character or repute; (3) it entails the discrediting or denigration of that mark.[872]

Thus, the Court of Justice makes the honesty of the use of a trade mark, above all, conditional on the absence of a likelihood of confusion in the broad sense. This interpretation of the concept of honest practices by the Court of Justice was rightly criticised in doctrine. Indeed, in the presence of only two similar signs, the likelihood of confusion is a condition of trade mark infringement. If it is not established, the latter cannot be retained under Article 10(2)(b) of Directive 2015/2436 or Article 9(2)(a) of Regulation 2017/1001, without the need to invoke Article 14. Hence, the absence of a likelihood of confusion cannot be a condition for the application of Article 14(2) without depriving it of its own efficiency as a real limitation of trade mark right.[873]

867. *Contra* Ebert-Weidenfeller, *Community Trade Mark ...*, pp. 384, 389; Kur, Senftleben, *European Trade Mark ...*, p. 434. The wording of the provisions does not provide any grounds for reversing the burden of proof.
868. *See* Bohaczewski, *Usage de nom ...*, pp. 84 et seq.
869. CJ, 23 February 1999, case C-63/97, *BMW*, para. 61.
870. de Candé, Phiquepal d'Arusmont, *Article 6 de la directive 89/104: la notion d'usage ...*, p. 296; Po Jen Yap, *Honestly, Neither Céline Nor Gillette Is Defensible!*, EIPR 2008, vol. 30, No. 7, p. 287.
871. This criterion was already provided for in the judgment of CJ, 23 February 1999, case C-63/97, *BMW*, para. 64.
872. CJ, 17 March 2005, case C-228/03, *Gillette*, para. 49. Moreover, the third party must not present its product as an imitation or replica of the product bearing the trade mark of which it is not the owner. This criterion applies only to the use of the trade mark to indicate the destination of a good or service.
873. *See* Grégoire Loiseau, *Droit de marque et droit au nom*, Bulletin Joly Sociétés 2011, No. 12, p. 954. The condition of honest practices cannot constitute a simple negation of the requirements for trade mark infringement. In the event that the right holder establishes a likelihood of confusion, the alleged infringer must have a possibility of defence. Otherwise, Article 14(1) and (2) of Directive 2015/2436 and Article 14(1) and (2) of Regulation 2017/1001 could never apply. Cf. Yap, *Essential Function ...*, p. 82; Bohaczewski, *Usage de nom ...*, p. 86. If the conditions for limiting the right to the trade mark are assessed after having established infringement a priori under Article 10(2)(b) of Directive 2015/2436 or Article 9(2)(c) of Regulation 2017/1001, the use likely to suggest that there is a commercial link between the

In the case of trade marks with a reputation, this first condition relating to the likelihood of indirect confusion is acceptable, since the infringement of the reputed trade mark does not depend on the existence of a danger of misleading the public as to the commercial origin of the goods or services. Nevertheless, similarly, in the view of the other criteria, it is difficult to indicate in which situations the alleged infringer of a reputed trade mark could avoid liability. In the event that the proprietor demonstrates an infringement of the reputed trade mark pursuant to Article 10(2)(c) of Directive 2015/2436 or Article 9(2)(c) of Regulation 2017/1001, apart from dilution, the disputed use either 'affects the value of the trade mark by taking unfair advantage of its distinctive character or repute' or 'entails the discrediting or denigration of that mark'. Indeed, the first criterion seems to correspond to the infringement by tarnishment, while the second criterion corresponds to the unfair advantage hypothesis. It should be stressed that in the light of the *Gillette* judgment, the existence of only one of the conditions listed by the Court of Justice is sufficient to exclude the honesty of the third party. Consequently, the conditions of honest practices imposed by the Court of Justice make the exceptions provided for in Article 14(1) of Directive 2015/2436 and Article 14(1) of Regulation 2017/1001, in most cases, practically impossible to implement on the ground of the special regime.[874] Moreover, the courts sometimes expressly admit that the existence of a commercial connection corresponds to the situation of the likelihood of confusion, whereas unfair advantage, on the one hand, and discredit and denigration, on the other hand, to the infringement of reputed trade marks.[875] Consequently, the exceptions provided for in Article 14(1) are only likely to apply in the case of dilution.[876] Indeed, if the right holder established only the infringement in the form of detriment to the distinctive character, the defendant could avoid liability since dilution is not covered by the criteria for assessing honest practices. However, even this assumption is not certain since the list of conditions for assessing honest practices provided by the Court of Justice is not exhaustive.[877]

In part of its case law, the Court of Justice links the honesty of the third party to the absence of a likelihood of confusion and, moreover, to the awareness of the alleged infringer. According to the *Anheuser-Busch* and *Céline* decisions, 'In assessing whether the condition of honest practice is satisfied, account must be taken first of the extent to which the use of the third party's trade name is understood by the relevant public, or at least a significant section of that public, as indicating a link between the third party's goods and the trade mark proprietor or a person authorised to use the trade mark, and secondly of the extent to which the third party ought to have been aware of that. Another factor to be taken into account when making the assessment is whether the

third party and the trade mark owner will always occur, unless the existence of that link is assessed *in concreto*, as in the field of unfair competition, taking into account factors likely to rule out the risk of confusion which are not taken into consideration in the examination of the trade mark infringement.

874. Simon Fhima, *Trade Mark Dilution* ..., p. 232; Caselli, *Il marchio che gode di rinomanza* ..., p. 214.
875. In Polish jurisprudence cf. SA Warsaw, 8 March 2016, case I ACa 793/15, *Tomatis*.
876. Simon Fhima, *Trade Mark Dilution* ..., p. 232.
877. *See* CJ, 17 March 2005, case C-228/03, *Gillette*, para. 49.

trade mark concerned enjoys a certain reputation in the Member State in which it is registered and its protection is sought, from which the third party might profit in selling his goods.'[878] The 'link' to which the Court refers seems to mean the likelihood of confusion *lato sensu* and not merely the link as a condition for infringement on the basis of the special regime. Thus, in accordance with the criteria resulting from these judgments, the third party could avoid liability by establishing that the public is not likely to be misled as to the commercial origin of the good or service designated by the disputed sign. For the same reason as the criteria of honest use provided for in the *BMW* and *Gillette* decisions, the solution is questionable in the field of trade mark infringement in the speciality.[879] In the case of reputed trade marks, the application of the conditions of honest use resulting from the *Anheuser-Busch* and *Céline* judgments can effectively allow the third party to avoid liability, in accordance with the function that the legislator gives to Article 14(1) and (2) which may then apply. That being said, the criterion of honest practices is flexible enough not to be reduced to the absence of likelihood of confusion. The disputed use can always be characterised as dishonest when the desire to benefit from the reputation of a reputed trade mark is manifest, even in the absence of any risk of confusion.[880] Moreover, as we have noted, according to the *Anheuser-Busch* and *Céline* judgments, the reputation of the trade mark is a factor to be taken into account in assessing the honesty of the use in question.

175. Prior use of the sign. Article 14(1) and (2) of Directive 2015/2436 and Article 14 of Regulation 2017/1001 are of real importance when the disputed sign is subsequent to the trade mark right. Conflicts with earlier signs, in particular, surnames, company names and trade names, should be settled on the basis of the provisions relating to relative grounds for refusal and invalidity of registration.[881] If the third party could not invoke his earlier right, in the absence of a likelihood of confusion at the time of filing of the mark which subsequently became reputed and enjoys extended protection, as we shall see, the prior use of the sign is likely to constitute due cause.[882]

878. CJ, 16 November 2004, case C-245/02, *Anheuser-Busch*, para. 83; CJ, 11 September 2007, case C-17/06, *Céline*, para. 34. *See also* CJ, 8 July 2010, case C-558/08, *Portakabin*, para. 67.

879. Cf. Tom Scourfield, *A Tale of Two Celines*, EIPR 2008, vol. 30, No. 2, p. 73. In order to ensure a possibility for the third party to raise limitations of trade mark rights, the third party's awareness of the possibility of infringing an earlier trade mark could constitute the essential criterion of honest practices. The assessment of honest practices would thus focus on the diligence of the defendant, on the acts performed by the defendant in order to avoid the likelihood of confusion. Cf. Yap, *Honestly, Neither Céline ...*, p. 292; Bohaczewski, *Usage de nom ...*, pp. 90-93. That said, it should be noted that the notion of awareness refers to the state of mind of the infringer, which is not relevant to trade mark infringement. Cf. de Candé, Phiquepal d'Arusmont, *Article 6 de la directive 89/104: la notion d'usage ...*, p. 297.

880. Cf. Zanella, *Les marques nominatives ...*, pp. 201-203. On the condition of honest practices cf. further Lorenzo Biglia, *Uso atipico del marchio altrui e rapporto di concorrenza,* Riv. Dir. Ind. 2006, I, pp. 195 et seq.

881. *See* Skubisz, *Prawo znaków ...*, p. 138; Szczepanowska-Kozłowska, *Używanie firmy jako naruszenie ...*, p. 6. Cf. also Ebert-Weidenfeller, *Community Trade Mark ...*, p. 383. Provided that the signs such as trade names, etc. are subject of prior rights opposable to registration of trade marks under national provisions.

882. *See* paras 191 et seq. *infra*.

In addition, the third party who exploited the disputed sign prior to the filing may invoke his local rights covered by national provisions interpreted in the light of Article 14(3) of Directive 2015/2436. This exception does not present any real specificities on the ground of the special regime. Moreover, since the use of the sign in the context of this exception is likely to be territorially limited, it should be more interesting for the third party to raise due cause characterised by prior use,[883] unless the use of the earlier sign does not satisfy the conditions arising from the case law of the Court of Justice on the basis of which due cause must be assessed, which will be examined below.

[2] Comparative Advertising

176. Conditions of lawfulness. Another exception that may be invoked against the proprietor of any trade mark, including a trade mark with a reputation, is the use of the sign in comparative advertising that satisfies the conditions of lawfulness provided for by Directive 2006/114[884] in Article 4 (formerly by Directive 84/450[885] in Article 3). Comparative advertising shall be permitted when, *inter alia*, pursuant to Article 4(d), it does not discredit or denigrate another's trade marks, and, pursuant to Article 4(f), it does not take unfair advantage of the reputation of a trade mark. Insofar as these conditions are particularly close to the special regime, I will discuss below the possibility for the alleged infringer of a reputed trade mark to invoke the use in accordance with the conditions of lawfulness of comparative advertising, likely to legitimise an a priori established infringement.

177. Broad definition of comparative advertising. Before moving on to the analysis, it is worth recalling the very broad definition of the concept of comparative advertising established by the Court of Justice. According to the *Toshiba* judgment, 'in order for there to be comparative advertising ... it is therefore sufficient for a representation to be made in any form which refers, even by implication, to a competitor or to the goods or services which he offers' and 'it does not matter that there is a comparison between the goods and services offered by the advertiser and those of a competitor'.[886]

883. Cf. Żelechowski, *'Uzasadniony powód' używania ...*, p. 87.

884. Directive 2006/114/EC of the European Parliament and of the Council of 12 December 2006 concerning misleading and comparative advertising, Official Journal L 376 of 27 December 2006.

885. Directive 84/450/EEC of the Council of 10 September 1984 relating to the approximation of the laws, regulations and administrative provisions of the Member States concerning misleading advertising, Official Journal L. 250 of 19 September 1984.

886. CJ, 23 October 2001, case C-112/99, *Toshiba*, para. 31. In other words, an advertisement can be qualified as comparative while it does not make any comparison. Jérôme Passa, *Les rapports entre droit des marques et droit de la publicité comparative: un risque d'affaiblissement de la protection de la marque*, Propr. ind. 2008, No. 10, étude 20, para. 4. Thus, any advertising that merely refers to a competitor is covered by Directive 2006/114 and, consequently, the exception is likely to be invoked against the advertiser by the proprietor of the trade mark, in the absence of a comparison. *See also* CJ, 12 June 2008, case C-533/06, *O2 Holdings*, para. 44. However, it must be noted that the solution is tempered by the wording of Article 4(b) and (c) of Directive 2006/114, which requires comparative advertising to compare goods or services.

178. Use as a trade mark. It should be also noted that the use of another's mark in comparative advertising constitutes use as a trade mark by the advertiser.[887] According the *O2 Holdings* judgment of the Court of Justice, 'use by an advertiser, in a comparative advertisement, of a sign identical with, or similar to, a competitor's mark may constitute use within the meaning of Article 5(1) and (2) of Directive 89/104'[888] – of Article 10(2) of Directive 2015/2436 (hence also of Article 9(2) of Regulation 2017/1001). Thus, use made to identify the competitor's products may be considered as use as a trade mark by the advertiser. As we have seen, the Court of Justice thus opted for a broad approach of use as a trade mark.[889] Today, the solution has normative value, since Directive 2015/2436 and Regulation 2017/1001 provide, respectively, in Articles 10(3)(f) and 9(3)(f) that using the sign in comparative advertising constitutes a form of use of the trade mark.

179. Likelihood of confusion. The absence of discredit or denigration of a trade mark and of unfair advantage taken of the reputation is included in Article 4 of Directive 2006/114 among the conditions for lawfulness of comparative advertising alongside the absence of likelihood of confusion. It should be noted that the latter must be given the same interpretation as in trade mark law. Consequently, where the conditions provided by Article 10(2)(b) of Directive 2015/2436 or Article 9(2)(b) of Regulation 2017/1001 are met, comparative advertising may not satisfy the requirement of lawfulness laid down in Article 4(h) of Directive 2006/114.[890]

Indeed, there can be no lawful comparative advertising without such a comparison. Passa, *Les rapports entre droit des marques …*, paras 5-6. *See also* CJ, 8 April 2003, case C-44/01, *Pippig Augenoptik*, para. 36.

887. *See* para. 132 *supra*.

888. CJ, 12 June 2008, case C-533/06, *O2 Holdings*, para. 33.

889. The solution was criticised because, in the light of earlier case law, it could be assumed that the condition of use as a trade mark meant that the third party had to use the sign at issue to designate his own goods or services. And it did not appear necessary for the proprietor of a trade mark to be able to take action under trade mark law in order to oppose comparative advertising which infringed the conditions of lawfulness. It could be sufficient if the proprietor could act only on the basis of unfair competition. The solution adopted by the Court of Justice and by the current legislature therefore allows to condemn, as an infringement of the trade mark, the author of unlawful comparative advertising targeting another's trade mark. Cf. Passa, *Les rapports entre droit des marques …*, para. 3.

890. *See* CJ, 12 June 2008, case C-533/06, *O2 Holdings*, paras 46 and 49. According to the Court of Justice, the same interpretation must be given to the term 'confusion' used in both Article 5(1)(b) of Directive 89/104 and Article 3a(1)(d) of Directive 84/450. The solution has not escaped criticism. Indeed, while in trade mark law the likelihood of confusion is assessed solely by comparing signs and goods or services, in comparative advertising law the assessment of the likelihood of confusion presupposes taking account of all the circumstances of the case, and therefore considering a comparative advertisement as a whole. Pursuant to Article 4(h) of Directive 2006/114, the likelihood of confusion may result from factors other than the use of a sign identical with, or similar to, a trade mark for identical or similar goods. The provision refers broadly to confusion 'between the advertiser and a competitor or between the advertiser's trade marks, trade names, other distinguishing marks, goods or services and those of a competitor'. It may therefore seem excessive to assert that taking into account of the likelihood of confusion when establishing that the trade mark right is enforceable necessarily implies a disregard of the condition of lawfulness of Article 4(h). Passa, *Les rapports entre droit des marques …*, para. 13. In this direction also Ryszard Skubisz, Jarosław Dudzik, *Używanie znaku towarowego konkurenta w reklamie porównawczej*, EPS 2008, No. 11, p. 39.

In the field of enhanced protection of trade marks with a reputation, the absence of likelihood of confusion cannot make an advertisement lawful. However, in the light of the first decisions of the Court of Justice on comparative advertising, it might seem that the right holder should always establish a likelihood of confusion in order to demonstrate an unfair advantage taken of the reputation, within the meaning of the Directive on comparative advertising. According to the *Toshiba* judgment, while assessing whether an advertisement is permitted it is necessary to determine whether the indication of the trade mark 'could cause the public to associate the equipment manufacturer, whose products are those identified, with the competing supplier, in that the public might associate the reputation of that manufacturer's products with the products of the competing supplier'.[891] The 'association' did not correspond to the concept of a 'link' used in the special regime since the Court required a likelihood of indirect confusion for comparative advertising to disregard the requirement of lawfulness relating to unfair advantage, now referred to in Article 4(f) of Directive 2006/114.[892] The solution was questionable. If the provision concerned indirect likelihood of confusion, the requirement provided for in Article 4(f) could not be distinguished from the condition related to the likelihood of confusion,[893] and the two conditions should not be confused when the Directive clearly distinguishes them.[894] The Court of Justice finally admitted that the advertiser is likely to take unfair advantage of the reputation of a competing trade mark in the absence of any likelihood of confusion. In the light of the *L'Oréal* judgment, all provisions should be considered independent; Article 4 of Directive 2006/114 does not require that there be a likelihood of confusion.[895] Thus, it is the condition of transfer of reputation that constitutes the main criterion for the illegality of comparative advertising and not the question of the creation of an association between operators.[896] The 'association' to which the previous case law of the Court of Justice refers may therefore correspond to the 'link' established in the mind of the public which is not likely to be misled.[897] Consequently, the case law on comparative advertising seems to have finally joined the jurisprudence which established the condition of existence of a link as a condition for the infringement of the trade mark with a reputation.

180. Unfair advantage. As regards the unfair advantage taken of the reputation, it should be noted that, according to the *Toshiba* judgment, the advertiser takes unfair advantage of the reputation attached to a trade mark when the public associates the

891. CJ, 23 October 2001, case C-112/99, *Toshiba*, para. 57.
892. CJ, 23 October 2001, case C-112/99, *Toshiba*, paras 59-60; CJ, 23 February 2006, case C-59/05, *Siemens*, paras 18-20.
893. *See* Passa, *Les rapports entre droit des marques ...*, paras 14-15.
894. Passa, *Traité de droit ...*, p. 501.
895. CJ, 18 June 2009, case C-487/07, *L'Oréal*, para. 74.
896. Passa, *Traité de droit ...*, p. 502.
897. This is how the French Court of Cassation interprets the condition of link allowing the advertiser to take advantage of the attractive power of a third party's sign, in the absence of a likelihood of confusion. *See* Cass. com., 30 March 2016, case 13-12.122, Contr. Conc. Cons. 2016, comment 164, of Marie Malaurie-Vignal.

reputation of the manufacturer's products with the products of the competing supplier.[898] The Court of Justice seems to give this expression the same meaning as in the field of the special regime, but, as we have seen, in that decision, the Court required the establishment of a likelihood of confusion. However, the *L'Oréal* judgment leaves no room for doubt: the expression 'take[s] unfair advantage' of that reputation, which is used in Article 4(f) of Directive 2006/114 and in Article 10(2)(c) of Directive 2015/2436 (hence also in Article 9(2)(c) of Regulation 2017/1001), must in principle be given the same interpretation.[899] The solution was criticised by some authors who consider that the unfair advantage referred to in the provision on comparative advertising should be interpreted in a more restrictive way so that the objective of the Directive on comparative advertising can be achieved.[900] It seems, however, that the legislator should not give two different meanings to the same notion. Moreover, it is difficult to understand how this distinction could be implemented in practice.

Thus, as observed by Simon Fhima, once unfair advantage is established, comparative advertising is unlawful, which the author criticised because of the broad appreciation of unfair advantage in trade mark law.[901] Nevertheless, in response to this criticism, it should be noted that this form of infringement of a reputed trade mark is likely to be assessed in the view of the particular nature of the use of the trade mark in comparative advertising and is not so easy to establish in this case. The Court of Justice noted in the *Siemens* judgment that 'the benefit of comparative advertising to consumers must necessarily be taken into account in determining whether an advertiser is taking unfair advantage of the reputation of a trade mark' and 'the benefit an advertiser derives from comparative advertising, which, by reason of its very nature, is self-evident in all cases, cannot alone be determinative of whether the conduct of such an advertiser is lawful'.[902] It seems that the condition of lawfulness should be considered to be disregarded where 'it is clear that comparative advertising is in reality merely a pretext to exploit the reputation of that mark in a parasitical manner'.[903]

Nevertheless, with regard to a particular hypothesis of use of another's trade mark in the comparison lists, it should be noted that, under the terms of the *L'Oréal* judgment, 'comparative advertising which presents the advertiser's products as an imitation of a product bearing a trade mark is inconsistent with fair competition and thus unlawful, any advantage gained by the advertiser through such advertising will have been achieved as the result of unfair competition and must, accordingly, be regarded as taking unfair advantage of the reputation of that mark'.[904] It is important to note that another condition of the lawfulness of comparative advertising is then also applied. Under Article 4(g) of Directive 2006/114, lawful comparative advertising may not present goods or services as imitations or replicas of goods or services bearing a

898. CJ, 23 October 2001, case C-112/99, *Toshiba*, para. 60.
899. CJ, 18 June 2009, case C-487/07, *L'Oréal*, para. 77.
900. Di Cataldo, *The Trade Mark with a Reputation ...*, p. 844.
901. Simon Fhima, *Trade Mark Dilution ...*, p. 234.
902. CJ, 23 February 2006, case C-59/05, *Siemens*, paras 24-25.
903. Opinion of Advocate General Paolo Mengozzi in case C-533/06, *O2 Holdings*, para. 57. Cf. also Passa, *Les rapports entre droit des marques ...*, para. 15.
904. CJ, 18 June 2009, case C-487/07, *L'Oréal*, para. 79.

protected trade mark. It follows that, since the condition laid down in Article 4(g) is not complied with, the condition relating to unfair advantage is also disregarded. Consequently, an infringement of a reputed trade mark can be established.[905]

181. Discredit and denigration. According to some authors, the situation is clearly different in the case of detriment to the distinctive character or repute. The terms 'discredit' or 'denigration', used in Article 4 of Directive 2006/114, would imply a more serious affection of the owner's interests than those used in trade mark law. Consequently, an infringement of a reputed trade mark could a priori be established, in the form of dilution or tarnishment, in accordance with Article 10(2)(c) of Directive 2015/2436 or Article 9(2)(c) of Regulation 2017/1001, but, in the absence of discredit or denigration, the use of the trade mark in comparative advertising could be legitimised by this limitation of trade mark right.[906]

It seems that the case of dilution should be distinguished from tarnishment. Indeed, it is not clear how a gradation could be established between the terms, on the one hand, 'discredit', 'denigration' and, on the other hand, 'detriment to repute', which is also referred to as 'tarnishment' or 'degradation'. Moreover, the concepts of 'discredit' and 'denigration' are sometimes used to characterise the detriment to the repute on the ground of the special regime. Finally, even if we could make such a distinction in theory, its application by the judge would be practically impossible.

However, it should be noted that Article 4 of Directive 2006/114 refers only to 'reputation' which should correspond to the concept of 'repute' of the mark within the meaning of Article 10(2)(c) of Directive 2015/2436 and Article 9(2)(c) of Regulation 2017/1001, but not to its distinctive character. Dilution is not covered by Article 4 of Directive 2006/114, which hence excludes the liability of the advertiser in the event of dilution when the advertisement meets all the conditions of lawfulness. This could also mean that comparative advertising is not likely to cause this type of detriment to the trade mark with a reputation.[907] The alleged infringer of a reputed mark could therefore successfully oppose this exception to the right holder who establishes only a simple dilution of his mark, without however demonstrating a more serious risk of damage to its image. Similarly, in the case of unfair advantage, this limitation of trade mark rights could be invoked against unfair advantage taken of the distinctive character. It is therefore necessary to distinguish between the two forms of unfair advantage which, in the field of the special regime, are presented together by the Court of Justice but, as we shall see further, can be dissociated.[908]

Thus, it must be noted that the defendant cannot rely on the exception based on the use of the disputed sign in comparative advertising against the proprietor who demonstrated the infringement in the form of tarnishment or unfair advantage taken of

905. Cf. Pollaud-Dulian, *Propriété intellectuelle. La propriété industrielle ...*, p. 966. On the use of trade marks in comparison lists *see also* Julien Canlorbe, *Les tableaux de concordance, la publicité comparative et le droit des marques: après l'arrêt 'L'Oréal c. Bellure' de la Cour de justice*, in: *Droit de propriété intellectuelle. Liber amicorum Georges Bonet*, Litec, Paris 2010, p. 117.
906. In this direction Di Cataldo, *The Trade Mark with a Reputation ...*, pp. 844-845.
907. Simon Fhima, *Trade Mark Dilution ...*, p. 234.
908. *See* paras 285 et seq. *infra*.

the repute, the terms used by Directive 2015/2436 (as well as Regulation 2017/1001) and Directive 2006/114 having the same meaning. The main question is under what conditions the use of a trade mark in a comparative advertisement is likely to damage repute or allow the advertiser to take unfair advantage. However, it is no longer a question of the limitations of the effects of the trade mark but of the characterisation of the infringement itself.

182. Limited practical importance. Finally, it should be noted that in fact the question of the use of trade marks in comparative advertising concerns the special regime of protection of trade marks with a reputation on a marginal basis since the invocation of extended protection will rarely be necessary. In comparative advertising, the advertiser normally uses an identical sign for identical goods or services. Consequently, the right holder may act primarily on the basis of the provisions relating to double identity.[909] Of course, any reputed trade mark also benefits from the protection provided for therein. Moreover, since the *L'Oréal* judgment, there is no doubt that, in the field of double identity, the trade mark is not only protected in its function as an indication of origin. Although the jurisprudence of the Court of Justice is particularly vague and difficult to interpret on this point, in case of trade marks with a reputation the affection of one of the newly recognised functions, in particular the communication, investment or advertising functions,[910] should be easy to establish.

The *L'Oréal* judgment shows itself that the importance of the special regime for condemning the use of a reputed trade mark in comparative advertising is limited. Admittedly, the Court of Justice pointed out that this regime is also applicable to the use of trade marks in comparative advertising, in the case at issue in comparison lists.[911] Nevertheless, the Court ruled on the conditions for the implementation of the infringement action concerning the use of trade marks for similar goods, in the case in question, for perfume bottles, and the conditions for lawfulness of comparative advertising were examined in the context of double identity.

A judgment of the Grand Instance Court of Paris is a good illustration of this problem.[912] In that case, the Court held that the operator of a website enabling Internet users to search for perfumes whose essential characteristics were identical to those of several leading mark perfumes took an unfair advantage of the reputation attached to those marks. According to the judgment, the defendant thus infringed the communication, investment and advertising functions of the marks in question. Since the marks were reproduced identically, the decision was based on the provisions relating to the double identity. Consequently, the claims founded on the special regime were rejected because they were based on the same facts as those that were condemned in the speciality, in the field of reproduction for identical goods.

909. *See* CJ, 18 June 2009, case C-487/07, *L'Oréal*, paras 55-56.
910. *See* CJ, 18 June 2009, case C-487/07, *L'Oréal*, para. 63.
911. CJ, 18 June 2009, case C-487/07, *L'Oréal*, para. 31.
912. TGI Paris, 11 April 2014, case 12/02594.

[B] Due Cause

183. Limitation specific to the special regime. Article 10(2)(c) of Directive 2015/2436 and Article 9(2)(c) of Regulation 2017/1001 provide for a specific exception in favour of third parties exploiting a reputed trade mark. Its unauthorised use can be condemned, because of detriment caused or unfair advantage, provided that it is made 'without a due cause'. In the light of the case law of the Court of Justice, due cause is intended to strike a balance between the interests of the proprietor of the trade mark and the interests of other economic operators in having signs capable of denoting their goods or services.[913]

This negative condition for the infringement of a reputed trade mark was for a long time poorly commented on in doctrine and rarely invoked in practice. Indeed, although the due cause exception has always been provided for by the European legislator, it has been envisaged as a real exception to the trade mark protection by the Court of Justice rather recently.[914]

According to the *Intel* and *Red Bull* judgments, 'where the proprietor of the mark with a reputation has demonstrated the existence of one of the forms of injury ... the onus is on the third party using a sign similar to the mark with a reputation to establish that he has due cause for using such a sign'.[915] The Court of Justice therefore considers that the assessment of the infringement and of the existence of a due cause is carried out separately and successively. The existence of a due cause constitutes a justification for an infringement a priori established.[916]

It should also be noted that the condition of due cause is autonomous from the other requirements for the infringement of a reputed trade mark. Due cause cannot be claimed in cases where the public does not establish a link or the right holder gave his consent to the use of the disputed sign, contrary to what may have been suggested by some authors.[917] Moreover, *de lege lata*, due cause is an exception specific to the special regime. The idea that the due cause could also be invoked in the case of double identity, where a function of the trade mark other than the distinctive function would be affected,[918] has no legal basis.

184. Flexible but restrictive interpretation. The Court of Justice interpreted the terms 'due cause' in particular in the *Red Bull* judgment. The approach of the Court of Justice presented in the decision favours a flexible interpretation of this concept likely to cover several situations, since the cases of due cause referred to in the judgment are not listed in an exhaustive manner. That said, a flexible interpretation does not mean

913. CJ, 6 February 2014, case C-65/12, *Red Bull*, paras 41-46. It is, however, unclear why the Court refers to striking a balance between the interests of the proprietor of the trade mark 'in safeguarding its essential function', since the protection of the distinctive function is not the subject matter of the special regime. Cf. Żelechowski, *'Uzasadniony powód' używania* ..., p. 81.
914. Cf. Passa, *Traité de droit* ..., p. 540.
915. CJ, 27 November 2008, case C-252/07, *Intel*, para. 39; CJ, 6 February 2014, case C-65/12, *Red Bull*, para. 44.
916. Passa, *Traité de droit* ..., p. 541; Caselli, *Il marchio che gode di rinomanza* ..., p. 139.
917. Cf. Caselli, *Il marchio che gode di rinomanza* ..., p. 132.
918. In this direction Kur, *Trade Marks Function* ..., p. 445.

that the Court approves of a broad interpretation of this negative condition of trade mark infringement.[919] According to the General Court, 'whether there is a due cause which makes it possible to use a mark which adversely affects a mark with a reputation is a matter which must be interpreted restrictively',[920] and the case law of the General Court shows that the argument based on the existence of a due cause is usually rejected.[921] Indeed, due cause is an exception to the exclusive trade mark right. Moreover, as it has been established, the defendant may also invoke other limitations provided for in Article 14(1) of Directive 2015/2436 or Article 14(1) of Regulation 2017/1001.[922]

In the light of the case law, it is possible to distinguish 'legitimate' justifications for the use of a reputed trade mark by a third party, in the sense that they actually can legitimise an a priori established infringement (§2.02[B][1]), and 'questionable' justifications, in other words, hypotheses which are sometimes cited in doctrine or in case law as due causes, but which, in fact, should not constitute limitations to the protection of the reputed trade mark (§2.02[B][2]).

[1] Legitimate Justifications of Due Cause

185. Objective reasons and subjective interests. Before the Court of Justice ruled on the meaning of the condition of due cause, the jurisprudence and doctrine often referred to the interpretation of this concept proposed by the Benelux Court of Justice in the famous *Claeryn* judgment of 1 March 1975.[923] European trade mark law is strongly inspired by Benelux law, which at the time of the drafting of Directive 89/104 was one of the most modern trade mark regimes in Europe.[924] The Benelux Court of Justice presented a strict approach to due cause. In the view of the *Claeryn* decision, due cause could only be invoked in two cases that can be referred to as 'objectively overriding reasons'. Such a restrictive interpretation of due cause can no longer be adopted under Directive 2015/2436 and Regulation 2017/1001. According to the Court of Justice, 'the concept of "due cause" may not only include objectively overriding reasons but may also relate to the subjective interests of a third party using a sign which is identical or similar to the mark with a reputation'.[925] Thus, the Court of Justice

919. Żelechowski, *'Uzasadniony powód' używania* ..., p. 82. Cf. Di Cataldo, *The Trade Mark with a Reputation* ..., pp. 834-835.
920. GC, 16 March 2016, case T-201/14, *Spa*, para. 65; GC, 1 March 2018, case T-85/16, *Adidas*, para. 56.
921. CFI, 16 April 2008, case T-181/05, *Citi*, para. 84; CFI, 25 March 2009, case T-21/07, *Spa*, para. 43; GC, 7 December 2010, case T-59/08, *La Perla*, paras 61-65; GC, 16 March 2016, case T-201/14, *Spa*, para. 66; GC, 5 July 2016, case T-518/13, *McDonald's*, paras 114-115; GC, 15 September 2016, case T-358/15, *Nina Ricci*, para. 84.
922. *See* Simon Fhima, *Trade Mark Dilution* ..., p. 229.
923. Cited by Cohen Jehoram, *La protection des marques* ..., p. 227. The mark *Claeryn* was famous in the Netherlands for juniper. A third party launched a cleaning product on the Dutch market under the name *Klarein*. The user of the sign Klarein invoked due cause for the use of the sign, since in Dutch the term means 'pure and clean', hence indicating the characteristics of the designated product.
924. *See* Gielen, *Harmonisation of Trade Mark Law in Europe* ..., p. 264.
925. CJ, 6 February 2014, case C-65/12, *Red Bull*, para. 45.

enshrined a more flexible approach to the assessment of due cause as a method of balancing the interests of the right holder and of the third party, leaving more freedom to the judge.[926]

However, objectively overriding reasons for using a reputed trade mark can still legitimise an a priori established infringement (§2.02[B][1][a]). Moreover, in the view of the *Red Bull* judgment, factual circumstances relating to prior use of the disputed sign by the third party may constitute a due cause (§2.02[B][1][b]). It should be noted that the list of justifications is not exhaustive. Nevertheless, apart from the objectively overriding reasons and previous use of the disputed sign, it is not easy to indicate what other situations may characterise a due cause.[927]

[a] Objectively Overriding Reasons

186. Necessity and rights of the third party. In the light of the *Claeryn* judgment of the Benelux Court of Justice, the objectively overriding reasons which may characterise a due cause are, on the one hand, the necessity for the third party to use the disputed sign (§2.02[B][1][a][i]) and, on the other hand, the exercise of the third party's own right over the disputed sign (§2.02[B][1][a][ii]).

[i] Necessity of Use of the Disputed Sign

187. Jurisprudence. According to the *Claeryn* decision, it is generally necessary to lay down as a condition that there is a need for the third party to make use of the sign, such that, despite the damage caused to the owner of the mark, the third party cannot reasonably be expected to refrain from using the sign.[928] Hence, the Benelux Court of Justice ruled that due cause was applicable only to cases where the use of a particular sign was an absolute necessity, strictly limiting the applicability of that condition. Moreover, the Court specified that the prior exploitation of the disputed sign was not such as to characterise a due cause.[929]

The same criteria for assessing the due cause exception were applied by the Office for Harmonisation in the Internal Market (OHIM) (at present EUIPO) in the famous *Hollywood* decision, according to which, for there to be a due cause, it is generally

926. Żelechowski, *'Uzasadniony powód' używania* ..., pp. 81-82.

927. For example, historical or geographical reasons for the disputed use do not justify the use of a sign identical or similar to a reputed trade mark, as ruled a French court in a case concerning the mark *Mont Blanc*. The defendant argued that his use of the sign *Mont Blanc* for alcoholic beverages was justified by the tradition of brewing activity in the regions of Savoie and Haute-Savoie and his desire to enjoy the image of purity and perfection associated with the mountains and the water of the glaciers. The Court pointed out that this could have been done in many other ways than by the use of a trade mark owned by a third party. TGI Valence, 2 November 2004, case 00/00953, *Mont Blanc*. The absence of a likelihood of confusion cannot obviously constitute a due case. *See* GC, 17 October 2018, case T-8/17, *Ballon d'or*, para. 145.

928. *See* Cohen Jehoram, *La protection des marques* ..., p. 228.

929. *See* Cohen Jehoram, Van Nispen, Huydecoper, *European Trademark Law* ..., p. 318.

necessary to establish as a condition that there is an obligation for the third party to use the sign in question.[930]

The necessity test is still applicable in the light of the case law of the General Court. It was implemented in two judgments of 25 March 2009 and 16 March 2016 (the latter being subsequent to the *Red Bull* decision), concerning the mark *Spa*. According to those judgments, the word 'spa' has not become so 'necessary' to the marketing of cosmetic products that the third party could not reasonably be required to refrain from the use of the mark.[931]

188. Assessment of necessity. It must be observed that the use of a sign identical or similar to a reputed trade mark can be only very rarely objectively necessary. The use of the disputed sign is actually necessary when it is required by a legal provision. Such obligations may arise, for example, from provisions relating to the composition of company names which can be found in national legislations, for example in Polish law.[932] That being said, this situation may also fall within the scope of the other situations likely to characterise a due cause, namely the exercise of the third party's own right, for instance, over its company name.

Justifications for the necessity of the disputed use which do not result from legal obligations are questionable. For example, some authors point out that, in the case of semi-descriptive or allusive marks, it is easier for the third party to demonstrate the need to use descriptive words.[933] However, as we have established, the use of a sign as a descriptive element shall not be considered as trade mark use. Consequently, already a priori there is no infringement of the trade mark.

[ii] Rights of the Third Party to the Disputed Sign

189. Rights to other distinctive signs. Apart from the situation in which the use of a reputed trade mark is necessary for the third party, in the *Claeryn* judgment, the Benelux Court of Justice ruled that the alleged infringer may oppose his own right over the exploited sign.[934] This may be another distinctive sign whose protection is recognised by the national legislator, such as a company name or a trade name, even if it is not protected by an exclusive right. In particular, the case of 'homonymy' can constitute a due cause.[935] Under the provisions of the former Directives and Regulations, homonymy was likely to fall within the general exception, applicable to all trade marks, relating to names. The latter term, as we have seen, covered the other distinctive signs used in the course of trade. However, Article 14(1)(a) of Directive 2015/2436 and Article 14(1)(a) of Regulation 2017/1001 reserve this limitation of trade

930. OHIM, BoA, 25 April 2001, case R-283/1999-3, *Hollywood*, para. 101.
931. CFI, 25 March 2009, case T-21/07, *Spa*, para. 43; GC, 16 March 2016, case T-201/14, *Spa*, para. 66.
932. Cf. para. 172 *supra*.
933. Casparie-Kerdel, *Dilution Disguised …*, p. 190.
934. Cohen Jehoram, *La protection des marques …*, p. 228.
935. *See* Bonet, *La protection des marques notoires …*, p. 204; Bouvel, *La protection des marques …*, para. 114.

mark rights to natural persons.[936] Consequently, a legal person is no longer entitled to invoke its 'rights' to the company name or trade name in order to avoid liability, on the basis of the provisions interpreted in the light of Article 14 of Directive 2015/2436 or Article 14 of Regulation 2017/1001. However, the cases in which it was previously accepted that a legal person could claim its right to the name, i.e. oppose its company name, trade name or shop name, *de lege lata*, could be invoked on the ground of the special regime as due causes.[937] It seems that the requirement of honest practices in industrial or commercial matters could apply *mutatis mutandis* to assess the merits of the defence of the third party based on a due cause, although, as we have seen, the implementation of this condition is complicated.[938] To this end, it should be possible to use the arguments previously developed by the courts in case law rendered pursuant to the former provisions on the limitation related to the use of the name. It was, for instance, considered that when a company identified itself personally and truly with the natural person, it should have the right to a commercial use of this name. In such case, the name holder should participate effectively in the company's activity and hold a majority or at least a significant share in the share capital.[939] Moreover, as we have noted, this could also be the case when the insertion of a name is required by the legal provisions relating to the company name.[940]

By contrast, the first name is not the subject of an exclusive right, the exercise of which could constitute a due cause. Thus, the choice of a first name as a distinctive sign cannot legitimise the infringement of a trade mark with a reputation.[941] This approach is confirmed by the case law of the General Court, in the light of which the fact that the sign at issue is the first name of the third party is not enough to constitute due cause for the use of the mark.[942]

190. Prior and subsequent use. The disputed use does not need to have occurred prior to the filing of the reputed mark. Any prior use, whether it is an unregistered trade mark or another distinctive sign, may characterise a due cause within the meaning of the *Red Bull* judgment which has a general scope. Distinguishing the case where the alleged infringer exercises his own right has its autonomous function when the use of the contested sign by the third party is subsequent to the filing of the opposed trade mark with a reputation. That being said, the combination of the exercise of a right by

936. *See* para. 172 *supra*.
937. It should be noted that if a third party can invoke due cause for using a sign, such as a trade name or a company name incorporating a partner's name, it cannot register such a sign as a trade mark. In the view of the case law, no unconditional right to the registration of a surname and, *a fortiori*, a first name as a trade mark is provided for by the legislation. GC, 25 May 2011, case T-397/09, *Ernst August Prinz von Hannover*, para. 29; GC, 15 September 2016, case T-358/15, *Nina Ricci*, para. 84.
938. *See* para. 174 *supra*.
939. Zanella, *Les marques nominatives ...*, p. 184.
940. *See* para. 172 *supra*.
941. Bouvel, *La protection des marques ...*, para. 114. In French jurisprudence *see* CA Versailles, 27 April 2006, case 05/03166, *Milka*.
942. CFI, 22 January 2015, case T-393/12, *Kenzo*, para. 21; CJ, 30 May 2018, cases 85/16 P and C-86/16 P, *Kenzo*, paras 83, 92-94. Cf. also GC, 17 October 2018, case T-8/17, *Ballon d'or*, para. 145.

the third party and the prior use of the sign can undoubtedly strengthen the argument that there is a due cause. A good example of a due cause resulting from prior use of a surname can be found in a judgment of the Paris Grand Instance Court concerning the trade mark *Michelin*.[943] The case involved a pastry chef named A. Michelin and the proprietor of the famous mark of tyre. The pastry chef had been operating a pastry shop under his name since 1880. Then, he contributed it to a company that adopted the corporate name *A. Michelin-Pâtisserie, chocolats, pains d'épices*. According to the Court, since the company had been operating peacefully under the name *Michelin* for several decades, the exploitation of the reputed mark *Michelin* was justified.[944] In the light of Article 14(1)(a) of Directive 2015/2436 and Article 14(1)(a) of Regulation 2017/1001, as we have seen, in such a case, a third company can no longer invoke its right to a name. However, a due case could be then established.

[b] Prior Use of the Disputed Sign

191. Obligation of tolerance of prior use. According to the *Red Bull* judgment, 'the proprietor of a trade mark with a reputation may be obliged to, pursuant to the concept of "due cause" ... tolerate the use by a third party of a sign similar to that mark in relation to a product which is identical to that for which that mark was registered, if it is demonstrated that that sign was being used before that mark was filed and that the use of that sign in relation to the identical product is in good faith'.[945] The wording of the operative part of the judgment is due to the circumstances of the case at issue and the questions referred by the Dutch judge for a preliminary ruling. Nevertheless, the judgment may have a more general scope and cover situations of prior use of identical signs for identical products and, *a fortiori*, identical or similar signs for similar and dissimilar products.[946]

The solution is not surprising. Indeed, prior use of the disputed sign was considered by the doctrine as due cause before the *Red Bull* judgment. Use prior to the acquisition of reputation by the trade mark and not to the date of filing of the latter was usually considered relevant.[947]

It should be noted that prior use of the sign does not exclude liability for infringement of the trade mark in the speciality.[948] Thus, prior use will not affect the assessment of the infringement in cases of double identity or likelihood of confusion. It can only legitimise the disputed use likely to be qualified as infringement of a reputed trade mark. It should also be pointed out that the Court of Justice did not recognise any

943. TGI Paris, 22 May 1991, PIBD 1991, No. 511, III, p. 683, Michelin.
944. *See* Bouvel, *La protection des marques ...*, para. 114.
945. CJ, 6 February 2014, case C-65/12, *Red Bull*.
946. *See* Żelechowski, *'Uzasadniony powód' używania ...*, p. 85.
947. *See* Caselli, *Il marchio che gode di rinomanza ...*, p. 130. In French case law cf. TGI Paris, 22 May 1991, PIBD 1991, No. 511, III, p. 683, *Michelin*.
948. However, filing of a mark previously used by a third party may be qualified as made in bad faith, which is a ground for invalidation and, in national legislations, can be a ground for refusal.

subjective right in the sign used. The right holder is only obliged to 'tolerate' the use of the sign by the third party.[949]

192. Possibility of claiming prior use. As regards the conditions under which prior use is likely to fall within the concept of due cause, it follows clearly from the *Red Bull* judgment that any use of a sign similar to a reputed trade mark prior to its filing, or more precisely to the date on which it acquired reputation, does not characterise due cause. In order to determine whether prior use is likely to constitute due cause, several factual elements must be taken into consideration. It should be noted that the interpretation of the *Red Bull* judgment is complicated because the Court's reasoning is inconsistent. According to the reasons of the decision, in order to assess due cause, two elements must be taken into account: first, how the sign has been accepted by, and what its reputation is with, the relevant public, and second, what was the intention of the person using the sign, hence whether he was acting in good faith. The good faith depends on the proximity between the goods and services in question and on the time when the sign was first used for a product identical to that designated by the earlier mark and when that mark acquired its reputation.[950] However, in the operative part, the Court points out that the prior use of the sign must be made in good faith, making it a general and sole condition for assessing due cause in the event of prior use, which is, this time, assessed by reference to three conditions listed in a non-exhaustive manner. Among those conditions, apart from, on the one hand, how the sign is accepted and what is its reputation, and, on the other hand, the degree of proximity between the goods, which were discussed in the motivation of the judgment, there appears, for the first time, a third condition relating to 'the economic and commercial significance' of the use of the disputed sign for that product designated by the reputed mark, which is, however, in no way explained by the Court.

193. Concept of good faith in private law and in trade mark law. Before examining further the criteria for assessing due cause referred to in the judgment, the meaning of the concept of good faith used by the Court of Justice should be analysed. Indeed, it is a concept, on the one hand, well known in private law, which has its origins in Roman law, and, on the other hand, used in trade mark law as a ground for invalidation.

Prima facie, the invocation of good faith can surprise because it could suggest that the infringement of a reputed trade mark would depend on the state of mind of the third party, in accordance with the understanding of good faith in general private law. This would be contrary to the principle that the trade mark infringement is assessed objectively. Some authors had pointed out that good faith should not constitute a due cause since the opposite would make the assessment of the infringement of the reputed trade mark subjective.[951] Commenting on the *Red Bull* judgment, Bonet observed that the good faith refers to a psychological consideration.[952] The author therefore seems to

949. CJ, 6 February 2014, case C-65/12, *Red Bull*, para. 46.
950. CJ, 6 February 2014, case C-65/12, *Red Bull*, paras 53-56.
951. Simon Fhima, *Trade Mark Dilution* ..., p. 231.
952. Georges Bonet, in: *Droit des marques et autres signes distinctifs. Chroniques*, Propr. intell. 2014, No. 52, pp. 294-295.

understand good faith in a subjective way, as this notion is traditionally defined in private law. According to an old definition, good faith means a state of mind such that one wrongly imagines having a right that does not actually exist.[953]

The notion of good, or rather bad, faith appears in Article 4(2) of Directive 2015/2436 and Article 59(1)(b) of Regulation 2017/1001 in the light of which a trade mark registered in bad faith can be invalidated. The concept is not defined and has been interpreted differently in national legislations.[954] One might think that under those provisions good faith should be assessed differently, namely in an objective manner. Good faith in the objective sense means that human behaviour should be assessed as appropriate or inappropriate. Hence, we do not examine the person's state of mind, but we assess whether his behaviour is in accordance with objective rules.[955] According to the jurisprudence of the Court of Justice, the concept of bad faith, as a ground for invalidation, is an autonomous concept of EU law.[956] The Court seems to have adopted an objective conception of good faith pursuant to the provisions related to the invalidation of trade marks.[957] Indeed, in the light of the *Lindt* judgment, good faith is assessed in particular based on the knowledge of the prior use of the sign filed by a third party and the intention of the applicant at the time of filing. The latter is a subjective factor which must be however determined 'by reference to the objective circumstances of the particular case'.[958]

Transposing this reasoning on the ground of due cause, it should be noted that, in the view of the *Red Bull* judgment, good faith is assessed on the basis of perfectly objective criteria.[959] There is therefore no need to refer to the subjective understanding of this concept adopted in general private law.

194. Criteria of assessment. As noted, in the operative part of the *Red Bull* judgment, the Court of Justice states, in a non-exhaustive manner,[960] three conditions for assessing good faith. First, it is necessary to take into account how the disputed sign has been 'accepted' by the relevant public and what is its 'reputation'. The two terms used by the Court are not very clear. There are also major differences between the language versions of the judgment, so it is difficult to say whether the concept of reputation should be linked to 'reputation' in the sense of the knowledge of the mark used in the special regime to define the mark subject to enhanced protection or perhaps

953. *See* Jules Wertheimer, *Des avantages attribués à la bonne foi relativement aux biens en droit civil*, thesis Paris 1899, p. 32.
954. Krystyna Szczepanowska-Kozłowska, *Znaki towarowe w Unii Europejskiej (cz. I)*, PPH 2004, No. 8, p. 9.
955. In Polish doctrine *see* Adam Szpunar, *Nadużycie prawa podmiotowego*, thesis Cracow 1947, p. 62.
956. CJ, 27 June 2013, case C-320/12, *Malaysia Diary*, para. 29.
957. Szczepanowska-Kozłowska, *System prawa prywatnego* ..., p. 618.
958. CJ, 11 June 2009, case C-529/07, *Lindt*, paras 38-42.
959. Cf. Żelechowski, *'Uzasadniony powód' używania* ..., p. 85.
960. For another circumstance likely to be taken into account in the assessment of due cause *see* CJ, 18 July 2013, case C-252/12, *Specsavers*, para. 49. According to the ruling, 'the fact that the third party making use of a sign which is alleged to infringe the registered trade mark is itself associated, in the mind of a significant portion of the public, with the colour or particular combination of colours which it uses for the representation of that sign can be relevant to determining whether the use of that sign has a "due cause"'.

to 'repute' of the mark, hence to qualitative criteria.[961] These terminological differences are confusing. Nevertheless, the concept used by the Court should not be given a meaning which would lead to higher requirements being imposed on the contested sign at issue than on the reputed mark covered by the extended protection. Thus, it seems that this sign must neither have a reputation among customers nor convey a particular image; it is sufficient if it is known to a part, not necessarily 'significant' within the meaning of the *Chevy* judgment, of the public concerned. Therefore, it must have been effectively exploited on the market for a certain period of time and have acquired some clientele. It should also be noted that this condition for assessing due cause is not a real criterion for examining the conduct of the third party; hence it is unclear why it may prove the latter's good faith.

Second, it is necessary to assess the intention of the person using the disputed sign. In the view of the reasons of the *Red Bull* judgment, this intention allows to establish good faith.[962] In this context, invoking good faith seems appropriate. It is indeed a question of assessing the behaviour of the third party. In assessing good faith here it is necessary to take account of the degree of proximity between the goods and services for which the disputed sign has been used and the product for which the reputed mark was registered, as well as to have regard for when that sign was first used for a product identical to that for which that mark was registered, and when that mark acquired its reputation.[963] Third, the Court must take account of the economic and commercial significance of the use of the contested sign for the product designated by the mark with a reputation.[964]

It should be stressed that these criteria are closely linked to the circumstances of the *Red Bull* case in which the defendant used the disputed sign *Bulldog* for hotel, restaurant and café services, involving the sale of drinks, prior to the registration of the reputed mark *Red Bull* of energy drinks. Subsequently, the user of the sign *Bulldog* extended the use of the sign to energy drinks. The conditions of proximity between the goods or services in dispute, the chronology of the first use of the disputed sign for an

961. In the Dutch version, which was the language of the proceeding, the Court uses the term *'reputatie'*, i.e. the term which appears in the Dutch text of the Directive but not to refer to the mark covered by the special regime – *'merk bekend'*, but to refer to tarnishment. This could suggest that the condition of 'reputation' referred to in the judgment should be assessed in the light of qualitative criteria. By contrast, the English version of the judgment uses the term 'reputation', the term used by the Directive to characterise the trade mark having a reputation, whereas degradation refers to the notion of 'repute'. The French version of the judgment uses an unknown term from the French text of Directive 2015/2436, of *'réputation'*, while the French provisions use the term *'renommée'*. The same is true in the Spanish version of the judgment, which refers to *'reputación'*, while the *'marca de renombre'* is the subject of the special regime and the term *'renombre'* is used to characterise tarnishment. By contrast, in the Polish version of the judgment, the Court uses the concept of *'renoma'*, i.e. the same notion as that used to describe the mark subject to extended protection – *'znak renomowany'*, as well as that used to characterise degradation – *'szkoda dla renomy'*. The same is true in the Italian version of the judgment, which refers to *'notorietà'* of the mark, the Directive using the terms *'marchio di notorietà'* and *'pregiudizio alla notorietà'*.
962. CJ, 6 February 2014, case C-65/12, *Red Bull*, paras 55-56.
963. CJ, 6 February 2014, case C-65/12, *Red Bull*, para. 56.
964. Again, this criterion does not seem relevant to assess the behaviour and therefore the good faith of the third party.

identical product and the economic significance of that use can only apply in cases where the defendant, before the filing of the reputed trade mark, and more precisely before the date on which it acquired reputation, used a similar sign for goods different from those in relation to which the proprietor claims the infringement and, subsequently, extended the use of the disputed sign to goods closer to those designated by the trade mark. In the light of the *Red Bull* judgment, where the goods in relation to which the sign at issue was originally used may be linked to the product for which the infringement is claimed, a due cause may be established. The use of that sign in relation to that latter product should appear to be a natural extension of the range of services and goods for which that sign already enjoys a certain reputation with the relevant public.[965] In addition, account must be taken of the chronology of the first use of the disputed sign for the product designated by the allegedly infringed mark and the acquisition of reputation by the latter. Thus, the extension of the use of the disputed sign must have taken place before the date on which the mark acquired reputation. Even more so, use may be justified if the third party began to exploit the sign for that product before the filing of the reputed trade mark.[966] By contrast, if the third party extends the exploitation of the disputed sign after the mark has acquired reputation, the argument relating to the extension of the activity cannot prosper. Finally, it is necessary to take into account the economic significance of the use of the disputed sign for the product designated by the trade mark, and therefore for the product in relation to which the third party has extended its exploitation. This directive is not perfectly clear.[967] It seems that the third party should have already acquired clientele for the product designated by the sign in question.

Apart from the particular case in which the defendant extends the exploitation of the disputed sign to goods or services designated by a reputed trade mark, it seems that the existence of due cause should be assessed in the light of the economic significance of the prior use of the sign by the third party. Consequently, if the defendant has not extended the use of the disputed sign after the acquisition of reputation by the allegedly infringed trade mark, and *a fortiori* after its filing, the defendant only has to establish the first condition imposed by the Court, of the acceptance and reputation of the disputed sign within the public.[968] Moreover, the use of that sign by the third party must not, in principle, have been challenged by the proprietor of the reputed mark. In other words, both signs should have coexisted peacefully on the market.[969]

965. CJ, 6 February 2014, case C-65/12, *Red Bull*, para. 57. This could be the case, according to the Court, in the *Red Bull* case, since energy drinks are products similar to food services and could therefore constitute a natural extension of the activity of the user of the *Bulldog* sign. Although one may wonder whether it is really frequent and natural for a restaurateur to manufacture energy drinks.
966. Żelechowski, *'Uzasadniony powód' używania* ..., p. 86.
967. Bonet, *Droit des marques* ..., p. 295.
968. According to the General Court, in the case of an EU trade mark, the disputed sign in question should have been previously used throughout the European Union market. GC, 5 July 2016, case T-518/13, *McDonald's*, para. 115; GC, 1 March 2018, case T-85/16, *Adidas*, para. 66; GC, 1 March 2018, case T-629/16, *Adidas*, paras 62 and 207. Cf. also CJ, 20 July 2017, case C-93/16, *Kerrygold*, para. 60. The solution seems strict.
969. GC, 5 July 2016, case T-518/13, *McDonald's*, para. 114; GC, 1 March 2018, case T-85/16, *Adidas*, paras 67 and 142-144.

195. Prior use and other limitations of trade mark rights. It should be noted that due cause characterised by prior use of the disputed sign may have a scope of application uncovered by the other limitations of the trade mark right. These may include both unregistered used trade marks and other distinctive signs exploited in the course of trade. Under several national laws, unregistered trade marks are not subject to exclusive rights.[970] Consequently, in principle, prior use of a sign identical or similar to a registered trade mark in those countries does not allow to request for invalidation of the latter, unless the third party can demonstrate that the right holder filed the mark in bad faith. As regards other distinctive signs, this will also depend on national legislations. In some jurisdictions, the third party may invoke a prior right and oppose the filing of a trade mark only in the speciality. Moreover, as we have seen, the prior use is not a circumstance taken into account in the jurisprudence of the Court of Justice when assessing the honest practices referred to in Article 14(2) of Directive 2015/2436 and Article 14(2) of Regulation 2017/1001.[971] Apart from due cause, prior use can only fall within the exception relating to prior local rights, but must then fulfil the specific conditions provided for by national laws and the use of the sign should be territorially limited.[972]

It should also be stressed that in the jurisdictions where unregistered trade marks are not subject to exclusive rights, the user of the sign should not be allowed in his defence to invoke prior use in order to bring a counterclaim based on national provisions related to unfair competition.[973] Otherwise, first, this would lead to providing for an additional limitation of the effects of the trade mark, unknown to the EU provisions, contrary to the principle of complete harmonisation of the scope of the trade mark right.[974] Indeed, according to the Court of Justice, 'a national court may not, in a dispute relating to the exercise of the exclusive right conferred by a trade mark, limit that exclusive right in a manner which exceeds the limitations arising from Articles 5 to 7 of the directive'[975] (nowadays of Articles 10, 14 and 15 of Directive 2015/2436). The solution imposed by the Court of Justice is in line with the idea that the exercise of an industrial property right should not be examined in the light of the rules on unfair competition and, therefore, that national provisions related to unfair competition cannot constitute a limitation of trade marks rights.[976] Second, the possibility of invoking prior use of the disputed sign in defence against any action for trade mark infringement, in and outside the speciality, would call into question the solution according to which prior use may be taken into account on the ground of due

970. Cf. von Bomhard, Geier, *Unregistered Trademarks ...*, pp. 686 et seq.
971. *See* para. 174 *supra*.
972. *See* para. 175 *supra*.
973. Cf. Michal Bohaczewski, *Les conflits entre les marques déposées et les marques d'usage en droit polonais: primauté du dépôt ou primauté de l'usage?*, RFPI 2019, No. 9, pp. 64-67.
974. Cf. CJ, 20 November 2001, cases C-414/99 to C-416/99, para. 39.
975. CJ, 19 September 2013, case C-661/11, *Nathan*, para. 55. Cf. also CJ, 6 October 2015, case C-500/14, para. 44.
976. Łukasz Żelechowski, *Kolizja prawa ochronnego na znak towarowy i reżimu ochrony oznaczeń odróżniających na podstawie ustawy o zwalczaniu nieuczciwej konkurencji – perspektywa w świetle orzecznictwa Trybunału Sprawiedliwości*, in: *Experientia docet. Księga jubileuszowa ofiarowana Pani Profesor Elżbiecie Traple*, Wolters Kluwer, Warsaw 2017, pp. 780-781.

cause, in the field of extended protection, provided that the conditions arising from the *Red Bull* judgment are met. Due cause is a special limitation of the effects of the trade mark provided by the regime reserved for trade marks with a reputation. It does not allow to avoid liability when the infringement of the trade mark right consists in double identity or likelihood of confusion. Indeed, it would be pointless to admit that prior use may, under certain conditions, characterise a due cause specific to the regime of enhanced protection if we admitted that the defendant may always invoke prior use against any action brought by the right holder, in and outside the speciality.

[2] Questionable Justifications of Due Cause

196. Absence of detriment and freedom of expression. Apart from the situations likely to allow the third party to actually avoid liability for the infringement of a reputed trade mark, it is possible to identify situations which were considered as due cause by the jurisprudence or doctrine, but that, in my opinion, should not characterise limitations of the extended protection of the trade mark. Thus, they are questionable justifications. Such cases constitute the absence of detriment to the trade mark caused by the disputed use (§2.02[B][2][a]). Another justification that appears illusory is the use of trade marks relating to the freedom of expression (§2.02[B][2][b]).

[a] Absence of Detriment Caused by the Use of the Disputed Sign

197. Questionable jurisprudence. Prior to the *Red Bull* judgment, the Court of Justice interpreted the due cause exception in the *Interflora* decision. According to this ruling, concerning a particular case of trade mark infringement on the Internet through the use of keywords, 'where the advertisement displayed on the Internet on the basis of a keyword corresponding to a trade mark with a reputation puts forward – without offering a mere imitation of the goods or services of the proprietor of that trade mark, without causing dilution or tarnishment and without, moreover, adversely affecting the functions of the trade mark concerned – an alternative to the goods or services of the proprietor of the trade mark with a reputation, it must be concluded that such use falls, as a rule, within the ambit of fair competition in the sector for the goods or services concerned and is thus not without "due cause"'.[977] In other words, in the field of the special regime, where the use of a reputed trade mark by a third party would not be detrimental to the distinctive character or repute, i.e. in the presence of mere unfair advantage, that third party would, 'as a rule', establish due cause. Thus, some authors argued that unfair advantage in itself is not sufficient to characterise an infringement of a trade mark with a reputation, for which one of the trade mark functions would need to be affected; hence there should be a detriment. The absence of affection of one of the functions would make it possible to retain the existence of due cause.[978]

---

977. CJ, 22 September 2011, case C-323/09, *Interflora*, para. 91.
978. Andrew Bailey, *Trade Mark Functions and Protection for Marks with a Reputation*, JIPLP 2013, vol. 8, No. 11, p. 874.

The solution is questionable and this analysis should not be approved. Detriment or unfair advantage, on the one hand, and due cause, on the other, are separate conditions of infringement of a trade mark with a reputation that require a distinct and successive assessment. The right holder must demonstrate a detriment or unfair advantage taken of the repute or distinctiveness of the mark, and subsequently the third party may establish the existence of a due cause that is likely to legitimise the a priori established infringement.[979] Pursuant to Article 10(2)(c) of Directive 2015/2436 and Article 9(2)(c) of Regulation 2017/1001, due cause constitutes an exception to any form of infringement of a reputed trade mark. However, according to the *Interflora* judgment, due cause can only legitimise the infringement in the form of unfair advantage. The existence of a detriment would exclude the possibility for the defendant to invoke due cause.[980] Consequently, the infringement of the trade mark in the form of unfair advantage would, as a rule, always be justified by a due cause. This would be a *contra legem* solution. Hence, the Court's reasoning is incorrect.[981] To say that in the absence of detriment there is due cause would mean that, on the one hand, in the event of dilution or degradation, the defendant would have no exception to raise as a defence, which would be contrary to law and would constitute an even narrower conception of due cause than that previously provided in the *Claeryn* decision. On the other hand, in cases where the right holder only shows unfair advantage taken of the distinctiveness or repute, there would automatically be due cause that the defendant would not even have to show, which would also not comply with the letter of the extended protection provisions.

198. Necessary limitation of the application of the solution. Therefore, the solution resulting from the *Interflora* judgment should have a narrow scope of implementation. It can only apply to the cases of use of trade marks as keywords. No general rule of assessing due cause should be deducted from the decision.

[b] Use of the Disputed Sign Falling under the Freedom of Expression

199. Use covered by the freedom of expression qualified as due cause. A justification for the use of a trade mark with a reputation is often sought in the field of the freedom of expression. It may concern use made in the context of freedom of creation and public information. The most controversial aspect of the conflict between the trade mark rights and the freedom of expression is the so-called trade mark parody. The question of whether the user of a trade mark can avoid liability for trade mark infringement because of the humorous or critical nature of its use, relying on the

979. Cf. Traple, *Reklama internetowa* ..., p. 421.
980. Caselli, *Il marchio che gode di rinomanza* ..., p. 136. Cf. also Ilanah Simon Fhima, *Due Cause*, JIPLP 2017, vol. 12, No. 11, p. 899.
981. Cf. Martin Senftleben, *The Perfect Match: Civil Law Judges and Open-Ended Fair Use Provisions*, American University International Law Review 2017, vol. 33, No. 1, p. 259. The author is less critical, and he seems to approve the idea that when a harm is caused to the mark, the possibility of relying on the due cause defence is excluded. Cf. also Senftleben, *European Trade Mark* ..., pp. 363-364.

freedom of expression, has long been a matter of concern in doctrine and divided case law.[982] The discussion concerns above all reputed marks that are particularly likely to be the subject of polemical or satirical use,[983] constituting the main target for parodists.[984] Since, in most cases, such use does not cause any likelihood of confusion as to the origin, the problem concerns above all the special regime.[985] As a result, the extended protection of the reputed trade marks is sometimes opposed to the freedom of expression.[986] Many European authors thus consider the use of trade marks relating to the freedom of expression as due cause.[987] Moreover, some scholars argued for the recognition of an additional specific limitation of trade marks rights related to parody, artistic expression, etc.[988] Introduction of such a limitation was discussed during the works on the last trade mark law reform in the EU but this suggestion was not followed.[989] It should be noted that use of a mark covered by the freedom of expression was expressly qualified as due cause in German jurisprudence, in the famous *Lila Postkarte* case, which was decided on 3 February 2005 by the Federal Court of Justice.[990]

---

982. Cf. in French doctrine Canlorbe, *L'usage de la marque ...*, pp. 400-403.
983. Federico Paesan, *La protezione dei marchi e la libertà d'espressione*, thesis Turin 2011, p. 64; Ilanah Simon Fhima, *Trade Marks and Free Speech*, IIC 2013, vol. 44, No. 3, p. 294.
984. Vincent Ruzek, *La parodie en droit des marques*, Propr. ind. 2005, No. 4, étude 11, para. 24; Isabelle Camus, *La parodie de marque: un défi mondial pour les marques de luxe qui en sont une cible privilégiée*, Propr. intell. 2015, No. 56, p. 241.
985. Caselli, *Il marchio che gode di rinomanza ...*, pp. 162-163.
986. Mohammad Amin Naser, *Trademarks and Freedom of Expression*, IIC 2009, vol. 40, No. 2, p. 196; Robert Burrell, Dev Saif Gangjee, *Trade Marks and Freedom of Expression: A Call for Caution*, IIC 2010, vol. 41, No. 5, pp. 545 et seq.
987. *See* Ellen Gredley, Spyros Maniatis, *Parody: A Fatal Attraction? Part 2: Trade Mark Parodies*, EIPR 1997, vol. 19, No. 8, p. 419; Piotrowska, *Renomowane znaki ...*, p. 92; Senftleben, *The Trademark Tower of Babel ...*, p. 63; Senftleben, *The Perfect Match ...*, pp. 262-263; Paesan, *La protezione dei marchi e la libertà ...*, pp. 156 et seq.; Szczepanowska-Kozłowska, *Swoboda wypowiedzi a prawo ...*, p. 17; Caselli, *Il marchio che gode di rinomanza ...*, p. 132; Gielen, *Trademark Dilution under European Law ...*, p. 728; Sabine Jacques, *A Parody Exception: Why Trade Mark Owners Should Get the Joke*, EIPR 2016, vol. 38, No. 8, p. 475; Jens Schovsbo, *'Mark My Words': Trademarks and Fundamental Rights in the EU*, UC Irvine Law Review 2018, vol. 8, No. 3, pp. 577 et seq.; Łukasz Żelechowski, *Invoking Freedom of Expression and Freedom of Competition in Trade Mark Infringement Disputes: Legal Mechanisms for Striking a Balance*, ERA Forum 2018, vol. 19, No. 1, pp. 128 et seq.
988. Ruzek, *La parodie en droit ...*, paras 6-10; Christophe Geiger, *Droit des marques et liberté d'expression (de la proportionnalité de la libre critique)*, D. 2007, No. 13, p. 884; Christophe Geiger, *Trade Marks and Freedom of Expression: The Proportionality of Criticism*, IIC 2007, vol. 38, No. 3, pp. 324-325. *See also* Martin Senftleben et al., *The Recommendation on Measures to Safeguard Freedom of Expression and Undistorted Competition: Guiding Principles for the Further Development of EU Trade Mark Law*, EIPR 2015, vol. 37, No. 6, p. 337. For the critics of the EU legislation in this respect cf. also Bereskin, *Anti-dilution ...*, p. 1754.
989. *See* Schovsbo, *'Mark My Words' ...*, pp. 568-569.
990. The case concerned marketing of postcards referring to the marks and an advertising campaign by the chocolate manufacturer of *Milka*. On a purple background, the purple colour being a registered trade mark of the plaintiff, the postcard showed, by ridiculing, elements used in the *Milka* advertising campaign, an idyllic landscape with mountains and cows accompanied by a poem attributed to a certain *Rainer Maria Milka*. The German court admitted due cause in this case, in the light of the fundamental freedom of artistic creation. *See* Bundesgerichtshof, 3 February 2005, case I ZR 159/02, GRUR 2005, p. 583. Cited by par Martin Senftleben, *Overprotection and Protection Overlaps in Intellectual Property Law: The Need for Horizontal*

200. Importance of the general conditions for trade mark infringement. Opposing the freedom of expression to the trade mark protection under EU law is, in my opinion, questionable and the presentation of the use of signs relating to the freedom of expression as due cause appears erroneous. The concerns that trade mark rights may prevent from engaging in some forms of free speech, such as parody or criticism,[991] seem excessive. It must be noted that the examination of possible conflicts between the freedom of expression and the trade mark rights is irrelevant when the use of the disputed sign is not made in the course of trade or to designate goods or services since these two conditions delimit the scope of exclusivity granted to the trade mark proprietors.[992] In most cases in which some authors seek use relating to the freedom of expression, there is no infringement of the trade mark constituted a priori, since the sign in question is not used in the course of trade or as a trade mark. Indeed, as some scholars rightly point out, in this debate we focus too quickly on the issue of resolving a conflict between the trade mark rights and the freedom of expression. It is better to settle this question in the field of trade mark law, avoiding considering the use covered by the freedom of expression as an infringement of the trade mark right.[993]

201. Condition of use in the course of trade. There is no doubt that the trade mark has an economic vocation. The monopoly conferred by registration is therefore restricted only to use made in the course of trade. French jurisprudence shows very well how this condition for infringement delimits the scope of trade mark rights and, as a result, guarantees the freedom of expression. Indeed, since the 1990s, some French courts highlighted the absence of a commercial purpose of the use of the trade mark in relation to the freedom of expression, in particular of the parodic use.[994] In the famous cases concerning the trade marks *Esso* and *Areva*, in which Greenpeace was accused of pasting the said trade marks to highlight the harmful influence of the activities of their owners on the environment, the Paris Court of Appeal dismissed the plaintiffs in the field of trade mark law on the grounds that the use of the trade marks in question clearly did not aim to promote the marketing of competing products or services but was

Fair Use Defences, in: Annette Kur, Vytautas Mizaras (eds), *Structure of Intellectual Property Law: Can One Size Fit All?*, Edward Elgar Publishing, Cheltenham-Northampton 2011, pp. 136 et seq. On this matter *see also* Senftleben, *The Perfect Match ...*, p. 262; Żelechowski, *Invoking Freedom ...*, p. 119.

991. Cf. Martin Senftleben, *Free Signs and Free Use: How to Offer Room for Freedom of Expression Within the Trademark System*, in: Christophe Geiger (ed.), *Research Handbook on Human Rights and Intellectual Property*, Edward Elgar Publishing, Cheltenham-Northampton 2016, p. 376.
992. Szczepanowska-Kozłowska, *Swoboda wypowiedzi a prawo ...*, p. 9.
993. Cf. Burrell, Gangjee, *Trade Marks and Freedom ...*, pp. 544 et seq.
994. *See* Emmanuel Baud, Stéphane Colombet, *La parodie de marque: vers une érosion du caractère absolu des signes distinctifs*, D. 1998, No. 23, pp. 227 et seq. Nevertheless, the solutions adopted by French courts at the time were various. *See* Ruzek, *La parodie en droit ...*, paras 11-15. For example, in a judgment concerning the publication by anti-smoking associations of posters presenting 'graphic diversions' of five cigarette marks, the Court of Cassation ruled that the use made on the disputed posters, for information and criticism purposes, was infringing. Cass. com., 21 February 1995, case 92-13.688.

purely polemical use made outside the course of trade.[995] French case law has finally established itself in favour of excluding trade mark law from the cases of use relating to the freedom of expression, for information or criticism purposes. Indeed, the Court of Cassation has ruled on several occasions[996] that condemning the use of a trade mark for polemical purposes is, where applicable, a matter of general tort liability and not of trade mark infringement. The decision is based on the absence of use in the course of trade.[997] As we have seen, the condition of use in the course of trade applies in the same way under the special regime of protection of the trade marks with a reputation.[998] The solution deserves approval. As previously observed, the use of the mark 'is indeed use in the course of trade, since it takes place in the context of commercial activity with a view to economic advantage and not as a private matter'.[999]

It should be stressed that the use of a trade mark in the course of trade must be made in the context of the marketing of a good or the provision of a service, in accordance with the purpose of the trade mark, which is to indicate the origin of a good or service.[1000] Indeed, the trade mark is protected as an indicator of the commercial origin and not a value in itself,[1001] in other words as a distinctive sign and not as a sign as such.[1002] Outside the economic context, the use of the trade mark is allowed. Consequently, in principle, any use of a sign for personal purposes within the company, for information purposes, artistic, educational or scientific purposes, parody, satire or polemic, etc., does not fall within the monopoly of the trade mark

995. CA Paris, 26 February 2003, PIBD 2003, No. 766, III, p. 323, D. 2003, p. 1831, comment of Bernard Edelman, Comm. com. élctr. 2003, comment 38, of Christophe Caron, Propr. intell. 2003, No. 3, p. 322, comment of Valérie-Laure Bénabou, Propr. intell. 2003, No. 9, p. 458, comment of Michel Vivant, Propr. ind. 2003, comment 40, of Pascale Tréfigny. On the *Esso* and *Areva* cases *see also* Christophe Geiger, *Marques et droits fondamentaux*, in: *Les défis du droit des marques au XXIe siècle. Actes du colloque en l'honneur du professeur Yves Reboul*, LexisNexis, Paris 2011, pp. 169-171.

996. Cass. civ. 1st, 8 April 2008, case 07-11.251, Bull. civ. I, No. 104, *Areva*; Cass. com., 8 April 2008, case 06-10.961, Bull. civ. IV, No. 79, *Esso*.

997. Canlorbe, *L'usage dans la vie des affaires ...*, p. 114.

998. *See* para. 128 *supra*. For instance, use of a mark in a film where a character wears a T-shirt showing a mark is not related to marketing of a product, hence is not made in the course of trade. Cf. TGI Paris, 10 November 2011, case 10/09164, *Dolce Gabbana*. This conclusion should have allowed the Court to dismiss the claims not only based on the infringement for likelihood of confusion but also in the field of the enhanced protection of trade marks with a reputation. Instead of doing so, the Court preferred to highlight that the advertising function of the mark was not affected, the defendant did not gain any commercial advantage and the use was made within the freedom of expression.

999. CJ, 12 November 2002, case C-206/01, *Arsenal*, para. 40.

1000. Of course, as we have seen, these may be acts of use that precede marketing, such as the stocking of marked goods, or acts that accompany it, such as advertising. *See* para. 128 *supra*.

1001. *See* Frédéric Pollaud-Dulian, *Protection de la marque et droit de liberté d'expression d'une association dans le cadre d'une campagne anti-tabac*, JCP 2006, No. 48, II, p. 10195.

1002. Cf. Christophe Geiger, *Fundamental Rights, a Safeguard for Coherence of Intellectual Property Law*, IIC 2004, vol. 35, No. 3, pp. 271-272; Geiger, *Droit des marques ...*, p. 884; Geiger, *Trade Marks and Freedom ...*, pp. 323-324. The author seems to agree that the condition of use in the course of trade allows to rule out infringement in many cases related to the freedom of expression. Nevertheless, according to the author, the notion of use in the course of trade is not clear in European case law. Consequently, invoking freedom of expression may be necessary.

owner.[1003] It is not then a question of arbitrating a conflict between the trade mark rights and the freedom of expression.[1004]

202. Condition of use as a trade mark. Use of a trade mark covered by the freedom of expression may of course take place in the context of the marketing of a good or service. In particular, the parody often contains a commercial element in the sense that the parodist derives an economic benefit from it.[1005] Consequently, use of trade marks relating to the freedom of expression may be qualified as use made in the course of trade.[1006] However, the contested use must also be made as a trade mark in order to establish infringement. Indeed, an act may be performed in the course of trade, but not as a trade mark, i.e. to designate goods or services and link them to a commercial origin.[1007] As we have pointed out, use as a trade mark means that the sign is exploited to designate a good marketed or service provided, in principle, by the infringer, except in specific cases where the sign is used to designate goods or services of the right holder that nevertheless remain related to the products of the infringer.[1008] Indeed, this is either an identical good, as in particular in the case of comparative advertising, or a service the subject of which is the right holder's good. However, when, for example, a journalist cites a trade mark in a press article, that trade mark may, of course, remind the public of the goods of its proprietor, but the sign is in no way used as a trade mark, since it is not used to designate the good marketed by the third party, in this case a newspaper, or for a good of the proprietor that would be related to the latter. Likewise, when a trade mark is presented in a work that is intended to be marketed, is therefore not entirely outside the course of trade, it is the condition of use as a trade mark that allows to rule out infringement. In this regard, it is worth quoting a judgment of the French Court of Cassation concerning a conflict between the trade mark *Décathlon* and a domain name identifying a website whose purpose was to make fun of the sporting activity of decathlon.[1009] The mark was clearly used in the course of trade. Nevertheless, the Court of Cassation refused to condemn the contested use in the field of extended protection, since it had not been made as a trade mark. According to the decision, ownership of a trade mark, even of a reputed one, consisting of a common

1003. *See* Pollaud-Dulian, *Propriété intellectuelle. La propriété industrielle* ..., p. 903; Senftleben, *European Trade Mark* ..., p. 279.

1004. *See* Passa, *Traité de droit* ..., pp. 292-293; Szczepanowska-Kozłowska, *Swoboda wypowiedzi a prawo* ..., pp. 11-12; Basire, *Les fonctions de la marque* ..., p. 211.

1005. On the different types of parodies *see* Naser, *Trademarks and Freedom* ..., pp. 193 et seq. Cf. also Paesan, *La protezione dei marchi e la libertà* ..., pp. 118 et seq.

1006. In some cases, the assessment may be complicated. For example, it could be considered that use of a trade mark for information purposes by a journalist in a press article is not made in the course of trade, since the use of the mark should itself have a commercial purpose; i.e., the mark should be used to promote the marketing of goods or services to the consumer. *See* Canlorbe, *Contrefaçon de marque* ..., para. 37. Nevertheless, one could argue that the publication of a press article for information or criticism is done in the course of trade. *See* Szczepanowska-Kozłowska, *Swoboda wypowiedzi a prawo* ..., p. 11. Such use is not indeed unrelated to the economic activity, since the mark is used in the context of the marketing of a product, in this case a newspaper. Cf. Canlorbe, *L'usage de la marque* ..., pp. 401-402.

1007. Passa, *Traité de droit* ..., p. 534.

1008. *See* para. 132 *supra*.

1009. Cass. com., 20 February 2007, case 05-10.319, *Décathlon*.

name, does not prohibit the use of this name in its usual sense. The judgment proves that trade mark law does not disregard the freedom of expression, that balances between the freedoms and property rights do exist.[1010]

Moreover, there are situations in which use of a sign is not made either in the course of trade or as a trade mark, for example the parodic use of a sign for militant purposes. Not only such use is foreign to the business activity, but, in addition, in many cases, it is not intended to designate, directly or indirectly, goods or services but rather the company itself, known under the name corresponding to the trade mark, as in the *Areva* and *Esso* cases.[1011]

Thus, the trade mark law itself, thanks to the general conditions for trade mark infringement, ensures the freedom of expression. As the trade mark right is unenforceable, the qualification of infringement of the trade mark right is necessarily excluded, without the defendant even having to invoke the freedom of expression in the field of trade mark law,[1012] since this defence assumes that an infringement of the trade mark right is a priori established.[1013]

203. Possible abuse of the freedom of expression. That said, there may be cases where a message related to the exercise of the freedom of expression is related to the course of trade and constitutes use as a trade mark.[1014] Such use may, in addition to its commercial nature, be in particular humorous. For example, in the event that a mark is mocked and exploited as an indication of origin of a good in the context of its marketing, as was the case in Italy of the mark *Diesel*, renowned in the field of clothing and ridiculed by a sign *Porco Diesel*, affixed to identical products,[1015] in France of the

1010. Christophe Caron, *Des frontières de la marque, de sa parodie et de sa territorialité*, Comm. com. électr. 2007, Nos 7-8, comment 93, para. 4.

1011. Passa, *Les conditions générales ...*, para. 18.

1012. The approach may be different in the national legislations which transposed Article 10(6) of Directive 2015/2436, former Article 5(5) of Directives 89/104 and 2008/95, allowing to provide for enhanced protection against the use of a sign other than use for the purposes of distinguishing goods or services. This is the case, in particular, in Benelux law. *See* Article 2.20(2)(d) of the Benelux Convention on Intellectual Property. Under those provisions, the freedom of expression can justify a due cause. Cf. Benelux Court of Justice, 14 October 2019, case A 2018/1/8, *Moët Hennessy v. Cedric Art.*

1013. Passa, *Les conditions générales ...*, para. 10. It should be noted that the absence of trade mark infringement does not exclude that the parodic use cannot be condemned on the basis of general tort liability if it is considered unlawful since consisting in an abuse of the freedom of expression and in particular a denigration of the product or service designated by the trade mark or of its proprietor. Passa, *Les conditions générales ...*, para. 10; Geiger, *Fundamental Rights ...*, p. 279; Passa, *Traité de droit ...*, p. 293; Pollaud-Dulian, *Propriété intellectuelle. La propriété industrielle ...*, p. 978; Canlorbe, *Contrefaçon de marque ...*, para. 33. For example, tort liability for abuse of freedom of expression was discussed in a case between a producer of tobacco and a French association for combating respiratory disease and tuberculosis, due to the use of stamps and posters by the latter. According to the judgment, by using elements of the packaging of *Camel* cigarettes, in a humorous manner, in posters and stamps distributed as part of a general prevention campaign aimed at adolescents, denouncing the dangers of tobacco consumption, a product harmful to health, the association, acting, in accordance with its purpose related to public health, by means proportionate to that purpose, did not abuse its right of free expression. Cass. civ. 2nd, 19 October 2006, case 05-13.489, Bull. civ. II, No. 282.

1014. Canlorbe, *L'usage dans la vie des affaires ...*, p. 114.

1015. Cited by Paesan, *La protezione dei marchi e la libertà ...*, pp. 136-137.

mark *Ricard*, renowned for alcohol beverages and registered for clothing, caricatured by the signs *Ringard* and *Smicard* affixed to T-shirts,[1016] or in Switzerland because of the use of the sign *Harry Popper*, referring to the mark *Harry Potter*, for condoms,[1017] it is difficult to understand why such use should be considered lawful. The third party cannot claim to have been motivated by a humorous intention; the parodic effect per se cannot serve as a criterion to legitimise the unauthorised use of a trade mark for commercial purposes.[1018] In such cases, the third party cannot benefit from any special treatment. The fact of presenting another person's trade mark in a parodic manner shall in no way exclude liability.[1019]

Similarly, it cannot be sufficient to qualify an expression as artistic for it to be lawful.[1020] When a use is of a commercial nature and can be considered as use as a trade mark, it is likely to infringe a trade mark right. Moreover, is it really possible to claim the 'freedom of expression' when a third party markets goods or provides services using a modified version of another person's trade mark? In order to invoke the freedom of expression, the third party should pursue a goal of general interest.[1021] As observed, a broad implementation of the freedom of expression may lead to its trivialisation.[1022] By pushing the debate to the point of absurdity, any modification of a mark could be considered as made within the freedom of artistic creation. When a third party uses a trade mark applied to a good in such a way as to enable the public to distinguish the origin of that good, it is no longer the freedom of expression that is at stake but freedom of trade and industry (or the related freedom of competition). There is no doubt, however, that trade mark rights constitute a legitimate limit to the latter. Nobody may invoke the freedom of trade and industry when infringing a trade mark right of another person. In such cases, invoking the freedom of expression shall be regarded as abusive.

204. Justified limitations of the freedom of commercial expression and constitutional value of trade mark rights. That being said, it needs to be stressed that the freedom of expression referred to in Article 10 of the European Convention on Human

1016. CA Paris, 11 May 2007, case 05/21446, *Ricard*. Provided that the signs have actually been used as a trade mark. Cf. Passa, *Traité de droit* ..., p. 534.
1017. Cited by Alberini, *L'exploitation de la renommée* ..., p. 426.
1018. Canlorbe, *L'usage de la marque* ..., pp. 407-408; Canlorbe, *L'usage dans la vie des affaires* ..., p. 114; Szczepanowska-Kozłowska, *Swoboda wypowiedzi a prawo* ..., p. 26. The Court of Rennes rightly observed that if the constitutional principle of freedom of expression allows, within certain limits, the use of elements diverted from a reputed trade mark to express in parodic form criticism of the goods designated by that trade mark or of the activity of the right holder, the use of such a mark by an economic operator in the course of trade, for the sole purpose of exploiting its repute to market its own goods, constitutes an infringement on the trade mark with a reputation. CA Rennes, 27 April 2010, case 09/00413, *Petit Navire*.
1019. In French jurisprudence *see* CA Paris, 21 November 1989, PIBD 1990, No. 481, III, p. 422, *Calèche*. According to the decision, the fact that the contested sign *Ca lèche* was a 'mockery mark' did not exclude infringement.
1020. Szczepanowska-Kozłowska, *Swoboda wypowiedzi a prawo* ..., p. 26.
1021. *See* in French jurisprudence CA Paris, 11 December 2015, case 14/23109, *Ricard*.
1022. Cf. Canlorbe, *L'usage de la marque* ..., p. 392.

Rights is interpreted broadly and the term 'expression' covers any form of communication of information or ideas regardless of their content or way of communication,[1023] including information of a commercial nature.[1024] Consequently, in certain cases, use made even as a trade mark and in the course of trade is likely to fall within the scope of the freedom of expression since it can be considered as 'expression' within the meaning of Article 10 EConvHR (European Convention on Human Rights). Apart from the situation of use of a mark which is at the same time humorous or artistic, this may include use of a mark in advertising or comparative advertising. Indeed, commercial advertising is a matter of freedom of expression.[1025] However, in the light of Article 10 EConvHR, advertising may be subject to several restrictions intended to prevent unfair competition and to ensure respect for the rights of others. Trade mark rights therefore constitute a justified restriction of the freedom of expression in advertising.

Thus, even if certain forms of trade mark use can be covered by the freedom of expression, commercial expressions should enjoy a more restricted freedom than expressions for public or artistic purposes, since they serve private economic interests and not the interests of the society as a whole. One could think that the interests of the third parties justified by the freedom of commercial expression, which may legitimise the use of another's trade mark, are already taken into account by the legislator, in an exhaustive manner, in Article 14 of Directive 2015/2436 and Article 14 of Regulation 2017/1001, providing for exceptions to trade mark rights. The freedom of expression should not therefore allow third parties to interfere with the trade mark rights of others beyond those limitations deriving from the law.[1026] Consequently, the trade mark right, including the right to a trade mark with a reputation, cannot be limited by the use of that mark by third parties, even if such use falls within the widely understood freedom of expression.[1027] This reasoning seems confirmed by the Court of Justice. According to a judgment rendered in the light of Directive 2008/95, 'save for the specific cases governed by Article 8 et seq. of that directive, a national court may not, in a dispute relating to the exercise of the exclusive right conferred by a trade mark, limit that exclusive right in a manner which exceeds the limitations arising from Articles 5 to 7 of the directive'.[1028] The defendant cannot therefore rely on a basis external to trade mark law in order to avoid liability for the infringement.[1029] Furthermore, it is in line with the jurisprudence of the Court of Justice in copyright matters, in the light of which other fundamental freedoms cannot justify a derogation from the holder's exclusive rights

1023. Pierre Wachsmann, *Liberté d'expression*, Fascicule 800, JurisClasseur 2008, paras 1-6; Szczepanowska-Kozłowska, *Swoboda wypowiedzi a prawo ...*, p. 7.
1024. *See* ECHR, 20 November 1989, case 10572/83, *Markt Intern Verlag GmbH and Klaus Beermann v. Germany*, para. 26.
1025. *See* ECHR, 24 February 1994, case 15450/89, *Casado Coca v. Spain*, para. 35.
1026. *See* Szczepanowska-Kozłowska, *Swoboda wypowiedzi a prawo ...*, pp. 24-25.
1027. *Contra* Jacques, *A Parody Exception ...*, p. 480. Cf. also Laure Marino, *Plaidoyer pour la liberté d'expression, droit fondamental de l'entreprise*, RTD com. 2011, No. 1, p. 1. The author argues in favour of the freedom of commercial expression, which could allow, as it seems, unlimited use of trade marks in comparative advertising.
1028. CJ, 19 September 2013, case C-661/11, *Nathan*, para. 55.
1029. Cf. Łukasz Żelechowski, *Funkcje znaku towarowego a naruszenie prawa ochronnego na znak towarowy (cz. II)*, PPH 2015, No. 6, p. 27.

beyond the exceptions or limitations provided by the European legislation.[1030] It seems accurate to state that, *mutatis mutandis* in trade mark law, the mechanisms allowing the different rights and interests of right holders and third parties to be balanced are contained in the provisions of Directive 2015/2436 and Regulation 2017/1001.[1031]

Furthermore, it needs to be stressed that the intellectual property rights are also fundamental rights whose value is, in addition, constitutional. In the light of the case law of the European Court of Human Rights (ECHR), the trade mark constitutes 'possession' within the meaning of Article 1 of Protocol No. 1 to the European Convention on Human Rights. Consequently, intellectual property is a fundamental right.[1032] This results also clearly from Article 17(2) of the Charter of Fundamental Rights of the EU. Thus, even if the freedom of expression in some situations is truly affected, this fundamental freedom also has its limits and must give way to other fundamental rights. As Caron rightly observed, it would be wrong to assume that, in the hierarchy of norms, the freedom of expression prevails over the trade mark rights. They both have equivalent value.[1033]

I therefore fully agree with the authors who point out that the conflict between the trade mark protection and the freedom of expression is less acute than it seems since the balance between the two can be found within the general conditions of trade mark infringement.[1034] Consequently, it is unnecessary to consider the existence of any additional exception to the trade mark rights.[1035] Directive 2015/2436 and Regulation 2017/1001 are therefore right not to refer to the freedom of expression as a limitation to the effects of the trade mark. For the same reason, it is inappropriate to invoke the freedom of expression as due cause. Indeed, use of a mark which is made in the course of trade and in order to indicate the commercial origin of goods or services, in principle of the third party, should not be considered as a fair use falling under the due cause exception. The interpretation delimitating the scope of the trade mark rights as enforceable only against use made in the economic context and as a trade mark constitutes an application of the trade mark law provisions made in a way that ensures

1030. CJ, 29 July 2019, case C-469/17, *Funke Medien*; CJ, 29 July 2019, case C-516/17, *Spiegel Online v. Volker Beck*.
1031. Cf. CJ, 29 July 2019, case C-469/17, *Funke Medien*, para. 58; CJ, 29 July 2019, case C-516/17, *Spiegel Online v. Volker Beck*, para. 43. Otherwise, the effectiveness of the harmonisation of the trade mark rights effected by the Directive would be endangered. Cf. CJ, 29 July 2019, case C-469/17, *Funke Medien*, paras 62-63; CJ, 29 July 2019, case C-516/17, *Spiegel Online v. Volker Beck*, paras 47-48.
1032. ECHR, 11 January 2007, case 73049/01, *Anheuser-Busch Inc. v. Portugal*.
1033. Christophe Caron, *Affaire Esso c/ Greenpeace: décision au fond*, Comm. com. électr. 2004, No. 4, comment 39, para. 3.
1034. Canlorbe, *L'usage de la marque …*, p. 447. *See also* Gredley, Maniatis, *Parody: A Fatal Attraction? …*, p. 419; Caron, *Affaire Esso c/ Greenpeace …*, para. 3. *Contra* Senftleben, *Adapting EU Trademark …*, pp. 146 et seq.
1035. Basire, *Les fonctions de la marque …*, p. 211.

full respect for the freedom of expression, in accordance with Recital 27 *in fine* of Directive 2015/2436 and Recital 21 *in fine* of Regulation 2017/1001.[1036]

1036. Recital 27 *in fine* of Directive 2015/2426 and Recital 21 *in fine* of Regulation 2017/1001 oblige to apply their provisions 'in a way that ensures full respect for fundamental rights and freedoms, and in particular the freedom of expression'. Some authors attach much importance to the last sentences of Recital 27 of Directive 2015/2426 and Recital 21 of Regulation 2017/1001, suggesting that they could justify further limitations of the trade mark rights. Cf. Schovsbo, *'Mark My Words'* ..., pp. 574 et seq.; Żelechowski, *Invoking Freedom* ..., pp. 117 et seq. In my opinion, this is however merely a general guidance for the interpretation of the provisions and the objective expressed therein can be fully achieved by a balanced interpretation of the basic conditions for trade mark infringement – use of the sign in the course of trade and as a trade mark. It does not allow to adopt a general limitation of trade mark rights which, in the field of the special regime, could characterise due cause. Indeed, the legislator decided not to introduce such a limitation.

CHAPTER 3

Forms of Infringement of Trade Marks with a Reputation

205. Distinction of the forms of infringement. Among the forms of infringement of trade marks with a reputation referred to in Article 10(2)(c) of Directive 2015/2436 and in Article 9(2)(c) of Regulation 2017/1001, a distinction must be made between those which consist in a detriment to the attractive power of the trade mark, related to the weakening of the ability of the mark to attract and retain customers (§3.01), and those which result in an unfair advantage taken of the attractive force of the mark (§3.02). I will characterise them and examine the conditions of their demonstration in civil infringement proceedings and administrative proceedings concerning the validity of marks. As regards the establishment of the forms of infringement of trade marks with a reputation, a reference should also be made to the criteria for assessing the existence of a link between the signs which are to be taken into account at the stage of the examination of the infringement itself. In this respect, the factors of assessment relating to the distinctive power of the mark are particularly relevant.[1037]

206. No restrictive interpretation. It is important to stress that the forms of infringement of reputed trade marks shall not be assessed in a restrictive way. If, in the light of Directive 2015/2436 and Regulation 2017/1001, the special regime provides for an exception to the principle of speciality, this does not allow to interpret it restrictively.[1038] It is not an 'exception' strictly speaking, in the sense of a limitation of the protection of the trade mark, like the limitations provided for in Article 14 of Directive and Article 14 of Regulation.[1039] This is a regime intended to delimit the scope of the

1037. *See* paras 156 et seq. *supra*.

1038. Such an idea was suggested by some French authors. Cf. Bonet, *La protection des marques notoires ...*, pp. 189 et seq.; Philippe Le Tourneau, *Parasitisme et marque notoire, ou de l'application du régime général de la responsabilité en présence d'une lacune du droit spécial*, Gaz. Pal. 2001, No. 90, p. 22; Bouvel, *La protection des marques ...*, para. 57.

1039. The rule of restrictive interpretation is sometimes challenged in relation to the limitations of the intellectual property rights. *See* Christophe Geiger, *Effectivité et flexibilité: deux impératifs*

right to the trade mark with a reputation. Indeed, the extended protection constitutes an 'exception' to the principle of freedom of trade and industry (freedom of competition) as well as the general protection of the trade mark within the limits of the speciality.

207. Exhaustive list of the forms of infringement. The list of the forms of infringements of reputed trade marks is exhaustive. In particular, a hypothesis of 'confinement' of the sign, also referred to as 'undermining the possibility of extension' or of 'economic expansion of company',[1040] does not constitute a form of infringement of a reputed trade mark. This type of detriment would consist in preventing the owner of the reputed trade mark from extending his field of activity to other areas of the market. However, the risk that the trade mark owner could not extend his activity does not constitute a detriment to the distinctive character or repute of the trade mark. Consequently, it should not be taken into account in the field of the special regime.[1041] Moreover, recognition of this type of detriment would call into question the principle of speciality of the mark as such.[1042] This concept would guarantee an absolute protection for any reputed trade mark, even if the conditions for assessing the forms of infringement provided for by the legislator were not met.[1043] Finally, the detriment in the form of confinement of the trade mark would often be highly hypothetical, since the trade mark owner would probably never offer goods or services which are completely outside his sphere of economic interests.[1044] Protection against the forms of infringement enshrined in the law appears sufficient to protect the reputed trade mark and, to a certain extent, to provide its owner with the possibility of extending its activity.

---

du droit des exceptions, RLDI 2013, No. 94, p. 41. Regarding limitations of copyright cf. however CJ, 16 July 2009, case C-5/08, *Infopaq*, para. 56.

1040. Cf. Jaton, *La protection des marques* ..., p. 51; Pérot-Morel, *L'extension de la protection* ..., p. 32; Portet, *Les marques notoirement connues* ..., p. 57; Brandt, *La protection élargie de la marque* ..., p. 173; Bonet, *La protection des marques notoires* ..., p. 198; Galli, *Funzione del marchio e ampiezza* ..., pp. 10-11; Frédéric Pollaud-Dulian, *Le point sur la protection des marques de renommée dans la jurisprudence de la Cour de justice des Communautés*, RJDA 2004, No. 3, chronique 232, p. 236; Bouvel, *Principe de spécialité* ..., p. 373; Canlorbe, *L'usage de la marque* ..., p. 124; Maetz, *Notoriété: essai sur l'appropriation* ..., p. 113. In French jurisprudence *see* CA Paris, 21 November 1991, PIBD 1992, No. 518, III, p. 174, *Orient-Express*; CA Paris, 31 October 1997, PIBD 1997, No. 650, III, p. 175, *Cosmopolitan*; CA Paris, 8 March 2002, PIBD 2002, No. 749, III, p. 409, *Zippo*; TGI Valence, 2 November 2004, case 00/00953, *Mont Blanc*; CA Paris, 16 December 2005, case 04/07547, *DMC*; it was however eventually rejected by the Court of Cassation, Cass. com., 20 February 2007, case 05-10.462, *Desperados*. In older American jurisprudence cf. Wolff, *Non-competing Goods* ..., p. 592.

1041. Passa, *Traité de droit* ..., p. 540.

1042. Canlorbe, *L'usage de la marque* ..., p. 124.

1043. In addition, it should be noted that if the infringement was to result in the third party's sole use of the disputed sign on the market, which the latter has not filed as a trade mark, this does not necessarily prevent the proprietor from exploiting his mark for the same goods, unless there is an effective likelihood of confusion on the market allowing the third party to invoke unfair competition. The owner also keeps the possibility of registering his trade mark for all these goods. In such a case, the success of a possible application for invalidity of the mark filed by the third party, as due to the bad faith, would not be obvious.

1044. Guglielmetti, *Marques ordinaires, notoirement connues* ..., p. 79. Cf. Simon Fhima, *Trade Mark Dilution* ..., pp. 193-194.

§3.01 FORMS OF INFRINGEMENT RESULTING FROM USE DETRIMENTAL TO THE TRADE MARK

208. Classic distinction. There are two forms of infringement of trade marks with a reputation which consist in harming the attractive power of the trade mark: detriment to the distinctive character - dilution (§3.01[A]) - and detriment to the repute - tarnishment (§3.01[B]). The distinction is classic. Both types of harm were recognised in the old case law and characterised by the doctrine.[1045] They are nowadays expressly provided by the European legislator and recognised by the Court of Justice.

[A] Detriment to the Distinctive Character (Dilution)

209. Controversy. As it has been established, the theory of dilution played an essential role in the process of recognising the extended protection of the trade marks with a reputation.[1046] Having said that, the detriment to distinctiveness, also referred to as 'whittling away' or 'blurring',[1047] is the most difficult form of violation of trade marks with a reputation to characterise. Indeed, dilution is controversial in theory and difficult to implement in practice. This concept caused much perplexity in the doctrine and misunderstanding on the part of judges.[1048] Admitting that a reputed trade mark should be protected against use by a third party of a sign likely to trivialise this mark would lead to confer exclusive rights to any trade mark, once it is qualified as having a reputation, if the public can establish a link between it and the disputed sign. Consequently, the recognition of dilution by the legislator is sometimes called into question, since the concept applied in an overly liberal manner is likely to grant absolute protection to trade marks with a reputation against any use of identical or similar signs by third parties.

Moreover, since dilution is based on the protection of the distinctive character of the mark, prima facie it seems related to the essential function of the mark and therefore to the hypothesis of the likelihood of confusion. Hence, the idea of the special protection against dilution a priori balances between the question of the risk of confusion and a simple reproduction or imitation of a reputed trade mark likely to create a link in the mind of the public. However, it is neither, falling somewhere in between. It is indisputable that, in order to establish dilution, on the one hand, no likelihood of confusion must be demonstrated and, on the other hand, the establishment of a link between the signs in dispute is not sufficient. Therefore, it is important to answer the question of what is the purpose of the special protection against dilution, which will allow us to clearly identify its role in trade mark law (§3.01[A][1]). Then, the difficult question of assessing the detriment to the distinctive character must be

1045. *See* paras 12 et seq. *supra*.
1046. *See* paras 13 et seq. *supra*.
1047. CJ, 27 November 2008, case C-252/07, *Intel*, para. 29. I use the term of 'dilution' to designate the detriment to the distinctive character, in accordance with the *Intel* judgment.
1048. Cf. Louis Harms, *Death of a Trade Mark Doctrine?: Dilution of Anti-dilution*, in: Lionel Bently, Catherine W. Ng, Giuseppina D'Agostino (eds), *The Common Law of Intellectual Property: Essays in Honour of Professor David Vaver*, Hurt Publishing, Oxford 2010, p. 380.

examined. Consideration should be given to a solution capable of ensuring enhanced protection of trade marks with a reputation, which will not reduce the demonstration of the infringement to the establishment of a simple association between the signs in the public mind (§3.01[A][2]).

[1] Subject of Protection of the Trade Mark Against Dilution

210. I will start by determining the purpose of the trade mark protection against dilution (§3.01[A][1][a]), and then distinguish it from other trade mark law concepts (§3.01[A][1][b]).

[a] Determination of the Subject of Protection

211. The purpose of the provisions on dilution is to protect the ability of the trade mark with a reputation to attract the attention of customers by creating instant associations (§3.01[A][1][a][i]). Since this form of infringement resides in the damage caused to the distinctive character of the mark, it is necessary to examine the relationship between the concept of dilution and the distinctive function (§3.01[A][1][a][ii]).

[i] Dilution and the Ability of the Trade Mark to Attract Consumers' Attention

212. Suggestive power of the reputed mark. The theory of dilution reflects the idea that the mere knowledge of a trade mark, which can make it highly distinctive, allows the mark to acquire a power of attraction.[1049] A mark which is strongly engraved in the public's mind gives it suggestive power that facilitates the purchasing process of goods or services for customers who often make irrational decisions based on the knowledge of the signs.[1050] Consequently, thanks to the knowledge of the trade mark, the public is likely to turn almost automatically to the goods or services covered by the sign.[1051] Indeed, the more a mark is in the foreground of memory, the more direct and suggestive are the rapprochements that the fact of reviewing the same or a similar mark provokes.[1052] Therefore, the mere fact that a trade mark is known and memorised by the public confers on it an important value, by making it an instrument of communication with customers, regardless of the goods or services for which the mark is registered.[1053]

Thus, the economic value protected by the special regime does not necessarily result from an exceptional image that the trade mark conveys, on which, as we will see,

1049. *See* Pérot-Morel, *Dégénérescence de la marque* ..., p. 51; Cohen Jehoram, Van Nispen, Huydecoper, *European Trademark Law* ..., p. 314.
1050. Pérot-Morel, *Dégénérescence de la marque* ..., p. 55.
1051. Maetz, *Notoriété: essai sur l'appropriation* ..., p. 110.
1052. Perent, *Marques notoirement connues* ..., p. 227.
1053. Anna Saraceno, in: Nicola Bottero, Massimo Travostino (eds), *Il diritto dei marchi d'impresa*, Utet Giuridica, Turin 2009, p. 157.

the concept of tarnishment is based. Dilution expresses the idea that the value of the mark depends not only on the quality of the goods or services designated by the sign but also on its uniqueness.[1054] Famous marks which are highly distinctive and create instant associations in the public mind are more attractive for customers, and this ability to attract the public is independent of the mark's repute.[1055] Moreover, the mere fame often suggests a certain amount of credit in customers' opinion. Consequently, the power of association resulting from the notoriety is coveted by other undertakings;[1056] in other words, third parties have an interest in using the power of attraction represented by the mark's celebrity.[1057] As one author noted, fame is in itself an appreciable advertising value, because 'the general public is always more attracted to a star than to a stranger'.[1058]

The special protection of the distinctive character of the trade mark should encourage the owners to make their marks popular with consumers.[1059] This allows the right holder to take direct benefits by imposing higher prices on goods or services similar to those offered on the market by his competitors.[1060] A mark is popular in particular when the goods or services designated by it are of good quality. Thus, the protection against dilution encourages investment in quality so that the mark not only has a distinctive power but also becomes a mark which enjoys a good repute. For the owners to be encouraged to invest in the quality of their goods or services, third parties must not be able to take advantage of the distinctive power and therefore the attractive strength that the mark represents.

The distinctiveness that creates instant associations in the consumer's mind is likely to be diluted if the mark begins to be used by different companies. Indeed, in the event of simultaneous use of a sign, the interplay of the association of ideas on which the commercial value of the mark is based is distorted.[1061] The suggestive effect of the mark is then considerably weakened. In addition, the fascination conveyed by the mark, thanks to its uniqueness, fades. As a result, the economic value of the mark is degraded.[1062] It must therefore be admitted that the fact that a trade mark no longer gives rise to immediate association with the goods or services for which it is registered and used undermines the commercial efforts made by the proprietor to develop his trade marks.[1063]

213. Ability of the mark to identify goods or services as coming from the proprietor. In the *Intel* judgment, the Court of Justice characterised the nature of the detriment to the distinctive character and ruled on the criteria for assessing the

1054. Schechter, *The Rational Basis* ..., p. 831.
1055. Strasser, *The Rational Basis* ..., p. 411.
1056. Maetz, *Notoriété: essai sur l'appropriation* ..., p. 110.
1057. Canlorbe, *L'usage de la marque* ..., p. 111.
1058. *Le grand public est toujours plus attiré par une vedette que par un inconnu.* Dassas, *L'élargissement de la protection* ..., p. 89.
1059. Strasser, *The Rational Basis* ..., p. 412.
1060. Simon Fhima, *Trade Mark Dilution* ..., pp. 118-119.
1061. Provided, of course, that there exists a link between the earlier mark and the disputed sign in the public mind.
1062. Pérot-Morel, *L'extension de la protection* ..., p. 30.
1063. GC, 22 May 2012, case T-570/10, *Wolf*, para. 64.

existence of dilution. According to the decision, a detriment to the distinctive character 'is caused when that mark's ability to identify the goods or services for which it is registered and used as coming from the proprietor of that mark is weakened, since use of the later mark leads to dispersion of the identity and hold upon the public mind of the earlier mark. That is notably the case when the earlier mark, which used to arouse immediate association with the goods and services for which it is registered, is no longer capable of doing so'.[1064] The use of the term 'notably' suggests that an immediate association is not necessary in order to establish dilution. However, it is difficult to accept that a trade mark which does not evoke an instant association in the public mind might be the subject matter of this type of infringement if the idea is to reserve the extended protection for a few specific cases of use of reputed trade marks, and to avoid conferring the benefits of the special protection on any trade mark qualified as reputed, once the existence of a link is demonstrated.

Thus, in the light of the case law of the Court of Justice, dilution consists above all in the loss of the ability to instantly identify goods or services as coming from the proprietor of the mark with a reputation.[1065] This immediate association is possible, especially in the case of unique trade marks.[1066] Consequently, the detriment to the distinctive character appears in particular when the trade mark loses its uniqueness.[1067] Having said that, a trade mark does not have to be unique in order to create an immediate association and therefore to be subject to dilution.[1068]

It should be noted that, in accordance with the *Intel* judgment, a detriment to the distinctive character exists when the ability of the mark to identify the goods or services for which it is registered and used 'as coming from the proprietor of that mark' is weakened.[1069] This observation by the Court allows to properly identify the nature of dilution. At first glance, it could be argued that it should simply consist in weakening the association in the public mind with a certain kind of good or service. The law would then protect the strength of the trade mark to symbolise a particular object, and dilution would be possible to retain as soon as the trade mark would be used for a dissimilar good or service. This was the classic interpretation of this concept.[1070] Jaton observed that as soon as the reputed trade mark has the advantage of being 'superiorly characteristic', the appearance of such a name immediately evokes a specific good to the public. In other words, according to the author, even alone, detached from the original good, it is sufficient to provoke the public to think of the product it usually designates, even when it is applied to other objects. Thus, he concludes, if other companies launch on the market goods bearing the same famous sign or a similar sign, the mark is likely to lose this characteristic power. It will no longer be the symbol of a

1064. CJ, 27 November 2008, case C-252/07, *Intel*, para. 29.
1065. *See* Bouvel, *Principe de spécialité* ..., p. 371; Bouvel, *La protection des marques* ..., para. 94.
1066. Regarding the concept of uniqueness of the trade mark *see* paras 167-168 *supra*.
1067. *See* Sara Caselli, *Il caso Wolf: la prova del pregiudizio alla capacità distintiva del marchio che gode di rinomanza e la nozione di 'modifica del comportamento economico del consumatore medio'*, Riv. Dir. Ind. 2014, No. 2, II, p. 173.
1068. *See* further para. 235 *infra*.
1069. CJ, 27 November 2008, case C-252/07, *Intel*, para. 29.
1070. Which seems to have been adopted by OHIM, BoA, 28 January 2014, case R 69/2013-4, *Camel*, para. 41.

specific object; the public will gradually develop the habit of associating several objects with one mark.[1071]

However, nowadays, the owners of reputed trade marks tend to take economic advantage of the reputation of their marks by diversifying production, either themselves or through subsidiaries and licence agreements.[1072] The wording of the *Intel* judgment leads to adopt a more nuanced understanding of the concept of dilution, which has the advantage of taking better account of the current economic context. Indeed, today, the owners of reputed trade marks often register and use their marks for many different goods and services. Consequently, how could they claim dilution as a result of the use of their marks by a third party for goods or services other than those normally designated by their marks, when they do so themselves, somehow diluting their marks?[1073] In addition, the reputed marks are protected against dilution because they often have a symbolic force of certain ideas or values that stand out from the goods or services they designate.[1074] For instance, the mark *Apple* represents an idea of modernity, makes consumers think of new technologies and the digital world, and the mark *Chanel* conveys ideas of prestige, luxury and refinement. The messages conveyed by such 'symbol marks' go beyond associations with a particular good, even if the ideas generated by those marks cannot be entirely detached from the goods for which they are used and known, or more generally from the market sectors to which they belong.[1075]

The Court of Justice therefore rightly points out in the *Intel* judgment that dilution consists in weakening the ability of the trade mark to identify the goods or services for which it is registered and used 'as coming from the proprietor of that mark'. Also in the *Interflora* decision, the Court held that 'detriment is caused to the distinctive character of a trade mark with a reputation when the use of a sign identical with or similar to that mark reduces the ability of the mark to distinguish the goods or services of its proprietor from those which have a different origin. At the end of the process of dilution, the trade mark is no longer capable of creating an immediate association, in the minds of consumers, with a specific commercial origin'.[1076] This shows that the Court applies a refined concept of dilution which is in a departure from the requirement of use that encroaches upon a mark's potential to evoke an immediate association with particular goods or services.[1077]

Thus, it is not enough for a reputed trade mark to be used for a good or service other than the one for which the mark has a reputation and to instantly evoke it in the

---

1071. Jaton, *La protection des marques ...*, p. 48.
1072. Durrande, *Note sous CA Paris 27 mai 1987 ...*, p. 530.
1073. On this question *see* Elizabeth C. Bannon, *The Growing Risk of Self-Dilution*, TMR 1992, vol. 82, No. 4, p. 570. Cf. OHIM, BoA, 8 January 2009, case R 226/2008-2, *Kiss*, para. 35.
1074. Cf. Schechter, *The Rational Basis ...*, p. 830.
1075. While the mark *Chanel* does not symbolise a specific good but a broader idea of prestige, this prestige is nevertheless linked to the sectors such as fashion or perfumery. This is why use of such a mark for a luxury good that is foreign to these areas, such as a car or a quality wine, is likely to dilute its distinctive character without being detrimental to its repute Cf. para. 222 *infra*.
1076. CJ, 22 September 2011, case C-323/09, *Interflora*, para. 76.
1077. Senftleben, *European Trade Mark ...*, p. 355.

mind of the public. The consumer must not attribute the origin of the third party's good or service to the right holder, but must stop associating the trade mark with a single commercial origin and start attaching it to several different commercial origins. Otherwise, where the consumer believes that the third party's good or service comes from the trade mark owner, the ability of the mark to identify the goods or services 'as coming from the proprietor of that mark' is in no way weakened. Such situation characterises likelihood of confusion and not dilution. This observation leads us to analyse dilution in the context of protecting the distinctive function of the trade mark and its relationship with the likelihood of confusion. Moreover, it should be pointed out that the wording referring to the ability of the mark to identify the goods or services 'as coming from the proprietor of that mark' does not imply in any way that the public must be able to identify the person who owns the mark. This only refers to the ability of the mark to indicate one commercial origin.

[ii] Dilution and the Distinctive Function of the Trade Mark

214. Absence of affection of the distinctive function. Since the special regime protects the distinctive character of the trade mark, it could appear that, in the case of dilution, it is the function of guaranteeing the origin that is affected. Indeed, several authors point out that dilution results in a violation of the distinctive function.[1078] As we have seen, however, under the special regime, the trade mark law does not serve to preserve the function of indication of origin but rather the economic (accessory) functions of the trade mark, in particular the advertising function, in its traditional sense.[1079] The protection granted by the special regime therefore does not concern the link established between a good or service and its source, but the use of the trade mark as a communication tool carrying a broader commercial message.[1080]

It should be recalled that the trade mark, in performing the distinctive function, allows the public to distinguish without possible confusion the goods or services designated by the mark from those of another origin.[1081] Thus, use of a sign by the third party is likely to undermine the distinctive function when it creates a likelihood of confusion in the mind of the public – when the mark no longer allows customers to distinguish the commercial origin of goods or services marketed by the third party from the goods or services of the trade mark owner.[1082] The infringement of a reputed trade mark in the form of dilution cannot be achieved by violating the origin function since the risk of confusion is not a condition of liability of the third party under the special regime. The opposite would lead to a misunderstanding of the spirit of this regime.[1083]

1078. *See* Simon Fhima, *Trade Mark Dilution* ..., p. 139; Bouvel, *Marque et renommée* ..., p. 130; Bailey, *Trade Mark Functions* ..., p. 872. Moreover, considering dilution by the prism of the distinctive function leads some authors to question the protection of the distinctive character of the mark outside the speciality. *See* Senftleben, *The Trademark Tower of Babel* ..., p. 65.
1079. *See* paras 3 and 135 *supra*.
1080. Opinion of Advocate General Eleanor Sharpston in case C-252/07, *Intel*, para. 13.
1081. CJ, 22 June 1976, case 119/75, *Terrapin v. Terranova*.
1082. *See* Strasser, *The Rational Basis* ..., p. 410; Cohen Jehoram, *The Function Theory* ..., p. 184.
1083. Pollaud-Dulian, *Le point sur la protection* ..., p. 233.

Indeed, as we have seen, it is when the public no longer associates the trade mark with a single commercial origin that the ability of the mark to identify the goods 'as coming from the proprietor of the mark' is weakened. In the event of dilution, the trade mark still provides information on the origin of the owner's goods or services and those of the third party. In consequence, the concept of dilution in no way translates into the protection of the distinctive function.[1084] Therefore, Basire is right that it is incorrect to consider dilution through the prism of the origin function. The Court of Justice, which does not make the special protection subject to a likelihood of confusion, demonstrates its willingness to consider the protection of the trade mark with a reputation otherwise than through its essential function.[1085] Indeed, if, on the one hand, dilution consists in weakening the ability of the trade mark to identify the goods or services 'as coming from the proprietor of the mark' and, on the other hand, harm to the distinctive function results in the creation of a likelihood of confusion, protection against dilution cannot be considered as a means of preserving the origin function.

This being said, it should be noted that the General Court has repeatedly noted that the primary function of a trade mark is unquestionably that of an 'indication of origin' which allows to 'better identify the risk' referred to by the provisions relating to the protection of trade marks with a reputation.[1086] The protection against dilution is therefore wrongly presented by the General Court as serving to preserve the distinctive function.[1087] Also the EUIPO sometimes refers to the 'dilution of the essential function'.[1088] The *Interflora* judgment, however, shows that the Court of Justice does not consider the detriment to the distinctiveness of the trade mark with a reputation as a case of violation of the function of indication of the origin. This results from the observation that 'in addition to a finding that the mark's function of indicating origin has been adversely affected' the referring court may find that the use made by the third party 'has also caused detriment to the distinctive character' of the mark.[1089]

215. Impossible coexistence with the likelihood of confusion. It follows from our analysis that dilution and the likelihood of confusion cannot coexist. However, although the Court of Justice has repeatedly confirmed that the likelihood of confusion is not a condition for the success of an action for infringement of a trade mark with a

1084. Strasser, *The Rational Basis* ..., p. 410.

1085. Basire, *Les fonctions de la marque* ..., pp. 289, 341-342.

1086. *See* CFI, 22 March 2007, case T-215/03, *VIPS*, para. 35; GC, 28 October 2010, case T-131/09, *Botox*, para. 90; GC, 25 January 2012, case T-332/10, *Viagra*, para. 57.

1087. GC, 22 May 2012, case T-570/10, *Wolf*, para. 50.

1088. EUIPO, BoA, 11 May 2018, case R 913/2017-1, *Mikado*, para. 114 (the appeal against this decision was overruled by the GC, 28 February 2019, case T-459/18).

1089. CJ, 22 September 2011, case C-323/09, *Interflora*, para. 83. However, in the *Red Bull* judgment, relating to the extended protection, the Court of Justice itself points out that the Directive 'is generally to strike a balance between the interest which the proprietor of a trade mark has in safeguarding its essential function, on the one hand, and the interests of other economic operators in having signs capable of denoting their products and services, on the other'. CJ, 6 February 2014, case C-65/12, *Red Bull*, para. 41. It was observed, with regard to this finding of the Court, that the special regime is not intended to protect the distinctive function. Cf. Żelechowski, *'Uzasadniony powód' używania* ..., p. 81. Indeed, this function is not relevant under the special regime, as the protection of trade marks with a reputation is not based on the preservation of the guarantee of identity of the origin.

reputation, and therefore also of an action based on dilution,[1090] as noted above, the Court considers that the likelihood of confusion may lead to infringement of the trade mark with a reputation.[1091] The risk of confusion could then characterise a detriment to distinctiveness. Some authors agree with this approach.[1092] The likelihood of confusion would then be a form of dilution. Likewise, some national courts have found that the infringement in the form of likelihood of confusion may also lead to dilution.[1093]

In this respect, it should be stressed that the theoretical concept of dilution is based on the assumption that there is no risk of confusion.[1094] Moreover, the detriment to the distinctive character results in principle from the use of an identical or similar sign for dissimilar goods or services.[1095] In the event of confusion, the public associates the origin of the goods or services designated by the disputed sign, in the broad sense of the term, with the trade mark owner. If this may have an effect on the distinctive character of the trade mark with a reputation, it can only strengthen the association between the mark and its proprietor.[1096] Indeed, the likelihood of confusion does not weaken the mark's ability to identify the goods or services as coming from their

1090. In this context, however, it is worth noting a surprising solution of the *Interflora* judgment (CJ, 22 September 2011, case C-323/09). The Court of Justice, after having reminded that the exercise of the right the trade mark with a reputation is not conditional upon there being a likelihood of confusion on the part of the relevant section of the public (para. 71), observes that the distinctive character of the mark is not reduced when the public can tell that the goods or services offered originate not from the proprietor of the trade mark but, on the contrary, from a competitor of that proprietor (para. 81). In fact, by this judgment, the Court allows the right holder to invoke dilution only if the clientele believes in a common origin of the two signs (*see* para. 82). The ruling was rightly criticised in doctrine. It is indeed difficult to understand how the provisions on dilution would then enhance the protection of trade marks with a reputation compared to the general regime when the origin function is affected. Jacques Azéma, *Usage d'une marque comme mot clé (suite ... mais sans doute pas fin)*, RTD com. 2012, No. 1, p. 103. If the right holder must establish a likelihood of confusion in order to demonstrate dilution, he will prove trade mark infringement under the general provisions and will no longer need to resort to the special regime. Darren Meale, *Interflora: The Last Word on Keyword Advertising?*, JIPLP 2012, vol. 7, No. 1, p. 13. Apart from the *Interflora* judgment, the texts do not in any way allow to consider the likelihood of confusion as a condition of dilution, and the entire case law of the Court of Justice confirms that the risk of confusion cannot be required under the special regime. Moreover, it must be said that the *Interflora* judgment is particularly obscure. As we have seen, the Court of Justice distinguished at the same time between the infringement of the distinctive function and between dilution. It follows that the risk of confusion, which characterises the harm to the distinctive function, is not required in order to demonstrate dilution.

1091. *See* para. 155 *supra*.

1092. According to Pollaud-Dulian, if the owner of the reputed trade mark demonstrates that there is a likelihood of confusion, he thereby establishes the existence of a link and of a detriment to the distinctive character. Pollaud-Dulian, *Les atteintes à la marque de renommée ...*, p. 7. Cf. also Bouvel, *Principe de spécialité ...*, p. 375. In addition, some authors consider it doubtful that dilution is possible without confusion. *See* Harms, *Death of a Trade Mark Doctrine ...*, p. 383.

1093. In French jurisprudence *see* CA Paris, 4 April 2014, case 13/18239, *Visa*. In Polish jurisprudence *see* SA Warsaw, 23 October 2012, case I ACa 373/12, *Nespresso*. Cf. also EUIPO, BoA, 11 May 2018, case R 913/2017-1, *Mikado*, para. 114.

1094. Wichers Hoeth, *Étude comparative ...*, p. 150; Brandt, *La protection élargie de la marque ...*, p. 155. *See* paras 13 et seq. *supra*.

1095. *See* Passa, *Traité de droit ...*, p. 537.

1096. Simon Fhima, *Trade Mark Dilution ...*, p. 101.

proprietor, does not lead to 'dispersion of the identity' of that mark.[1097] By contrast, dilution presupposes that the public no longer perceives a trade mark as a sign that designates goods as coming from one single commercial origin, which reduces the immediate association with the trade mark owner. Consequently, the mark's ability to identify the goods or services as originating from the proprietor, its distinctiveness, is weakened. Hence, the two situations are mutually exclusive, constituting two quite distinct forms of trade mark infringement unlikely to overlap.[1098] Their coexistence is therefore logically impossible.[1099]

[b] Distinction of Dilution from Other Trade Mark Law Concepts

216. Need for distinction. Dilution needs to be distinguished from, on the one hand, the concept of degeneration, which, like dilution, is linked to the weakening of the distinctive character (§3.01[A][1][b][i]), and, on the other, from tarnishment. The latter, the second type of infringement of a trade mark with a reputation consisting in detriment, is a much less questionable concept and, more importantly here, according to some authors, it is likely to cover the situations of dilution. Hence, it is necessary to properly characterise the additional protection of the reputed trade mark against the harm caused to the distinctive character (§3.01[A][1][b][ii]).

[i] Dilution and Trade Mark Degeneration

217. Closeness of both concepts. There is a concept in trade mark law which at first glance appears similar to dilution. It can be referred to as 'degeneration'. This is the case where the trade mark loses its distinctive character by becoming a common (generic) designation of a good in trade and, as a result, can be revoked.[1100] In order to perform the function of guaranteeing the identity of the origin, a sign must have a distinctive character that constitutes a condition for the validity of the mark. Thanks to distinctiveness, a sign can play the role of a trade mark, which is to enable customers

1097. Both were incorrectly linked by OHIM, BoA, 28 January 2014, case R 69/2013-4, *Camel*, para. 41. The reasoning, according to which there is a risk that the public will be led to believe that the goods bearing the contested sign originate from the right holder and that the consumers will be less inclined to associate the reputed mark with the right holder, is contradictory.

1098. In Anglo-Saxon doctrine, it has been suggested that it would be possible for some consumers to perceive the goods as coming from the holder, which would characterise confusion, while others would be aware that the goods have two different origins, which could cause dilution. According to Simon Fhima, this only shows that an infringement of the reputed trade mark and an infringement for likelihood of confusion can be established in the same case, but confusion neither causes nor is a form of prejudice to the distinctive character of the reputed trade mark. *See* Simon Fhima, *Trade Mark Dilution* ..., p. 101. However, it should be recalled that trade mark infringement is assessed by reference to the average consumer who cannot at the same time be and not be misled. The assessment of the infringement in the light of the perception of the sign by the average consumer excludes such a double qualification of the same fact.

1099. This observation applies *mutatis mutandis* to the unfair advantage taken of the distinctive character.

1100. *See* Articles 20(a) of Directive 2015/2436 and 58(1)(b) of Regulation 2017/1001.

to associate goods or services with common commercial origin. The sign does not fulfil the distinctive function when it is not perceived by the public as an indicator of origin.[1101]

There is clearly a relationship between dilution and degeneration since both of them are based on the weakening of the distinctive character of the trade mark.[1102] Therefore, since dilution and degeneration refer to distinctiveness, they are often considered as close.[1103] The case when the trade mark becomes a generic sign would therefore constitute a type of dilution.[1104] Degeneration would then be an extreme form of dilution, which is not required in order to establish the latter, for which the degree of harm to distinctiveness may be much lower.[1105] Also in the light of the *Interflora* judgment, it may seem that dilution could result in the sign becoming generic. According to the Court of Justice, 'the use, by a third party in the course of trade, of a sign identical with or similar to a trade mark with a reputation reduces the latter's distinctiveness and is thus detrimental to the distinctive character of that trade mark for the purposes of Article 5(2) of Directive 89/104[1106] or ... of Article 9(1)(c) of Regulation No 40/94,[1107] when it contributes to turning the trade mark into a generic term'.[1108]

218. Famous marks. Both concepts concern in principle famous marks. Those that become generic are considered to reach the summit of popularity,[1109] which can lead to ruining the mark.[1110] Indeed, a mark can be so successful that it becomes in everyday language the generic designation of the type of good or service it covers.[1111] Some authors point out that in the absence of reputation a mark cannot become a customary designation.[1112] In principle, this observation can be accepted in the view of the broad definition of the trade mark with a reputation. However, if the reputation was to be assessed more rigorously than by reference to the general public, degeneration of a non-reputed mark would be perfectly conceivable. A sign used in a very narrow area by specialists in a particular field could, in their view, become a customary sign, without being known to the general public. Thus, it should be stressed that the mark's reputation in itself cannot give it a customary character. It all depends on how the sign is perceived by the public.[1113] The perception of the sign as a generic term by the clientele is therefore the only real criterion for degeneration.

1101. *See* Passa, *Traité de droit* ..., p. 99; Kur, *European Trade Mark* ..., p. 531.
1102. Simon, *Dilution by Blurring* ..., p. 73.
1103. Cf. Skrzydło-Tefelska, *Community Trade Mark* ..., p. 288, who uses the term 'blurring sensu largo' in order to refer to both of them. The author stresses, however, that they are two separate phenomena.
1104. Gielen, *Trademark Dilution in the European Union* ..., p. 229.
1105. Cf. Simon Fhima, *Trade Mark Dilution* ..., p. 118.
1106. Article 10(2)(c) of Directive 2015/2436.
1107. Article 9(2)(c) of Regulation 2017/1001.
1108. CJ, 22 September 2011, case C-323/09, *Interflora*, para. 79.
1109. Bertrand, *De la marque notoire* ..., p. 11; Pérot-Morel, *Notoriété et renommée* ..., p. 464; Kur, *European Trade Mark* ..., p. 531.
1110. Brandt, *La protection élargie de la marque* ..., p. 32.
1111. Passa, *Traité de droit* ..., p. 262.
1112. Lefranc, *La renommée en droit* ..., p. 149.
1113. Passa, *Traité de droit* ..., pp. 263-264.

219. Differences. The distinctive character covered by the protection against dilution, however, implies that the mark arouses immediate associations with a good or service as coming from its proprietor; thus the public still needs to perceive the sign as a trade mark.[1114] As it has been established, detriment to the distinctive character under the special regime occurs when the public risks no longer associating the origin of the goods or services designated by the trade mark with its owner but attaching it to several different sources of commercial origin. Nevertheless, the mark is still perceived by the public as an indicator of the commercial origin; it does not lose its ability to perform the distinctive function. Hence, while the provisions relating to degeneration protect the essential function, in the case of dilution, it is always about affecting the economic (accessory) functions of the mark, in particular the advertising function, in its traditional sense. Consequently, the concept of 'distinctive character', to which the provisions relating to the extended protection refer, cannot be given the same meaning as the one given to it in trade mark law in general.[1115] Indeed, in the field of dilution, the 'distinctive character', understood as the ability of the trade mark to enable the consumer to distinguish the goods or services designated as to their commercial origin, is in no way harmed. Therefore, outside the speciality the term of distinctiveness gains a new meaning and must be understood as the ability of the trade mark to arouse immediate associations with the goods or services designated as originating from its owner. Degeneration refers to the initial distinctive character of the trade mark, which is a condition for its validity, since it results in the loss of the mark's ability to perform the origin function.

Moreover, it should be noted that, in the event of degeneration, the earlier trade mark and the disputed sign must be used for the same goods or services, which, in principle, is not the case for dilution.[1116] The situations in which the use of the disputed sign is likely to dilute the trade mark and at the same time lead to its degeneration will therefore be quite rare. Furthermore, dilution is possible when a trade mark gives rise to immediate associations with the goods or services as originating only from its owner, i.e. when it is exploited exclusively by the right holder, and when a third party begins to use an identical or similar sign likely to destroy that instant association. Degeneration, however, in principle results from the simultaneous use of a sign by many different undertakings. Eventually, of course, their roles in trade mark law are completely different: prohibiting dilution allows the right holder to defend the trade mark, while degeneration leads to the loss of trade mark rights by revocation.

In conclusion, it must be noted that an act which may be qualified as dilution is likely to lead to the degeneration of the trade mark when the disputed sign is used for the same goods or services. The weakening of distinctiveness may result in the loss of any distinctive character of the mark when customers perceive the sign as a generic term. However, degeneration itself is no longer really a type of dilution. In the event of dilution, the public no longer perceives the trade mark as a sign that designates the

1114. *See* Baeumer, *La protection de la marque ...*, p. 570.
1115. In this direction Simon Fhima, *Trade Mark Dilution ...*, p. 98. Cf. also Ricolfi, *Trattato dei marchi ...*, pp. 765-766.
1116. Simon Fhima, *Trade Mark Dilution ...*, pp. 117-118. Cf. Simon, *Dilution by Blurring ...*, p. 74.

goods or services as originating only from the owner, while in the case of degeneration, the public no longer perceives the trade mark as an indicator of the commercial origin of the goods or services.

[ii] Dilution and Tarnishment

220. Distinction by the law. *De lege lata*, there is no doubt that there are two types of detriment which constitute two forms of injury giving rise to liability under the special regime – detriment to the distinctive character and to the repute. Both are clearly distinguished in the jurisprudence of the Court of Justice and of the General Court.[1117]

221. Doctrinal debates. Tarnishment which, still in the 1980s, was very rarely invoked before courts in European countries and almost forgotten by the doctrine[1118] today appears more important. Nowadays, dilution is sometimes somewhat neglected by authors. For instance, Bonet seems to include it in the detriment to the repute, considering dilution to be a lower level of the latter.[1119] In addition, the role of dilution and the special protection against harm to distinctiveness are sometimes challenged in doctrine. According to Senftleben, a particularly distinctive character of the trade mark is inseparably linked to its reputation. Therefore, according to the author, the concept based on uniqueness and immediate association with the trade mark owner adds little to the system of protection of trade marks having a reputation, which would primarily serve to protect the image of the mark.[1120] Likewise, other authors seem to consider both concepts are inseparable,[1121] or question the existence of infringement in the absence of harm to the repute or of a risk of a transfer of the image conveyed by the mark.[1122]

222. Different concepts. However, it must be noted that tarnishment is a form of infringement distinct from dilution since the distinctiveness and repute of the trade mark constitute two different subjects of protection under the special regime.[1123] Dilution consists only in a dispersion of the distinctive character of the sign, while detriment to the repute consists in the creation of associations incompatible with the image of the mark.[1124] Tarnishment appears to be more serious than dilution since it is

1117. In national jurisprudences, their distinction is often less clear. Until recently, French courts, as suggested by former Article L. 713-5 CPI, did not differentiate between detriment to the distinctive character and to the repute. Passa, *Traité de droit* ..., para. 384, p. 539. Nowadays, courts distinguish both forms of detriment. Cass. com., 1 March 2011, case 10-14.967, D. 2012, p. 1364, comment of Sylviane Durrande, RTD com. 2011, p. 328, comment of Jacques Azéma, *Agatha*; CA Paris, 11 May 2012, PIBD 2012, No. 967, III, p. 556, *Must*. Likewise, Polish courts sometimes do not assess both detriments separately. WSA Warsaw, 8 December 2014, case VI SA/Wa 1359/14, *Montblanc*.

1118. Brandt, *La protection élargie de la marque* ..., p. 179. Cf. para. 19 *supra*.

1119. Bonet, *La protection des marques notoires* ..., p. 200.

1120. Senftleben, *The Trademark Tower of Babel* ..., p. 68.

1121. Laporte-Legeais, *Clair-obscur sur la marque renommée* ..., para. 10.

1122. Skubisz, *Naruszenie praw z rejestracji* ..., pp. 445-446.

1123. Cf. Senftleben, *The Trademark Tower of Babel* ..., p. 55.

1124. Regarding tarnishment *see* paras 239 et seq. *infra*.

linked to a real deterioration of the mark's image in the minds of the public.[1125] The doctrine emphasises the importance of trade mark protection against dilution.[1126] In this respect, it has been observed that the uniqueness of the mark is sometimes more important for the success of a good than the actual quality of the good it designates.[1127] Naturally, both types of detriment often overlap. However, it is clear that the two forms of injury do not coincide perfectly. The *contra legem* approach, which tends to include dilution into tarnishment, would have the effect of restricting the scope of the provisions on the extended protection. These are intended to protect the attractive power of the trade mark, which is a broader concept than that of repute and may result not only from the image of the sign but also from its high distinctiveness.

In criticising the concept of dilution, Senftleben gives as an example of an invented situation of the use of the mark *Mercedes* for products such as baths, cakes and shoes. The author notes that, in such cases, the owner has no interest in claiming dilution, as customers are not likely to be misled as to the commercial origin of the third party's goods. Since the trade mark still fulfils its function of indicating the origin, he says, the distinctive character is therefore not affected. In order to invoke special protection, the owner may raise the detriment to the repute of the mark.[1128] However, as Gielen observed, the proposed approach does not take into account the economic functions of trade marks related to their distinctiveness.[1129] First, as we have pointed out, in the context of the special regime, detriment to the distinctive character does not in any way result in a likelihood of confusion, as the two are in fact mutually exclusive. Second, invoking tarnishment is not always conceivable in cases of use of marks having a reputation for dissimilar goods or services. Detriment to the repute requires that the owner establish that the use of the disputed sign is likely to damage the image of the mark.[1130]

It is easy to imagine, even taking the example of the mark *Mercedes* used for cakes, that if the latter are of very good quality, sold in beautiful packaging, in elegant pastries, at high prices, etc., the right holder could have difficulty proving a detriment to the repute of his mark. Indeed, the use of his mark by the third party would not have any negative influence on its image. We can also cite an old American case concerning the use of the mark *Tiffany* by a film production company. It was observed that this use did not affect the jeweller's reputation. However, it jeopardised the mark's advertising value by diluting its potential to attract customers.[1131]

Tarnishment is also difficult to establish when the third party uses a trade mark having a reputation accompanied by its own trade marks and the latter themselves enjoy an indisputable reputation. An interesting case can be found in an older decision

1125. Passa, *Traité de droit* ..., p. 542.
1126. *See* Dassas, *L'élargissement de la protection* ..., p. 90; Pérot-Morel, *Notoriété et renommée* ..., p. 472.
1127. Cf. Dassas, *L'élargissement de la protection* ..., p. 90, and cited authors.
1128. Senftleben, *The Trademark Tower of Babel* ..., p. 69.
1129. Gielen, *Trademark Dilution in the European Union* ..., p. 230.
1130. *See* paras 247 et seq. *infra*.
1131. Cited by Callmann, *Unfair Competition* ..., p. 462.

of the Paris Court of Appeal.[1132] The house Yves Saint Laurent marketed a perfume under the name *Champagne*, which is a registered geographical designation of origin. Such a use is likely to be condemned in the field of dilution but not in the field of tarnishment. It is indeed unlikely that the use of the term *Champagne* by Yves Saint Laurent was negative for the image of the designation, weakening its appeal, since the mark *Yves Saint Laurent* conveys its own image of refinement.[1133]

Moreover, there is no doubt that the trade mark with a reputation does not need to be a mark of luxury or prestige. It is worth recalling one of the first German decisions condemning dilution, of 11 September 1924, in the *Odol* case.[1134] This mark, famous at the time for toothpastes, was used by a manufacturer of cutlery. The mark was therefore hardly a luxury mark, and the third party's goods were not of poor quality or of a nature likely to tarnish the image of the *Odol* mark. Indeed, the idea calling into question the importance of dilution is based on an erroneous assumption that a trade mark having a reputation is a mark of high quality, or even prestige or luxury. However, this way of understanding the concept of the mark with a reputation is contrary to the letter of the law and finds no approval in the jurisprudence, as the definition of the reputed mark ignores qualitative criteria.[1135] It must be noted that the legislator, having introduced protection against dilution, clearly expressed the desire to condemn acts that are not detrimental to the repute of the trade mark or do not confer a profit on the third party.[1136] Limiting the protection of trade marks with a reputation to the protection of the image of the sign is incompatible with the idea that strong distinctiveness constitutes an important economic value worthy of protection. In all these cases, the power of the mark to symbolise a good or service or a more general idea, which nevertheless remains linked to certain goods or services or certain areas of activity,[1137] is weakened. Consequently, *de lege lata*, the idea of limiting protection of marks under the special regime solely to the repute is inadmissible, and *de lege ferenda*, such a limitation of protection of trade marks with a reputation does not seem justified.[1138]

1132. CA Paris, 15 December 1993, D. 1994, p. 145, comment of Philippe Le Tourneau, JCP 1994, II, p. 22229, comment of Frédéric Pollaud-Dulian, *Yves Saint-Laurent*.
1133. *See* Hervé Maccioni, *L'image de marque: Émergence d'un concept juridique?*, JCP 1996, No. 21, I, p. 3934, para. 21. Cf. further as regards the unfair advantage para. 282 *infra*.
1134. Cited by Baeumer, *La protection de la marque ...*, p. 550.
1135. *See* para. 53 *supra*.
1136. Cf. further para. 263 *infra*.
1137. *See* para. 213 *supra*.
1138. Due to the differences between dilution and tarnishment, one may wonder why the two are protected under a common special regime. The explanation is quite obvious. Both apply in cases where there is no likelihood of confusion. *See* Simon Fhima, *Trade Mark Dilution ...*, p. 160. If we consider that the reputed trade marks deserve an extended protection, going beyond the risk of confusion, it makes sense to create a common regime of enhanced protection. It would be possible to imagine two distinct regimes of protection, on the one hand, for highly distinctive trade marks, protected against the weakening of their attractiveness resulting from popularity, and, on the other hand, for trade marks giving rise to positive associations, marks of quality, prestige, protected against the deterioration of their image. Hence, it would be possible to create two different concepts of trade marks protected outside the speciality, one assessed solely on the basis of quantitative criteria, the other also on the basis of qualitative criteria. However, this would only complicate the law unnecessarily, since

223. Single act of use. Finally, it was observed in doctrine that, unlike dilution, which results from a gradual process, a single act of use could be sufficient to characterise tarnishment.[1139] However, as regards the possibility of invoking the infringement of a trade mark with a reputation, there is no real difference between the two forms of detriment. An isolated act of use by a third party is sufficient to establish both the risk of dilution and degradation. As we shall see, the establishment of a risk is sufficient to demonstrate the infringement and a first act of use of the disputed sign can constitute dilution.[1140]

[2] Establishment of Dilution

224. Requirement of a change in the economic behaviour. According to the *Intel* judgment, 'detriment to the distinctive character of the earlier mark is caused when that mark's ability to identify the goods or services for which it is registered and used as coming from the proprietor of that mark is weakened, since use of the later mark leads to dispersion of the identity and hold upon the public mind of the earlier mark. It follows that proof that the use of the later mark is or would be detrimental to the distinctive character of the earlier mark requires evidence of a change in the economic behaviour of the average consumer of the goods or services for which the earlier mark was registered consequent on the use of the later mark, or a serious likelihood that such a change will occur in the future'.[1141] Thus, dilution must be assessed in relation to a change in the economic behaviour of the customers concerned by the trade mark with a reputation.[1142] This is a requirement arising from consumer law which does not appear in any way in the provisions relating to trade marks and which is likely to make it more difficult to prove detriment to the distinctive character. Prima facie, in the view of this requirement, it is very difficult to demonstrate dilution. I will examine the reasons for such an increase in the standard of proof of detriment to the distinctive character of the mark (§3.01[A][2][a]) and then consider a flexible interpretation of this requirement in order not to deprive the concept of dilution of its role (§3.01[A][2][b]).

---

the conditions of infringement, in particular those relating to the assessment of the link, are partly identical. Therefore, the regulation of the two types of detriment to the reputed trade mark by the same special regime is entirely justified. This should not, however, call into question the need for an appropriate distinction between the two forms of injury, as the particular conditions of application of each are different.

1139. Simon Fhima, *Trade Mark Dilution ...*, pp. 159-160.

1140. *See* para. 230 *infra*.

1141. CJ, 27 November 2008, case C-252/07, *Intel*, paras 76-77. *See also* e.g. GC, 27 November 2014, case T-173/11, *Carrera*, para. 53.

1142. Regarding the relevant public by reference to which dilution needs to be assessed cf. para. 151 *supra*.

[a] *Justification of the Requirement of a Change in the Economic Behaviour of the Consumer*

225. Risk of conferring absolute monopolies to reputed marks. The requirement of a change in the economic behaviour of the average consumer concerned by the trade mark has the effect of restricting the access of the owners of reputed trade marks to the extended protection. It should be recalled that the definition of the trade mark with a reputation is not very selective and, consequently, the action for infringement under the special regime is a priori easy to bring.[1143]

The imposition of a requirement not provided for in the legal provisions in order to demonstrate a detriment to the distinctive character is due to the difficulty of applying the concept of dilution. As Simon Fhima observed, as an abstract theory serving to protect the distinctive character of the trade mark with a reputation, dilution is very attractive, but its implementation and proof of this type of harm are particularly difficult.[1144] Indeed, any act of reproduction or imitation of a trade mark having a reputation by a third party for dissimilar goods or services, to a certain extent, reduces its distinctiveness. Nevertheless, admitting it as unlawful use would lead to granting total protection to trade marks with a reputation against any exploitation by third parties.[1145] Hence, the concept of dilution interpreted too liberally would ensure absolute protection of reputed trade marks since the right holder would then enjoy an unlimited monopoly over the mark as soon as the public established a link between the signs in dispute. Evidence of the reputation of the trade mark and of the existence of a link in the public mind would then be sufficient in order to demonstrate infringement. This would call into question the logic of the special regime that condemns unlawful use of reputed marks only in well-defined cases and the ratio of distinguishing the other forms of infringement. Invoking tarnishment or unfair advantage would then become redundant. Moreover, a liberal interpretation of dilution would be likely to unduly undermine the freedom of commerce and industry (freedom of competition).[1146] In this respect, dilution constitutes a specific form of infringement of trade marks with a reputation. The problem does not arise in the field of tarnishment or unfair advantage since it is obvious that their demonstration cannot be limited to the establishment of a simple link between the signs in dispute.

Thus, the recognition of the criterion of a change in consumer behaviour is explained by the desire to ensure that the protection of trade marks with a reputation would not result in condemning any use of a reputed mark by a third party.[1147] For that

1143. Pollaud-Dulian, *Marque de renommée. Histoire ...*, p. 51.
1144. Simon Fhima, *Trade Mark Dilution ...*, p. 151.
1145. Passa, *Traité de droit ...*, p. 538. The courts point out that the purpose of the provisions on the extended protection is not to prevent use of any mark which is identical with a mark with a reputation or similar to it. CFI, 25 May 2005, case T-67/04, *Spa*, para. 40; CFI, 30 January 2008, case T-128/06, *Camel*, para. 49; CFI, 22 March 2007, case T-215/03, *VIPS*, para. 46. *See also* CJ, 30 April 2009, case C-136/08, *Camel*.
1146. *See* Bouvel, *Marque et renommée ...*, pp. 130-131.
1147. Caselli, *Il caso Wolf: la prova del pregiudizio ...*, p. 165. Cf. also Pascale Tréfigny-Goy, *Un monogramme bien défendu ... Ou quand une jaquette se prend une veste!*, Propr. ind. 2008, No. 6, comment 39.

reason, the restriction of protection resulting from the *Intel* judgment could be approved.[1148] The risk of excessive protection is then largely excluded. It is however necessary to determine which acts of use are likely to affect the distinctiveness of the mark by modifying the public perception of the sign.[1149]

Indeed, national courts sometimes consider that the infringement of the trade mark with a reputation is constituted as soon as the public concerned can establish a link between the trade mark and the disputed sign.[1150] In the French jurisprudence, it was also repeatedly held that the loss of exclusivity over the sign constituting a reputed trade mark is in itself a harm that should be compensated.[1151] Nevertheless, accepting that the loss of exclusivity characterises the infringement of a trade mark with a reputation leads to admitting that the owner of a reputed mark could prevent any third party from exploiting an identical or similar sign to designate dissimilar goods or services since the use of such a sign necessarily causes a loss of exclusivity.[1152] This problem further demonstrates the jurisprudence of the French Court of Cassation prior to the *Intel* judgment. In a decision of 20 February 2007, the Court of Cassation held that the existence of trivialisation, without further proof other than the evidence required to establish the link, was sufficient to condemn dilution.[1153] In a ruling of 11 March 2008,[1154] with regard to a comment by the Paris Court of Appeal that the detriment must be assessed not only on the basis of an infringement of the reputed trade mark by trivialising it, because in such a case any imitation of a reputed mark would be detrimental, but also by a real search for harm, the Court of Cassation noted that it resulted from its findings that the use of the contested sign in this case was detrimental to the distinctive character of the reputed mark, by its trivialisation, which constituted precisely the harm caused. Commenting on the solution of the judgment, Passa pointed out that the Court of Cassation probably meant to say that a detriment to the distinctive character existed precisely in the case at issue, in particular because of the great reputation of the earlier trade mark.[1155] Thus, the second ruling would suggest that, even before the *Intel* judgment, the Court of Cassation considered that the mere use of a sign identical or similar to a reputed trade mark did not automatically lead to the reprehensible dilution on the ground of the special regime. One might think that the Court of Cassation required the demonstration of a trivialisation of the earlier trade

1148. Bouvel, *Marque et renommée ...*, p. 131.
1149. Simon Fhima, *Trade Mark Dilution ...*, p. 140.
1150. TGI Paris, 2 March 2012, case 10/14345, *Louis Vuitton*.
1151. *See* e.g. CA Paris, 18 February 1993, PIBD 1993, No. 546, III, p. 393, *Château d'Yquem*; CA Angers, 7 June 1996, PIBD 1996, No. 619, III, p. 530, Ann. propr. ind. 1996, p. 34, comment of Paul Mathély, *Château d'Yquem*; TGI Paris, 20 February 1998, PIBD 1998, No. 654, III, p. 280, *Crunch*.
1152. Bouvel, *Principe de spécialité ...*, p. 371; Bouvel, *La protection des marques ...*, para. 95.
1153. Cass. com., 20 February, 2007, case 05-10.462, *Desperados*.
1154. Cass com., 11 March 2008, case 06-15.594, D. 2008, p. 917, comment of Jeanne Daleau, Propr. intell. 2008, No. 28, p. 360, comment of Jérôme Passa, Propr. ind. 2008, comment 39, of Pascale Tréfigny-Goy, *Louis Vuitton*.
1155. Passa, *Traité de droit ...*, pp. 539-540. *See also* Jérôme Passa, *Le régime spécial de protection de la marque renommée et l'exigence d'un usage à titre de marque*, Propr. intell. 2008, No. 28, pp. 360 et seq. The author also raises the question of the use of the disputed sign as a trade mark, which was questionable in the circumstances of the case.

mark, which could be described as 'serious'. Hence, the exploitation of a sign identical or similar to a reputed mark would not automatically be detrimental; the owner of the latter would have to prove particular circumstances, such as a strong reputation of his trade mark, a high *ab initio* distinctiveness or its uniqueness. The solution appears to balance the interests of the owners of the marks with a reputation and other undertakings.

226. Consumer law criterion. The Court of Justice went further by imposing the requirement to prove a change in the economic behaviour of the consumer, in order to emphasise that the existence of a link in itself does not lead to infringement.[1156] However, use of the formula of a change in the economic behaviour of the trade mark owner's customers is questionable. The requirement of this form of proof was rejected by the Advocate General.[1157] The term appeared in the judgment because of the preliminary questions addressed to the Court of Justice. It is not by chance that the British judge referred to it since British courts had implemented this criterion in their national case law beforehand.[1158] The criterion of a change in the economic behaviour comes from consumer law. It was first used in Directive 84/450 concerning misleading advertising.[1159] Then, this requirement reappeared in Article 5(2)(b) of Directive 2005/29 of 11 May 2005 concerning unfair commercial practices.[1160] The requirement of a change in the economic behaviour of customers is therefore specific to consumer law. Is this criterion well suited to trade mark law, based on different principles, intended to protect the interests of the trade mark owners? I tend to answer in the negative.

In addition, it should be noted that a criterion of 'affecting the economic behaviour' of the consumers concerned had been used by the Court of Justice in a judgment of 28 January 1999,[1161] rendered in a specific field of wine names, regarding

1156. *See* Simon Fhima, *Trade Mark Dilution* ..., p. 142.
1157. Opinion of Advocate General Eleanor Sharpston in case C-252/07, *Intel*, para. 74.
1158. Middlemiss, Warner, *The Protection of Marks* ..., p. 331.
1159. Pursuant to Article 2(2), misleading advertising means: 'any advertising which in any way, including its presentation, deceives or is likely to deceive the persons to whom it is addressed or whom it reaches and which, by reason of its deceptive nature, is likely to affect their economic behaviour or which, for those reasons, injures or is likely to injure a competitor'.
1160. Directive 2005/29/EC of the European Parliament and of the Council of 11 May 2005 concerning unfair business-to-consumer commercial practices in the internal market and amending Council Directive 84/450/EEC, Directives 97/7/EC, 98/27/EC and 2002/65/EC of the European Parliament and of the Council and Regulation (EC) No. 2006/2004 of the European Parliament and of the Council ('Unfair Commercial Practices Directive'), Official Journal L 149 of 11 June 2005. Pursuant to Article 5(2)(b), a commercial practice shall be unfair if: 'it materially distorts or is likely to materially distort the economic behaviour with regard to the product of the average consumer whom it reaches or to whom it is addressed, or of the average member of the group when a commercial practice is directed to a particular group of consumers'.
1161. CJ, 28 January 1999, case C-303/97. According to the operative part of the judgment, Article 13(2)(b) of Regulation 2333/92 'is to be interpreted as meaning that, for the prohibition laid down by that provision to be applied, it is not sufficient to determine that a brand name which contains a word appearing in the description of one of the products mentioned in that provision is, in itself, likely to be confused with that description. It is also necessary to establish that use of the brand name is in fact likely to mislead the consumers concerned and thus affect their economic behaviour. In that respect, it is for the national court to refer to the

Article 13(2)(b) of Regulation 2333/92 of 13 July 1992 on the description and presentation of sparkling wines.[1162] However, this provision refers to the likelihood of confusion, and it is questionable whether evidence used to examine the likelihood of confusion is appropriate for the assessment of dilution.[1163]

The approach adopted by the Court of Justice, which applies a requirement specific to consumer law, close to unfair competition law, is difficult to reconcile with the European concept of the extended protection, which falls within the scope of exclusive trade mark rights. However, given the importance of the jurisprudence of the Court of Justice in interpreting national laws and the Regulation on EU trade marks, national courts and trade mark offices cannot refuse to apply this criterion. Nevertheless, in order for dilution to still fulfil the function assigned to it by the legislator, i.e. to ensure that the provisions relating to the distinctive character can apply, the requirement for a change in the economic behaviour must be interpreted in a flexible manner.

[b] Flexible Interpretation of the Requirement of a Change in the Economic Behaviour of the Consumer

227. Necessity and method. The requirement of proof of a change in the economic behaviour of the consumer, interpreted restrictively, would amount to requiring the trade mark owner to establish an actual loss of customers as a result of the allegedly unlawful use of the disputed sign by the third party. Since such an interpretation of the requirement of a change in the economic behaviour is in no way in line with the traditional conditions for assessing trade mark infringement and would call into question the special protection of trade marks against dilution, it is necessary to argue for a flexible interpretation of this requirement (§3.01[A][2][b][i]). It remains to consider how the trade mark owners can establish dilution in accordance with the case law of the Court of Justice (§3.01[A][2][b][ii]).

[i] Necessity of a Flexible Interpretation

228. Critics. The requirement of proof of a change in the economic behaviour was widely criticised in doctrine. Favourable opinions are quite rare.[1164] The formula was

presumed expectations in regard to that information on the part of an average consumer who is reasonably well informed and reasonably observant and circumspect'.

1162. Council Regulation (EEC) No. 2333/92 of 13 July 1992 laying down general rules for the description and presentation of sparkling wines and aerated sparkling wines, Official Journal L 231 of 13 August 1992.

1163. *See* Simon Fhima, *Trade Mark Dilution* ..., pp. 149-150. That being said, this decision may be of interest to our subject because, unlike the *Intel* judgment, it contains at least some guidance on how the change in the economic behaviour can be assessed, such as the establishment of an expert report or opinion poll, which could be used to demonstrate it in the area of dilution. *See* CJ, 28 January 1999, case C-303/97, para. 37.

1164. *See* however Martin Senftleben, *Trade Mark Protection: A Black Hole in the Intellectual Property Galaxy?*, IIC 2011, vol. 42, No. 4, p. 385; Senftleben, *Adapting EU Trademark* ..., pp. 151-152. The author emphasises that the extended protection of the trade marks with a reputation should remain exceptional. Cf. also Andreas Breitschaft, *Intel, Adidas & Co: Is the*

considered questionable,[1165] it was argued that the requirement has no legal basis,[1166] that it proves the power of the Court of Justice of creating legal norms.[1167] Many authors point out that the requirement is vague and obscure.[1168] Indeed, when reading the judgment, it is difficult to understand what it covers. It is therefore questionable whether it is worth producing legal standards that are inapplicable because of their lack of intelligibility.[1169] It must be noted that the *Intel* judgment gives no indication on how to prove a change in the economic behaviour of the consumer.[1170] Moreover, since the Court of Justice only requires the establishment of a risk of detriment to distinctiveness in order to demonstrate dilution, it is difficult to understand why a change in the economic behaviour of the average consumer is necessary.[1171] In general, in trade mark law, the right holder is not required to demonstrate that he has lost customers in order to establish infringement.[1172] In addition, the holder would then have to prove that the loss of customers is due to the disputed use.[1173] This evidence is clearly not simple to present.[1174] Indeed, the requirement imposed by the *Intel* judgment applied strictly would make it almost impossible to prove dilution,[1175] thus would lead to a partial petrification of the protection of trade marks with a reputation,[1176] by de facto paralysing a part of the provisions of the Directive and of the Regulation on EU trade marks.[1177] This would undoubtedly be a step backwards in the special protection of trade marks having a reputation, in which the theory of dilution played an essential role. Some national judgments show that the requirement of proof of a change in the economic behaviour of the customers, interpreted, as it seems, strictly, makes the establishment of dilution extremely complicated.[1178]

Jurisprudence of the European Court of Justice on Dilution Law in Compliance with the Underlying Rationales and Fit for the Future?, EIPR 2009, vol. 31, No. 10, p. 503; Louise O'Callaghan, *Intel-Ligent Way Forward? The ECJ Rules on Dilution*, JIPLP 2009, vol. 4, No. 4, p. 239; Skubisz, *Kolizja późniejszego znaku ...*, p. 36.

1165. Pollaud-Dulian, *Les atteintes à la marque de renommée ...*, p. 7.
1166. Colin Davies, *To Buy or Not to Buy: The Use of a Trade Mark as a Communication Tool Rather than as a Link Between the Product and Its Source – A Further Consideration of the Concept of Dilution*, EIPR 2013, vol. 35, No. 7, p. 379.
1167. Bouvel, *La protection des marques ...*, para. 100.
1168. Middlemiss, Warner, *The Protection of Marks ...*, p. 328; Simon Fhima, *Trade Mark Dilution ...*, p. 148; Bouvel, *Marque et renommée ...*, p. 131.
1169. Bouvel, *La protection des marques ...*, para. 100.
1170. Caselli, *Il caso Wolf: la prova del pregiudizio ...*, p. 177.
1171. Folliard-Monguiral, *CJCE, arrêt Intel ...*, para. 6.
1172. Davies, *To Buy or Not to Buy ...*, p. 379.
1173. Cf. Darren Meale, Joel Smith, *Enforcing a Trade Mark when Nobody's Confused: Where the Law Stands after L'Oréal and Intel*, JIPLP 2010, vol. 5, No. 2, p. 102.
1174. Georges Bonet, *Protection de la marque renommée*, Propr. intell. 2010, No. 37, p. 654; Bereskin, *Anti-dilution ...*, p. 1749.
1175. Cohen Jehoram, Van Nispen, Huydecoper, *European Trademark Law ...*, p. 317; Barton Beebe, *Intellectual Property Law and the Sumptuary Code*, Harv. L. Rev. 2010, vol. 123, No. 4, p. 856. Cf. also Passa, *Les grands arrêts ...*, pp. 616-617.
1176. *See* Maetz, *Notoriété: essai sur l'appropriation ...*, p. 113.
1177. Christophe Caron, *Les marques renommées face à la dilution de leur caractère distinctif*, Comm. com. électr. 2009, No. 2, comment 14.
1178. *See* in French jurisprudence: CA Paris, 8 November 2013, case 11/00737 and Cass. com., 7 June 2016, case 14-16.885, *Visa*; in Polish jurisprudence: SA Warsaw, 6 April 2011, case I ACa

229. Intention of the Court of Justice. The evidence required by the judge to demonstrate dilution cannot be impossible to establish. It should be stressed, as the Advocate General did in the *Intel* case, that the judge's interpretative work should, as far as possible, aim for a fair balance between the different interests of rights holders and other market participants.[1179] By requiring evidence that is impossible to establish, while protection against dilution is expressly guaranteed by the law, the Court of Justice would undermine that balance to the detriment of trade mark owners. It should be also borne in mind that the current Article 10(2)(c) of Directive 2015/2436, as well as Article 9(2)(c) of Regulation 2017/1001, must be interpreted in the light of the overall scheme and objectives of the system of which it is a part.[1180] One of the objectives of the special regime is to protect the trade mark against the detriment to its distinctive character. The jurisprudence cannot call into question the effectiveness of a significant part of the regime of protection of trade marks with a reputation enshrined by the legislator. I am not going to enter into the debate on the role of the Court of Justice in the interpretation of European law, on its 'power to create legal norms',[1181] and I will certainly not question its importance and the obligation of national judges to respect its case law. Nevertheless, the power of the Court of Justice remains with the judiciary. The role of the interpreter of the law, the judge, is to seek and respect the will of the legislator, taking into account the purpose of the rule of law,[1182] in order to achieve the objectives adopted by the legislator, which excludes the power to challenge or amend a decision taken by the legislator. The search for the legislator's intention, the *ratio legis*, remains the cardinal method of interpreting texts.[1183] In this case, the provisions explicitly express the desire to condemn the use of trade marks with a reputation which is detrimental to the distinctive character, and therefore to condemn dilution. The European legislator provided for an enhanced system of protection for trade marks having a reputation and the judge cannot contest the ratio of a normative act by an interpretation tending to make it inapplicable, which would empty its provisions of their substance by imposing a kind of *probatio diabolica*. Therefore, it should be admitted that the intention of the Court of Justice was certainly not to question the protection of the trade mark against dilution, but to 'rationalise' its demonstration.

Moreover, challenging the protection of reputed trade marks against dilution by imposing a requirement impossible to meet would have the effect of undermining the consistency of the jurisprudence of the Court of Justice, which requires that a significant value be attributed to dilution. As we have seen, in the view of the broad

866/10, *Delicje*; WSA Warsaw, 8 December 2014, case VI SA/Wa 1359/14, *Montblanc*; and Dutch jurisprudence cited by Gielen, *Trademark Dilution under European Law* ..., p. 721.

1179. Opinion of Advocate General Eleanor Sharpston in case C-252/07, *Intel*, para. 32.

1180. *See* CJ, 9 January 2003, case C-292/00, *Davidoff*, para. 24.

1181. Cf. Bouvel, *La protection des marques* ..., para. 100.

1182. *See* François Terré, *Introduction générale au droit*, 9th ed., Dalloz, Paris 2012, pp. 435 et seq.

1183. Pascale Deumier, *Introduction générale au droit*, 2nd ed., LGDJ, Paris 2013, pp. 102-103. On the famous Montesquieu's formula according to which the judges are only 'the mouth that pronounces the words of the law; inanimate beings who cannot moderate its force or rigour' (*la bouche qui prononce les paroles de la loi; des êtres inanimés qui n'en peuvent modérer ni la force ni la rigueur*), *see* Deumier, *Introduction générale* ..., p. 85.

definition of the trade mark with a reputation enshrined in the *Chevy* judgment,[1184] it must be admitted that, in the context of the special regime, not only prestigious trade marks that convey an image of excellence but also all marks known to a significant part of the public concerned are protected, in accordance with the assumption that popularity of the sign itself confers on it an economic value worthy of protection. Consequently, the protection of trade marks with a reputation is not limited to the protection of their repute, against acts detrimental to the image of the sign or allowing third parties to take unfair advantage of it.

230. No requirement of proof of an actual damage. The establishment of trade mark infringement is never dependent on the right holder demonstrating that he actually suffered damage, in particular as a result of a loss of customers.[1185] This is not the case in the field of infringement within the speciality. Similarly, as we shall see, no actual harm or advantage must be proven in order to establish the other forms of infringement of trade marks with a reputation. There is no argument that would justify a different solution in the case of dilution. Indeed, in order to establish the infringement of a mark having a reputation, the risk of harm or profit is sufficient.[1186] Although Article 10(2)(c) of Directive 2015/2346 and Article 9(2)(c) of Regulation 2017/1001 explicitly do not suggest the possibility of acting against a simple risk,[1187] since they refer to the use which 'takes unfair advantage' or 'is detrimental', the jurisprudence of the Court of Justice confirms that the establishment of a risk of harm or advantage is sufficient. While the *Intel* judgment concerns the interpretation of the provisions relating to the relative grounds for invalidity, the solution also applies to the interpretation of the provisions relating to the infringement of reputed trade marks.[1188] According to the *Intel* judgment, in order to benefit from the extended protection, 'the proprietor of the earlier trade mark is not required ... to demonstrate actual and present injury to its mark. ... When it is foreseeable that such injury will ensue from the use which the proprietor of the later mark may be led to make of its mark, the proprietor of the earlier mark cannot be required to wait for it actually to occur in order to be able to prohibit that use. The proprietor of the earlier mark must, however, prove that there is a serious risk that such an injury will occur in the future'.[1189] The establishment of a serious risk of infringement is therefore quite sufficient to condemn the use of a trade mark with a reputation by a third party. The notion of 'serious' risk should mean a risk that is not hypothetical.[1190] Moreover, a first use of the disputed mark may suffice to cause actual

---

1184. *See* para. 56 *supra*.
1185. Davies, *To Buy or Not to Buy ...*, p. 379.
1186. Bonet, *La protection des marques notoires ...*, p. 198; Canlorbe, *L'usage de la marque ...*, p. 123.
1187. Bouvel, *Marque et renommée ...*, p. 129.
1188. *See* CJ, 27 November 2008, case C-252/07, *Intel*, paras 24-25. Moreover, proof of a change in the economic behaviour of the average consumer must be appropriate both for the examination of conflicts with an earlier trade mark with a reputation, as a ground for invalidity, in cancellation proceedings, or in opposition proceedings, i.e. in cases where no use of the disputed sign has yet taken place. Cf. Opinion of Advocate General Eleanor Sharpston in case C-252/07, *Intel*, para. 84.
1189. CJ, 27 November 2008, case C-252/07, *Intel*, para. 38.
1190. Gielen, *Trademark Dilution in the European Union ...*, p. 228.

and present detriment to the distinctive character of the earlier mark or to give rise to a serious likelihood that such detriment will occur in the future.[1191]

The solution is in full compliance with Article 16(3) of the TRIPS Agreement. As we have seen, this provision is considered to recognise the special protection of reputed trade marks on international level, since it explicitly refers to the protection of marks beyond the speciality.[1192] It should be stressed that the interpretation of Directive 2015/2436 and of Regulation 2017/1001 must be in line with the TRIPS Agreement. Article 16(3) of the latter explicitly refers to protection against use made by a third party if the interests of the trade mark owner 'are likely to be damaged' by such use.[1193] Thus, the establishment of actual and present harm cannot be required on the part of the owner in order to demonstrate the infringement of the trade mark with a reputation.

231. No immediate effect of dilution. Furthermore, according to the *Interflora* judgment, for the proprietor of a trade mark with a reputation to be effectively protected against dilution, Article 10(2)(c) of Directive 2015/2436 and Article 9(2)(c) of Regulation 2017/1001 'must be interpreted as entitling the proprietor to prevent all use of a sign identical with or similar to that trade mark which reduces the distinctiveness of the mark, without it being required to wait for the end of the process of dilution, that is to say, the total loss of the trade mark's distinctive character'.[1194] Indeed, the weakening of the value of the trade mark due to the use by a third party does not necessarily take place from the outset. Sometimes it takes years for this effect to occur.[1195] To quote Jaton, dilution acts in a surreptitious way. 'It is pernicious like a slow poison, unlike confusion which causes damage that is usually immediately noticeable.'[1196] Thus, dilution can only influence the behaviour of customers, who turn away from the goods or services covered by the mark, after a certain period of time. At first, it is only possible to consider that dilution will have the effect of limiting the number of new customers, which is very difficult to establish.[1197] Proof of a risk must therefore be sufficient; otherwise protection against dilution would become ineffective and could not take place at the time when it is really necessary, i.e. from the very beginning of the use of the disputed sign, at the first stage of trade mark's dilution.[1198] It would be economically unjustified, also from the point of view of the infringer who has invested in promoting his sign and has acquired his own clientele, if the right holder had to wait years before being entitled to bring an action for trade mark infringement.

1191. CJ, 27 November 2008, case C-252/07, *Intel*, para. 75.
1192. *See* para. 39 *supra*.
1193. Cf. Cohen Jehoram, Van Nispen, Huydecoper, *European Trademark Law ...*, p. 307.
1194. CJ, 22 September 2011, case C-323/09, *Interflora*, para. 77.
1195. Troller, *La marque de haute renommée ...*, p. 79.
1196. Jaton, *La protection des marques ...*, p. 49. '*Elle est pernicieuse comme un poison lent, au contraire de la confusion qui provoque un dommage en général immédiatement sensible*'.
1197. Passa, *Traité de droit ...*, p. 539.
1198. Pollaud-Dulian, *Les atteintes à la marque de renommée ...*, p. 7.

[ii] Method of the Flexible Interpretation

232. Broad sense of the formula. The expression referring to the 'economic behaviour' is sufficiently vague to allow for several interpretations,[1199] and since establishment of a risk of a change in the consumer's behaviour is sufficient, infringement can be assessed more flexibly.[1200] Indeed, an excessively strict requirement of proof of dilution would be likely to deprive trade marks with a reputation of a part of the special protection.[1201]

A flexible interpretation of the requirement of a change in the behaviour of the consumer is possible in the light of a judgment of the Court of Justice of 10 May 2012 in the *Botox* case.[1202] According to this ruling, 'the proprietor of the earlier mark is not required to demonstrate actual and present harm to its mark but must, however, adduce prima facie evidence of a future risk, which is not hypothetical, of unfair advantage or detriment, and such a conclusion may be established, in particular, on the basis of logical deductions made from an analysis of the probabilities and by taking account of the normal practice in the relevant commercial sector as well as all the other circumstances of the case'.[1203]

233. Autonomous assessment based on logical deductions. Trying to give a meaning to the *Intel* decision, which would not call into question the protection of the trade mark against dilution, Gielen further observed that the requirement of proof of a change in the economic behaviour, which appears in the operative part of the *Intel* judgment, should not be read in isolation from its entire text.[1204] This interpretation was applied by the General Court in a judgment of 22 May 2012 concerning the mark *Wolf*.[1205] According to the General Court, which adopted the formula established by the Court of Justice in the *Botox* judgment, a risk of dilution can be proven 'in particular, on the basis of logical deductions'. Then, the General Court attempted to challenge the value of the requirement of a proof of a change in customers' behaviour. In the light of the decision, 'It cannot, however, be required that, in addition to those elements, the

1199. Caron, *Les marques renommées face à la dilution* ..., comment 14.

1200. Passa, *Traité de droit* ..., p. 539. This is why it was even observed that, because of the broad discretion given to the judge, the *Intel* solution had the potential to work in practice. Middlemiss, Warner, *The Protection of Marks* ..., p. 326.

1201. As it was rightly observed in Polish jurisprudence. *See* SO Warsaw, 30 July 2012, case XXII GWzt 18/10, *My Little Pony*.

1202. CJ, 10 May 2012, case C-100/11 P, *Botox*. *See* Gielen, *Trademark Dilution in the European Union* ..., p. 233.

1203. CJ, 10 May 2012, case C-100/11 P, *Botox*, para. 95. Cf. earlier CFI, 25 May 2005, case T-67/04, *Spa*, para. 40; CFI, 10 May 2007, case T-47/06, *Nasdaq*, para. 54; GC, 28 October 2010, case T-131/09, *Botox*, para. 91.

1204. According to Gielen, a global and combined reading of the decision should be adopted. Recognition of the requirement would logically develop the previous remarks in which the Court of Justice refers to the various factors for assessing the link and the infringement itself, such as the degree of the trade mark's reputation, its distinctive character or its uniqueness. Thus, it should be possible for the right holder to establish dilution as soon as he demonstrates that the use of the disputed sign is likely to lead to the dispersion of the identity of his mark. This would be sufficient evidence of a risk of a change in the consumer's economic behaviour. Gielen, *Trademark Dilution in the European Union* ..., pp. 232-233.

1205. GC, 22 May 2012, case T-570/10, *Wolf*.

proprietor of the earlier mark must show an additional effect, caused by the introduction of the later mark, on the economic behaviour of the average consumer of the goods or services for which the earlier mark was registered.' Regarding the requirement of a change in the economic behaviour, the Court considered that it 'is established if the proprietor of the earlier mark has shown ... that the mark's ability to identify the goods or services for which it is registered and used as coming from the proprietor of that mark is weakened, since use of the later mark leads to dispersion of the identity and hold upon the public mind of the earlier mark'.[1206]

This interpretation of the solution imposed by the *Intel* judgment appears clear and convincing. Nevertheless, the Court of Justice did not share the opinion of the General Court in that case and annulled its judgment by a decision of 14 November 2013.[1207] The ruling of the Court of Justice remains however very obscure.[1208] On the one hand, the Court of Justice points out that the requirement of a proof of a change in the economic behaviour is not 'merely an explanation' but is 'autonomous'[1209] and 'lays down an objective condition. That change cannot be deduced solely from subjective elements such as consumers' perceptions'.[1210] What 'objective' evidence does the Court of Justice require? This is impossible to tell. If the right holder provides unquestionably 'objective' evidence, for example, based on a decrease in turnover, this is no longer a proof of a risk of detriment but of actual harm. However, the Court itself is content with a simple likelihood of dilution to establish infringement, which it reaffirms each time. On the other hand, the judgment contains findings which in fact enshrine a flexible interpretation of the requirement of a change in the economic behaviour. The Court of Justice clearly admits that the legal provisions and case law 'do not require evidence to be adduced of actual detriment, but also admit the serious risk of such detriment, allowing the use of logical deductions'. Then, the Court of Justice partially approves the ruling of the General Court. Referring to the *Botox* judgment, it points out that such deductions, which must not be the result of mere suppositions, must be founded on 'an analysis of the probabilities and by taking account of the normal practice in the relevant commercial sector as well as all the other circumstances of the case'.[1211] It seems that the General Court is criticised for not having conducted a separate analysis of the risk of a change in consumer behaviour.[1212] It can be assumed that the Court of Justice annulled the judgment of the General Court because the latter had only examined the existence of a link between the signs in dispute and had failed

1206. GC, 22 May 2012, case T-570/10, *Wolf*, paras 52-54.
1207. CJ, 14 November 2013, case C-383/12 P, *Wolf*. Following the annulment and referral of the case, the General Court dismissed the dilution claim. GC, 5 February 2015, case T-570/10 RENV, *Wolf*, para. 40.
1208. Cf. Arnaud Folliard-Monguiral, *CJUE, arrêt Tête de Loup: dilution et comportement économique*, Propr. ind. 2014, No. 1, comment 5, para. 3.
1209. CJ, 14 November 2013, case C-383/12 P, *Wolf*, para. 35. Cf. Bouvel, *La protection des marques ...*, para. 100.
1210. CJ, 14 November 2013, case C-383/12 P, *Wolf*, para. 37. Cf. Yann Basire, Adrien Bouvel, in: Franck Macrez et al., *Un an de jurisprudence de la Cour de justice et du Tribunal de l'Union européenne en propriété industrielle*, Propr. ind. 2014, No. 11, chron. 9, para. 10.
1211. CJ, 14 November 2013, case C-383/12 P, *Wolf*, paras 42-43.
1212. *See* CJ, 14 November 2013, case C-383/12 P, *Wolf*, para. 44.

to justify its decision by reference to a change in the consumer behaviour, as the courts and trade mark offices should do since the *Intel* judgment, instead of challenging the autonomous value of the formula. The *Wolf* judgment once again reflects the concern not to grant unlimited monopolies to reputed trade marks, which could harm competition. It was reiterated that the link between the signs per se is not sufficient to establish dilution.[1213] The fact that the Court of Justice emphasises that the assessment may be based on logical deductions indeed supports the view that no evidence establishing economic loss is required but that the analysis of the requirement of a change in the economic behaviour must be purely normative.[1214]

234. Requirement of immediate associations. The 'logical deductions' that allow to establish a risk of dilution are therefore sufficient. They can be based on the factors for assessment relating to the examination of the existence of a link.[1215] Indeed, the Court of Justice applies the criteria used to examine the link between the signs in order to assess the infringement itself.[1216] The courts and trade mark offices must nevertheless make an autonomous assessment of the existence of a link between the signs and of dilution. Obviously, this may lead to examining the same facts twice. However, as the Advocate General pointed out in the *Intel* case, the relevant factors for assessment may be taken into account in a different way at the second stage of the analysis, when one turns to assess the presence or likelihood of infringement, and in particular of dilution. 'It may be the case that the public will more readily establish a link between the two marks if the earlier mark has a "huge" reputation and is "unique in respect of any goods or services" ... However, those facts seem more relevant when assessing the existence of free-riding, blurring or tarnishment.'[1217]

Indeed, establishment of dilution requires evidence that is in no way necessary to prove the existence of a link, even if it can be demonstrated based on factors that may be taken into account in the assessment of the link – that of an instant association caused by the trade mark. As we have seen, dilution occurs when the public is likely to perceive a mark associated with one commercial origin as indicating several different sources of origin.[1218] The detriment to the distinctive character of the mark appears when the mark is no longer able to evoke immediate associations with the goods or services as coming from their proprietor. A mark likely to be diluted, to quote Troller's words, used by the author in order to define the reputed trade mark, 'must impose itself without having to intervene either a reasoning or the evocation of a memory'; 'it must emerge as a reflex'.[1219] Hence, the more immediate and strong the evocation of the

1213. *See* CJ, 14 November 2013, case C-383/12 P, *Wolf*, paras 40-41.
1214. Gielen, *Trademark Dilution under European Law* ..., p. 722.
1215. *See* paras 138 et seq. *supra*.
1216. CJ, 27 November 2008, case C-252/07, *Intel*, para. 68. Cf. also Skrzydło-Tefelska, *Community Trade Mark* ..., p. 290.
1217. Opinion of Advocate General Eleanor Sharpston in case C-252/07, *Intel*, paras 45-50. *See also* Simon Fhima, *Trade Mark Dilution* ..., p. 141.
1218. *See* para. 213 *supra*. *See also* Simon Fhima, *Trade Mark Dilution* ..., p. 101.
1219. Troller, *La marque de haute renommée* ..., p. 76. '*Doit s'imposer sans qu'ait à intervenir ni un raisonnement, ni l'évocation d'un souvenir. Elle doit surgir comme un réflexe*'.

mark by the sign in dispute is, the greater the risk of dilution.[1220] A trade mark that gives rise to immediate associations must certainly have a high degree of distinctiveness. Indeed, it is then likely that the instant association with the right holder will be weakened by the presence of other similar signs.[1221]

235. Uniqueness of the mark. In this respect, the 'uniqueness' of the trade mark appears to be of major importance.[1222] According to the *Intel* judgment, the ability of a trade mark to identify the goods or services for which it is registered and used as coming from the proprietor of that mark and, therefore, its distinctive character are all the stronger if that mark is unique.[1223] The Court of Justice emphasises the role of uniqueness at the stage of assessing the infringement.[1224] The jurisprudence of the General Court confirms that the uniqueness of the trade mark is a factor facilitating the establishment of the existence of an infringement, in particular of dilution.[1225] Also, the EUIPO and some national judges link dilution to the loss of uniqueness by the trade mark.[1226] In consequence, the doctrine raises that detriment to the distinctive character is intended to be invoked in particular by the owners of trade marks which are unique on the market.[1227]

As we have seen, according to the Court of Justice, a mark is unique when 'the word of which it consists has not been used by anyone for any goods or services other than by the proprietor of the mark for the goods and services it markets'.[1228] This approach to the concept of uniqueness, assessed taking into account the other marks on the market, but regardless of the meaning of the mark, appears to be the most appropriate in trade mark matters.[1229] Nevertheless, the meaning of the sign can be of importance and enhance the risk of dilution. Ensuring special protection against dilution to 'original' marks that have no meaning in everyday language would correspond to Schechter's concept who advocated for strengthening the protection of 'arbitrary, invented or fanciful' marks.[1230] Similarly, Dassas considered that a mark which does not exclusively refer to the good it designates, but to a first name, a character, etc., cannot be subject to dilution.[1231] Thus, it may be accepted that it is more likely to establish dilution when the sign composing the mark is not a word belonging

1220. *See* CJ, 27 November 2008, case C-252/07, *Intel*, para. 67.
1221. *See* Opinion of Advocate General Eleanor Sharpston in case C-252/07, *Intel*, para. 72. Cf. CFI, 30 January 2008, case T-128/06, *Camel*, para. 56. Both the intrinsic distinctiveness and the one related to the use are concerned. *See* CFI, 10 May 2007, case T-47/06, *Nasdaq*, para. 58.
1222. Cf. similarly under Swiss law, Alberini, *L'exploitation de la renommée* ..., pp. 221-222.
1223. CJ, 27 November 2008, case C-252/07, *Intel*, para. 56.
1224. CJ, 27 November 2008, case C-252/07, *Intel*, para. 74.
1225. CFI, 25 May 2005, case T-67/04, *Spa*, para. 44; GC, 16 December 2010, cases T-345/08 and T-357/08, *Botox*, para. 85.
1226. OHIM, BoA, 28 January 2014, case R 69/2013-4, *Camel*, paras 37-38. In French jurisprudence *see* TGI Valence, 2 November 2004, case 00/00953, *Mont Blanc*. In Polish jurisprudence *see* SA Wrocław, 3 October 2007, case I ACa 767/07, *Velux*.
1227. Cohen Jehoram, Van Nispen, Huydecoper, *European Trademark Law* ..., p. 313.
1228. CJ, 27 November 2008, case C-252/07, *Intel*, para. 56.
1229. *See* para. 167 *supra*.
1230. Schechter, *The Rational Basis* ..., pp. 828-830.
1231. Dassas, *L'élargissement de la protection* ..., p. 88.

to the common language.[1232] According to the General Court, when a mark has no inherent meaning, but is a fanciful term with which the public will be faced only in relation to the goods covered by the widely known earlier trade mark, it is more probable that use of a similar sign will result in dilution of the distinctive character of the widely known earlier trade mark.[1233] By contrast, in the General Court's view, 'the risk of dilution appears, in principle, to be lower if the earlier mark consists of a term which, because of a meaning inherent in it, is very common and frequently used, irrespective of the earlier mark consisting of the term at issue'.[1234]

Consequently, if several similar marks coexist on the market, it is difficult for the owner to establish that dilution of his trade mark is due to the disputed sign. In addition, the actions undertaken by the right holder may have some impact on the possibility of demonstrating harm to distinctiveness. First, if the trade mark has been exploited by other undertakings without the owner's reaction, it may be complicated to demonstrate that the use of the sign by the third party attacked has damaged the distinctive character of the sign which had already lost its distinctiveness, allowing immediate associations with the goods or services as coming from the owner. In addition, the right holder may himself contribute to the dilution of his trade mark, in particular by granting licences for several different goods,[1235] because the public may not associate all these goods with one commercial origin. As noted above, trade mark owners often extend their activities into new areas of business. When the public associates the origin of all the goods coming from the right holder with the latter, as we have seen, the use of the mark by a third party for a different good, in the absence of any likelihood of confusion, may lead to dilution. However, if the third party demonstrates that the public does not associate all the goods designated by the trade mark and marketed with the consent of the right holder with the latter, the risk of dilution of the trade mark by the disputed use can easily be ruled out. Accordingly, the action based on dilution may be dismissed. Nevertheless, the hypothesis seems rather theoretical. The trade mark would have to be used by the right holder and his licensees for goods that are in no way related to each other.[1236]

Having said that, the uniqueness of the trade mark is not a condition *sine qua non* for dilution. Even where a trade mark with a reputation is not unique, the use of an identical or similar sign may be such as to weaken the distinctive character of the mark.[1237] *A fortiori*, trade marks that are unique, according to the definition resulting from the *Intel* judgment, but have an inherent meaning, may be diluted. However, they must then enjoy an exceptional reputation and the word the mark consists of should not be widely used. The General Court observed, with regard to a mark having a

1232. Cf. Isabelle Meunier-Cœur, *Notoriété et renommée de la marque*, Propr. ind. 2006, étude 12, para. 43.
1233. GC, 28 October 2010, case T-131/09, *Botox*, para. 99. In French jurisprudence *see* CA Paris, 28 September 2011, case 09/21842, *Nutella*.
1234. CFI, 22 March 2007, case T-215/03, *VIPS*, para. 38; GC, 28 October 2010, case T-131/09, *Botox*, para. 98.
1235. *See* Simon Fhima, *Trade Mark Dilution ...*, p. 148.
1236. Moreover, it seems that such evidence could in principle only be provided by means of a survey.
1237. CJ, 27 November 2008, case C-252/07, *Intel*, paras 72-73.

plurality of meanings and being able to refer to something other than the owner of the mark, that if the absence of polysemy is a factor in recognising the strong distinctive character of a mark, the polysemy of a mark is not, in itself, likely to affect the strong distinctive character of a mark.[1238] Using once again the example of the mark *Mercedes*,[1239] this sign seems to evoke an instantaneous association, although the mark is not fanciful, constituting a female first name that is nevertheless rarely used in most European countries. On the contrary, it would be difficult to envisage dilution of the mark *Dupont* in France since, even though it undoubtedly has a reputation in relation to lighters and accessories for smokers, the name is intrinsically banal,[1240] as it is a very common family name.

236. Relevant public. Another factor that should be examined is the relevant public targeted by the third party. It must be admitted that if the contested sign designates goods or services directed at a limited public, the risk of dilution of the earlier mark through the dispersion of its identity and its hold upon the public mind is reduced.[1241] According to the General Court, 'the risk that the use of an identical or similar trade mark would be detrimental to the distinctive character of a widely known earlier trade mark is greater where that other mark will be used in respect of goods intended for a wide public'.[1242] In addition, the greater the number of goods or services for which the third party exploits the disputed sign, the greater the risk of dilution.[1243]

Moreover, the comparison of the public concerned by the signs in dispute seems to be important for the assessment of dilution and remains in line with the requirement of a proof of a change in the economic behaviour of the consumer. Azéma even pointed out that a change in consumer's behaviour can only occur when the goods or services identified by the contested sign, without being similar to those covered by the mark with a reputation, remain within the same economic sector.[1244] However, a simple overlap of the publics concerned should allow to establish a change in the behaviour of the consumer of the good designated by the earlier trade mark, since he is then exposed to the good or service under the disputed sign. Hence, it should be sufficient if one of the signs in dispute was aimed at the general public, for there to be a possible overlap of publics and therefore dilution, regardless of whether the economic sectors to which the goods or services belong are close. Nevertheless, too important differences between the sectors are indeed likely to rule out dilution, since the nature of the goods or services in question may also be a relevant factor in assessing the risk of a change in consumer behaviour. Jaton rightly observed that the need for protection against dilution disappears when, for example, a mark known for aircraft is affixed to an ordinary product because the attractive power of the mark plays no role when

1238. GC, 27 October 2016, case T-625/15, *Spa*, para. 59.
1239. *See* para. 168 *supra*.
1240. Cf. Dassas, *L'élargissement de la protection ...*, p. 189.
1241. CFI, 22 March 2007, case T-215/03, *VIPS*, para. 63.
1242. GC, 28 October 2010, case T-131/09, *Botox*, para. 100.
1243. In French jurisprudence *see* CA Angers, 7 June 1996, PIBD 1996, No. 619, III, p. 530, *Château d'Yquem*.
1244. Jacques Azéma, *Protection d'une marque renommée pour des produits différents*, RTD com. 2009, No. 1, p. 117.

purchasing an aircraft, and therefore the owner of the mark loses the interest in maintaining the distinctive power of his sign.[1245]

This being said, it should be noted that the comparison of the specialities of the two signs concerned must be more flexible than in the event of the likelihood of confusion since the trade mark with a reputation is protected beyond the speciality.[1246] Moreover, it must be admitted that too much similarity between the goods or services in question, *a fortiori* their identity, which leads to a likelihood of confusion, is in no way likely to weaken the immediate association with the goods or services as originating from the trade mark owner. If the public associates the origin of these goods or services with the right holder, this immediate association can only be strengthened. Hence, the General Court is wrong when it says that 'the fact that competitors use somewhat similar signs for identical or similar goods compromises the immediate connection that the relevant public makes between the signs and the goods at issue, which is likely to undermine the earlier mark's ability to identify the goods for which it is registered as coming from the proprietor of that mark'.[1247] This finding is contradictory.[1248] Dilution of the trade mark with a reputation cannot be dependent on the similarity of the goods or services designated by that trade mark with those covered by the disputed sign.[1249] In most cases, the similarity of the goods or services excludes dilution. Indeed, dilution is the most classic form of trade mark infringement outside the speciality, particularly well suited to the exploitation of an identical or similar sign for dissimilar goods or services.

237. Affection of the immediate associations. In consequence, establishment of a high distinctive character of a trade mark which evokes an immediate association in the mind of the public with the goods or services as originating from the proprietor and a risk of weakening that association because of the contested use makes it possible to prove a risk of a change in the economic behaviour of the consumer and hence dilution.[1250] The OHIM (nowadays EUIPO) very rightly observed that, when the consumers of the goods for which the reputed mark is protected and known will be less inclined to associate it immediately with the right holder, this must be considered a change in their economic behaviour.[1251] This instantaneous association is a criterion for assessment specific to dilution, even if it can be demonstrated on the basis of factors that may already be taken into account at the stage of examining the link. Moreover, it should be noted that the criterion of a change in the customer's behaviour was initially used in British case law precisely to assess the existence of a link between the signs.[1252]

1245. Jaton, *La protection des marques* ..., p. 50.
1246. *See* Bouvel, *Marque et renommée* ..., p. 127.
1247. GC, 22 May 2012, case T-570/10, *Wolf*, para. 62.
1248. Moreover, this would blur the distinction between infringement for likelihood of confusion and the extended protection provided for reputed trade marks against the use of the mark for dissimilar goods. *See* opinion of Advocate General Eleanor Sharpston in case C-252/07, *Intel*, para. 59.
1249. *See* CFI, 22 March 2007, case T-215/03, *VIPS*, para. 64.
1250. In this direction Szczepanowska-Kozłowska, *System prawa handlowego* ..., p. 345.
1251. OHIM, BoA, 28 January 2014, case R 69/2013-4, *Camel*, para. 41.
1252. *See* Middlemiss, Warner, *The Protection of Marks* ..., p. 331.

Indeed, any evidence aimed at establishing a change in the economic behaviour of the consumer, thus dilution, can *a fortiori* be used to demonstrate the existence of a link. Once a link has been established, the judge must then make an independent assessment of the relevant factors in order to examine whether the mark arouses an immediate association, a circumstance that is in no way necessary to establish the existence of a link. One may think that once a link has been established, when the trade mark enjoys a high reputation in the public mind, it should be relatively easy to demonstrate the detriment to the distinctive character of the trade mark, in particular when the signs are identical.[1253] I can therefore only agree with a recent judgment of the Paris Court of Appeal which insisted that an actual and present detriment to distinctiveness is not required by the *Intel* judgment and retained dilution on the ground that the trade mark in question might no longer give rise to an immediate association with the right holder's goods.[1254]

238. Loss of turnover. Although the right holder does not have to demonstrate any decrease in turnover,[1255] he can always try to provide such evidence. However, the task appears very complicated. As Durrande pointed out, when the reputed trade mark is taken over to identify dissimilar goods, it is possible that the disruption created by the third party may not immediately result, or even never result in a loss of turnover.[1256] Thus, the importance of proof based on turnover cannot be overemphasised.[1257]

[B] Detriment to the Repute (Tarnishment)

239. The second form of infringement of the trade mark with a reputation consists in the detriment to the repute of the mark, in other words, to its image or good reputation. This type of injury is also referred to as 'tarnishment', 'degradation'[1258] or 'dilution by

1253. Gielen, *Trademark Dilution in the European Union* ..., p. 226.
1254. CA Paris, 25 April 2017, case 16/08758, *Maisons du monde*. *See also* CA Paris, 11 December 2015, case 14/23109, *Ricard*.
1255. Cf. TGI Paris, 7 July 2016, case 15/05226, *Burberry*. In this case, the Court appears to have required such evidence. However, an actual loss can only be relevant at the stage of assessing the reparable damage. Davies, *To Buy or Not to Buy* ..., p. 379. *See* further Middlemiss, Warner, *The Protection of Marks* ..., p. 332.
1256. Sylviane Durrande, *Droit des marques*, D. 2010, No. 14, p. 851. This explains, according to the author, why, in the view of the *Intel* judgment, the trade mark owner is not required to provide proof of an effective and actual infringement, but of the existence of elements allowing to conclude that there is a serious risk that such an infringement will occur in the future. By contrast, according to the author, a change in the behaviour of the consumer is a reliable criterion if the mark is used to identify identical goods because, in this case, a part of the public will turn away, voluntarily or not, from the goods distributed by the owner of the reputed mark to those of the third party, and dilution of the sign will result, almost immediately, in a decrease in the turnover generated by the use of the mark. This last idea is debatable because the author seems to think of confusion and not dilution.
1257. Moreover, it is very uncertain whether a drop in sales results from the use of the disputed sign. Simon Fhima, *Trade Mark Dilution* ..., p. 148. Indeed, the probative value of such evidence will always be easily questionable.
1258. CJ, 18 June 2009, case C-487/07, *L'Oréal*, para. 40.

tarnishment'.[1259] Compared to the detriment to the distinctive character, the ratio of the protection against degradation is less controversial[1260] (§3.01[B][1]). The assessment of the detriment to the repute is also less difficult since there is no doubt that the criteria applied to examine this form of infringement are different from those used to assess the existence of a link between the signs (§3.01[B][2]).

[1] Subject of Protection of the Trade Mark Against Tarnishment

240. Image of the mark. In the case of tarnishment, it is the repute (good reputation) in the true sense of the word that is protected against injury, which is synonymous with the image that the mark conveys to the public (§3.01[B][1][a]). This image is a priori inherent to the mark. However, the concepts of repute, good reputation and image are not specific to trade mark matters. I will therefore address the question of whether the repute can be the subject of an autonomous subjective right, thus have a sort of double legal nature, as some authors have suggested (§3.01[B][1][b]).

[a] Repute as the Image of the Trade Mark

241. Concept of repute. The English version of Directive 2015/2436 and of Regulation 2017/1001 use two different words: 'reputation', in order to designate the trade mark subject to the extended protection, and 'repute', to describe the injury consisting in tarnishment, which, as already observed, is not the case in several other language versions.[1261] Hence, the repute does not, unlike the reputation, refer to the degree of knowledge of the mark.[1262] The repute needs to be appreciated based on qualitative criteria,[1263] as referring to the mark's power of attraction,[1264] and must therefore be interpreted more strictly, as a synonymous with a positive image of the mark.[1265] Consequently, the expression of detriment to the repute needs to be understood in the sense of harm to the image of the trade mark.[1266] Indeed, the repute branch of the extended protection serves the preservation of positive associations that are attached to a trade mark.[1267] The repute refers to all positive imaginations of customers about the goods or services designated by the mark. Any image is likely to be targeted. The repute

1259. Bouvel, *La protection des marques* ..., para. 85. I will avoid using the latter, coming from American trade mark law, not to confuse the form of harm in question with the detriment to the distinctive character which, under European law, is referred to as dilution.

1260. For a critical view on condemning tarnishment cf. however Michael Handler, *What Can Harm the Reputation of a Trademark? A Critical Re-evaluation of Dilution by Tarnishment*, TMR 2016, vol. 106, No. 3, pp. 639 et seq.

1261. *See* para. 55 *supra*.

1262. Cf. Bouvel, *Principe de spécialité* ..., p. 368.

1263. Cf. Szczepanowska-Kozłowska, *System prawa handlowego* ..., p. 345.

1264. Skrzydło-Tefelska, *Community Trade Mark* ..., p. 291; Senftleben, *European Trade Mark* ..., p. 357.

1265. Cf. Maetz, *Notoriété: essai sur l'appropriation* ..., p. 94; Ricolfi, *Trattato dei marchi* ..., pp. 772-773.

1266. Bouvel, *La protection des marques* ..., para. 84.

1267. Senftleben, *European Trade Mark* ..., p. 357.

is a broad concept that can refer to physical characteristics of the goods under the mark, such as their durability, reliability or quality of the materials from which they are manufactured, as well as intangible characteristics, such as the luxury or prestige associated with the mark.[1268]

Thus, degradation results in a harm to the image of the trade mark. This form of infringement expresses the idea that if the consumer begins to associate the mark with something unpleasant, incompatible with its image or with a product of poor quality, this mark will inevitably be damaged by ricochet, even in the absence of a likelihood of confusion.[1269] Several situations that will be discussed in more detail below can characterise degradation. Since the detriment to the repute consists in a harm to the image conveyed by the mark, the trade mark owner who invokes tarnishment needs to establish that his mark benefits from the image claimed.[1270] In other words, the right holder should demonstrate that the mark evokes values or positive messages to the public, hence that his mark enjoys a good reputation which is likely to be tarnished.[1271] To this end, the right holder may submit several types of evidence, such as press articles attesting to the alleged image. He can demonstrate the importance of the distribution of advertising campaigns, the commercial success that goods bearing the mark may have had during their distribution, participation in specialised trade shows or official events, etc. Evidence likely to establish the quality of the goods or services designated by the mark, such as awards or distinctions granted to the owner, is also relevant. In addition, the trade mark's image can be demonstrated using public surveys. The image of luxury or exclusivity can be established by selective marketing or marketing in small quantities by the owner wishing to avoid excessive popularisation of the mark. Thus, the right holder may prove that he addresses a demanding clientele which searches for luxury and exclusivity.[1272]

242. Image of the mark outside the special regime. It should be noted that in trade mark law the concept of harm to the image of the mark does not appear only in the field of extended protection. This concept is not reserved for trade marks with a reputation within the meaning of the law. Any mark can enjoy a good image, a repute, without being sufficiently known to be qualified as having a reputation. Thus, the image of the trade mark is not protected solely under the special regime. Indeed, the likelihood of confusion is perfectly likely to be detrimental to the image of the mark.[1273] In the field of double identity, detriment to the repute can characterise the harm to one of the economic functions recognised by the Court of Justice. In addition, harming the trade

1268. Szczepanowska-Kozłowska, *System prawa handlowego* ..., p. 345. Cf. OHIM, BoA, 23 November 2010, case R 240/2004-2, *Waterford*, para. 87; OHIM, BoA, 12 March 2012, case R 297/2011-5, *Kappa*, para. 35.

1269. Pérot-Morel, *L'extension de la protection* ..., p. 31.

1270. *See* OHIM, BoA, 23 November 2010, case R 240/2004-2, *Waterford*, para. 89.

1271. Cf. Bouvel, *Principe de spécialité* ..., p. 369.

1272. Rodà, *Les conséquences civiles de la contrefaçon* ..., pp. 237-238.

1273. Cf. Gaëtan Cordier, *L'atteinte à l'image de marque dans l'évaluation du préjudice de la contrefaçon*, Comm. com. électr. 2007, No. 11, étude 29, paras 11-15.

mark's reputation may constitute a ground for excluding the effect of exhaustion of trade mark rights.[1274]

[b] Legal Nature of the Repute

243. Distinction of the image of the mark as a separate asset. Some authors suggest that the repute of the trade mark, the 'mark image', understood as the image it enjoys among customers, could itself have a special legal nature in relation to the trade mark. It could be therefore a distinct object of a property right, thus economic right, over the reputation or of a personal (moral) right. The mark image is sometimes defined as an intangible asset consisting of all representations that tend to make a mark's reputation stand out in the eyes of the public and that results from numerous investments, in particular in advertising and marketing.[1275]

244. Image inseparable from the mark. Without discussing arguments that could be raised in this respect under national laws, such as the principle of *numerus clausus* of property rights or, more generally, of exclusive rights enforceable *erga omnes* accepted in some national legislations,[1276] the image of the mark, the repute, cannot be considered as a separate asset that can be freely disposed of, which could be subject of a property right. Reputation is only transferable with the mark which enjoys that reputation. The image of the mark is indeed strictly linked to the mark itself, being inseparable from it. For the same reason, the image of the mark cannot be considered as subject of a distinct moral right. A personal right is by definition inherent to the person of its owner and is therefore non-transferable. By contrast, the reputation of the mark, which is inseparable from it, is likely to be transferred with the mark. The reputation cannot therefore constitute an attribute distinct from the mark, a separate asset. Moreover, it is difficult to understand how recognising such an additional right would enhance the protection of the trade mark since the damage to the reputation of the trade mark is an element of the prejudice resulting from the infringement of the trade mark right.[1277]

245. Concepts of reputation and image within the speciality. It was recently raised by an author that the regime of protection of reputed trade marks is impregnated by concepts external to trade mark law such as 'reputation', 'image' or 'identity', generally reserved for personality rights. The enhanced protection of the reputed trade mark would thus be justified by this personalist aspect.[1278] With regard to the notion of identity, it should be noted that it is specific to the protection of the trade mark within

---

1274. Regarding this last question *see* Georges Bonet, *La protection de l'image de la marque dans la jurisprudence de la Cour de justice*, in: *Les défis du droit des marques au XXIe siècle. Actes du colloque en l'honneur du professeur Yves Reboul*, LexisNexis, Paris 2011, pp. 105 et seq. In French jurisprudence *see* e.g. Cass. com., 4 October 2011, case 10-20.914, *Chanel*.

1275. Maccioni, *L'image de marque: Émergence d'un concept …*, para. 3; Rodà, *Les conséquences civiles de la contrefaçon …*, p. 231.

1276. For example, under Polish law *see* Promińska, *Prawo własności …*, p. 23.

1277. Cf. Passa, *Contrefaçon et concurrence …*, p. 185.

1278. Basire, *Les fonctions de la marque …*, pp. 298-300.

the speciality, since it serves to designate the essential function of the mark – the function of guaranteeing the identity of the commercial origin. It is true, however, that the concept of image is traditionally used with respect to personality rights. Nevertheless, in the field of trade marks, this notion is synonymous with good reputation or repute. The protection of the reputation is in no way unrelated to the traditional protection of the trade mark in the speciality. On the contrary, it is strictly linked to its protection against the likelihood of confusion. This is a classic approach. Already by a judgment of 28 May 1822, the French Court of Cassation condemned the infringement which could only be done with the intention of benefiting from the reputation of the infringed trade mark.[1279] According to a judgment of 12 July 1845 of the Court of Cassation, the exclusive use of the trade mark is guaranteed, in order to ensure the exclusive enjoyment of the advantages and the customers who attach importance to the commercial reputation.[1280] Similarly, in the old doctrine, under the French law of 23 June 1857, Rendu noted that the owner of a trade mark has the right to enjoy alone the benefit of the reputation acquired by his goods; he has the right to prevent a third party from usurping the benefit of that reputation by using the distinctive sign of the goods.[1281] Bédarride specified that the purpose of infringement can only be to create, through confusion, the means to benefit from the reputation of the mark.[1282] This is why damage to the reputation of the trade mark is indeed an element of the prejudice resulting from infringement.[1283] Thus, the idea of protecting the image created by the trade mark is inherent to the protection of the trade mark right, whether within or outside the speciality. Only in the latter case, the image of the mark is protected independently of the likelihood of confusion in the mind of the public, as a result of a link established among customers, the protection of which is reserved for marks qualified as reputed. However, there is nothing extraordinary in this concept from the point of view of trade mark law, and in particular there is nothing extrapatrimonial in taking into account the reputation, and therefore the associations that the trade mark generates, which influence its economic value.

246. Distinction of the reputation of the right holder. That being said, a distinction must be made between the reputation of the trade mark itself and the reputation of its owner. The latter is indeed a personality right of the proprietor, thus subject of a separate personal (moral) right. The reputation of the trade mark owner can undoubtedly be linked to the reputation of his mark. The infringement of the trade mark is likely to damage the image of its owner where such a trade mark makes it possible to identify his person. In this case, reputation may indeed constitute a distinct asset. Nevertheless, it is then the image of the holder, and not of the mark per se. When a mark allows to identify its proprietor, and consequently the infringement may be detrimental to the

1279. Cited by Bédarride, *Commentaire des lois sur les brevets …*, p. 54.
1280. Cited by Bédarride, *Commentaire des lois sur les brevets …*, pp. 58-59.
1281. Rendu, *Traité pratique des marques …*, p. 5.
1282. Bédarride, *Commentaire des lois sur les brevets …*, pp. 161-162. *See also* Fauchille, *De ce qu'il faut entendre par des industries …*, p. 270.
1283. Passa, *Contrefaçon et concurrence …*, p. 185.

image of the right holder, a moral prejudice, referred to in Article 13(1)(a) of Directive 2004/48, is likely to occur.

[2] Establishment of Tarnishment

247. Concept. Once the image of the mark has been established,[1284] the owner must demonstrate that the disputed use made by the third party has damaged or is likely to damage that image. According to the *L'Oréal* judgment of the Court of Justice, detriment to the repute of the trade mark 'is caused when the goods or services for which the identical or similar sign is used by the third party may be perceived by the public in such a way that the trade mark's power of attraction is reduced. The likelihood of such detriment may arise in particular from the fact that the goods or services offered by the third party possess a characteristic or a quality which is liable to have a negative impact on the image of the mark'.[1285] Thus, in most cases, degradation is assessed in the light of the goods or services designated by the disputed sign (§3.01[B][2][a]). However, a detriment to the repute can sometimes be established without taking into account those goods or services (§3.01[B][2][b]).

248. Question of applicability of the criterion of a change in the economic behaviour. Several solutions applicable to dilution are adopted in the field of tarnishment since both consist in detriment. Hence, no actual damage is required in order to establish the infringement[1286] and tarnishment is assessed within the public concerned by the earlier trade mark.[1287] What about the requirement of a change in the economic behaviour of the average consumer? Is it applicable in the field of degradation? In its case law, the Court of Justice applies this condition only in the context of dilution.[1288] However, this criterion appears to be theoretically applicable also to the assessment of tarnishment.[1289] Indeed, one could assume that it is implicitly implemented by the judges, since the idea of condemning detriment to the image of trade marks with a reputation is justified by the fact that reducing the attractiveness of a mark weakens its power to encourage purchasing and, consequently, influences the behaviour of the consumers. The courts sometimes point out that, because of infringement of a trade mark with a high value, the customers are diverted from articles bearing the discredited mark.[1290] It is considered that, in the event of a detriment to the image of the trade mark, the goods designated by it are discredited among the public, so that the right

1284. *See* para. 241 *supra*.
1285. CJ, 18 June 2009, case C-487/07, *L'Oréal*, para. 40.
1286. CJ, 27 November 2008, case C-252/07, *Intel*, para. 38. Cf. para. 230 *supra*.
1287. CJ, 27 November 2008, case C-252/07, *Intel*, paras 34-35. Regarding the relevant public by reference to which tarnishment needs to be examined cf. further para. 151 *supra*.
1288. This is also the approach of some national courts. In French jurisprudence *see* e.g. CA Paris, 16 January 2015, case 14/03650, *p.a.p.* Cf. however CA Paris, 8 November 2013, case 11/00737 and Cass. com., 7 June 2016, case 14-16.885, *Visa*; CA Paris, 16 February 2016, case 15/00086, *Linkedin*.
1289. Some authors indeed consider that this requirement should also apply to tarnishment. *See* Senftleben, *European Trade Mark ...*, p. 352.
1290. In French jurisprudence *see* CA Paris, 9 November 1983, Ann. propr. ind. 1983, p. 152, *Chanel*.

holder will sell less than previously; hence, the trade mark no longer has the same advertising effect.[1291] Thus, by condemning tarnishment, the courts clearly censure the fact that customers risk losing interest in the goods or services designated by the mark, in other words, changing their economic behaviour.

[a] Tarnishment Related to the Goods or Services Bearing the Disputed Sign

249. Two types of detriment. As it was ruled by the Court of Justice, the likelihood of detriment to the repute 'may arise in particular from the fact that the goods or services offered by the third party possess a characteristic or a quality which is liable to have a negative impact on the image of the mark'.[1292] It is therefore above all a question of using a sign identical or similar to a reputed trade mark for goods or services having characteristics incompatible with the image conveyed by that mark (§3.01[B][2][a][ii]). Such detriment can also occur when the disputed sign is used for goods or services of poor quality (§3.01[B][2][a][i]).

[i] Use of the Disputed Sign for Goods or Services of Bad Quality

250. Examples from case law. Detriment to the repute of a trade mark arises when it is reproduced or imitated by a third party for goods or services of bad quality, because such use, by a ripple effect, reflects on the reputation of the infringed trade mark.[1293] In this regard, in the famous *Hollywood* decision, the OHIM (nowadays EUIPO) stated that a trade mark will be tarnished when the consumer's ability to associate it with the goods or services for which it is registered is diminished by the fact that the reputed mark might be linked with goods of poor quality.[1294]

Thus, use of a mark designating a luxury good for a 'low-end' product is likely to damage the image of the infringed mark. French case law clearly condemns this type of damage to a reputed trade mark. It was held, for instance, that the use of a trade mark associated with high-quality goods in relation to everyday quality goods is likely to result in a degradation of the trade mark.[1295] More recently, the Paris Court of Appeal condemned the imitation of a mark associated with high-end products by a sign designating cheap, low-quality products.[1296]

In this respect, to a certain extent, it is possible to use the case law relating to the infringement due to the likelihood of confusion, condemning the deterioration of the

1291. Wichers Hoeth, *Étude comparative* ..., pp. 144-145.
1292. CJ, 18 June 2009, case C-487/07, *L'Oréal*, para. 40.
1293. Pérot-Morel, *L'extension de la protection* ..., p. 31.
1294. OHIM, BoA, 25 April 2001, case R-283/1999-3, *Hollywood*, para. 86. *See also* OHIM, BoA, 23 November 2010, case R 240/2004-2, *Waterford*, para. 88.
1295. TGI Bobigny, 12 October 1988, PIBD 1989, No. 454, III, p. 238, *Moustache*.
1296. CA Paris, 25 April 2017, case 16/08758, *Maisons du monde*.

image of the mark, according to which the use of a mark with a high reputation for products of low or ordinary quality damages the mark's image of quality or prestige.[1297]

251. Similarity of the goods or services. Contrary to the cases where the goods or services are by their nature incompatible with the image conveyed by the trade mark, in the case of poor quality goods or services, they may be identical or similar if the differences between the signs exclude the likelihood of confusion. That said, it should be pointed out that the poor quality of the goods or services designated by the disputed sign is likely to harm the repute of the trade mark, whatever the nature of those goods or services.[1298] Differences between goods or services cannot exclude degradation. The General Court sometimes overemphasises the question of proximity of goods or services for the establishment of the detriment to the repute. According to its case law, where the opposing signs designate very different goods, it would be unlikely that the goods covered by the contested sign, even if they prove to be of lower quality, would reduce the attractiveness of the earlier trade mark.[1299] This approach is questionable. If the public establishes a link between the signs in dispute, it risks transferring its disappointment as to the quality of the goods or services designated by the contested sign to the reputed trade mark, whatever the nature of those goods or services may be. In addition, the requirement of proximity between the goods or services would call into question the principle of the extended protection. Finally, as soon as the goods are identical or similar, it is normally possible to establish trade mark infringement due to the likelihood of confusion.

[ii] Use of the Disputed Sign for Goods or Services Incompatible with the Image Conveyed by the Trade Mark

252. Concept. Detriment to the repute of the trade mark is possible in particular when, irrespective of the quality of the infringer's goods or services, the latter exploits the disputed sign in a way that calls into question a particular image conveyed by the earlier trade mark, taking into account the characteristics of the goods or services covered by it.[1300] In consequence, the reputed mark ceases to convey a desirable message to the public.[1301]

In this respect, the OHIM (nowadays EUIPO) distinguished two situations. It was held that, first, 'tarnishment may occur when the reputed mark is linked to goods which evoke undesirable or questionable mental associations which conflict with the associations or image generated by legitimate use of the reputed trade mark by its

1297. In French jurisprudence *see* Cass. com., 9 February 1999, case 96-19.660; Cass. com., 18 December 2001, 99-13.384, *Galway*; CA Paris, 9 March 1983, Ann. propr. ind. 1983, p. 105, *Chanel*; in Polish jurisprudence *see* SN, 12 October 2005, case III CK 160/05, *Braun*.

1298. Of course, provided that the public establishes a link between the signs in dispute.

1299. CFI, 25 May 2005, case T-67/04, *Spa*, para. 49.

1300. *See* Promińska, *Własność przemysłowa* ..., pp. 525-526; Sironi, *Codice della proprietà* ..., pp. 383-384.

1301. OHIM, BoA, 3 July 2006, case R 334/2005-2, *Derbi*, para. 42.

proprietor', or, second, 'when the reputed mark is linked to goods which are incompatible with the quality and prestige associated with that mark, even though it is not a matter of inappropriate use of the mark itself'.[1302] It seems that both cases refer to the incompatibility of the goods or services designated by the disputed sign with the image conveyed by the earlier trade mark. The first concerns cases where the reputed mark is used for an 'unpleasant' product. Hence, tarnishment allows to condemn the use of a reputed trade mark for goods or services which provoke a reaction of annoyance or displeasure, are intended for dubious use or 'inspire a feeling of disgust or mockery'.[1303] The second case concerns situations where the good or service is not per se unpleasant, but is an ordinary product, whereas the mark is a prestigious mark associated with luxury or excellent quality. It should be, however, noted that, in both cases, infringement is due to the incompatibility of the good or service of the third party with the image conveyed by the earlier trade mark with regard to the nature and characteristics of the goods or services designated by the latter. A good or service is never, in an abstract way, unpleasant, by evoking 'undesirable or questionable mental associations'. In order to assess whether the contested use is indeed inappropriate, it is necessary to take into account the good or service designated by the earlier trade mark. For example, if the third party reproduces or imitates a reputed mark by using it for detergents, such use may give rise to undesirable associations when the earlier mark is known in relation to whisky, as it was in the famous *Claeryn* case.[1304] However, this will not be the case when the earlier trade mark designates a product close to detergents. Similarly, an incompatibility may exist if, as in the *Hollywood* case, a manufacturer of cigarettes uses a mark of chewing gum. However, detriment does not have to occur when he uses a mark of clothing. In a dispute between a manufacturer of clothing and a manufacturer of cigarettes, the General Court ruled that the harmfulness of tobacco to health does not automatically lead to the loss of attraction for the public of a mark associated with clothing. Thus, the use of a mark of clothing for cigarettes as such does not weaken its repute.[1305] Similarly, according to the OHIM, alcohol, which is not dangerous to health when consumed with moderation, does not have per se negative connotations.[1306] Thus, it was, for instance, decided that there is no antagonism between wines and clothing covered by the earlier mark *Versus* of Versace, which enjoy an image of luxury and of a sexy style aimed at young people, since the image generally conveyed by wines is not negative.[1307]

Therefore, what is sought in the case of the detriment to the repute of the trade mark is the existence of an incompatibility between the goods or services covered by the contested sign and the characteristics associated with the goods or services

1302. OHIM, BoA, 25 April 2001, case R-283/1999-3, *Hollywood*, para. 86; OHIM, BoA, 23 November 2010, case R 240/2004-2, *Waterford*, para. 88.
1303. Jaton, *La protection des marques ...*, p. 40.
1304. About this case *see* para. 185 *supra*.
1305. GC, 18 November 2015, case T-606/13, *Mustang*, paras 62-65.
1306. OHIM, BoA, 2 April 2009, case R 677/2008-2, *Banania*, paras 36-39.
1307. OHIM, BoA, 26 January 2010, case R 582/2009-1, *Versus*, paras 56-57. It was also held that there is no antagonism between glassware and wine. OHIM, BoA, 23 November 2010, case R 240/2004-2, *Waterford*, para. 91.

designated by the reputed trade mark or, more generally, with the image conveyed by that mark.[1308] In other words, there must be an antagonism between the goods or services covered by the two signs likely to tarnish the image of the mark.[1309] Indeed, in many cases, the nature of the good or service designated by the disputed sign is itself incompatible with the image of the earlier trade mark. It must be noted that the goods or services designated by the conflicting signs are then dissimilar,[1310] as in the field of dilution, where the weakening of the immediate association with the designated goods or services normally results from the use of the disputed sign for dissimilar goods or services. Thus, the forms of injury to trade marks with a reputation consisting in detriment are by their nature adapted above all to the cases of unlawful use of the sign in the absence of similarities between the goods or services.

253. Examples from case law. I will now refer to some examples from case law illustrating tarnishment. In administrative proceedings, the OHIM (nowadays EUIPO) held that a mark reputed for motorcycles could be tarnished if a similar sign was used for gambling machines.[1311] It was also decided that the mark *Kappa*, reputed for sports clothing which conveys an image of a healthy lifestyle, would be affected if a similar mark was used for tobacco since smoking is universally known to damage health.[1312] According to the OHIM, the mark *Chivas Regal*, recognised as a quality whisky, manufactured with care and deliberation, expensive, purchased by people with good taste would be tarnished by the use of a similar sign for foodstuff for animals.[1313] The General Court admitted the existence of an antagonism between cleaning products, containing toxic substances dangerous to health, and cosmetics and held that the public risks to make a negative connection between the marks in dispute.[1314]

Regarding civil infringement proceedings, it is worth mentioning a few cases from the rich French jurisprudence relating to the incompatibility of images. The French courts condemned the use of a renowned trade mark *Must* of Cartier, enjoying a prestigious image in the luxury sector, for light therapy devices, referring to the medical universe closely associated with pathologies and ageing. According to the decision, a device used to blur stretch marks is likely to tarnish the image conveyed by the mark *Must*.[1315] According to the Paris Court of Appeal, the use of the sign *Nu bella* for nutritional supplements for medical use, dietetic products, dietary supplements or meal substitutes was likely to damage the image of the mark *Nutella*, renowned for its delicacies products, which are not sought by consumers for their dietary properties. The Court observed that the damage to reputation was due to the fact that the

1308. Brandt, *La protection élargie de la marque ...*, p. 176.
1309. CFI, 25 May 2005, case T-67/04, *Spa*, para. 48; CFI, 30 January 2008, case T-128/06, *Camel*, para. 62. *See also* Cass. com., 1 March 2011, case 10-14.967, *Agatha*.
1310. Cf. Simon Fhima, *Trade Mark Dilution ...*, p. 162.
1311. OHIM, BoA, 3 July 2006, case R 334/2005-2, *Derbi*, para. 43.
1312. OHIM, BoA, 12 March 2012, case R 297/2011-5, *Kappa*, paras 37-40. Cf. also OHIM, Opposition Division, 15 April 2014, opposition B 2 168 840, *Apple*, p. 12-13.
1313. OHIM, BoA, 26 March 2003, case R 165/2002-1, *Chivas Regal*, para. 60.
1314. GC, 8 June 2017, case T-341/13 RENV, *SO ...?*, para. 91.
1315. CA Paris, 11 May 2012, case 11/12836, PIBD 2012, No. 967, III, p. 556, *Must*.

characteristics of the goods in dispute were radically opposed.[1316] The use of the trade mark *American Express* for clothing and shoes was condemned by the Paris Court of Appeal on the grounds that the use of this sign was likely to reduce the prestige of the trade mark to which the public associated the ideas of seriousness and quality.[1317] The French Court of Cassation condemned the use of a trade mark linked to the theme of innocence and youth for press material of a pornographic nature, which was likely to damage the image of the trade mark in question by degrading it.[1318] The Paris Grand Instance Court considered detrimental to the repute of the mark *Facebook*, designating the famous social network, the use of the sign *Fuckbook* for a libertine dating site. According to the decision, the *Facebook* mark was devalued by the association between it and the dating site in question.[1319] Based on two other cases decided in France, it could be also assumed that an incompatibility may exist when a trade mark targeting the jewellery sector is applied to dog products,[1320] or when a mark of excellent quality wine is used for cleaning preparations and washing substances.[1321]

The trade marks of luxury or prestige are a special category of marks. According to the OHIM, the image conveyed by the famous *Monogram LV* of Louis Vuitton, of luxury, glamour and exclusivity, being a synonymous for excellency in relation to leather goods and craftwork, was incompatible with technical and industrial products, such as electric meters, scientific microscopes, battery accumulators, cash registers for supermarkets.[1322] In general, the use of a mark of luxury for everyday consumer products can damage its image of exclusivity, high quality or prestige.[1323] For example, according to the Paris Court of Appeal, the use of the mark *Must* of Cartier in relation to chewing gum, which is a daily consumer product, necessarily caused damage to Cartier by undermining the attractiveness of this mark, its economic value and the image of prestige attached to it.[1324] Indeed, the use of a mark associated with excellence for a commonplace product, moreover when it is marketed at a low price, is likely to damage the image of prestige conveyed by the mark.[1325] In the field of the special regime, the price of the product offered under the disputed sign may be taken into account in assessing the infringement.[1326] The use of a trade mark associated with excellent quality for cheap products of insignificant value is likely to tarnish the repute of the mark.[1327]

1316. CA Paris, 28 September 2011, 09/21842, *Nutella*.
1317. CA Paris, 21 February 1989, PIBD 1989, No. 461, III, p. 450, *American Express*.
1318. Cass. com., 14 January 2003, case 00-10.656, *Classe mannequin*. It seems, however, that the disputed sign was used as the title of an article and not as a trade mark.
1319. TGI Paris, 13 June 2013, case 10/11174, *Facebook*.
1320. Cf. Cass. com., 1 March 2011, case 10-14.967, *Agatha*.
1321. Cf. CA Paris, 18 February 1993, PIBD 1993, No. 546, III, p. 393, *Château d'Yquem*. Cf. also OHIM, BoA, 30 July 2009, case R 1513/2008-1, Merci, para. 42.
1322. OHIM, BoA, 6 October 2011, case R 2124/2010-1, *Monogram LV*, paras 28-30.
1323. GC, 2 December 2015, case T-528/13, *Kenzo*, paras 35-36.
1324. CA Paris, 29 September 2004, case 03/18019, *Must*.
1325. CA Paris, 17 September 2008, case 07/06803, *Moët*.
1326. Cf. Rodà, *Les conséquences civiles de la contrefaçon ...*, p. 235.
1327. In Polish jurisprudence SA Poznań, 21 October 2004, case I ACa 752/04, *Ritz*.

254. Positive image of the disputed sign. It should be noted that the disputed sign may itself enjoy a well-established image, or may be used by the infringer in association with a trade mark of the latter being a renowned mark.[1328] This circumstance does not exclude degradation, as long as the respective images of the conflicting signs are incompatible. In such case, the image of the disputed sign, which is positive in the eyes of the infringer's customers, may have a negative impact on the image of the earlier trade mark among the consumers concerned by it.

[b] Tarnishment Independent of the Goods or Services Bearing the Disputed Sign

255. Two types of detriment. In some situations, detriment may be caused to the image of the mark without this being linked to the goods or services designated by the disputed sign. This is particularly the case when the sign constituting the earlier trade mark is altered, in particular in a negative form (§3.01[B][2][b][i]). Detriment to the repute is also possible because of the conditions of use of the disputed sign which may have a degrading effect on the image of the mark (§3.01[B][2][b][ii]).

[i] Alteration of the Sign Constituting the Trade Mark

256. Alteration of the mark in a negative form. The reputed mark's verbal or figurative element may be amended or altered in a negative way,[1329] which ridicules it in the eyes of the customers, and therefore causes a damage to the image of the mark. Such cases are rare in practice. However, it is worth mentioning a judgment rendered by the Paris Court of Appeal, in which several imitations of the trade mark *Ricard* were condemned.[1330] In this case, the defendant marketed T-shirts bearing the signs *Smicard, Ringard, Tricard, Zonard, Flicard* and *Petard*. The Court dismissed the claims of Pernod Ricard in the field of infringement within the speciality, since there was no likelihood of confusion because of the intellectual differences between the signs, but held that there was a degradation of the image of the *Ricard* mark. Indeed, tarnishment resulted solely from the alteration of the mark, the goods designated by the signs in dispute being in no way incompatible with the image conveyed by the *Ricard* mark. Similarly, the Rennes Court of Appeal condemned alterations of the trade marks *Petit Navire* and *Le Bon Goût du Large* by the use of the signs *Petit Chavire* and *Le Mauvais Goût du Large* on T-shirts.[1331] Another example can be found in a decision of the Turin

1328. Cf. CA Paris, 25 September 2009, case 08/11638, *Baccarat*. In this case, in the field of infringement within the speciality, the judge condemned the use of a mark of luxury and refinement by a third party who used it in association with his own trade mark whose repute was not disputed.

1329. *See* OHIM, BoA, 25 April 2001, case R-283/1999-3, *Hollywood*, para. 86; OHIM, BoA, 23 November 2010, case R 240/2004-2, *Waterford*, para. 88.

1330. CA Paris, 11 May 2007, case 05/21446, *Ricard*. Cf. also TGI Paris, 25 September 2014, case 13/03117, *Ricard*.

1331. CA Rennes, 27 April 2010, case 09/00413, *Petit Navire*.

Court of 9 March 2006, by which the Italian court condemned, in similar circumstances, the use of the sign *Porco Diesel* on T-shirts, as damaging the image of the trade mark *Diesel*, renowned in the fashion industry.[1332] It also seems that an alteration detrimental to the trade mark *Facebook* could have been retained by the Paris Court in the aforementioned decision concerning the sign *Fuckbook.*[1333]

257. Primitive imitation of the mark. Apart from the situations in which the mark is altered in a negative way which ridicules it, the repute of the mark can be affected when the sign is subject to a primitive imitation by the third party, inconsistent with the image of excellence conveyed by the mark.[1334]

[ii] Degrading Conditions of Use of the Disputed Sign for the Image of the Trade Mark

258. Concept. Some authors observed that the use of reprehensible sales methods is likely to damage the image of the mark.[1335] The courts sometimes also consider that the use of a trade mark associated with high-quality goods for everyday quality products, 'under very ordinary conditions of sale', can lead to degradation of the mark.[1336]

More generally, detriment to the repute could be considered because of the conditions of use of trade marks likely to tarnish the image of the earlier mark, linked to the presentation of the mark in a degrading context. An interesting example was a case between Louis Vuitton and the singer Britney Spears, who used the famous *Monogram LV* in a videoclip. A French court condemned, on the ground of tarnishment, an attack on the image of luxury conveyed by the mark which 'appeared far from the image represented by Britney Spears'.[1337] Thus, the conditions of presentation of the mark were considered detrimental to the image of the mark. It should be noted that the disputed use must however always be made in the course of trade and as a trade mark, which implies that it must be linked to the marketing of a good or the provision of a service.[1338]

259. Relevant criterion of a trade mark infringement? A priori one might think that it is uncertain whether the conditions of marketing of the goods or services designated by the disputed sign, or more generally of its use, can be taken into account in assessing the infringement of a trade mark with a reputation which, pursuant to Article 10(2)(c) of Directive 2015/2436 and Article 9(2)(c) of Regulation 2017/1001, constitutes a

1332. Cited by Caselli, *Il marchio che gode di rinomanza ...*, pp. 166-167. However, it should be pointed out that, in the case in question, the use of the sign *Porco Diesel* was condemned on the ground of infringement for likelihood of confusion.
1333. TGI Paris, 13 June 2013, case 10/11174, *Facebook*. As we have seen, the motivation of the decision is based more on the association between the mark *Facebook* and a dating site which was incompatible with the image of the mark.
1334. *See* TGI Paris, 22 December 2017, case 16/17522, *Yves-Saint Laurent.*
1335. Jaton, *La protection des marques ...*, p. 40. Cf. Rodà, *Les conséquences civiles de la contrefaçon ...*, pp. 234-235.
1336. TGI Bobigny, 12 October 1988, PIBD 1989, No. 454, III, p. 238, *Moustache.*
1337. TGI Paris, 14 November 2007, case 06/12785, *Monogram LV.*
1338. *See* paras 131 et seq. *supra.*

violation of the exclusive right to the trade mark. In principle, infringement of trade mark rights cannot be assessed on the basis of criteria unrelated to the signs and goods or services designated by them. Prima facie in the field of infringement in the speciality it is always a question of assessing the likelihood of confusion in an abstract way, by comparing, on the one hand, the earlier trade mark such as registered and the disputed sign such as used and, on the other hand, the goods or services for which the trade mark is registered and those for which the disputed sign is used. If, as part of the overall assessment of the likelihood of confusion, criteria such as the conditions under which the goods or services are marketed are taken into consideration, it is only with a view to establishing the similarity between the goods or services which should, in the light of the jurisprudence of the Court of Justice, be assessed subjectively.[1339] The infringement of a trade mark with a reputation is also assessed by reference to the comparison of the signs and, where appropriate, taking into account criteria resulting from the comparison of the goods or services concerned. Indeed, based on the nature of the goods or services in dispute, it is necessary to examine whether a transfer of reputation is possible in order to establish an unfair advantage. Similarly, degradation is often appreciated, as we have just seen, by reference to the incompatible nature of the goods or services designated by the conflicting signs. The latter may have no relevance, as in the field of dilution, where it is necessary to examine the ability of the trade mark to evoke an instant association in the public mind, or in the case of the alteration of the sign condemned in the field of tarnishment. In all these cases, criteria external to the signs, or to the goods or services, are not taken into account. This is indeed the logic of trade mark infringement. Thus, one might think that the conditions of use of the disputed sign do not constitute a suitable criterion for assessing trade mark infringement, hence that they could only be taken into account in the context of parasitism (freeriding) under the relevant national provisions of tort law or special legislations related to unfair and parasitic competition.

However, this reasoning does not seem justified. Indeed, it should be noted that the consideration of the conditions of use of trade mark is not entirely irrelevant to the assessment of trade mark infringement within the speciality. It is implicitly taken into account in the field of double identity in cases where the exhaustion of trade mark rights is ruled out. In the light of the case law of the Court of Justice, the use of another's trade mark in advertising which damages the reputation of the trade mark may constitute a ground for exclusion from the rule of exhaustion of trade mark rights.[1340] Moreover, the Court of Justice expressly ruled that exhaustion may be excluded where the damage to the reputation of the trade mark is linked to the conditions under which the goods designated by it are marketed.[1341] Hence, it seems that *a fortiori* under the special regime detriment to the repute may be assessed in the light of the conditions of use of the disputed sign, and in particular of the conditions of

1339. Likewise, if the reputation of the mark is taken into account, it is the reputation of the mark such as registered. *See* paras 114 et seq. *supra*.
1340. CJ, 4 November 1997, case C-337/95, *Dior v. Evora*, para. 46.
1341. CJ, 23 April 2009, case C-59/08, *Dior v. Copad*, paras 56-59. Cf. Passa, *Traité de droit* ..., p. 486.

marketing of goods or the provision of services designated by the latter. Harm to the reputation resulting from the conditions of use should be possible, as in the judgments of the Court of Justice related to exhaustion, in particular where the infringed trade mark is a prestigious mark conveying an image of luxury. Indeed, it is in these circumstances that a damage to the image linked to the conditions of use is normally likely to appear.

§3.02 FORMS OF INFRINGEMENT RESULTING FROM TAKING UNFAIR ADVANTAGE OF THE TRADE MARK

260. Theory of parasitism. Article 10(2)(c) of Directive 2015/2436 and Article 9(2)(c) of Regulation 2017/1001 condemn use that allows the third party to take unfair advantage of the repute or distinctive character of a trade mark with a reputation. According to the *L'Oréal* judgment, 'as regards the concept of "taking unfair advantage of the distinctive character or the repute of the trade mark", also referred to as "parasitism" or "free-riding", that concept relates not to the detriment caused to the mark but to the advantage taken by the third party as a result of the use of the identical or similar sign. It covers, in particular, cases where, by reason of a transfer of the image of the mark or of the characteristics which it projects to the goods identified by the identical or similar sign, there is clear exploitation on the coat-tails of the mark with a reputation'.[1342] Moreover, the Court specified that 'where a third party attempts, through the use of a sign similar to a mark with a reputation, to ride on the coat-tails of that mark in order to benefit from its power of attraction, its reputation and its prestige, and to exploit, without paying any financial compensation and without being required to make efforts of his own in that regard, the marketing effort expended by the proprietor of that mark in order to create and maintain the image of that mark, the advantage resulting from such use must be considered to be an advantage that has been unfairly taken of the distinctive character or the repute of that mark'.[1343]

The Court of Justice enshrined the formula 'ride on the coat-tails' (in French '*se placer dans le sillage*'), clearly influenced by the theory of parasitism developed in French doctrine and case law.[1344] Nevertheless, parasitism under the European special regime seems to correspond particularly well to the concept derived from German case law of the 1980s which condemned the fact of taking unfair advantage of the reputation of a famous trade mark, in the absence of any likelihood of confusion or damage to the attractive power of the trade mark, in the event of transfer of the image of reputation to the goods of the third party designated by the disputed sign.[1345]

1342. CJ, 18 June 2009, case C-487/07, *L'Oréal*, para. 41.
1343. CJ, 18 June 2009, case C-487/07, *L'Oréal*, para. 49.
1344. *See* para. 27 *supra*. That said, under French law, the idea of parasitism was developed in order to characterise the fault of the trade mark usurper – *a sine qua non* condition of civil liability. For the latter to be established, it was also necessary to identify the damage suffered by the trade mark owner. This is of course not the approach enshrined by the European legislature, which condemns the mere fact of taking unfair advantage of a third party's trade mark, irrespective of the existence of damage to its proprietor.
1345. *See* Simon Fhima, *Exploring the Roots* ..., pp. 31-32.

It should be stressed that this form of infringement of the trade mark with a reputation is autonomous from those consisting in a detriment (§3.02[A]). After having analysed this issue, I will examine the question of the establishment of unfair advantage (§3.02[B]).

[A] Autonomous Nature of the Unfair Advantage

261. Concept based on benefit. The nature of unfair advantage is quite different from dilution and degradation since it is based on the benefit obtained by the third party and not on the detriment caused to the trade mark owner. It is important to stress the absence of interdependence between the different types of infringement of trade marks with a reputation (§3.02[A][1]) and to explain the reasons why the legislator condemns use of trade marks with a reputation by third parties in the absence of any prejudice (§3.02[A][2]).

[1] Absence of Interdependence Between the Forms of Infringement of Trade Marks with a Reputation

262. Irrelevance of detriment. *De lege lata*, taking unfair advantage of the distinctive character or repute of another's mark constitutes an autonomous form of infringement of the trade mark with a reputation. Indeed, just one of those three types of injury suffices for the special regime to apply, hence 'an advantage taken by a third party of the distinctive character or the repute of the mark may be unfair, even if the use of the identical or similar sign is not detrimental either to the distinctive character or to the repute of the mark or, more generally, to its proprietor'.[1346] In consequence, the proprietor of a mark with a reputation is not required, in order to claim enhanced protection, to prove detriment to the distinctive character or repute of that mark, where a third party, by using a sign identical or similar to that mark, takes unfair advantage of its reputation.[1347] Having said that, there is no doubt that the three forms of infringement of trade marks with a reputation are likely to coexist.[1348] It should be noted that the case law, including the jurisprudence of the European instances, is not always clear on the distinction between the different types of injury.[1349]

Some authors, admitting that detriment is not required to establish unfair advantage, find that infringement of a trade mark with a reputation always results in a

1346. CJ, 18 June 2009, case C-487/07, *L'Oréal*, paras 42-43. *See* Yves Reboul, *L'arrêt de la Cour de justice du 18 juin 2009. L'Oréal-Bellure: comment résister à la rançon de la gloire!*, Légicom 2010/1, No. 44, pp. 7-8.

1347. CJ, 6 February 2014, case C-65/12, *Red Bull*, para. 40.

1348. In French jurisprudence *see* e.g. TGI Paris, 28 June 1990, PIBD 1990, No. 490, III, p. 727, *Monte Cristo*; CA Rennes, 27 April 2010, PIBD 2010, No. 922, III, p. 493; CA Paris, 25 April 2017, case 16/08758, *Maisons du monde*. Cf. Pollaud-Dulian, *Propriété intellectuelle. La propriété industrielle ...*, p. 1082.

1349. For example, in a judgment of 16 December 2010, the General Court recalled that there are three distinct types of infringement, based its analysis first and foremost on dilution, but finally, as it seems, deduced the unfair advantage and the detriment to the repute of the mark. GC, 16 December 2010, case T-345/08, *Botox*, paras 81-88.

damage.[1350] Unfair advantage may, however, occur without detriment to the distinctive character or repute. It is sufficient to consider the use of a reputed mark which is not 'unique', and therefore particularly susceptible to dilution,[1351] for a good of an excellent quality, in no way incompatible with the image of the earlier mark, so that any degradation is excluded. In such case, in the absence of detriment to distinctiveness or repute, a mere unfair advantage may characterise infringement of the trade mark having a reputation. The case law shows that arguments based on dilution and tarnishment can be dismissed, while an unfair advantage is established.[1352] Similarly, the existence of a detriment does not imply the existence of an unfair advantage. In particular, harm to the reputation clearly cannot prejudge an unfair advantage made by the third party, since if the goods in question are incompatible, no transfer of the positive associations is likely to take place.[1353]

263. Overlap with dilution. Unfair advantage is not likely to cover all the cases which consist in detriment to the distinctive character. According to Senftleben, who, as we have seen, questions the protection of the trade mark against dilution, the situations which are not qualified as tarnishment characterise unfair advantage. The author considers a case of use of the mark *Mercedes* for good quality products that do not give rise to negative associations for the reputed trade mark, but notes that such cases can be resolved on the basis of the unfair advantage taken of the repute. Consequently, the concept of detriment to the distinctive character would be unnecessary, as infringement of trade marks with a reputation would always consist in a detriment to the repute or unfair advantage taken of the image of the mark.[1354] In the case of unfair advantage, however, as it will be established, it should be proven that the 'characteristics normally associated with a mark with a reputation' for the goods in question can be 'considered in themselves to be such as to bring any advantage' to the goods of the third party.[1355] Associations aroused by a mark, which are positive from the point of view of the public concerned by the goods or services designated by the mark, do not necessarily have this effect in a completely different sector of the market. A mark creates very specific associations related to the characteristics of the relevant goods or services that are not necessarily sought by consumers in other sectors. Associations linked to the *Mercedes* mark, likely to attract the interest of the car customers, may have no effect on the behaviour of the consumers of cakes, shoes or medicines. Hence, for instance, the case of use of the trade mark of a stock market index to designate clothing is more a matter of dilution than of unfair advantage.[1356] As it has been ruled, the characteristics usually associated with a trade mark registered for goods made of luxury metals, furniture, works of art and decorative objects are not likely to bring an advantage to the

1350. *See* Albert Chavanne, *Marques notoires. Principe de la spécialité*, RTD com. 1991, No. 4, p. 588; Cohen Jehoram, Van Nispen, Huydecoper, *European Trademark Law* ..., p. 310.
1351. *See* para. 235 *supra*.
1352. *See* GC, 13 May 2015, case T-363/13, *Clinique*, para. 91.
1353. Simon Fhima, *Trade Mark Dilution* ..., p. 163.
1354. Senftleben, *The Trademark Tower of Babel* ..., pp. 69-70. Cf. paras 221-222 *supra*.
1355. CFI, 22 March 2007, case T-215/03, *VIPS*, para. 73.
1356. Cf. TGI Paris, 14 November 1991, PIBD 1992, No. 518, III, p. 185, *Dow Jones*.

pharmaceutical, veterinary and chemical products covered by the contested sign.[1357] Moreover, it should be recalled that the reputed trade mark is not necessarily a mark of luxury or great prestige. The distinction between dilution and unfair advantage is even clearer if one takes as an example a mark such as *Volkswagen* which probably has a reputation but does not necessarily have to allow the third party to benefit from its repute if it is exploited for lipsticks or shoes. Such use could, however, weaken the association created in the consumer's mind and thus be detrimental to the distinctive character of the trade mark. This being said, the coexistence of dilution and unfair advantage is perfectly possible.[1358]

Furthermore, it should be stressed that unfair advantage is not always possible to claim since it is assessed in relation to the customers of the third party. If the allegedly infringed trade mark is a mark intended for a specialised public, the judge may reject the unfair advantage appreciated in relation to the general public. Thus, it may be easier to invoke degradation or dilution. However, it should be noted that, particularly because of the controversies surrounding the concept of dilution, courts often prefer to base their decisions on unfair advantage,[1359] the assessment of which appears more flexible. However, some decisions that retained unfair advantage are questionable in the view of the goods at issue and of the risk of transfer of the image conveyed by the infringed trade mark, whereas the use condemned was such as to characterise a detriment to the distinctive character of the trade mark.[1360]

Therefore, unfair advantage appears to be the easiest form of infringement of a trade mark with a reputation currently to be demonstrated but also to be justified by the Court (or trade mark office). Since it is sufficient to establish one of the three forms of infringement of the trade mark with a reputation, the courts and trade mark offices often retain an unfair advantage without assessing the existence of the two forms of detriment, considering that it is not necessary to rule on them,[1361] sometimes in cases where the decision could also perfectly be pronounced based on a detriment, and in particular on dilution.[1362] The solution can be accepted with regard to administrative proceedings. However, it is questionable in proceedings concerning infringement of trade marks with a reputation, since the establishment of a detriment to the distinctiveness or to the repute is likely to characterise the reparable prejudice, or at least to increase its scope, and thus to influence the amount of damages.

1357. CA Paris, 11 May 2012, case 11/12836, PIBD 2012, No. 967, III, p. 556, *Must*.

1358. *See* TGI Paris, 28 June 1990, PIBD 1990, No. 490, III, p. 727, *Monte Cristo*; CA Paris, 4 November 1993, RJDA 1994, No. 94/6, p. 579, *Monte Cristo*. The Court ruled that the use of the mark *Monte Cristo*, renowned for cigars, by a producer of rums and brandy, affected the distinctive character of the mark and allowed the disputed sign to benefit from the prestige of the mark among high-end tobacco smokers by associating it with products that were also high-end.

1359. Cf. Bently, Sherman, *Intellectual Property* ..., p. 886.

1360. *See* NSA, 26 June 2013, case II GSK 484/12, *Orlen* – a mark famous for fuels used by a manufacturer of computers; Cass. com., 7 June 2016, case 14-16.885, *Visa* – a mark famous for credit cards used by a manufacturer of perfumes. Cf. para. 280 *infra*.

1361. GC, 7 December 2010, case T-59/08, *La Perla*, para. 70; TGI Paris, 6 December 2013, case 13/14248, *Vente privée*.

1362. *See* e.g. GC, 22 January 2015, case T-393/12, *Kenzo*, para. 58.

[2] Rationale for Condemning Unfair Advantage

264. Controversy. The recognition of the unfair advantage as a form of injury to the trade mark with a reputation is controversial. This is not a new question. Indeed, undue profit, as an autonomous form of infringement, is not a recent concept invented by the European legislator in Directive 89/104. The historical draft amendments to the Paris Convention were aimed at the illegitimate profit which in itself was sufficient to condemn any use of a trade mark intended to benefit from the reputation of a sign of another person.[1363] For several decades, the doctrine has been wondering whether the exploitation of the attractive power of a trade mark could in itself constitute a ground for an extended protection. As observed, it generally answered in the affirmative, qualifying as unlawful the fact of benefiting from the advertising power that the famous mark inspires among the public.[1364] However, some authors were against it. Jaton criticised the idea that the unjustified advantage of the third party could be sufficient in order to establish infringement of a famous mark. According to the author, the law deals with undeserved benefits only in relation to the detriment of legally protected interests. Consequently, wrongfulness cannot be based on the benefit obtained, but must lie solely in the harm caused to interests worthy of protection.[1365] Similarly, in Wichers Hoeth's view, taking advantage of the reputation of a famous trade mark was not as such an unlawful act since in commerce everyone can benefit from the results obtained by others and this in itself does not cause damage to the owner of the earlier trade mark.[1366] Also according to Dassas, there was nothing wrong with following others if no harm was caused.[1367] At present, particularly in the Anglo-Saxon doctrine, some authors consider that when there is no likelihood of confusion, dilution or degradation, the owner of the trade mark with a reputation does not suffer any damage. Therefore, by condemning the mere unfair advantage, the law would protect the creation of a simple association between the signs in the public mind, which would excessively limit the freedom of trade and industry (freedom of competition).[1368] Thus, according to these opinions, the special regime can only be applied provided that the disputed use is detrimental to the proprietor of the trade mark.

265. Illegitimate enrichment. Currently, the European legislator condemns undeserved benefits regardless of any detriment. The approach is in line with the theory of parasitism in the light of which the reputation of a trade mark is a legitimate source of profits and it would be unfair to let third parties misappropriate it.[1369] Thus, the law

1363. *See* para. 31 *supra*.
1364. Brandt, *La protection élargie de la marque* ..., p. 181.
1365. Jaton, *La protection des marques* ..., pp. 46-47.
1366. Wichers Hoeth, *Étude comparative* ..., p. 192.
1367. Dassas, *L'élargissement de la protection* ..., p. 90. Cf. German authors cited by Brandt, *La protection élargie de la marque* ..., pp. 186-188.
1368. Seán Mc Guinness, *Observations on Free Riding after L'Oréal v Bellure*, JIPLP 2013, vol. 7, No. 12, p. 892. Cf. also Simon Fhima, *Trade Mark Dilution* ..., pp. 194 et seq.; Carys J. Craig, *Perfume by Any Other Name May Smell as Sweet ... But Who Can Say?: A Comment on L'Oreal v. Bellure*, Intellectual Property Journal 2010, vol. 22, pp. 326 et seq.; Bereskin, *Anti-dilution* ..., p. 1752.
1369. Cf. Le Tourneau, *Le parasitisme dans tous ses états* ..., para. 9.

condemns a form of enrichment that could be described as illegitimate.[1370] Many authors have observed that benefiting free of charge from the reputation of another's mark without due cause and without any compensation is an illegitimate enrichment.[1371] This enrichment consists in saved expenses. The trade mark with a reputation permeates the consumer's subconscience, positively influences the buyer and encourages him to take a special interest in the product bearing a famous sign.[1372] It is therefore tempting to use a famous mark, first for the advertising economy, and then to benefit immediately from the impact of the mark on the public.[1373] The General Court pointed out that the use of a mark with a reputation enables the third party 'to introduce its own trade mark on the market without incurring any great risk and the costs – in particular advertising costs – of launching a newly created mark'.[1374] The use of a reputed mark gives the third party the possibility to acquire customers without any own efforts for the promotion or quality of the product.[1375] The unfair advantage can also consist in the enrichment of the infringer that has saved the expenses that he should have incurred in order to legally exploit another person's trade mark.[1376] This enrichment is unjustified not only vis-à-vis the owner of the reputed trade mark but also vis-à-vis the competitors.[1377] Indeed, the third party makes undeniable savings and gives itself undeserved advantages over competitors, by distorting the free play of fair competition.[1378]

266. Loyalty in the course of trade. Since in the case of the unfair advantage any impoverishment of the trade mark owner is irrelevant, the recognition of this form of infringement of trade marks with a reputation is considered to be justified by the need to preserve loyalty between undertakings against parasitic acts. The European legislator assumes that it is not only unfair to create a likelihood of confusion or otherwise harm a third party, but also, under certain conditions, it is unfair to only take an advantage of the attractive power of another's mark. Preserving the loyalty of trade would reveal a moral appreciation; the law would then tend to protect the 'morality of business'.[1379] Indeed, according to many authors, the idea of parasitism embodied in

1370. Cf. Senftleben, *European Trade Mark* ..., p. 338.
1371. *See* e.g. Jacq, *Réflexions sur les marques* ..., p. 191.
1372. *See* Brandt, *La protection élargie de la marque* ..., pp. 181-182.
1373. *See* Portet, *Les marques notoirement connues* ..., pp. 46, 54; Brandt, *La protection élargie de la marque* ..., p. 189.
1374. GC, 29 March 2012, case T-369/10, *Beatles*, para. 73.
1375. In Polish jurisprudence SN, 12 October 2005, case III CK 160/05, *Braun*.
1376. In Polish jurisprudence *see* SN, 10 August 2006, case V CSK 237/06, *Hortex*.
1377. Cf. Simon Fhima, *Trade Mark Dilution* ..., p. 192.
1378. Brandt, *La protection élargie de la marque* ..., pp. 181, 189. Since in the case of unfair advantage, the legislator condemns a form of illegitimate enrichment, the concept evokes the idea of unjust enrichment known in general private law (*see* e.g. Article 1303 of the French Civil Code; § 812 of the German Civil Code; Article 405 of the Polish Civil Code). However, it should be pointed out that it cannot be the latter since, in the case of unjust enrichment, enrichment and correlative impoverishment must coexist. In the field of unfair advantage, impoverishment is ignored. Enrichment shall be condemned independently of any transfer between the assets of the parties to the dispute. *See* Marie-Laure Izorche, *Les fondements de la sanction de la concurrence déloyale*, RTD com. 1998, No. 1, p. 17, para. 72; Mc Guinness, *Observations on Free Riding* ..., p. 895.
1379. Cf. Le Tourneau, *Le parasitisme dans tous ses états* ..., para. 1.

the concept of unfair advantage is linked to a moral or ethical assessment.[1380] Moreover, the language of the Court of Justice used in the *L'Oréal* judgment would suggest a degree of 'moral censorship'.[1381] The solution would then be based on the principle that it would be immoral to allow a third party to enrich himself at the expense of the owner of a trade mark with a reputation, by allowing him to benefit from the latter's investments.

In this regard, it is worth noting that some authors express their scepticism about referring to morality in the interpretation of legal provisions. In Polish doctrine, Szpunar considered that there is no one morality but there are just and unjust moralities. Since moral questions are probably more complicated than legal questions, according to the author, the doctrine does not make it any easier to refer to moral rules. Thus, condemning the unfair advantage, like condemning the abuse of rights to which the author referred, could be considered rather as a postulate of equity and not of morality.[1382] To the equity referred Pérot-Morel. In her view, in terms of strict justice, the mere idea of illegitimate profit is sufficient to condemn any use of a famous trade mark of another undertaking operating in a remote sector, with the clear aim of obtaining, without any effort, a considerable benefit from the reputation of the sign.[1383] Moreover, the unfair advantage was in the past condemned on the ground of parasitism as contrary to honest commercial practices. However, honest practices are not necessarily linked to morality. One might think that morality refers to a person's state of mind, while honest practices refer to human behaviour. Consequently, when the judge rules on honest practices, his assessment is objective, and not made from an ethical point of view.[1384] It would therefore be rather a rule of law aimed at commercial probity, subject to a purely objective assessment. Moreover, as we shall see, the assessment of the unfair advantage is now carried out by reference to perfectly objective criteria, regardless of the intention of the third party. Thus, condemning unfair advantage taken of the repute or distinctiveness would be aimed at punishing an excessive use of the freedom of trade and industry, which is limited by the conduct contrary to the rules of professional integrity.[1385]

267. Incentive to invest and innovate. From an economic point of view, it is agreed that trade marks are used to promote innovation and business investment. The trade mark protects the investment that its owner has made in the goods or services associated with it and, in so doing, provides an economic incentive to continue to innovate and invest.[1386] The protection of this aspect of the mark appears necessary for

1380. *See* Pérot-Morel, *L'extension de la protection* ..., p. 29; Guglielmetti, *La tutela di marchi* ..., p. 289; Urszula Promińska, in: Urszula Promińska (ed.), *Prawo własności przemysłowej*, 2nd ed., Difin, Warsaw 2005, p. 269; Skubisz, *Znaki towarowe – ewolucja* ..., p. 19; Christophe Caron, *Marque renommée: pas de risque de confusion*, Comm. com. électr. 2016, No. 6, comment 50, para. 1.
1381. Simon Fhima, *Trade Mark Dilution* ..., p. 199.
1382. *See* Szpunar, *Nadużycie prawa* ..., p. 9.
1383. Pérot-Morel, *L'extension de la protection* ..., p. 29.
1384. Cf. Szpunar, *Nadużycie prawa* ..., p. 64.
1385. Cf. Passa, *Contrefaçon et concurrence* ..., p. 14.
1386. *See* opinion of Advocate General Miguel Poiares Maduro in cases C-236/08-C-238/08, *Louis Vuitton v. Google*, para. 96. Cf. Simon Fhima, *Trade Mark Dilution* ..., p. 193.

the development of competition and therefore for the interests of companies and the economy in general.[1387]

268. Prejudice subject to compensation. It should be noted that the establishment of infringement of a trade mark with a reputation in the form of unfair advantage does not imply the absence of prejudice liable to compensation. Indeed, a clear distinction must be made between the detriment as an event giving rise to liability and the prejudice subject to damages.[1388] The prejudice may, for instance, include various costs incurred by the right holder. Moreover, under Directive 2004/48, damages for trade mark infringement are not limited by the principle of full compensation. The concept of damages used in Article 13(1)(a) of the Directive includes 'unfair profits' which therefore constitute an element of assessment of the compensation. These may include all profits resulting from the acts of infringement regardless of the actual economic prejudice suffered by the right holder.[1389]

Finally, it is important to note that taking advantage of a trade mark with a reputation is not in itself prohibited. This profit must also be taken 'unfairly' by the third party.[1390] This is the case where the conditions for establishing this form of injury are met.

[B] Establishment of the Unfair Advantage

269. Unfairness of the advantage. The owner of a trade mark with a reputation who invokes infringement in the form of unfair advantage must demonstrate that the third party has unfairly benefited from the attractive power of his mark. Use of a reputed mark by a third party is not necessarily unlawful, even if it confers a benefit on the third party. Indeed, if the third party uses a famous mark to designate his own goods or services, it is always possible to speak of a profit characterised by savings in expenses. It is only when the conditions for establishing the advantage taken of the repute (§3.02[B][1]) or the distinctive character (§3.02[B][2]) are met that such an advantage can be qualified as unfair.

270. Objective assessment. Before addressing this question, it should be acknowledged that the assessment of the unfair advantage, as of every form of trade mark infringement, is objective. No intentional elements are required. Hence, it is not necessary to demonstrate an intent to harm the right holder.[1391] Some authors argue that, in the *L'Oréal* judgment, the Court of Justice underlined the role of the third party's intention, and therefore of a subjective criterion, in the assessment of unfair advantage.[1392] Nevertheless, the behaviour of the third party, the attempt to 'ride on

1387. *See* Skubisz, *Znaki towarowe – ewolucja* ..., p. 19.
1388. *See* Passa, *Traité de droit* ..., p. 549.
1389. In some national legislations, recovery of profits of the infringer is an independent remedy. *See* Kur, *European Trade Mark* ..., p. 685.
1390. Bently, Sherman, *Intellectual Property* ..., p. 884.
1391. TGI Paris, 20 March 2007, case 04/15814, *Free*.
1392. *See* Cohen Jehoram, Van Nispen, Huydecoper, *European Trademark Law* ..., p. 309; Meale, Smith, *Enforcing a Trade Mark* ..., p. 102.

the coat-tails' under the terms of the *L'Oréal* judgment,[1393] as we will see, is assessed based on objective criteria. Infringement in the form of unfair advantage is established when the purpose or effect of the link that the disputed use establishes with the reputed mark in the mind of the public enables its author to take advantage of the attractive power attached to the mark.[1394] Hence, the intention is irrelevant in order to demonstrate infringement, as the holder is not required to prove that the defendant acted deliberately. That being said, the Court will probably tend to take this circumstance into account,[1395] and it must be noted that a parasitic intention can often be characterised. Use of a reputed trade mark is normally explained by the intention to benefit from the attractive power of that mark.[1396] However, it should also be stressed that this intention in itself should not be sufficient in order to establish infringement.

271. Relevant public and global assessment. It is important to recall that, contrary to the detriment to the distinctive character and to the repute, the existence of unfair advantage is assessed by reference to the consumers targeted by the disputed sign and not by the earlier mark.[1397] As in the case of each form of infringement of a reputed trade mark, in order to determine whether the use of the third party's sign takes unfair advantage of the distinctive character or repute of the trade mark, 'it is necessary to undertake a global assessment, taking into account all factors relevant to the circumstances of the case'.[1398] All factors for assessing the existence of a link, in particular those relating to the distinctiveness of the trade mark,[1399] are relevant. Indeed, the stronger the mark's distinctive character and reputation are, the easier it will be to accept that an injury occurred.[1400] The criteria of proximity of goods or services, and in particular the overlap of the targeted publics, are also relevant. As observed, a mark known to a limited group of public is less likely to be the subject of unfair advantage than a mark known to the general public.[1401]

272. Question of applicability of the criterion of a change in the economic behaviour. As it will be established, the Court of Justice imposed specific criteria for assessing the unfair advantage, which consist, in particular, in examining whether there is a transfer of the image associated with the earlier trade mark to the goods or services bearing the disputed sign marketed by the third party. In assessing unfair advantage, the case law does not refer to the criterion of a change in the economic behaviour of customers developed in relation to dilution. However, some authors

---

1393. CJ, 18 June 2009, case C-487/07, *L'Oréal*, para. 49.
1394. Passa, *Traité de droit ...*, p. 545.
1395. Cf. CJ, 18 June 2009, case C-487/07, *L'Oréal*, para. 47; CJ, 18 July 2013, case C-252/12, *Specsavers*, para. 40.
1396. Brandt, *La protection élargie de la marque ...*, p. 189. Cf. also CJ, 22 September 2011, case C-323/09, *Interflora*, para. 86.
1397. CJ, 27 November 2008, case C-252/07, *Intel*, para. 36.
1398. CJ, 18 June 2009, case C-487/07, *L'Oréal*, para. 44. The colour in which the proprietor has used the mark not registered in colour can be taken into account in the global assessment. CJ, 18 July 2013, case C-252/12, *Specsavers*, para. 41.
1399. *See* paras 160 et seq. *supra*.
1400. CJ, 18 June 2009, case C-487/07, *L'Oréal*, para. 44.
1401. Bouvel, *La protection des marques ...*, para. 109. *See* CA Versailles, 27 April 2006, case 05/03166, *Milka*. Cf. para. 154 *supra*.

suggested that this requirement should also apply to the unfair advantage.[1402] Prima facie, one could argue that, in this case, it is less a question of demonstrating a change in the behaviour of an already existing clientele than of creating a new one. However, the trade mark infringement must be assessed by reference to the 'average consumer' concerned. By reference to this abstract person, we can speak of a change in the behaviour of the consumer targeted by the goods or services bearing the disputed sign. Consequently, it is possible to adapt the requirement of a change in economic behaviour on the ground of unfair advantage, arguing that it would then be a matter of establishing a change in the behaviour of the public designated by the disputed sign by reference to which the unfair advantage must be assessed. The change will be characterised by the fact that the public is attracted by the disputed sign itself and buys the goods or services identified by it on the grounds that it bears a sign similar to a trade mark with a reputation.[1403] Of course, the right holder does not have to demonstrate that the third party has actually attracted new customers, in other words, prove that the injury has actually occurred. He must establish the existence of elements allowing to conclude that there is a serious risk that such an infringement will occur.[1404] Thus, as in the case of degradation, it can be accepted that the right holder who establishes the conditions for unfair advantage demonstrates a risk of a change in the behaviour of the third party's public, even if, as we have seen, the expression is not well adapted to trade mark law. The opinion that the condition of a change in the economic behaviour of the public concerned applies to the field of unfair advantage can therefore be accepted, but rather for the sake of consistency of the special regime, with no impact on the assessment of trade mark infringement.

[1] Unfair Advantage Taken of the Repute

273. Concept of transfer of the image of the mark. In the light of the *L'Oréal* judgment, the concept of unfair advantage covers, in particular, cases where there is a transfer of the image of the mark or of the characteristics which it projects to the goods identified by the disputed sign.[1405] This wording seems particularly suitable for assessing the unfair advantage taken of the mark's repute. The distinction between the 'image' and the 'characteristics' of the mark is not entirely clear. It seems that the image of the mark is made up of the characteristics that the public associates with it. It is precisely this transfer of positive associations regarding the characteristics, more generally of the image of the mark, that characterises infringement.

The image may be transferred under specific circumstances. Apart from the reputation of the trade mark, the relationship between the goods or services in question and their characteristics must be taken into account. A trade mark as famous as it is

---

1402. *See* Arnaud Folliard-Monguiral, *CJCE, arrêt Bellure: publicité comparative et tableaux de concordance*, Propr. ind. 2009, No. 9, comment 51; Ricolfi, *Trattato dei marchi …*, p. 1282. *Contra* Skrzydło-Tefelska, *Community Trade Mark …*, p. 293.

1403. Cf. GC, 16 March 2016, case T-201/14, *Spa*, para. 57.

1404. GC, 29 March 2012, case T-369/10, *Beatles*, paras 61-62.

1405. CJ, 18 June 2009, case C-487/07, *L'Oréal*, para. 41.

does not confer an absolute monopoly.[1406] It does not guarantee success in all areas of industry. The General Court pointed out that 'it cannot be assumed that each mark with a reputation conveys, by the mere fact of its reputation, an image of prestige or superior quality'.[1407] It is necessary to examine whether the image conveyed by the mark in question increases the power of attraction of the third party's goods or services likely to attract the interest of the customers targeted by the latter, taking into account the qualities of his goods or services. To this end, it is necessary to establish the characteristics that are associated with the trade mark and to demonstrate that those characteristics are likely to be transferred to the goods or services of the third party in the commercial sector concerned.[1408] In other words, unfair advantage requires proof of an association of the disputed sign with positive qualities of the earlier trade mark, which could 'give rise to manifest exploitation or parasitism' by the disputed sign.[1409]

Thus, the trade mark owner who claims unfair advantage needs to demonstrate the nature of that advantage, by establishing which associations are likely to be transferred to the goods or services designated by the disputed sign. Similarly, the courts or trade mark offices must justify their decisions by reference to the possibility of a transfer of the image. It is not sufficient to state that the use of a similar sign gives an unfair advantage since the third party intentionally imitates a reputed mark in order to exploit its power of attraction,[1410] or that the third party could take advantage of the investments made by the trade mark proprietor in order to create an attractive image of his own sign and attract customers.[1411] The national courts, like the European instances, must specify which associations conveyed by the earlier trade mark may benefit the third party.

274. Relevant image of the mark. A transfer of the image is likely to appear when the goods or services identified by the signs in dispute, although not necessarily similar, refer to similar ideas, for example because of the composition of the goods. In a dispute opposing a manufacturer of mineral waters and manufacturer of cosmetics, it was decided that the image of the mark of water and the message it conveys relate to health, beauty, purity and richness in minerals. This image may also apply to cosmetic products inasmuch as those products are intended to protect, take care of and clean the skin and their purpose is that of beauty. Consequently, there exists 'a risk of a free-riding transfer of the advertising effort made by the proprietor of the earlier mark'.[1412] It was also admitted that the image of prestige related to sports events can be transferred to various goods and services which have a link with sport.[1413] Neighbouring modes of use can facilitate the transfer of the image. With regard to the use of a

1406. Simon Fhima, *Trade Mark Dilution* ..., p. 199.
1407. CFI, 22 March 2007, case T-215/03, *VIPS*, para. 58.
1408. *See* GC, 5 February 2015, case T-570/10 RENV, *Wolf*, para. 57.
1409. CFI, 30 January 2008, case T-128/06, *Camel*, para. 65.
1410. Cf. Passa, *Traité de droit* ..., p. 546.
1411. Cf. Skubisz, *Glosa* ..., p. 148.
1412. GC, 16 March 2016, case T-201/14, *Spa*, paras 59-62. *See also* GC, 5 May 2015, case T-131/12, *Spa*, para. 54; in Belgian jurisprudence, CA Bruxelles, 16 September 2016, case 2011/AR/1184, *Spa*.
1413. GC, 17 October 2018, case T-8/17, *Ballon d'or*, para. 139.

trade mark with a reputation of automobiles by a manufacturer of sound and image transmission equipment and mobile navigation equipment, the General Court held that there was a risk of transfer of the image since the goods identified by the contested sign could be used in automobiles and that they could be associated with technology and mobility in the same way as automobiles covered by the earlier trade mark.[1414]

275. Similarity of the goods or services. An unfair advantage is likely to arise when the goods or services covered by the signs in dispute are similar, *a fortiori* when they are identical, particularly in cases where the signs are not sufficiently similar to prove likelihood of confusion and hence infringement within the speciality, because of conceptual differences, but a link can be established between them. In such cases, the transfer of the image is difficult to question.[1415] Indeed, the associations raised by the earlier trade mark concern the characteristics sought by the purchasers of the goods designated by the sign at issue. Thus, the idea that when the disputed sign is used for identical or very similar goods, the establishment of a mere link is sufficient to characterise the infringement, by allowing a transfer of positive associations likely to confer an unfair advantage on the third party using the disputed sign,[1416] can be accepted, but only if the image conveyed by the earlier trade mark is demonstrated.[1417] Therefore, the establishment of a link in itself is never sufficient to prove infringement. The right holder is required to demonstrate that his trade mark has a good reputation, a positive image that can be transferred and confer an advantage on the third party. An advantage is then conceivable, in particular when the third party's activity is associated with low-quality products, while the owner markets products of high quality, and therefore the mark enjoys a good reputation. The third party thus benefits from the mark's attractiveness and repute.[1418] Finally, besides such situations, use of a reputed trade mark for an identical or similar good or service is likely to be resolved on the ground of likelihood of confusion, so that there is no need to invoke the special regime of extended protection.

This being said, according to the case law, the criterion of similarity of the goods or services appears more relevant in the case of unfair advantage than in the case of the forms of injury consisting in detriment. Although the fact that the goods or services are completely different in no way excludes infringement in the form of unfair advantage,[1419] in the light of the requirement of a transfer of the image related to the

1414. GC, 27 November 2014, case T-173/11, *Carrera*, para. 70.
1415. Cf. e.g. TGI Paris, 24 May 2018, case 16/15779, *Facebook*.
1416. In Polish jurisprudence e.g. CA Gdańsk, 15 October 2014, case I ACa 373/14, *Adidas*. Cf. CFI, 16 April 2008, case T-181/05, *Citi*, paras 82-83.
1417. *See* GC, 1 March 2018, case T-629/16, *Adidas*, paras 184-187; GC, 1 March 2018, case T-85/16, *Adidas*, para. 118.
1418. *See* CA Paris, 25 April 2017, case 16/08758, *Maisons du monde*.
1419. *See* GC, 2 October 2015, case T-624/13, *Darjeeling*, para. 139; GC, 26 June 2019, case T-651/18, *Hawkers*, paras 55-56. In the second decision, it seems that there was, however, a proximity between the goods being fashion accessories (*see* para. 57 of the judgment), eyewear and sunglasses for the earlier mark, and jewellery and watches for the contested mark. In fact, in case of trade marks with a reputation, those goods should be considered similar since the consumer is familiar with the well-established practice of marketing them by the same or economically linked undertakings. Cf. further paras 114-115 *supra*.

characteristics of the goods or services, the existence of a proximity between them helps to establish parasitism. For instance, the General Court pointed out that the image conveyed by the mark *Botox* refers to a skin made smooth through the elimination of wrinkles. Thus, by using a similar mark for magazines and specialised medical or scientific journals, consumers may be led to buy goods of that type, thinking that they will find in them the clues or advice of specialists proposing, *inter alia*, courses of action against the ageing of the skin.[1420] A trend for trade marks present in one market to evolve towards other markets and business sectors can be relevant.[1421] Sometimes the reasoning goes far. In a case concerning the use of the trade mark *Beatles* for vehicles, wheelchairs and other apparatus made for sick and disabled persons, the General Court observed that the mark *Beatles* is synonymous with youth and a certain counterculture of the 1960s. That very positive image portrayed by the earlier mark could benefit the goods covered by the contested mark, since the relevant public, on account specifically of the handicap in question, would be particularly attracted by the very positive image of freedom, youth and mobility associated with the earlier mark, especially since a part of the public targeted by the goods concerned by the disputed sign belongs to the generation of persons who knew the goods bearing the earlier mark in the 1960s and some of whom may now be concerned by the goods covered by the contested sign.[1422] The criterion of destination to a particular clientele may be relevant. A French court ruled that an unfair advantage was taken of a trade mark famous for games and video consoles, used for clothing, caps and sports shoes, directly aimed at young customers who use games and consoles.[1423] Another example of a broad appreciation of the unfair advantage can be found in a decision condemning the use of a mark known in relation to chocolate, attached in the public mind to a product 'considered as a delicacy and therefore pleasant', by a third party for clothing, since it could allow the third party to enjoy the 'idea of a pleasant everyday consumer product'.[1424]

276. Marks of luxury and prestige. The trade marks that enjoy the image of luxury or prestige associated with excellent quality of the designated goods or services constitute a special category of marks. The use of such trade marks often allows to benefit from the aura of prestige enjoyed within the consumers who associate them with products of excellent quality.[1425] In this regard, the General Court observed that since the goods identified by the signs in dispute 'project images of luxury, glamour, good taste, success, and social status' and target consumers having a sophisticated taste, the

1420. GC, 28 October 2010, case T-131/09, *Botox*, para. 95.
1421. GC, 11 April 2019, case T-655/17, *Zara*, para. 51. Cf. however a very questionable judgment of GC, 5 June 2018, case T-111/16, *Prada*, paras 49-55.
1422. GC, 29 March 2012, case T-369/10, *Beatles*, paras 71-72.
1423. TGI Paris, 24 February 1994, PIBD 1994, No. 568, III, p. 328, *Sega*.
1424. TGI Paris, 20 February 1998, PIBD 1998, No. 654, III, p. 280, *Crunch*.
1425. In French jurisprudence *see* TGI Paris, 28 June 1990, PIBD 1990, No. 490, III, p. 727, *Monte Cristo*; TGI Paris, 14 November 1991, PIBD 1992, No. 518, III, p. 185, *Dow Jones*; TGI Paris, 19 November 1992, PIBD 1993, No. 540, III, p. 208, *Porsche*; Cass. com., 4 July 1995, case 93-16.355, PIBD 1995, No. 597, III, p. 497, *Orient-Express*; Cass com., 11 March 2008, case 06-15.594, *Louis Vuitton*.

'undisputable allure' associated with the earlier mark can be transferred to other luxury goods.[1426] Likewise, when the goods identified by the sign in dispute may be sold as luxury goods, the third party may take advantage of the link which exists with the earlier reputed mark 'in order to associate his sign with the renown of the earlier mark and take unfair advantage of that mark's reputation, benefitting from the image of luxury and exclusivity which that mark conveys'.[1427] The doctrine also points out this particular situation characterised by an attempt to benefit from the image of luxury of the mark.[1428] It should be noted that it is not the establishment of a simple link that is then condemned.[1429] Indeed, the right holder must always provide additional proof of an excellent, at the very least positive, image of the allegedly infringed trade mark. Hence, no automatism can be allowed; a luxury mark is not necessarily unavailable in all areas of industry.[1430] Nevertheless, the demonstration of a prestigious image enjoyed by the trade mark makes it relatively easy to establish that the third party could unduly benefit from it, since such an image may constitute an important advantage in a large number of market sectors.

277. Graphic presentation. Transfer of the image can occur with regard to the graphic presentation of the disputed sign. In a judgment of the General Court, it was held that the mark *Nina Ricci*, renowned in the field of perfumery, conveyed floral, romantic and classic concepts. The disputed sign, registered for clothing, in its graphic presentation, conveyed, like the mark *Nina Ricci*, floral and romantic concepts, referring to Shakespeare's romantic universe. As a result, an unfair advantage of the repute was condemned.[1431] The romantic connotations were considered relevant in the area of perfumery, covered by the earlier trade mark, and clothing, identified by the disputed sign.

278. Advantage with regard to only part of the goods or services. It should be noted that an unfair advantage may be established in relation to only part of the goods or services covered by the disputed sign. It is indeed necessary to take into account the associations created by the reputed trade mark in the view of the goods or services for which the trade mark enjoys a particular image. This criterion has already been used in the past by the OHIM (nowadays EUIPO), *inter alia*, in the above-mentioned decision in the *Hollywood* case. The sign in question, which referred to chewing gum and enjoyed an image of sport, vitality and *joie de vivre*, was registered by a manufacturer of tobacco and tobacco accessories. The Office pointed out that the registration of the sign in question for cigarettes would allow the applicant to benefit from this image, in

1426. GC, 22 January 2015, case T-393/12, *Kenzo*, paras 56-57.
1427. GC, 2 December 2015, case T-528/13, *Kenzo*, para. 33.
1428. Cohen Jehoram, Van Nispen, Huydecoper, *European Trademark Law ...*, p. 311.
1429. Cf. Pascale Tréfigny-Goy, *Un monogramme bien défendu ... Ou quand une jaquette se prend une veste!*, Propr. ind. 2008, No. 6, comment 39, para. 7.
1430. *See* Arnaud Folliard-Monguiral, *Arrêt Kenzo: de la mode aux vignes*, Propr. ind. 2015, No. 3, comment 19, para. 3.
1431. GC, 15 September 2016, case T-358/15, *Nina Ricci*, paras 74-76.

the view of the promotion and marketing strategies implemented by manufacturers of cigarettes. However, this image would not be transferred to lighters and matches.[1432]

279. Irrelevant image of the mark. In the light of the case law, the associations that may be transferred to the goods or services designated by the contested sign may be varied and can be widely appreciated. Intrinsic natures entirely different from the goods or services in dispute must not prevent the Court from considering a risk of transfer of the reputation. However, where the image conveyed by the earlier trade mark is not relevant, given the characteristics of the third party's goods or services, no transfer of the image can be demonstrated. For example, the good quality of lighting products is not likely to be transferred to foodstuffs,[1433] and the characteristics conveyed by a mark of a fast-food chain are not relevant for computer programming services.[1434] The characteristics usually associated with a well-known mark of cigarettes cannot in itself be considered suitable for making a profit from roasted coffee, even if, according to the Court of First Instance (nowadays General Court), these products can sometimes be consumed together and thus be associated, to a certain extent, both with moments of conviviality and relaxation.[1435]

280. Dilution cases. As we have pointed out, in cases where unfair advantage is impossible to demonstrate, sometimes it might be more likely to establish a detriment. Moreover, as we have seen, courts and trade mark offices often prefer to base the decisions on the unfair advantage taken of the repute.[1436] However, some decisions are questionable. For example, the French Court of Cassation admitted that the mark *Visa*, renowned in the field of credit cards, conveys qualities of trust and excellence, which are also expected by the normally attentive and informed consumer of perfumery and luxury cosmetics products.[1437] It seems very doubtful that the average consumer is really attracted to a fragrance that conveys confidence in the financial field. This situation appears to be a good illustration of dilution,[1438] or, alternatively, we will see the difference, of the unfair advantage taken of the distinctive character. Similarly, if the mark *Orlen* enjoys a reputation in Poland in relation to gas and fuels,[1439] the transfer of the image conveyed by this mark to food products appears unlikely.[1440] The idea that unfair advantage can also be taken of that mark because of its use for computers and software[1441] is also unconvincing. It is doubtful that consumers of these

1432. OHIM, BoA, 25 April 2001, case R-283/1999-3, *Hollywood*, paras 123-125.
1433. *See* GC, 30 September 2016, case T-430/15, *Sylvania*, para. 46. However, in this case, the infringement of the reputed trade mark was already excluded at the stage of establishing the existence of a link.
1434. CFI, 22 March 2007, case T-215/03, *VIPS*, para. 73.
1435. CFI, 30 January 2008, case T-128/06, *Camel*, para. 66.
1436. *See* para. 263 *supra*.
1437. Cass. com., 7 June 2016, case 14-16.885, *Visa*.
1438. Which, in this case, was rejected because of the absence of evidence of a change in consumers' economic behaviour, strictly assessed.
1439. Cf. NSA, 27 February 2008, case II GSK 359/07, *Orlen*.
1440. *See* Skubisz, *Glosa* ..., p. 148.
1441. NSA, 26 June 2013, case II GSK 484/12, *Orlen*.

products are attracted by the image of a mark of fuels. Such cases are more a matter of dilution.

281. Marks with an exceptionally high reputation. It should be also stressed that, according to the General Court, in the case of marks with an exceptionally strong reputation, the probability of a future, non-hypothetical risk of unfair advantage being taken of that mark by the disputed sign is so obvious that the opposing party does not need to put forward and prove any other fact to that end.[1442] The solution, or at least the wording, appears questionable in the light of the jurisprudence of the Court of Justice. It is always preferable to determine the image conveyed by the mark, which can indeed sometimes be deduced from the mark's exceptional reputation.

282. Positive image of the disputed sign. It is perfectly conceivable that the third party may take an unfair advantage of the repute of another's trade mark, even if he owns himself a sign enjoying a positive or even prestigious image. Practice shows that there are disputes between owners or users of signs, both of which benefit from established images or are even both renowned names. This was the case, for example, of the use by the house Yves Saint Laurent of the appellation *Champagne* for perfumes.[1443] The French court accepted the parasitic nature of this use, noting that no detriment to the reputation of the sign *Champagne* was demonstrated. The use of this appellation by Yves Saint Laurent was certainly not negative in terms of image for the name *Champagne*. Nevertheless, Yves Saint Laurent could have benefited from its exceptional image.[1444] Another example of a case where the sign of the third party enjoyed itself a well-established reputation can be found in a judgment of the French Court of Cassation of 4 February 2014, rendered in the field of parasitic competition under the provisions on general tort liability.[1445] In this case, the house Christian Dior brought an action for parasitism against the house Salvatore Ferragamo because of the use by the latter of elements of the bottle, packaging and advertisements of the perfume *Miss Dior*. The Court decided that Salvatore Ferragamo, whose name is undeniably renowned itself, could take advantage of the recognition of the product *Miss Dior* in order to market its own perfumes under the name *Signorina*.

283. Keyword advertising. The general rules of assessment of the unfair advantage are hardly applicable to the cases of use of reputed marks as keywords. Some specific rules were therefore developed in the case law. According to the Court of Justice, an

---

1442. GC, 18 November 2015, case T-606/13, *Mustang*, para. 28; GC, 2 October 2015, case T-624/13, *Darjeeling*, para. 134; GC, 2 December 2015, case T-528/13, *Kenzo*, para. 32; GC, 16 March 2016, case T-201/14, *Spa*, para. 58; GC, 10 October 2019, case T-428/18, *McDonald's*, para. 96.

1443. CA Paris, 15 December 1993, D. 1994, p. 145, comment of Philippe Le Tourneau, JCP 1994, II, p. 22229, comment of Frédéric Pollaud-Dulian, *Champagne*. On this judgment and the history of the appellation *Champagne see* Caroline Lampre, *Le champagne ou le parfum de la renommée*, D. 1994, No. 27, p. 213. Cf. further para. 222 *supra*.

1444. Hervé Maccioni, *L'image de marque: étude juridique de la notoriété commerciale*, Economica, Paris 1995, pp. 55-58.

1445. Cass. com., 4 February 2014, case 13-11.044, Propr. ind. 2014, comment 53, of Jacques Larrieu, Contrats conc. cons. 2014, comment 90, of Marie Malaurie-Vignal, *Miss Dior*. Cf. also CA Paris, 21 October 2015, case 13/08861, *Cartier v. L'Oréal*.

unfair advantage is particularly likely in cases in which 'internet advertisers offer for sale, by means of the selection of keywords corresponding to trade marks with a reputation, goods which are imitations of the goods of the proprietor of those marks'.[1446] It must be, however, observed that the situations of use of reputed marks as keywords should in fact rarely concern the special regime of extended protection. In most cases, the third party uses an identical sign for identical goods or services. Thus, they should be resolved in the field of infringement within the speciality, and in particular pursuant to the provisions relating to double identity. Indeed, use of a reputed mark in keyword advertising should, in principle, affect one of the economic (accessory) functions of the mark.[1447] Invoking the special regime becomes then redundant.[1448]

284. Actual use of the sign filed for registration by the third party. In administrative proceedings, the assessment of the unfair advantage is, in principle, made based on the application for registration of the sign by the third party. However, in the light of the jurisprudence, the actual use of the mark applied for may be taken into account in the assessment. The General Court considers that the behaviour of the third party, identified in the course of the actual use of the sign, constitutes a relevant concrete element for the purposes of establishing the existence of a risk of unfair advantage being taken of the repute.[1449]

[2] Unfair Advantage Taken of the Distinctive Character

285. Distinction. Pursuant to Article 10(2)(c) of Directive 2015/2436 and Article 9(2)(c) of Regulation 2017/1001, infringement of a trade mark with a reputation may consist in an unfair advantage taken of the distinctive character or repute. Thus, the provisions provide *expressis verbis* for two distinct types of infringement. The Court of Justice does not, however, make the distinction between the advantage taken of the distinctiveness and of the repute.[1450] The doctrine raises the point that such a distinction would be difficult to apply in practice.[1451] We have seen that the unfair advantage taken of the repute exists when there is a transfer of the image. In part of the case law of the General Court, the transfer of the image is presented as a necessary condition for unfair advantage and thus the only hypothesis of infringement of the trade mark with a reputation, in the absence of detriment.[1452] Nevertheless, according to the *L'Oréal* judgment, the concept of unfair advantage covers 'in particular' cases where there is a transfer of the image of the mark or of the characteristics which it

1446. CJ, 22 September 2011, case C-323/09, *Interflora*, para. 90. *See also* CJ, 23 March 2010, cases C-236/08 to C-238/08, *Google France v. Louis Vuitton*, paras 102-103.
1447. Cf. CJ, 22 September 2011, case C-323/09, *Interflora*, para. 66.
1448. On the complementary role of the special regime *see* paras 118 et seq. *infra*.
1449. GC, 1 March 2018, case T-85/16, *Adidas*, paras 44 and 123.
1450. *See* CJ, 27 November 2008, case C-252/07, *Intel*, para. 33.
1451. Passa, *Traité de droit ...*, p. 544. In this direction also Simon Fhima, *Trade Mark Dilution ...*, p. 201.
1452. *See* CFI, 22 March 2007, case T-215/03, *VIPS*, para. 40; GC, 27 November 2014, case T-173/11, *Carrera*, para. 53.

projects to the goods identified by the disputed sign.[1453] Hence, it can be deduced that other cases allow to establish an unfair advantage and then characterise the advantage taken of the distinctive character. This view is in accordance with the letter of the European legislation.

The distinction between the two types of unfair advantage enshrined in the texts was envisaged long before the harmonisation of trade mark law in the EU. In examining the advantage that could be made by the infringer of a reputed trade mark, in 1961, Jaton distinguished two situations: the 'impression of quality' (*impression de qualité*) and the 'feeling of familiarity' (*sentiment de connu*),[1454] which seem to correspond to both forms of the unfair advantage. The 'impression of quality' would characterise the advantage taken of the repute, while the 'feeling of familiarity' would constitute the advantage taken of the distinctive character. Indeed, at least in theory, a distinction is perfectly conceivable. There are many marks that have a very high degree of distinctiveness without enjoying a special image.[1455]

De lege lata, while the unfair advantage taken of the repute consists in a transfer of positive associations, the advantage taken of the distinctive character results from the fact that, thanks to the use of a mark known to the public, the third party's goods or services are better visible on the market. It allows him to distinguish more effectively his offer and attract the public's attention, which does not necessarily lead to a transfer of the image.[1456] Indeed, in some cases, such a transfer is not possible. One may, for instance, think that the mark *Coca-Cola* does not allow to benefit from its repute when it is used for products such as medical equipment[1457] or wine.[1458] It confers however an advantage over other products on the market since it definitely makes it easier to attract consumers' attention.

An advantage taken of the distinctive character can therefore be characterised in the case of the use of highly distinctive marks, even if there is no transfer of the image with regard to the characteristics of the goods or services covered by the conflicting signs, and therefore the qualities sought by consumers. For example, it can be assumed that the use of the mark *L'Oréal* for pasta would not make it possible to create a transfer of associations, but would make it easier for the third party to distinguish his product from pasta marketed by his competitors. Moreover, under the special regime, the trade mark does not have to enjoy an exceptional image. One author gave the example of the mark *Audi*, which, in his opinion, is certainly very well known but does not have a repute. Therefore, if this mark is used by a manufacturer of lipsticks, he will not benefit from a particular image. Nevertheless, the decision to use a famous trade mark, instead

1453. CJ, 18 June 2009, case C-487/07, *L'Oréal*, para. 41.

1454. Jaton, *La protection des marques* ..., p. 44. However, it should be noted that the author was critical of the idea that the third party could take a profit in the absence of confusion.

1455. Cohen Jehoram, Van Nispen, Huydecoper, *European Trademark Law* ..., pp. 308-309. The authors give as an example the mark *Lidl*.

1456. Cf. Ricolfi, *Trattato dei marchi* ..., pp. 780-781, 1273; Szczepanowska-Kozłowska, *System prawa handlowego* ..., p. 346; Marcus H.H. Luepke, *Taking Unfair Advantage or Diluting a Famous Mark: A 20/20 Perspective on the Blurred Differences Between U.S. and E.U. Dilution Law*, TMR 2008, vol. 98, No. 3, pp. 814-816.

1457. Simon Fhima, *Trade Mark Dilution* ..., p. 190.

1458. Piotrowska, *Renomowane znaki* ..., p. 35.

of an unknown sign, gives him an advantage, as the public's attention is more easily attracted. Hence, the third party takes an advantage of the distinctive character of the reputed trade mark.[1459]

286. Examples from case law. There are few examples of decisions in which unfair advantage taken of the distinctive character was accepted. Some can be found in German jurisprudence. Several authors cite in particular a few judgments relating to the use of highly distinctive marks, such as *Nivea*, *American Express* or *Mars*, by manufacturers of condoms, in which the courts clearly condemned the use intended to benefit from the distinctiveness of the marks in question.[1460] In French case law, the Versailles Court of Appeal held an unfair advantage taken of a very distinctive trade mark, *Milka*, emphasising the third party's aim to make himself known on the market and to allow him to present his activity.[1461] The reasoning seems to correspond to the idea of unfair advantage taken of the distinctive character. The latter was explicitly referred to by the Paris Court in a decision concerning the use of a trade mark belonging to Louis Vuitton by a manufacturer of fasteners for skateboards. According to the Court, by manufacturing or marketing the said products, the defendant undoubtedly intended to take advantage of the distinctive character of the mark.[1462]

One could see a kind of recognition of the two forms of unfair advantage in the jurisprudence of the General Court in the light of which 'unfair advantage has been taken of the distinctive character or the repute of the earlier mark where there is clear exploitation and free-riding on the coat tails of a famous mark or an attempt to trade upon its reputation'.[1463] The attempt to trade upon the reputation would refer to the advantage taken of the repute, while the reference to 'clear' exploitation and freeriding could also cover the advantage taken of the distinctive character, thus cases where the benefit is derived from an instant association that the mark is likely to create in the mind of the public. Nevertheless, the EU instances hardly ever apply the distinction between the two forms of advantage in their decisions, and in general base the rulings on the repute even when the cases assessed are rather related to the distinctiveness of the earlier mark and not its particular image. For instance, one could argue that use of the very distinctive mark of a social network *Twitter* for T-shirts is rather a situation of taking unfair advantage of the immediate associations with this famous sign than of a risk of transfer of characteristics conveyed by it.[1464]

287. Relation with dilution. While the advantage taken of the repute requires a transfer of positive associations resulting from the image of the mark, this transfer being strictly linked to the characteristics of the goods or services in question and the

1459. Strasser, *The Rational Basis* ..., pp. 411-412.
1460. *See* Büscher, *Famous and Well-Known Marks* ..., p. 4-188; Simon Fhima, *Trade Mark Dilution* ..., p. 190.
1461. CA Versailles, 27 April 2006, case 05/03166, *Milka*.
1462. TGI Paris, 19 October 2012, case 11/04505, *Louis Vuitton*.
1463. GC, 29 March 2012, case T-369/10, *Beatles*, para. 63.
1464. Cf. OHIM, BoA, 16 March 2012, case R 1074/2011-5, *Twitter*, paras 40-41.

image conveyed by the mark, the advantage taken of the distinctive character consists in exploiting the mere distinctiveness of the mark due to its exceptional popularity on the market and therefore its ability to attract public attention through the sole distinctive power. Hence, the unfair advantage taken of the distinctive character would presuppose that the mark is capable of evoking an immediate association in the minds of customers.[1465] Some famous marks, especially those that are unique, attract consumers' attention particularly well. And this ability to attract the public is independent of the mark's repute.

It is thus possible to characterise an unfair advantage taken of the distance character that is not always encompassed by the advantage taken of the repute. The unfair advantage related to the distinctiveness would therefore not be a superfluous concept. However, this form of infringement of a reputed trade mark seems to be subject to the same conditions of assessment as dilution. Indeed, with regard to the example of the use of the mark *Audi* for lipsticks, the author observed that the third party takes an advantage of the distinctive character of the famous trade mark and at the same time the uniqueness of this mark is reduced. He seems to admit that in this case the detriment is inseparable from the advantage.[1466]

Consequently, prima facie, the situations relating to the advantage taken of the distinctiveness are covered by the detriment to the distinctive character. Thus, the problem of distinguishing the unfair advantage taken of the distinctiveness does not really result from the fact that it cannot be distinguished from the advantage taken of the repute. It is rather because, unlike the forms of infringement related to the repute where a clear distinction can be made, it is difficult to see how the concept of the advantage taken of the distinctive character could broaden the scope of protection of trade marks with a reputation in relation to dilution. Where a third party uses a highly distinctive mark that allows an immediate association with goods or services as coming from the right holder, if the third party can benefit from it, a priori this necessarily implies that the distinctive character of the mark is put at risk.

Nevertheless, it should be noted that, although dilution and the advantage taken of the distinctive character will usually coexist, they are assessed by reference to differently determined publics. Thus, if it is unlikely that a mark known only in a very narrow sector of activity will confer an unfair advantage,[1467] its use for a good aimed at the general public is likely to harm the distinctive character of the mark appreciated by this limited group of consumers. However, in cases where the earlier trade mark would be known to the public at large and the disputed sign would be aimed at a specialised public, the infringement would probably be easier to establish among the public targeted by the disputed sign. It would then be easier to demonstrate an unfair

1465. Bouvel, *La protection des marques* ..., para. 110. *See also* Bouvel, *Principe de spécialité* ..., p. 378. The author nevertheless points out that an advantage may be taken of the distinctive character of a trade mark when it is original, consisting of terms that have no inherent meaning. As we have seen, however, for a mark to be unique, it does not need to be original. *See* para. 167 *supra*.

1466. Strasser, *The Rational Basis* ..., pp. 411-412.

1467. Promińska, *Odpowiedzialność naruszającego* ..., pp. 693-694.

advantage than a detriment.[1468] Consequently, it is necessary to distinguish the unfair advantage taken of the distinctive character as the fourth form of infringement of trade marks with a reputation, since the situations covered by it are not always encompassed by the other types of infringement provided by the law.

1468. Regarding the establishment of the existence of a link cf. para. 154 *supra*.

Conclusion

The current rules of special protection constitute a coherent regime which appears to achieve satisfactorily the objective of extending the protection of the trade mark with a reputation beyond the speciality and in the absence of a likelihood of confusion. The judicial and administrative authorities must however interpret the law in such a way as to respect the clearly expressed wish of the legislature to condemn acts of unauthorised use of reputed marks which are detrimental to the distinctive character or the repute of the mark or which take unfair advantage of it. In particular, in the view of the jurisprudence of the Court of Justice which requires the proprietors to demonstrate a change in the economic behaviour of the average consumer in order to prove dilution, a balanced interpretation is necessary as regards the establishment of this form of infringement.[1469]

It is difficult to predict the direction in which the special regime will develop. Since it guarantees a satisfactory protection from the normative point of view, and taking into account the recent reform of trade mark law in the EU, we should not expect that the texts relating to the protection of the reputed trade mark will change in the near future. To my knowledge, there are no initiatives tending to strengthen the trade mark protection outside the field of the speciality at the international level either. Moreover, it seems unlikely that changes to the Paris Convention or the TRIPS Agreement will be made in this respect. The latter already provides, in Article 16(3), for an extension of the protection of well-known trade marks beyond the risk of confusion. Its wording, rather general and less precise than the European provisions, seems sufficient because of the divergences between the legislations of the signatories of the TRIPS Agreement that have adopted their own special regimes. There are, for example, major differences between the approach taken in the EU and the American regime of protection of the 'famous marks'. In particular, the latter does not condemn the mere taking advantage of another's trade mark in the absence of a likelihood of confusion.[1470]

In the EU, one thing is certain: the development of the regime of protection of the trade mark with a reputation will depend above all on the case law of the Court of

1469. *See* paras 228-231 *supra*.
1470. *See* Simon Fhima, *Trade Mark Dilution …*, p. 189.

Justice. History shows that the Court of Justice is however often unpredictable in this area. While, in the *Intel* judgment,[1471] the Court was severe vis-à-vis the proprietors of reputed trade marks by requiring a proof of a change in the economic behaviour of consumers in order to establish dilution, in the *L'Oréal* judgment,[1472] it imposed a less strict interpretation of tarnishment and unfair advantage. Therefore, it is impossible to say whether, in its future case law, the Court of Justice will tend to strengthen the rights of the proprietors or to weaken them by, respectively, a more liberal or more restrictive interpretation of the conditions for infringement of the trade mark with a reputation. That being said, the main issues of enhanced protection, regarding the concept of the trade mark with a reputation and the prerequisites of infringement, appear to be settled. New preliminary questions relating to the special regime will therefore probably deal with more specific problems. An important issue, however, that should be clarified, is whether, and under what conditions, the prohibition of infringing use of an EU reputed trade mark should extend to the entire territory of the EU.[1473] It would also be hardly surprising if, for example, a national court referred a question to the Court of Justice as to whether the use of a reputed trade mark covered by the freedom of expression can constitute a due cause. The issue of the relationship between trade mark rights and the freedom of expression is still discussed in Europe, and many authors are in favour of the recognition of the freedom of expression as a due cause. In my view, on the one hand, the conflict between trade mark rights and the freedom of expression is often illusory, and, on the other hand, the commercial freedom of expression needs to be limited by trade mark rights.[1474] Nevertheless, it is impossible to predict what approach the Court of Justice would take. A positive answer to such a question could have important consequences for the protection of reputed trade marks in the sense of weakening the rights of their proprietors.

There should be no doubt that the Member States of the EU need to guarantee extended protection in accordance with the European legislation. The reputed trade mark must therefore be protected on the basis of the exclusive trade mark right.[1475] The fact that the special regime is based on the trade mark right should imply a reasoning adapted to the assessment of infringement of the exclusive right, including infringement of EU trade marks which have a unitary effect in the whole territory of the EU. However, it should be noted that the interpretation made by the Court of Justice itself is sometimes influenced by reasoning specific rather to the unfair competition law. In particular, the requirement of a proof of a change in the consumer behaviour is definitely closer to the latter. Moreover, while, in the case of infringement of the EU trade mark in the field of speciality, the likelihood of confusion is assessed independently of the fact that the trade mark is not used in the Member State where the proprietor claims infringement, in the *Impulse* judgment,[1476] the Court of Justice made the examination of infringement of an EU trade mark with a reputation conditional on

1471. CJ, 27 November 2008, case C-252/07, *Intel.*
1472. CJ, 18 June 2009, case C-487/07, *L'Oréal.*
1473. *See* para. 72 *supra.*
1474. *See* paras 199 et seq. *supra.*
1475. *See* para. 123 *supra.*
1476. CJ, 3 September 2015, case C-125/14, *Impulse.*

its presence in the Member State in which the proprietor invokes enhanced protection. The Court thus makes the assessment of infringement of the reputed trade mark dependent on the actual use of the trade mark in the Member State concerned, even if the trade mark has a reputation in another Member State and therefore, in principle, in the EU.

Finally, it should be stressed that the current regime of enhanced protection, constituting a form of consecration of the concept of parasitism (freeriding), should have an impact on the interpretation and implementation of the national provisions related to unfair competition and parasitism. It seems that, in order to ensure the coherence of the legal system, the conditions for infringement of the trade mark with a reputation should apply *mutatis mutandis* in the field of parasitism, at least in the cases where it is possible. On the one hand, national provisions related to freeriding should not allow to protect more easily trade marks which do not meet the requirements of the special regime provided by the European trade mark law. On the other hand, unregistered signs used as trade marks or other distinctive elements of products, in fact perceived by the consumers as indicators of commercial origin, should not benefit from a wider protection. Since the problem is outside the jurisdiction of the Court of Justice, the work of interpretation is with the national courts. In this respect, adoption of special provisions on parasitism at the EU level seems unlikely, at least in the near future. Moreover, such legislative interventions do not seem necessary. The general rules on freeriding, properly interpreted, can ensure a balance between the freedom of trade and industry and the need to eliminate acts which do not respect the rules of fair competition. Indeed, we can hope that, as Pouillet said more than a century ago, the courts, the guardians of commercial loyalty, will always be able, even in the absence of precise rules, to recognise and punish acts which are contrary to them.[1477]

1477. Pouillet, *Traité des marques de fabrique ...*, p. 716. '*Les tribunaux, gardiens de la loyauté commerciale, sauront toujours, même en l'absence des règles précises, reconnaître et punir les actes qui y sont contraires*'.

Bibliography

Alberini Alain, *L'exploitation de la renommée de la marque d'autrui. Du risque de confusion au risque d'association*, CEDIDAC, Lausanne 2015.

Allart Henri, Allart André, *Traité théorique et pratique des marques de fabrique et de commerce*, Arthur Rousseau, Paris 1914.

Amar Moise, *Dei nomi, dei marchi e degli altri segni e della concorrenza nell'industria e nel commercio*, Unione Tipografico-Editrice, Turin 1893.

Anemaet Lotte, *The Many Faces of the Average Consumer: Is It Really So Difficult to Assess Whether Two Stripes Are Similar to Three?*, IIC 2020, vol. 51, No. 2, p. 187.

Anfossi-Divol Joan, *L'usage et l'enregistrement, éléments essentiels de l'harmonisation du droit des marques*, Presses Universitaires, Strasbourg 2003.

Angelini Fabio, Verducci Galletti Simone, *If You Remove It, You Use It: The Court of Justice of the European Union on Debranding – On the Mitsubishi v. Duma Judgment by the Court of Justice of the European Union*, TMR 2019, vol. 109, No. 5, p. 875.

Assaf Katya, *Protection of Trade Marks Against Dilution: A Semiotic Perspective*, JIPLP 2009, vol. 4, No. 9, p. 643.

Azéma Jacques, *Défaut de distinctivité de la marque*, RTD com. 2013, No. 4, p. 693.

Azéma Jacques, *Existence de la contrefaçon de marque*, RTD com. 2016, No. 4, p. 729.

Azéma Jacques, *L'incidence des dérives du parasitisme sur le régime des droits de propriété industrielle (à propos de quelques décisions récentes)*, in: *Études de droit privé. Mélanges offerts à Paul Didier*, Economica, Paris 2008, p. 1.

Azéma Jacques, *Marques et signes distinctifs traditionnels: Enseigne, nom commercial, dénomination sociale*, in: *Les défis du droit des marques au XXIe siècle. Actes du colloque en l'honneur du professeur Yves Reboul*, LexisNexis, Paris 2011, p. 19.

Azéma Jacques, *Marques renommées et marques notoires en droit européen et en droit français*, in: Werra de Jacques (ed.), *Marques notoires et de haute renommée. Well-Known and Famous Trademarks*, Schulthess Verlag, Zurich 2011, p. 23.

Azéma Jacques, *Portée du droit de marque*, RTD com. 2015, No. 2, p. 267.

Azéma Jacques, *Protection des marques renommées*, RTD com. 2015, No. 2, p. 270.

Azéma Jacques, *Protection d'une marque renommée pour des produits différents*, RTD com. 2009, No. 1, p. 117.

Azéma Jacques, *Usage de la dénomination dans son sens commun*, RTD com. 2014, No. 4, p. 795.

Azéma Jacques, *Usage d'une marque comme mot clé (suite... mais sans doute pas fin)*, RTD com. 2012, No. 1, p. 103.

Azéma Jacques, in: Azéma Jacques, Galloux Jean-Christophe, *Droit de la propriété industrielle*, 6th ed., LGDJ, Paris 2006.

Azzi Tristan, *Étendue géographique de la notoriété d'une marque*, D. 2008, No. 5, p. 322.

Baeumer Ludwig, *La protection de la marque de haute renommée en droit français et en droit allemand*, Rev. Inter. Dr. Comparé 1962, p. 549.

Baeumer Ludwig, in: Mostert Frederick W. et al., *Famous and Well-Known Marks*, INTA, New York 2004.

Bailey Andrew, *Trade Mark Functions and Protection for Marks with a Reputation*, JIPLP 2013, vol. 8, No. 11, p. 868.

Bannon Elizabeth C., *The Growing Risk of Self-Dilution*, TMR 1992, vol. 82, No. 4, p. 570.

Basire Yann, *La réforme du droit des marques en Europe: quid novi?*, Europe 2016, No. 5, étude 4.

Basire Yann, *Les fonctions de la marque: essai sur la cohérence du régime juridique d'un signe distinctif*, LexisNexis, Paris 2014.

Basire Yann, Bouvel Adrien, in: Macrez Franck et al., *Un an de jurisprudence de la Cour de justice et du Tribunal de l'Union européenne en propriété industrielle*, Propr. ind. 2014, No. 11, chronique 9.

Baud Emmanuel, Colombet Stéphane, *La parodie de marque: vers une érosion du caractère absolu des signes distinctifs*, D. 1998, No. 23, p. 227.

Baz Miguel Angel, Elzaburu de Alberto, in: Mostert Frederick W. et al., *Famous and Well-Known Marks*, INTA, New York 2004.

Bédarride Jassuda, *Commentaire des lois sur les brevets d'invention, sur les noms des fabricants et des lieux de fabrication, sur les marques de fabrique et de commerce*, t. III, Imprimerie et Librairie Générale de Jurisprudence Cosse et Marchal, Paris-Aix 1869.

Beebe Barton, *Intellectual Property Law and the Sumptuary Code*, Harv. L. Rev. 2010, vol. 123, No. 4, p. 809.

Bellan Alberto, *Different Degrees of Similarity Between Normal and Reputed Trade Marks Lead to Separate Assessment*, JIPLP 2015, vol. 10, No. 6, p. 393.

Bently Lionel, Sherman Brad, *Intellectual Property Law*, Oxford University Press, Oxford 2009.

Bereskin Daniel R., *Anti-dilution/Anti-free-Riding Laws in the United States, Canada, and the EU: Bridges Too Far?*, TMR 2011, vol. 101, No. 6, p. 1710.

Bertrand André R., *De la marque notoire à la marque renommée*, RDPI 1992, No. 44, p. 11.

Bertrand André R., *Droit des marques. Signes distinctifs, Noms de domaine*, Dalloz, Paris 2005.

Biglia Lorenzo, *Alcuni problemi sull'affinità dei prodotti e sul giudizio di confondibilità fra marchi*, Riv. Dir. Ind. 1982, II, p. 42.

Biglia Lorenzo, *Uso atipico del marchio altrui e rapporto di concorrenza*, Riv. Dir. Ind. 2006, I, p. 195.

Binctin Nicolas, *Droit de la propriété intellectuelle*, LGDJ, Paris 2010.

Blum Rudolf E., *La marque de 'haute renommée'. Une réponse*, PI 1954, p. 110.

Bodenhausen Georg Hendrik Christiaan, *Guide to the Application of the Paris Convention for the Protection of Industrial Property*, BIRPI, Geneva 1968.

Bodenhausen Georg Hendrik Christiaan, *Problèmes actuels concernant la protection internationale de la propriété industrielle*, PI 1950, p. 84.

Bohaczewski Michal, *Les conflits entre les marques déposées et les marques d'usage en droit polonais: primauté du dépôt ou primauté de l'usage?*, RFPI 2019, No. 9, p. 61.

Bohaczewski Michal, *Usage de nom comme contrefaçon de marque en droit de l'Union européenne*, Les cahiers de propriété intellectuelle 2015, vol. 27, No. 1, p. 61.

Bomhard von Verena, Geier Artur, *Unregistered Trademarks in EU Trademark Law*, TMR 2017, vol. 107, No. 3, p. 677.

Bonet Georges, *Du risque de confusion par l'utilisation d'un signe ressemblant à celui d'une marque renommée*, RTD eur. 2004, No. 4, p. 706.

Bonet Georges, *La protection de l'image de la marque dans la jurisprudence de la Cour de justice*, in: *Les défis du droit des marques au XXIe siècle. Actes du colloque en l'honneur du professeur Yves Reboul*, LexisNexis, Paris 2011, p. 105.

Bonet Georges, *La protection des marques notoires dans le Code de la propriété intellectuelle*, in: *Jean Foyer, auteur et législateur: leges tulit, jura docuit: écrits en hommage à Jean Foyer*, PUF, Paris 1997, p. 189.

Bonet Georges, *La très prochaine réforme du droit des marques dans l'Union européenne*, Propr. intell. 2015, No. 54, p. 4.

Bonet Georges, *Les conditions strictes de l'usage autorisé de la marque d'autrui selon la CJCE*, Propr. intell. 2005, No. 16, p. 277.

Bonet Georges, *Les trois âges de la fonction de la marque. Selon la jurisprudence de la Cour de justice*, Propr. intell. 2012, No. 43, p. 154.

Bonet Georges, *Protection de la marque renommée*, Propr. intell. 2010, No. 37, p. 654.

Bonet Georges, *Protection de la marque renommée contre l'usage d'un signe identique ou similaire pour des produits ou services non identiques ou similaires*, RTD eur. 2004, No. 1, p. 110.

Bonet Georges, *Protection d'un signe constituant une marque renommée contre l'usage qui en est fait par un tiers non autorisé à des fins autres que la distinction de produits ou services*, RTD eur. 2004, No. 1, p. 119.

Bonet Georges, *Note sous CA Nancy 26 juin 1974*, JCP 1975, p. 18178.

Bonet Georges, in: *Droit des marques et autres signes distinctifs. Chroniques*, Propr. intell. 2014, No. 52, p. 294.

Bouche Nicolas, *L'objet spécifique du droit de marque*, D. 2000, No. 6, p. 103.

Bouvel Adrien, *Étendue de la protection des marques renommées en droit communautaire*, JCP E 2003, No. 36, p. 1249.

Bouvel Adrien, *La construction du droit des marques par la Cour de justice à la lumière contentieux relatif au référencement payant des sites*, in: Christophe Geiger (ed.), *La contribution de la jurisprudence à la construction de la propriété intellectuelle en Europe*, LexisNexis, Paris 2013.

Bouvel Adrien, *La protection des marques renommées*, Fascicule 7320, JurisClasseur 2016.

Bouvel Adrien, *Marques et renommée. À propos de l'arrêt 'Intel', rendu par la Cour de justice des communautés européennes le 27 novembre 2008 (aff. C-252/07)*, in: *Les défis du droit des marques au XXIe siècle. Actes du colloque en l'honneur du professeur Yves Reboul*, LexisNexis, Paris 2011, p. 123.

Bouvel Adrien, *Principe de spécialité et signes distinctifs*, Litec, Paris 2004.

Brandt Dominique, *La protection élargie de la marque de haute renommée au-delà des produits identiques et similaires. Étude de droit comparé*, Librairie Droz, Geneva 1985.

Braun Antoine, Cornu Emmanuel, *Précis des marques*, 4th ed., Larcier, Bruxelles 2004.

Breitschaft Andreas, *Intel, Adidas & Co: Is the Jurisprudence of the European Court of Justice on Dilution Law in Compliance with the Underlying Rationales and Fit for the Future?*, EIPR 2009, vol. 31, No. 10, p. 497.

Burrell Robert, Gangjee Dev Saif, *Trade Marks and Freedom of Expression: A Call for Caution*, IIC 2010, vol. 41, No. 5, p. 544.

Burrell Robert, Handler Michael, *Reputation in European Trade Mark Law: A Re-examination*, ERA Forum 2016, vol. 17, No. 1, p. 85.

Büscher Wolfgang, in: Mostert Frederick W. et al., *Famous and Well-Known Marks*, INTA, New York 2004.

Calboli Irene, *'Marchio che gode di notorietà': una discutabile pronuncia della Corte di Giustizia delle Communità Europee*, Riv. Dir. Ind. 2000, II, p. 261.

Callmann Rudolf, *Unfair Competition Without Competition?*, Univ. Pen. Law Rev. 1947, vol. 95, No. 4, p. 443.

Camus Isabelle, *La parodie de marque: un défi mondial pour les marques de luxe qui en sont une cible privilégiée*, Propr. intell. 2015, No. 56, p. 241.

Candé de Patrice, *Amélioration de la protection des marques renommées depuis les arrêts 'Davidoff' et 'Adidas' de la Cour de justice des Communautés européennes*, Propr. ind. 2004, No. 4, chronique 7.

Candé de Patrice, *L'usage d'un signe à titre de marque*, D. 2003, No. 11, p. 755.

Candé de Patrice, Phiquepal d'Arusmont Alix, *Article 6 de la directive 89/104: la notion d'usage honnête, le cheval de Troie de la concurrence déloyale du droit communautaire*, Propr. intell. 2008, No. 28, p. 291.

Canlorbe Julien, *Contrefaçon de marque. Usage illicite de la marque*, Fascicule 7513, JurisClasseur 2016.

Canlorbe Julien, *L'usage dans la vie des affaires, condition nécessaire de la contrefaçon des marques*, Légicom 2010/1, No. 44, p. 107.

Canlorbe Julien, *L'usage de la marque d'autrui*, Litec, Paris 2008.

Canlorbe Julien, *Les tableaux de concordance, la publicité comparative et le droit des marques: après l'arrêt 'L'Oréal c. Bellure' de la Cour de justice*, in: *Droit de propriété intellectuelle. Liber amicorum Georges Bonet*, Litec, Paris 2010, p. 117.

Canlorbe Julien, in: *Droit des marques et autres signes distinctifs. Chroniques*, Propr. intell. 2015, No. 57, p. 436.

Caron Christophe, *Affaire Esso c/ Greenpeace: décision au fond*, Comm. com. électr. 2004, No. 4, comment 39.

Caron Christophe, *Des frontières de la marque, de sa parodie et de sa territorialité*, Comm. com. électr. 2007, Nos 7-8, comment 93.

Caron Christophe, *Les marques renommées face à la dilution de leur caractère distinctif*, Comm. com. électr. 2009, No. 2, comment 14.

Caron Christophe, *Les nouvelles frontières du parasitisme*, Comm. com. électr. 2006, No. 12, comment 153.

Caron Christophe, *Marque renommée: pas de risque de confusion*, Comm. com. électr. 2016, No. 6, comment 50.

Carty Hazel, *Les marques jouissant d'une renommée méritent-elles une protection particulière?*, PIBD 1998, No. 653, II, p. 79.

Caselli Sara, *Il caso Wolf: la prova del pregiudizio alla capacità distintiva del marchio che gode di rinomanza e la nozione di 'modifica del comportamento economico del consumatore medio'*, Riv. Dir. Ind. 2014, No. 2, II, p. 160.

Caselli Sara, *Il marchio che gode di rinomanza*, thesis Parma 2014.

Casparie-Kerdel Sabine, *Dilution Disguised: Has the Concept of Trade Mark Dilution Made Its Way into the Laws of Europe?*, EIPR 2001, vol. 23, No. 4, p. 185.

Chavanne Albert, *Le délit d'usage de marque et son évolution*, in: *Mélanges dédiés à Paul Mathély*, Litec, Paris 1990, p. 101.

Chavanne Albert, *Les marques notoirement connues ou de haute renommée*, in: *Études de droit contemporain*, Éditions Cujas, Paris 1966, p. 301.

Chavanne Albert, *Marques notoires. Principe de la spécialité*, RTD com. 1991, No. 4, p. 588.

Chavanne Albert, in: Burst Jean-Jacques, Chavanne Albert, *Droit de la propriété industrielle*, 5th ed., Dalloz, Paris 1998.

Chavanne Albert, Azéma Jacques, *Réflexions sur les marques figuratives*, in: *Mélanges offerts à Jean-Jacques Burst*, LexisNexis, Paris 1997, p. 39.

Clavier Jean-Pierre, *Marques et droits des tiers – (vers un droit des 'marques-médias')*, Propr. ind. 2004, No. 7, étude 13.

Cohen Jehoram Herman, *La protection des marques contre l'usage pour des produits différents: la loi Benelux, un exemple pour l'Europe?*, PI 1978, p. 224.

Cohen Jehoram Tobias, *The Function Theory in Trade Mark Law and the Holistic Approach of the ECJ*, in: *Verbindend recht, liber amicorum K. F. Haak*, Kluwer, Alphen aan den Rijn 2012, p. 177.

Cohen Jehoram Tobias, Van Nispen Constant, Huydecoper Tony, *European Trademark Law: Community Trademark Law and Harmonized National Trademark Law*, Wolters Kluwer, Alphen aan den Rijn 2010.

Cordier Gaëtan, *L'image de marque et le préjudice de contrefaçon*, Cah. dr. entr. 2007, No. 4, dossier 25.

Cornish William R., *Intellectual Property*, 3th ed., Sweet & Maxwell, London 1996.

Cuonzo Gabriele, *Il caso 'Krizia': revirement della Corte di Appello di Milano sulla tutela dei marchi dei creatori del gusto e della moda*, Riv. Dir. Ind. 1991, II, p. 44.

Dassas Georges, *Conditions et effets de la notoriété*, in: *Le nouveau droit des marques en France*, Colloque IRPI 1991, No. 10, p. 27.

Dassas Georges, *L'élargissement de la protection des marques en droit français, allemand et international*, Librairies techniques, Paris 1976.

Davies Colin, *To Buy or Not to Buy: The Use of a Trade Mark as a Communication Tool Rather than as a Link Between the Product and Its Source – A Further Consideration of the Concept of Dilution*, EIPR 2013, vol. 35, No. 7, p. 373.

Davison Mark, Di Giantomasso Frank, *Use as a Trade Mark: Avoiding Confusion when Considering Dilution*, EIPR 2009, vol. 31, No. 9, p. 443.

Desbois Henri, *La protection des marques notoires ou de haute renommée en l'absence de confusion entre les produits, à propos de l'affaire Mazda*, in: *Mélanges en l'honneur de Daniel Bastian*, t. II, Librairies techniques, Paris 1974, p. 13.

Desbois Henri, *Note sous CA Paris 8 déc. 1962*, D. 1963, p. 408.

Deumier Pascale, *Introduction générale au droit*, 2nd ed., LGDJ, Paris 2013.

Dhenne Matthieu, *Appréciation comparée du risque de confusion entre marques en jurisprudence française et communautaire*, Propr. ind. 2007, No. 4, étude 10.

Di Cataldo Vincenzo, *The Trade Mark with a Reputation in EU Law: Some Remarks on the Negative Condition 'Without Due Cause'*, IIC 2011, vol. 42, No. 7, p. 833.

Dinwoodie Graeme B., *Dilution as Unfair Competition: European Echoes*, Oxford Legal Studies Research Paper 2013, No. 37, p. 1.

Durrande Sylviane, *Droit des marques*, D. 2010, No. 14, p. 851.

Durrande Sylviane, *La définition d'une marque renommée*, D. 2002, No. 13, p. 1132.

Durrande Sylviane, *Note sous CA Paris 27 mai 1987*, D. 1986, p. 527.

Dusolier Raymond, *Note sous CA Paris 12 juill. 1955*, Ann. propr. ind. 1956, p. 128.

Dusolier Raymond, *Note sous CA Paris 8 déc. 1962*, Ann. propr. ind. 1963, p. 148.

Ebert-Weidenfeller Andreas, in: Hasselblatt Gordian N. (ed.), *Community Trade Mark Regulation. A Commentary*, C.H. Beck Hart Nomos, Munich-Oxford 2015.

Fauchille Paul, *De ce qu'il faut entendre par des industries ou des commerces similaires en matière de marques de fabrique*, Ann. dr. comm. 1890, p. 267.

Feer Verkade D.W., *Unfair Use of and Damage to the Reputation of Well-Known Trademarks, Trade Names and Indications of Source: A Contribution from Benelux*, IIC 1986, vol. 17, No. 6, p. 768.

Folliard-Monguiral Arnaud, *Arrêt Adidas: trompettes de la renommée ou trompettes de Jericho?*, Propr. ind. 2018, No. 5, comment 34.

Folliard-Monguiral Arnaud, *Arrêt Kenzo: de la mode aux vignes*, Propr. ind. 2015, No. 3, comment 19.

Folliard-Monguiral Arnaud, *Arrêt Mustang: ternissement de la renommée et tabac*, Propr. ind. 2016, No. 1, comment 3.

Folliard-Monguiral Arnaud, *Arrêt Puma: preuve de la renommée et pratique décisionnelle*, Propr. ind. 2016, No. 11, comment 75.

Folliard-Monguiral Arnaud, *CJCE, arrêt Bellure: publicité comparative et tableaux de concordance*, Propr. ind. 2009, No. 9, comment 51.

Folliard-Monguiral Arnaud, *CJCE, arrêt Intel: que reste-t-il de la dilution?*, Propr. ind. 2009, No. 1, comment 3.

Folliard-Monguiral Arnaud, *CJUE, arrêt Tête de Loup: dilution et comportement économique*, Propr. ind. 2014, No. 1, comment 5.

Folliard-Monguiral Arnaud, *Conditions et effets de la coexistence de marques en droit communautaire*, Propr. ind. 2006, No. 9, étude 24.

Franceschelli Remo, *Concorrenza parassitaria*, Riv. Dir. Ind. 1956, I, p. 265.

Franceschelli Remo, *Dei marchi notori, del modo come si construiscono i principi giuridici consolidati, e della fortuna delle sentenze*, Riv. Dir. Ind. 1961, II, p. 396.

Franceschelli Remo, *È proprio vero che il nome Champagne è in Italia di libera appropriazione come marchio a designare qualunque prodotto che non sia vino spumante?*, Riv. Dir. Ind. 1989, II, p. 21.

Franceschelli Remo, *La concurrence parasitaire en Italie*, in: *La concurrence parasitaire en droit comparé. Actes du Colloque de Lausanne*, Libraire Droz, Geneva 1981, p. 7.

Friedmann Danny, *The Uniqueness of the Trade Mark: A Critical Analysis of the Specificity and Territoriality Principles*, EIPR 2016, vol. 38, No. 11, p. 677.

Galli Cesare, *Funzione del marchio e ampiezza della tutela*, Guiffrè, Milan 1996.

Galli Cesare, *I limiti di protezione dei marchi rinomati nella giurisprudenza della Corte di Giustizia C.E.*, Riv. Dir. Ind. 2004, II, p. 137.

Geiger Christophe, *Droit des marques et liberté d'expression (de la proportionnalité de la libre critique)*, D. 2007, No. 13, p. 884.

Geiger Christophe, *Effectivité et flexibilité: deux impératifs du droit des exceptions*, RLDI 2013, No. 94, p. 41.

Geiger Christophe, *Fundamental Rights, a Safeguard for Coherence of Intellectual Property Law*, IIC 2004, vol. 35, No. 3, p. 268.

Geiger Christophe, *Marques et droits fondamentaux*, in: *Les défis du droit des marques au XXIe siècle. Actes du colloque en l'honneur du professeur Yves Reboul*, LexisNexis, Paris 2011, p. 163.

Geiger Christophe, *Trade Marks and Freedom of Expression: The Proportionality of Criticism*, IIC 2007, vol. 38, No. 3, p. 317.

Geoffray Bertrand, *La protection des marques renommées en droit communautaire*, Propr. ind. 2008, No. 5, étude 11.

Geoffray Bertrand, in: *Droit des marques et autres signes distinctifs. Chroniques*, Propr. intell. 2009, No. 38, p. 130.

Ghidini Gustavo, Cavani Giovanni, *On the Scope of Protection of Renowned Trade Marks*, Queen Mary Journal of Intellectual Property 2018, vol. 8, No. 4, p. 273.

Gielen Charles, *Harmonisation of Trade Mark Law in Europe: The First Trade Mark Harmonisation Directive of the European Council*, EIPR 1992, vol. 14, No. 9, p. 262.

Gielen Charles, *On the Limitations of Rights under European Trade Mark Law*, in: Beier Dietrich, Brüning-Petit Laurence, Heath Christopher (eds), *Festschrift für Jochen Pagenberg*, Carl Heymanns Verlag, Cologne 2006, p. 129.

Gielen Charles, *The Relevance of 'Association' for Trade Mark Conflicts*, in: von Bomhard Verena, Pagenberg Jochen, Schennen Detlef (eds), *Harmonisierung des Markenrechts: Festschrift für Alexander von Mühlendahl*, Carl Heymanns Verlag, Cologne 2005, p. 207.

Gielen Charles, *Trademark Dilution in the European Union*, in: Daniel R. Bereskin (ed.), *International Trademark Dilution*, Thomson Reuters, New York 2013.

Gielen Charles, *Trademark Dilution under European Law*, TMR 2014, vol. 104, No. 3, p. 693.

Gilliéron Philippe, *Les marques notoirement connues et les marques de haute renommée en droit suisse*, in: Werra de Jacques (ed.), *Marques notoires et de haute renommée. Well-known and famous trademarks*, Schulthess Verlag, Zurich 2011, p. 37.

González-Bueno Carlos, *Marcas notorias y renombradas en la ley y la jurisprudencia*, La Ley, Madrid 2005.

Gredley Ellen, Maniatis Spyros, *Parody: A Fatal Attraction? Part 2: Trade Mark Parodies*, EIPR 1997, vol. 19, No. 8, p. 412.

Griffiths Andrew, *The Trade Mark Monopoly: An Analysis of the Core Zone of Absolute Protection under Art.5(1)(a)*, IPQ 2007, No. 3, p. 312.

Guglielmetti Giannantonio, *La tutela di marchi di alta rinomanza*, Riv. Dir. Ind. 1980, I, p. 281.

Guglielmetti Giannantonio, *Marques ordinaires, notoirement connues et de haute renommée: différences entre ces trois figures et la portée de leur protection*, ZNUJ 1981, No. 22, p. 74.

Guglielmetti Giovanni, *Il caso Camel: une correzione del trend?*, Riv. Dir. Ind. 1995, II, p. 308.

Haas de Charles, *La 'contrefaçon' de la marque notoire en droit comparé américain, européen et français: une leçon américaine encore mal comprise*, Propr. intell. 2003, No. 7, p. 138.

Haas de Charles, *La fonction d'identification de la marque, la bonne fonction essentielle qui éclipse toutes les autres*, Propr. intell. 2013, No. 46, p. 4.

Handler Michael, *What Can Harm the Reputation of a Trademark? A Critical Re-evaluation of Dilution by Tarnishment*, TMR 2016, vol. 106, No. 3, p. 639.

Harms Louis, *Death of a Trade Mark Doctrine?: Dilution of Anti-dilution*, in: Bently Lionel, Ng Catherine W., D'Agostino Giuseppina (eds), *The Common Law of Intellectual Property: Essays in Honour of Professor David Vaver*, Hurt Publishing, Oxford 2010, p. 379.

Hoffmann Emmanuelle, Bouchard Laure, *Les spécificités du luxe*, Propr. intell. 2015, No. 56, p. 232.

Humblot Benoît, *Droit des marques: de l'influence ou non du risque de confusion sur la similitude et vice versa*, RLDI 2011, No. 72.

Izorche Marie-Laure, *Les fondements de la sanction de la concurrence déloyale*, RTD com. 1998, No. 1, p. 17.

Jacq Fernand, *La référence à un nom commercial ou à une marque déposée, pour désigner des pièces détachées, est-elle licite?*, Ann. propr. ind. 1928, p. 121.

Jacq Fernand, *Pièces détachées, marques et noms commerciaux*, PI 1930, p. 39.

Jacq Fernand, *Réflexions sur les marques notoires*, PI 1952, p. 189.

Jacq Fernand, *Subtilités dans le domaine des marques*, PI 1955, p. 231.

Jacq Fernand, *Note sous CA Paris 23 nov. 1937*, Ann. propr. ind. 1939, p. 269.

Jacques Sabine, *A Parody Exception: Why Trade Mark Owners Should Get the Joke*, EIPR 2016, vol. 38, No. 8, p. 471.

Jaeger-Lenz Andrea, in: Hasselblatt Gordian N. (ed.), *Community Trade Mark Regulation. A Commentary*, C.H. Beck Hart Nomos, Munich-Oxford 2015.

Jaton Michel, *La protection des marques de haute renommée au regard du droit suisse*, thesis Lausanne 1961.

Klimkevičiūtė Danguolė, *The Legal Protection of Well-Known Trademarks and Trademarks with a Reputation: the Trends of the Legal Regulation in the EU Member States*, University of Wroclaw, Social Sciences Studies 2010, vol. 7, No. 3, p. 229.

Kraus Alfred, Zoll Fryderyk, *Polska ustawa o zwalczaniu nieuczciwej konkurencji*, Poznan 1929.

Kur Annette, *Borderline Cases of Trademark Protection: A Study in German Trademark Law on the Eve of Amendment*, IIC 1992, vol. 23, No. 4, p. 485.

Kur Annette, *Trade Marks Function, Don't They? CJUE Jurisprudence and Unfair Competition Principles*, IIC 2014, vol. 45, No. 4, p. 434.

Kur Annette, *Trademark Functions in European Union Law: Also Containing a Comment on CJEU case C-129/17, Mitsubishi v. Duma*, Max Planck Institute for Innovation & Competition Research Paper 2019, No. 19-06.

Kur Annette, *Well-Known Marks, Highly Renowned Marks and Marks Having a (High) Reputation: What's It All About?*, IIC 1992, vol. 23, No. 2, p. 218.

Kur Annette, in: Kur Annette, Senftleben Martin, *European Trade Mark Law: A Commentary*, Oxford University Press, Oxford 2017.

Kur Annette, Senftleben Martin, *European Trade Mark Law: A Commentary*, Oxford University Press, Oxford 2017.

Lachacinski Thibault, Fajgenbaum Fabienne, *Quelle marque notoire ou renommée au XXIe siècle?*, Légicom 2010/1, No. 44, p. 39.

Ladas Stephen P., *Lettre des États-Unis*, PI 1951, p. 152.

Lampre Caroline, *Le champagne ou le parfum de la renommée*, D. 1994, No. 27, p. 213.

Lancrenon Thibault, *La marque communautaire renommée*, Légicom 2010/1, No. 44, p. 51.

Laporte-Legeais Marie-Eugénie, *Clair-obscur sur la marque renommée: dix ans d'application de la loi du 4 janvier 1991*, JCP E 2001, No. 39, p. 1514.

Larrieu Jacques, *La saisie-contrefaçon et l'action spéciale en responsabilité civile de l'article L. 713-5 du Code de la propriété intellectuelle*, Propr. ind. 2007, No. 6, comment 58.

Le Stanc Christian, *Le domaine public, le libre accès, incluant la liberté d'imiter comme un principe légal ou un concept oublié?*, ATRIP, Munich 2008, p. 1.

Le Tourneau Philippe, *Le parasitisme dans tous ses états*, D. 1993, No. 42, p. 310.

Le Tourneau Philippe, *Parasitisme et marque notoire, ou de l'application du régime général de la responsabilité en présence d'une lacune du droit spécial*, Gaz. Pal. 2001, No. 90, p. 22.

Lefranc David, *La renommée en droit privé*, Defrénois, Paris 2004.

Loiseau Grégoire, *Droit de marque et droit au nom*, Bulletin Joly Sociétés 2011, No. 12, p. 954.

Luepke Marcus H.H., *Taking Unfair Advantage or Diluting a Famous Mark: A 20/20 Perspective on the Blurred Differences Between U.S. and E.U. Dilution Law*, TMR 2008, vol. 98, No. 3, p. 789.

Maccioni Hervé, *L'image de marque: Émergence d'un concept juridique?*, JCP 1996, No. 21, I, p. 3934.

Maccioni Hervé, *L'image de marque: étude juridique de la notoriété commerciale*, Economica, Paris 1995.

Maetz Claude-Albéric, *Notoriété: essai sur l'appropriation d'une valeur économique*, Presses Universitaires, Aix-Marseille 2010.

Mansani Luigi, *La nozione di rischio di associazione fra segni nel diritto comunitario dei marchi*, Riv. Dir. Ind. 1997, I, p. 133.

Marino Laure, *L'affaire l'Oréal: le droit des marques et la publicité comparative sous le sceau du parasitisme*, JCP 2009, No. 31, p. 180.

Marino Laure, *Plaidoyer pour la liberté d'expression, droit fondamental de l'entreprise*, RTD com. 2011, No. 1, p. 1.

Marry Georges, *De la contrefaçon en matière de propriété industrielle, littéraire et artistique*, thesis Paris 1899.

Mathély Paul, *La protection de la marque renommée*, Ann. propr. ind. 1996, p. 31.

Mathély Paul, *Le droit français des signes distinctifs*, Librairie du Journal des notaires et des avocats, Paris 1984.

Mathély Paul, *Note sous CA Paris 27 mai 1987*, Ann. propr. ind. 1987, p. 3.

Mazurek Michał, in: Skubisz Ryszard (ed.), *System prawa prywatnego*, t. 14B, *Prawo własności przemysłowej*, 2nd ed., C.H. Beck, Warsaw 2017.

Mc Guinness Seán, *Observations on Free Riding after L'Oréal v Bellure*, JIPLP 2013, vol. 7, No. 12, p. 890.

McCarthy J. Thomas, *Dilution of a Trademark: European and United States Law Compared*, TMR 2004, vol. 94, No. 6, p. 1163.

Meale Darren, *Interflora: The Last Word on Keyword Advertising?*, JIPLP 2012, vol. 7, No. 1, p. 11.

Meale Darren, Joel Smith, *Enforcing a Trade Mark When Nobody's Confused: Where the Law Stands after L'Oréal and Intel*, JIPLP 2010, vol. 5, No. 2, p. 96.

Meunier-Cœur Isabelle, *Notoriété et renommée de la marque*, Propr. ind. 2006, No. 4, étude 12.

Michalak Arkadiusz, Witkowska Monika, in: Michalak Arkadiusz (ed.), *Prawo własności przemysłowej. Komentarz*, C.H. Beck, Warsaw 2016.

Middlemiss Susie, Warner Steven, *The Protection of Marks with a Reputation: Intel c CPM*, EIPR 2009, vol. 31, No. 6, p. 326.

Monteiro José, Ruzek Vincent, *L'usage du signe à des fins autres que celle de distinguer les produits et services d'un opérateur économique*, Propr. ind. 2007, No. 4, étude 9.

Mostert Frederick W., in: Mostert Frederick W. et al., *Famous and Well-Known Marks*, INTA, New York 2004.

Naser Mohammad Amin, *Trademarks and Freedom of Expression*, IIC 2009, vol. 40, No. 2, p. 188.

O'Callaghan Louise, *Intel-Ligent Way Forward? The ECJ Rules on Dilution*, JIPLP 2009, vol. 4, No. 4, p. 237.

Offner Eric D., *International Trademark Protection*, Fieldston Press, New York 1965.

Paesan Federico, *La protezione dei marchi e la libertà d'espressione*, thesis Turin 2011.

Passa Jérôme, *Caractérisation de la contrefaçon par référence aux fonctions de la marque: la Cour de justice sur une fausse piste*, Propr. ind. 2011, No. 1, étude 1.

Passa Jérôme, *Contrefaçon de marque: condition d'usage à titre de marque dans l'hypothèse de l'emploi du signe litigieux en complément de la marque principale du défendeur*, RTD com. 2019, No. 2, p. 377.

Passa Jérôme, *Contrefaçon de marque par suppression?*, RTD com. 2019, No. 2, p. 379.

Passa Jérôme, *Contrefaçon et concurrence déloyale*, Litec, Paris 1997.

Passa Jérôme, *Déchéance pour défaut d'usage sérieux: usage sous une forme modifiée dans l'hypothèse de l'emploi d'un signe verbal sur le produit dont la forme seule est enregistrée comme marque*, RTD com. 2019, No. 2, p. 372.

Passa Jérôme, *L'appréciation abstraite du risque de confusion en matière de contrefaçon de marque*, in: *Le droit de la propriété intellectuelle dans un monde globalisé. Mélanges en l'honneur du Professeur Joanna Schmidt-Szalewski*, LexisNexis, Paris 2014, p. 237.

Passa Jérôme, *L'usage de la marque d'un tiers pour décrire les caractéristiques de produits concurrents*, D. 2002, No. 41, p. 3137.

Passa Jérôme, *L'usage de marque dans la jurisprudence récente de la CJCE*, RJDA 2003, No. 3, p. 195.

Passa Jérôme, *La contrefaçon de marque et l'exigence d'une mise dans le commerce*, Propr. ind. 2008, No. 5, étude 10.

Passa Jérôme, *Le régime spécial de protection de la marque renommée et l'exigence d'un usage à titre de marque*, Propr. intell. 2008, No. 28, p. 360.

Passa Jérôme, *Les conditions générales d'une atteinte au droit sur une marque*, Propr. ind. 2005, No. 2, étude 2.

Passa Jérôme, *Les 'familles' de marques dans la jurisprudence européenne: surcroît de protection ou trompe-l'œil?*, Propr. intell. 2015, No. 54, p. 16.

Passa Jérôme, *Les nouvelles fonctions de la marque dans la jurisprudence de la Cour de justice: portée? Utilité?*, Cah. dr. entr. 2012, No. 1, dossier 5.

Passa Jérôme, *Les rapports entre droit des marques et droit de la publicité comparative: un risque d'affaiblissement de la protection de la marque*, Propr. ind. 2008, No. 10, étude 20.

Passa Jérôme, *Précisions sur la protection de la marque non exploitée et non encore sujette à déchéance*, JCP 2017, No. 10, p. 253.

Passa Jérôme, *Traité de droit de la propriété industrielle*, t. I, 2nd ed., LGDJ Paris 2009.

Passa Jérôme, in: Vivant Michel (ed.), *Les grands arrêts de la propriété intellectuelle*, 2nd ed., Dalloz, Paris 2015.

Perent Robert, *Marques notoirement connues et marques dites 'de haute renommée'*, thesis Paris 1960.

Pérot-Morel Marie-Angèle, *L'extension de la protection des marques notoires*, RTD com. 1966, p. 9.

Pérot-Morel Marie-Angèle, *Dégénérescence de la marque par excès de notoriété*, in: *Mélanges en l'honneur de Daniel Bastian*, t. II, Librairies techniques, Paris 1974, p. 49.

Pérot-Morel Marie-Angèle, *Les difficultés d'application de l'article 6 bis de la Convention d'Union de Paris relatif à la protection internationale des marques notoires*, Riv. Dir. Ind. 1981, I, p. 34.

Pérot-Morel Marie-Angèle, *Notoriété et renommée: unité ou dualité de concept en droit des marques?*, in: *Mélanges offerts à Jean-Jacques Burst*, LexisNexis, Paris 1997, p. 463.

Piotrowska Joanna, *Renomowane znaki towarowe i ich ochrona*, C.H. Beck, Warsaw 2001.

Pollaud-Dulian Frédéric, *De quelques avatars de l'action en responsabilité civile dans le droit des affaires*, RTD com. 1997, No. 3, p. 349.

Pollaud-Dulian Frédéric, *Le point sur la protection des marques de renommée dans la jurisprudence de la Cour de justice des Communautés*, RJDA 2004, No. 3, chronique 232.

Pollaud-Dulian Frédéric, *Les atteintes à la marque de renommée. À propos de l'arrêt Intel de la Cour de justice des Communautés européennes du 27 novembre 2008*, Gaz. Pal. 2009, No. 90, p. 7.

Pollaud-Dulian Frédéric, *Marque de renommée. Histoire de la dénaturation d'un concept*, Propr. intell. 2001, No. 1, p. 43.

Pollaud-Dulian Frédéric, *Propriété intellectuelle. La propriété industrielle*, Economica, Paris 2011.

Pollaud-Dulian Frédéric, *Protection de la marque et droit de liberté d'expression d'une association dans le cadre d'une campagne anti-tabac*, JCP 2006, No. 48, II, p. 10195.

Portet Hélène, *Les marques notoirement connues ou de haute renommée selon la Convention de Paris et la loi française du 31 décembre 1964*, thesis Paris 1975.

Pouillet Eugène, *Traité des marques de fabrique et de la concurrence déloyale en tous genres*, 6th ed., Imprimerie et Librairie Générale de Jurisprudence Marchal et Billard, Paris 1912.

Promińska Urszula, *Odpowiedzialność naruszającego prawo ochronne na znak towarowy*, in: *Odpowiedzialność cywilna. Księga pamiątkowa ku czci Profesora Adama Szpunara*, Wolters Kluwer, Cracow 2004, p. 681.

Promińska Urszula, *Prawo z rejestracji znaku towarowego, treść i naruszenie*, thesis Lodz 1994.

Promińska Urszula, *Ustawa o znakach towarowych. Komentarz*, PWN, Warsaw 1998.

Promińska Urszula, in: Adamczak Alicja, Szewc Andrzej (ed.), *Konwencja paryska o ochronie własności przemysłowej. Komentarz*, Wolters Kluwer, Warsaw 2008.

Promińska Urszula, in: Nowińska Ewa, Promińska Urszula, Szczepanowska-Kozłowska Krystyna, *Własność przemysłowa i jej ochrona*, LexisNexis, Warsaw 2014.

Promińska Urszula, in: Promińska Urszula (ed.), *Prawo własności przemysłowej*, 2nd ed., Difin, Warsaw 2005.

Reboul Yves, *L'arrêt 'Davidoff' de la Cour de justice des Communautés européennes du 9 janvier 2003: Schisme... ou 'Yalta' de la protection des marques renommées?*, Propr. ind. 2003, No. 3, comment 17.

Reboul Yves, *L'arrêt de la Cour de justice du 18 juin 2009. L'Oréal-Bellure: comment résister à la rançon de la gloire!*, Légicom 2010/1 No. 44, p. 5.

Rendu Ambroise, *Traité pratique des marques de fabrique et de commerce et de la concurrence déloyale*, Imprimerie et Librairie Générale de Jurisprudence Cosse et Marchal, Paris 1858.

Ricolfi Marco, *Trattato dei marchi. Diritto europeo e nazionale*, Giappichelli, Turin 2015.

Rodà Caroline, *Les conséquences civiles de la contrefaçon des droits de propriété industrielle*, LexisNexis, Paris 2011.

Roubier Paul, *Le droit de la propriété industrielle*, t. II, Sirey, Paris 1954.

Ruzek Vincent, *La parodie en droit des marques*, Propr. ind. 2005, No. 4, étude 11.

Saint-Gal Yves, *Concurrence déloyale et concurrence parasitaire (ou agissements parasitaires)*, RIPIA 1956, p. 19.

Saint-Gal Yves, *Concurrence et agissements parasitaires en droit français et belge*, in: *La concurrence parasitaire en droit comparé. Actes du Colloque de Lausanne*, Libraire Droz, Geneva 1981, p. 133.

Saint-Gal Yves, *Importance économique des droits de propriété industrielle*, RIPIA 1968, No. 76, p. 50.

Saraceno Anna, in: Bottero Nicola, Travostino Massimo (eds), *Il diritto dei marchi d'impresa*, Utet Giuridica, Turin 2009.

Schechter Frank I., *The Rational Basis of Trademark Protection*, Harv. L. Rev. 1927, vol. XL, p. 813.

Schlosser Ralph, Maradan Claudia, in: Werra de Jacques, Gilliéron Philippe (eds), *Propriété intellectuelle. Commentaire romand*, Helbing Lichtenhahn Verlag, Basel 2013.

Schmidt-Szalewski Joanna, *La commercialisation d'un produit non protégé n'est pas une faute*, Propr. ind. 2004, No. 1, comment 10.

Schmidt-Szalewski Joanna, *Les relations entre contrefaçon et concurrence déloyale*, Propr. ind. 2008, No. 11, comment 91.

Schmidt-Szalewski Joanna, *Notion d'usage contrefaisant d'une marque*, RTD eur. 2007, No. 4, p. 689.

Schmidt-Szalewski Joanna, *Régime de la marque notoire ou renommée*, RTD eur. 2008, No. 4, p. 938.

Schmidt-Szalewski Joanna, in: Schmidt-Szalewski Joanna, Pierre Jean-Luc, *Droit de la propriété industrielle*, 7th ed., LexisNexis, Paris 2007.

Schovsbo Jens, *'Mark My Words': Trademarks and Fundamental Rights in the EU*, UC Irvine Law Review 2018, vol. 8, No. 3, p. 555.

Schricker Gerhard, *La tutela della Ausstattung e del marchio celebre nella Germania Federale*, Riv. Dir. Ind. 1980, I, p. 254.

Scourfield Tom, *A Tale of Two Celines*, EIPR 2008, vol. 30, No. 2, p. 71.

Seeling G.W., *Protecting 'Famous Brands' in Germany*, EIPR 1989, vol. 11, No. 5, p. 158.

Sena Giuseppe, *Brevi note sulla funzione del marchio*, Riv. Dir. Ind. 1989, I, p. 5.

Sena Giuseppe, *Confondibilità fra segni e confondibilità fra prodotti o servizi nella giurisprudenza comunitaria: alcune considerazioni pertinenti e impertinenti*, Riv. Dir. Ind. 2004, I, p. 201.

Senftleben Martin, *Adapting EU Trademark Law to New Technologies: Back to Basics?*, in: Geiger Christophe (ed.), *Constructing European Intellectual Property Achievements and New Perspectives*, Edward Elgar Publishing, Cheltenham-Northampton 2013, p. 137.

Senftleben Martin, *Free Signs and Free Use: How to Offer Room for Freedom of Expression Within the Trademark System*, in: Christophe Geiger (ed.), *Research Handbook on Human Rights and Intellectual Property*, Edward Elgar Publishing, Cheltenham-Northampton 2016.

Senftleben Martin, *Overprotection and Protection Overlaps in Intellectual Property Law: The Need for Horizontal Fair Use Defences*, in: Kur Annette, Mizaras Vytautas (eds), *Structure of Intellectual Property Law: Can One Size Fit All?*, Edward Elgar Publishing, Cheltenham-Northampton 2011, p. 136.

Senftleben Martin, *The Perfect Match: Civil Law Judges and Open-Ended Fair Use Provisions*, American University International Law Review 2017, vol. 33, No. 1, p. 231.

Senftleben Martin, *The Trademark Tower of Babel: Dilution Concepts in International, US and EC Trademark Law*, IIC 2009, vol. 40, No. 1, p. 45.

Senftleben Martin, *Trade Mark Protection: A Black Hole in the Intellectual Property Galaxy?*, IIC 2011, vol. 42, No. 4, p. 383.

Senftleben Martin, in: Kur Annette, Senftleben Martin, *European Trade Mark Law. A Commentary*, Oxford University Press, Oxford 2017.

Senftleben Martin et al., *The Recommendation on Measures to Safeguard Freedom of Expression and Undistorted Competition: Guiding Principles for the Further Development of EU Trade Mark Law*, EIPR 2015, vol. 37, No. 6, p. 337.

Simon Ilanah, *Embellishment: Trade Mark Use Triumph or Decorative Disaster?*, EIPR 2006, vol. 28, No. 6, p. 323.

Simon Fhima Ilanah, *Dilution by Blurring: A Conceptual Roadmap*, IPQ 2010, No. 1, p. 44.

Simon Fhima Ilanah, *Due Cause*, JIPLP 2017, vol. 12, No. 11, p. 897.

Simon Fhima Ilanah, *Exploring the Roots of European Dilution*, IPQ 2012, No. 1, p. 25.

Simon Fhima Ilanah, *Protection of Well-Known and Famous Marks in the United States and United Kingdom*, in: Werra de Jacques (ed.), *Marques notoires et de haute renommée. Well-Known and Famous Trademarks*, Schulthess Verlag, Zurich 2011, p. 1.

Simon Fhima Ilanah, *Trade Marks and Free Speech*, IIC 2013, vol. 44, No. 3, p. 293.

Simon Fhima Ilanah, *Trade Mark Dilution in Europe and the United States*, Oxford University Press, Oxford 2011.

Sironi Giulio E., in: Vanzetti Adriano (ed.), *Codice della proprietà industriale*, Giuffrè, Milan 2013.

Sitko Joanna, *Trade Marks with a Reputation and Famous Marks: Differences in Approach Between the European Union, Poland and the United States in Relation to the Principle of Speciality*, Queen Mary Journal of Intellectual Property 2017, vol. 7, No. 3, p. 331.

Skrzydło-Tefelska Ewa, in: Hasselblatt Gordian N. (ed.), *Community Trade Mark Regulation. A Commentary*, C.H. Beck Hart Nomos, Munich-Oxford 2015.

Skrzydło-Tefelska Ewa, Żuk Mateusz, in: Hasselblatt Gordian N. (ed.), *Community Trade Mark Regulation. A Commentary*, C.H. Beck Hart Nomos, Munich-Oxford 2015.

Skubisz Ryszard, *Funkcje znaku towarowego*, in: *Księga pamiątkowa z okazji 80-lecia rzecznictwa patentowego w Polsce*, Polska Izba Rzeczników Patentowych, Warsaw 2001, p. 163.

Skubisz Ryszard, *Glosa do wyroku NSA z dnia 27 lutego 2008 r. (II GSK 359/07)*, PS 2009, No. 4, p. 138.

Skubisz Ryszard, *Kolizja późniejszego znaku towarowego z wcześniejszym renomowanym znakiem towarowym*, EPS 2009, No. 2, p. 33.

Skubisz Ryszard, *Naruszenie praw z rejestracji renomowanych znaków towarowych (w świetle dyrektywy o znakach towarowych)*, in: Łazowski Adam, Ostrihansky Rudolf (eds), *Współczesne wyzwania europejskiej przestrzeni prawnej. Księga pamiątkowa dla uczczenia 70. Urodzin Profesora Eugeniusza Piontka*, Zakamycze, Warsaw 2005, p. 145.

Skubisz Ryszard, *Prawo znaków towarowych. Komentarz*, Wydawnictwa Prawnicze, Warsaw 1997.

Skubisz Ryszard, *Wielkość terytorium używania znaku jako przesłanka powstania prawa do znaku towarowego powszechnie znanego*, EPS 2008, No. 1, p. 40.

Skubisz Ryszard, *Znaki towarowe – ewolucja przedmiotu ochrony prawnej*, PPH 2008, No. 12, p. 16.

Skubisz Ryszard, in: Skubisz Ryszard (ed.), *System prawa prywatnego*, t. 14 B, *Prawo własności przemysłowej*, 2nd ed., C.H. Beck, Warsaw 2017.

Skubisz Ryszard, Dudzik Jarosław, *Używanie znaku towarowego konkurenta w reklamie porównawczej*, EPS 2008, No. 11, p. 36.

Sobol Agata, *Marchio notorio e decadenza*, Riv. Dir. Ind. 2009, II, p. 217.

Sotriffer Gioacchino, *Protezione allargata del marchio di rinomanza e prodotti affini*, Riv. Dir. Ind. 2010, II, p. 108.

Strasser Mathias, *The Rational Basis of Trademark Protection Revisited: Putting the Dilution Doctrine into Context*, Forham Intell. Prop., Media and Ent., L. J. 2000, vol. 10, No. 2, p. 375.

Szczepanowska-Kozłowska Krystyna, *Czy znak renomowany zawsze ma renomę?*, Glosa 2016, No. 2, p. 51.

Szczepanowska-Kozłowska Krystyna, *Swoboda wypowiedzi a prawo ochronne na znak towarowy*, ZNUJ 2013, No. 119, p. 5.

Szczepanowska-Kozłowska Krystyna, *Używanie firmy jako naruszenie prawa ochronnego na znak towarowy*, PPH 2008, No. 10, p. 5.

Szczepanowska-Kozłowska Krystyna, *Wyczerpanie praw własności przemysłowej. Patent i prawo ochronne na znak towarowy*, C.H. Beck, Warsaw 2003.

Szczepanowska-Kozłowska Krystyna, *Znaki towarowe w Unii Europejskiej (cz. I)*, PPH 2004, No. 8, p. 4.

Szczepanowska-Kozłowska Krystyna, in: Nowińska Ewa, Szczepanowska-Kozłowska Krystyna (eds), *System prawa handlowego*, t. III, *Prawo własności przemysłowej*, C.H. Beck, Warsaw 2015.

Szpunar Adam, *Nadużycie prawa podmiotowego*, thesis Cracow 1947.

Terré François, *Introduction générale au droit*, 9th ed., Dalloz, Paris 2012.

Tomassini E., *Il nome Camel come marchio celebre, protezione allargata e principio di specialità*, Riv. Dir. Ind. 1990, II, p. 213.

Traple Elżbieta, *Reklama internetowa (adwords) jako uzasadniona przyczyna użycia cudzego znaku towarowego*, in: *Problemy polskiego i europejskiego prawa prywatnego. Księga pamiątkowa Profesora Mariana Kępińskiego*, Wolters Kluwer, Warsaw 2012, p. 407.

Tréfigny Pascale, *Action en contrefaçon et action en concurrence déloyale. L'évolution de la jurisprudence la plus récente face au parasitisme*, in: *Le droit de la propriété intellectuelle dans un monde globalisé. Mélanges en l'honneur du Professeur Joanna Schmidt-Szalewski*, LexisNexis, Paris 2014, p. 343.

Tréfigny Pascale, *La saisie-contrefaçon offerte aux marques renommées...*, Propr. ind. 2007, No. 5, comment 39.

Tréfigny-Goy Pascale, *Un monogramme bien défendu... Ou quand une jaquette se prend une veste!*, Propr. ind. 2008, No. 6, comment 39.

Troller Alois, *La marque de haute renommée*, PI 1953, p. 73.

Troller Alois, *Précis du droit de la propriété immatérielle*, Helbing & Lichtenhahn, Basel 1978.

Vanzetti Adriano, *Funzione e natura giuridica del marchio*, Riv. Dir. Comm. 1961, I, p. 17.

Vanzetti Adriano, Di Cataldo Vincenzo, *Manuale di diritto industriale*, 4th ed., Giuffrè, Milan 2003.

Vilmart Christine, *La CJCE arbitre le match en faveur de la marque renommée*, Gaz. Pal. 2003, No. 135, p. 6.

Vivant Michel, *Marque et fonction sociale de la marque. Ou quand la réalité passe par le rêve?*, in: *Les défis du droit des marques au XXIe siècle. Actes du colloque en l'honneur du professeur Yves Reboul*, LexisNexis, Paris 2011, p. 145.

Vivant Michel, *Prendre la contrefaçon au sérieux*, D. 2009, No. 25, p. 1839.

Vivant Pierre, *Marque notoire et marque renommée: une distinction conforme au droit des marques*, D. 2010, No. 37, p. 2496.

Wachsmann Pierre, *Liberté d'expression*, Fascicule 800, JurisClasseur 2008.

Welkowitz David S., *Trademark Dilution*, Bloomberg, Washington 2002.

Wertheimer Jules, *Des avantages attribués à la bonne foi relativement aux biens en droit civil*, thesis Paris 1899.

Wichers Hoeth Leo, *Étude comparative de quelques aspects de l'usage de la marque*, thesis Leyden 1963.

Wiszniewska Irena, *Znaki towarowe w prawie własności przemysłowej*, PPH 2001, No. 12, p. 3.

Włodarczyk Wojciech, *Użycie oznaczenia 'w charakterze znaku towarowego' (w orzecznictwie ETS)*, PiP 2009, No. 11, p. 92.

Wojcieszko-Głuszko Ewa, *Ochrona prawna znaków towarowych powszechnie znanych na tle prawnoporównawczym*, ZNUJ 1995, No. 65, p. 3.

Wojcieszko-Głuszko Ewa, in: Skubisz Ryszard (ed.), *System prawa prywatnego*, t. XIV B, *Prawo własności przemysłowej*, 2nd ed., C.H. Beck, Warsaw 2017.

Wolff John, *Non-competing Goods in Trademark Law*, Columb. L. Rev. 1937, vol. 37, No. 4, p. 582.

Yap Po Jen, *Essential Function of a Trade Mark: from BMW to O2*, EIPR 2009, vol. 31, No. 2, p. 81.

Yap Po Jen, *Honestly, neither Céline nor Gillette is Defensible!*, EIPR 2008, vol. 30, No. 7, p. 286.

Yap Po Jen, *Making Sense of Trade Mark Use*, EIPR 2007, vol. 29, No. 10, p. 420.

Zanella Christine, *Les marques nominatives*, Litec, Paris 1995.

Zoll Fryderyk, *À propos de la loi polonaise du 2 août 1926 concernant la répression de la concurrence déloyale*, PI 1927, p. 64.

Zolynski Célia, *La protection étendue de la marque renommée en droit de l'Union européenne*, D. IP/IT 2016, No. 2, p. 94.

Żelechowski Łukasz, *Funkcje znaku towarowego a naruszenie prawa ochronnego na znak towarowy (cz. I)*, PPH 2015, No. 5, p. 4.

Żelechowski Łukasz, *Funkcje znaku towarowego a naruszenie prawa ochronnego na znak towarowy (cz. II)*, PPH 2015, No. 6, p. 20.

Żelechowski Łukasz, *Infringement of a Community Trade Mark: Between EU-Wide and Non EU-Wide Scope of Prohibitive Injunctions*, EIPR 2013, vol. 5, p. 287.

Żelechowski Łukasz, *Invoking Freedom of Expression and Freedom of Competition in Trade Mark Infringement Disputes: Legal Mechanisms for Striking a Balance*, ERA Forum 2018, vol. 19, No. 1, p. 115.

Żelechowski Łukasz, *Kolizja prawa ochronnego na znak towarowy i reżimu ochrony oznaczeń odróżniających na podstawie ustawy o zwalczaniu nieuczciwej konkurencji – perspektywa w świetle orzecznictwa Trybunału Sprawiedliwości*, in: *Experientia docet. Księga jubileuszowa ofiarowana Pani Profesor Elżbiecie Traple*, Wolters Kluwer, Warsaw 2017, p. 767.

Żelechowski Łukasz, *'Uzasadniony powód' używania oznaczenia kolidującego z renomowanym znakiem towarowym*, Glosa 2014, No. 3, p. 75.

Żelechowski Łukasz, in: Kostański Piotr, Żelechowski Łukasz, *Prawo własności przemysłowej*, C.H. Beck, Warsaw 2014.

Żuraw Monika, *Znak towarowy jako przedmiot ochrony – uwagi o użyciu oznaczenia 'w charakterze znaku towarowego'*, Studia Iuridica 2010, No. 52, p. 165.

Index

T

U

W

www.ingramcontent.com/pod-product-compliance
Lightning Source LLC
Chambersburg PA
CBHW071242230926
51849CB00001B/196
* 9 7 8 9 4 0 3 5 2 0 2 1 6 *